JAMAICA, 1830–1930

JAMAICA, 1830 – 1930

A STUDY IN ECONOMIC GROWTH

by

GISELA EISNER

GREENWOOD PRESS, PUBLISHERS
WESTPORT, CONNECTICUT

Library of Congress Cataloging in Publication Data

Eisner, Gisela.
Jamaica, 1830-1930; a study in economic growth.

Reprint of the ed. published by Manchester University Press, Manchester, Eng.
Bibliography: p.
1. Jamaica--Economic conditions. I. Title.
HC157.J2E35 1974 330.9'7292'04 73-15054
ISBN 0-8371-7157-1

Published by the University of Manchester at the University Press

Reprinted with the permission of Manchester University Press

Reprinted in 1974 by Greenwood Press, Inc.,
51 Riverside Avenue, Westport, Conn. 06880

Library of Congress catalog card number 73-15054
ISBN 0-8371-7157-1

Printed in the United States of America

10 9 8 7 6 5 4 3 2

PREFACE

The purpose of this book is to see how far national income accounting can help us to understand long-term historical change. This task involves two problems: is it possible to prepare meaningful estimates for an historical period and, if so, do they increase our insight into economic development?

As to the problem of computing national income estimates, it is surprising how much can be done without too much guessing. Jamaica is, in this respect, specially favoured because it formed the subject of many commissions of enquiry and of a great many books —an advantage of having so often been so controversial an island. No claim as to the absolute accuracy of the estimates is made. The quality of the data naturally varies for different aspects of economic activity. For example, we have very little information about the output of ground provisions which accounts for about one-third of total output. All the same, sufficient figures have been found to give fair confidence that the estimates are not wildly out.

It must be remembered that one of the advantages of national income accounting is that one estimate checks another. Figures of population, acreages, wages, costs, consumer expenditures, imports, exports, etc., are all called upon and used in such a way that inconsistencies tend to show up. Because of inadequate data we are not able to make all the independent checks that national income statisticians expect to be able to make. Thus we cannot check the accuracy of totals through independent estimates of output, income and expenditure. But we are able to make many checks through individual figures and to decide which to accept and which to reject with rather more confidence than can be felt by historians using other methods. For example, R. M. Martin[1] estimated the value of output of 'Domestic Manufactures' (i.e. carpentering, tailoring, smithing etc., for the local market) at £2 million in 1834. The number of workers in these occupations at this date was only about 12,000. Per capita output was thus about £167 p.a. As most of the raw materials used in producing furniture, clothing, etc., were imported, average incomes were practically the same as average output. But this would

[1] *Statistics of the Colonies of the British Empire*, London, 1839.

mean that the incomes of carpenters, tailors, etc.—mainly free coloured and slave workers—were considerably above those earned by white employees on sugar estates; clearly an impossibility. When we came to estimate slaves' incomes, we found that pro-slavery writers, such as A. Barclay,[1] put forward estimates of slaves' cash earnings, which do not appear reasonable in relation either to other workers' earnings or to possible levels of output.

The other main advantage of national income accounting is perspective. National income estimates, for example, tell us the relative importance of production for export and for the home market, the distribution of income between the various classes of the community and the share of the government in national income. The importance of this is that such estimates enable us to assess the effect on the whole economy of changes in the various sectors and thus avoid the risk of exaggerating or minimizing changes such as might result from taking single statistical series. We can illustrate this point by Jamaican Customs Returns. The value of exports from Jamaica fell by nearly 60 per cent between 1832 and 1850. How important was this fall? Did it represent a fall in total production of the same order or of 40 per cent or 20 per cent or only 10 per cent? Similarly, the statistics show that the value of exports doubled in the forty years following the introduction of the banana as an export crop in 1869. The questions to which we should like answers are: was this growth greater than that in production for the home market? Was it matched by growth in the public sector? And was it accompanied by expansion in manufacturing industry?

The success of the method is to be judged not merely by the estimates in Part I but also by the use made of them in Part II. There we have collected much other statistical material, and used it, together with the national income estimates, to give a brief long-term statistical account of Jamaican development.

This study does not claim to be an exhaustive economic history of Jamaica. Whole fields of history are omitted. Thus, very little is said about the shaping of economic policy, the study of which takes the historian into government minutes and files. There is a great deal of material on this subject in the Public Record Office and much work remains to be done, especially for the years following the change in government in 1865. Other big gaps waiting to be filled are the histories of estates and individuals. In their absence the section on

[1] *Practical View of the Present State of Slavery*, London, 1827.

enterprise in this study proved very difficult to write. No attempt is made either to follow the trade cycle, or the course of events from day to day or year to year. The goal is broad trends of economic change.

Within this limited field no more is claimed for this study than can normally be claimed for the use of statistics in history, namely that it is helpful to get the quantities right; in other words, the method of national income accounting improves perspective.

Part II has benefited in various ways from recent discussions of the theory of growth. This explains why more than usual emphasis is given to such matters as attempts to measure investment, the relationship between saving and the distribution of income, the productive importance of education, and similar topics. Unfortunately, not enough is known about enterprise in Jamaica in the second half of the nineteenth century, or about investment opportunities, for this study to be very helpful in improving the theory of growth itself.

The work for this study was done while I was a member of the Economic Research Section of the University of Manchester, 1951–6. My first acknowledgment is therefore due to this University for making the research possible and also for generously enabling me to visit Jamaica during the winter of 1953–4. I should also like to thank the staffs of the following institutions: Arts Library, University of Manchester; Central Library, Manchester; Public Record Office; Colonial Office Library; Royal Empire Society; Newspaper Library, British Museum, and the West India Reference Library. My visit to Jamaica was made very pleasant through the kindness and hospitality of many. I am particularly grateful to Mr. D. T. M. Girvan, Secretary of the Jamaica Agricultural Society, Mr. C. D. Hutchins of the Department of Agriculture and Mr. E. B. Hamilton of the Education Department for enabling me to see so much of the island. My thanks are also due to Miss Phyllis Deane for reading and commenting on the typescript and to my husband for checking it. My greatest debt, however, is to Professor W. A. Lewis, who initiated this study and gave me constant help and encouragement.

March, 1958

CONTENTS

CONTENTS

LIST OF TABLES

PART ONE

SUMMARY TABLES

PART TWO

LIST OF TABLES

DIAGRAM

LIST OF ABBREVIATIONS

BBJ	Blue Book(s) of Jamaica
BPP	British Parliamentary Papers
Col. Rep.	Colonial Report(s)
CP	Census(es) of Population
CR	Customs Returns
HBJ	Handbook(s) of Jamaica
JA	Jamaica Almanack
JBC	Jamaica Banana Commission
JBPA	Jamaica Banana Producers' Association
PAIJ	Papers relative to the Affairs of the Island of Jamaica
PPSC	Past and Present State of H.M. Colonies
PWI	Papers relating to the West Indies
REJ	Revenue and Expenditure (Jamaica)
RWIC	Royal West India Commission
SCP	Select Committee on Sugar and Coffee Planting
SIC	Sugar Industry Commission
SSIJ	Statistics of the Sugar Industry of Jamaica
STC	Statistical Tables for the Colonies
WISC	West India Sugar Commission

Note: Throughout the book national income years are shown in italics to distinguish them from ordinary years. For a definition of national income years, see Chapter I, A.

FOREWORD

by W. ARTHUR LEWIS

Principal of the University College of the West Indies

MRS. EISNER'S experiment has succeeded beyond all hope and expectation. Her painstaking searches have yielded far more good statistical material than was thought to exist. The national income technique has proved its value in arranging, disciplining, cross-checking and rejecting a mass of material, drawn from many sources. And this bit of history, of which our knowledge was vague and impressionistic, has now acquired clear quantitative perspectives.

Historians no longer argue about the role of statistics in writing history. Statistics are about masses and averages. They are no substitute for historical writing about the individuals who change history. Mrs. Eisner has been handicapped by the comparative absence of that other kind of historical writing about Jamaica. She would have liked to know more about the lives and acts of Jamaicans who influenced history; of Governors, planters, middle-class politicians; small banana farmers, Chinese grocers, and others who helped to make Jamaica what she is. Here is plenty of work for a generation of scholars, working in the Public Record Office, in the Jamaican archives, and in the records of individuals. Public policy will be found in the written records, but for the lives and acts of private individuals we shall have largely to rely on oral statements by people who are growing older every day, so our scholars have not much time to lose. Mrs. Eisner's contribution, in mapping the broad flow of economic activity, provides an indispensable background for innumerable intensive studies.

Those who expect history to consist of facts may be somewhat surprised by the number of guesses which Mrs. Eisner has had to incorporate into her statistics. Neither the national income specialist nor the professional historian will share this surprise. They, on the contrary, will be amazed to see how many good figures there are. All historical writing consists of making the best guess one can from the available materials, and this is true even when one is trying to calculate last year's national income in Britain or in the United

States, where statistics are ample. The chief value of the national income approach is that it provides automatic cross-checks, so that the unreliability of some figures become obvious, and the appropriateness of others can be deduced.

Of its kind, this is a model study. It is also a pioneer. If there were a similar book about England in the nineteenth century, or about the United States of America, or any country of continental Europe, we would know much more about the economic history of the nineteenth century. Mrs. Eisner's performance would be remarkable even if she were merely proceeding on well-trodden paths; that she was writing a new kind of book must be remembered when assessing her achievement.

II

The book speaks for itself and needs no commendation from me. I will use the space accorded to me to wrestle with the big problem which it leaves unsolved: Why was Jamaica's economic performance not better?

Let us start with 1870. By then Jamaica had settled down after the upheavals of emancipation, more than thirty years earlier, and of free trade, about twenty years earlier. The sugar industry was reasonably prosperous, and the first shipments of bananas had been made. The old unstable political system had been swept away, leaving power in the hands of a series of relatively able Governors. The island was a part of the modern world; as much so as Argentina or Australia; more so than Japan or Russia. Why did it get left behind?

The performance was unimpressive. The average annual increase in production per head was 0·2 per cent from 1870 to 1890, 0·5 per cent from 1890 to 1910, and 0·7 per cent from 1910 to 1930 (Table LVI). That there was progressive improvement is good. The low rate between 1870 and 1890 was to some extent due to the slump in the sugar industry. However, the later rates, while better than India's or Egypt's, were low in comparison with Japan's or Western Europe's.

More ominous was the failure of the economy to cope with population growth, which laid the foundations of the acute unemployment which the island is now experiencing. The average annual rate of population increase between 1870 and 1930 was only 1·2 per cent; but, after about 1880, this was more than could be absorbed by agriculture. In consequence, the proportion of the occupied population engaged in agriculture fell steadily after 1881, when it was 67·5 per cent, to 55·3 per cent in 1921, and probably 54·1 per cent in 1930.

A fall in the proportion engaged in agriculture is a feature of all progressive economies. However, where economic conditions are healthy, the reason for the fall in the proportion is increasing economy in producing food for home consumption. This was not the situation in Jamaica. There was no evidence in Jamaica of productivity rising in that part of the agricultural sector which produced food for the home market. Indeed, one of the principal reasons why productivity in the economy as a whole increased so slowly was that there was practically no productivity increase in home food production, in which more than half of the agricultural population was engaged. In Jamaica the proportion of the population engaged in agriculture declined not because the demand for food failed to keep pace with productivity, but because the cultivable area was limited.

Matters came to a head in the 1880's because of the substitution of the banana for sugar. Sugar is highly labour-intensive, while the banana is not. Because of adverse prices, the share of sugar in exports fell from 45 per cent in 1870 to 8 per cent in 1910; while the share of bananas in exports rose from 1 per cent to 52 per cent. This was good for national income, since bananas were more productive than sugar, but it was very bad for agricultural employment. Total acreage under cultivation increased considerably between 1871 and 1891; but thereafter increased more slowly than population, at the same time as labour requirements per acre were falling. Large areas remained which could be cultivated at some cost, especially with irrigation, drainage, or terracing; but by the end of the century the limits of easy cultivation were already in sight.

In a progressive economy the decline in the proportion engaged in agriculture is matched by increases in the proportions in manufacturing industry and in the more remunerative forms of service. In Jamaica, on the contrary, these categories showed little relative increase. The share of agriculture declined 12 points between 1881 and 1921. The largest offset to this was in the share of domestic service, which rose 7 points, to absorb as much as 18 per cent of the working population. Petty commerce also rose by 3 points, thus doubling the relative number of traders. This is the form which 'disguised unemployment' takes in an economy where agriculturists work for wages, and where therefore the labour surplus is not kept on the farms. Actually, since more than one-half of the agricultural population consisted of family farmers, we can also safely assume that a fair amount of disguised unemployment also accumulated on the small-holdings. It would not be excessive to guess that, already in 1930 more than one-eighth of the working population was already in disguised unemployment.

The failure of the more productive sectors of the economy to grow showed up in a low level of investment, which was at once cause and effect. Even at its best, in 1930, gross investment was only 10 per cent of the gross domestic product (Table LXII), with 45 per cent of this in residential building, and only just over a quarter in equipment. At this level, net investment (5 to 6 per cent) would keep pace with population growth (1·5 per cent), and leave room for only a small increase in production per head.

Jamaica's problem can be approached by asking why, as agricultural opportunities failed to expand sufficiently, there was not more investment to bring land under cultivation, and failing this, greater expansion of employment in manufacturing industry and in the more remunerative services. The solutions have to be sought both on the side of demand and on the side of supply.

III

On the side of demand, Jamaica could easily have found a market for more agricultural products if more land had been brought under cultivation. The market for sugar was depressed, but all other export markets could have absorbed greater quantities at current prices, which were acceptable—bananas, coffee, cocoa, spices. The home market could also have taken more food—in 1930 as much as 9 per cent of national income was being spent on imported food, much of it on livestock products which could have been supplied at home. The failure here lay on the side of supply, rather than of demand.

When we turn to the demand for manufactures and for services, the first factor to note is the extent to which the gains in productivity were eroded by adverse changes in the terms of trade. The terms of trade improved between 1870 and 1890, partly because of increases in the prices of coffee and logwood, partly because of the shift from sugar towards the more remunerative banana, and partly because the 'great depression' reduced the prices of imports from Britain and from North America. Thereafter the terms of trade moved adversely, from 137 in 1890 to 100 in 1910 and to 84 in1930. As a result, though productivity increased by 27 per cent between 1890 and 1930, consumption per head increased only by 13 per cent in the same period (even though consumption increased slightly relatively to production).

This pattern of price behaviour is common to most tropical countries. Since tropical commercial agriculture (sugar, tea, cocoa, coffee, bananas, rubber, etc.) is small relatively to the production of food for home consumption, the elasticity of supply of commercial crops is very high at prices yielding little more than farmers can earn by producing food for themselves. Hence, so long as productivity is constant in subsistence production, practically all the benefit of increases in productivity in the commercial crops accrues to the consumer and not to the producer. The individual country can benefit by keeping ahead of the average for the tropical world, and will lose if it falls behind; but tropical producers, taken as a whole, do not benefit from higher productivity in commercial crops, so long as productivity remains constant in subsistence food production. Greater productivity is offset by adverse terms of trade.

The second factor holding down demand for manufactures and for the more remunerative services was the failure of productivity to increase in the sector producing food for the home market. If the average food farmer had had a larger income, he could have afforded to buy more manufactures and services. This argument must be treated carefully. If farmers had deluged the market with food, they would have become not richer but poorer. As we have noted, there was scope for replacing much of the imported food, and this could have been done without spoiling the market. Import replacement apart, higher output per person would produce higher income per person only if there was a relative decline in the number of food producers, associated with expansion in sectors producing for export, or substituting for imports, or creating and serving new home demands. Given balanced growth in this sense, the food farmers would be able to buy more manufactures and services, and the rest of the community would buy more food.

Why did small-holders not become more efficient in producing food for the home market? Because nobody taught them how to do so. Nineteenth-century Jamaica was not seized with the spirit of the scientific revolution. Even the planters did not begin to pay serious attention to productivity until the sharp fall in the price of sugar at the end of the century forced them to do so; and even then many found an easy way out in converting from sugar to bananas. Small farmers do not innovate; they imitate. But it was not until the very end of the century that the Government began to take agricultural research seriously, and promoted the extension work of the Jamaica Agricultural Society. The failure of agricultural efficiency must be attributed to the backwardness of Jamaican thought.

A third element in the slow growth of the more remunerative service employments was the low level of taxation, and the consequent poverty of the public services. (Where unemployment exists, total employment is increased by taxing some people and using the proceeds to employ others.) In particular, education and medicine provided relatively little employment. This also was due to the backwardness of Jamaican thought which, in 1900, had retrogressed as compared with 1840. For in 1840, Jamaicans were just emerging from a period in which medical service was supplied to the great majority of the population (slaves). It was also assumed in 1840, at least by the Baptists and by the British Government, that schools could and should be provided for nearly all Jamaican children. This is what I meant by saying earlier that Jamaica was a part of the modern world. If it did not provide itself with needed public services this was not because the idea of providing such services was strange to those who were prominent in the island's affairs. It was because they set their faces against the times.

We cannot explain the failure of employment to grow adequately in manufacturing industry and in remunerative services simply by failure of demand, since there was a considerable demand for manufactures, which was met by imports. In 1930 about 12 per cent of the national income was spent on imported consumer manufactures, of which over 40 per cent was textiles. It is therefore necessary to examine deficiencies on the side of supply.

IV

More employment could have been provided in agriculture if more had been invested in making marginal lands suitable for cultivation. There was indeed some investment in irrigation, but it was not enough. The deficiency was partly private and partly public. Plantation owners were active investors in land. However, much of the required investment was beyond the capacity of the small farmers, who were more numerous than agricultural labourers. What was needed was large public investment in irrigation, reclamation, drainage, terracing, conservation, afforestation, and feeder roads to make land available for the small farmers. Considerable headway was made with investment in roads, but not much thought was given to other forms of public investment.

Neither does shortage of natural resources explain the failure to make adequate progress in manufacturing industry. Jamaica is not less well endowed with natural resources than is Japan, which was forging ahead from 1870. No particular natural resource is required to manufacture light consumer goods, such as textiles. Jamaica did not have cheap power, but power is a very small element in the cost of this type of production.

Investing in land or in factories would have required capital. Nevertheless, the low level of savings is not a plausible explanation, since Jamaica had always had easy access to the British capital market. If manufacturing industry had been deemed profitable, the necessary capital would have been found. Besides, lack of saving is a circular explanation for lack of capitalist activity. The people who save most are those who invest in industry. Jamaica would have saved more if it had had more industry. Lack of industry was not due to lack of domestic saving. As for public investment in land, some part could have been financed directly out of taxes; the rest could have been borrowed in the London market, and would have paid for itself by increasing the national output, thus making possible the payment of water charges and other contributions to sinking funds.

In our day a high level of wage costs has been advanced as a factor retarding industrialization. This is not a decisive obstacle, since in production for the home market it can largely be offset by tariffs or by import quotas. In any case, it does not fit the period covered in this book. There were then no trade unions. Wages were flexible, and moved up and down by large amounts, in response to changes in the demand for labour. Female labour, suitable for textile factories, was available in abundance for a pittance. In Jamaica around 1900 the level of wages cannot have been a significant deterrent to investment.

Lack of skills is more relevant, but must be considered at different levels. Education was poorly developed; much worse than in the rest of the British West Indies. This was not important at the lowest level. A factory worker can be taught the necessary skills without learning to read and write; neither in Britain nor in Japan was the Industrial

Revolution founded upon mass literacy. Neither do farmers need literacy to acquire new productive skills, as Japan had already amply demonstrated by 1914. The deficiency of education was more important at higher levels. It was especially important at secondary school level, since the secondary schools supply the clerical, book-keeping, semi-technical and supervisory levels of any economy. Society needs relatively few university graduates, and can import what it needs; but to have to import large numbers of secondary school products imposes a large burden on an economy. This burden Jamaica carried throughout the period examined in this book, and it helps to explain why her costs were relatively high. This, however, is only a surface explanation. For if entrepreneurs find that shortage of school products is raising their costs, all they have to do is to see to it that more schools are built. If Jamaica was handicapped by lack of schools, one has to ask, why did not her entrepreneurs have more schools built?

The answer is presumably a failure of entrepreneurship itself. If Jamaica had had capitalists interested in developing local industries, they would have influenced the Government to build schools, to impose higher tariffs, to improve the public utilities, or whatever they felt to be the deficiency. These things did not happen because Jamaicans did not think in terms of developing industrial employment. The island had always lived off agricultural exports, and the speed with which the banana displaced sugar at the end of the century showed that its farmers, large and small, were still fairly quick at adjusting to changing opportunities in the export market. Production of manufactures for the home market is a different entrepreneurial skill. The island did not possess it, and would not develop it until after the Second World War.

V

If this analysis is right, Jamaica did not cope with her economic problems in the half century before 1930 because her leaders did not try to cope with them. They failed especially at five points: to help the small farmers to be more productive; to invest public funds in opening up marginal lands for small settlers, by irrigation, drainage, and conservation; to provide enough secondary education; to raise taxes for the social services; and to take the steps required for producing consumer manufactures. This cannot be attributed to 'the evils of colonialism'. The nationalist Jamaican leaders of the day, of whatever race, were not much concerned about the economic and social questions which are here discussed; they were preoccupied with questions of political power, and with protecting their respective middle or upper class positions. On the contrary, the British Governors were usually more enlightened than the Jamaican spokesmen, and were hampered by the politicians' preoccupation with keeping taxes low. Not until the 1930's did Jamaica find among her own people spokesmen whose primary concern was economic and social development. Every society is to some extent a prisoner of its past. Jamaica entered the twentieth century with an assortment of ideas derived from the first half of the nineteenth century. Catching up has been a costly process.

University College of the West Indies,
Jamaica
October 1959

PART I

NATIONAL INCOME ESTIMATES *1832–1930*

CHAPTER 1

INTRODUCTION

THE purpose of Part I is to obtain national income estimates that will make possible quantitative appraisal of economic change during the period 1830 to 1930. The choice of such a long period and the quality of the available data inevitably raise various problems.

A. THE SELECTION OF YEARS

As explained in the Preface we are interested mainly in long-term trends and do not need a continuous series of yearly estimates. For this purpose it is sufficient to have estimates that give an indication of the general trend—provided care is taken to avoid dates that might be unrepresentative of the period. Estimates at twenty-year intervals, beginning in 1830, seemed a good solution since they allowed changes to make themselves felt. Furthermore, the choice of such long intervals meant that each of the selected years could represent a notional year—one typical of the period. This had the added advantage that data that are available only for a period separated by only a year or two from the chosen one could be incorporated in the estimates so long as account was taken of any intervening changes.

There remained the problem of eliminating short-term fluctuations. The export trade was subject to considerable year to year fluctuations and thereby affected other sectors of the economy. An examination of the major export crops—sugar, rum and coffee—showed a cycle in exported quantities averaging about three years in duration. To eliminate these fluctuations we have calculated an average of three successive years with the chosen year as the mid-year. The ideal was to calculate a three-year average for the output of all other sectors of the economy, but in practice this proved possible only for external trade, public administration, wage rates in later years and a few other data which appeared annually in the BBJ and other statistical returns.

Thus, although the choice of years fell on 1830, 1850, 1870, 1890, 1910 and 1930, each annual estimate represents an average of three for most of the values: e.g. 1850 is based on data for 1849, 1850 and 1851. Only in the first year was this not possible. It is only in 1832 that the CR begin to differentiate between imports and exports of the several West Indian colonies. Moreover, in that year and the following the BBJ have rather fewer blank pages than on previous occasions. Accordingly, 1832 and 1833 had to replace the original choice of 1830. In order to distinguish national income years, as here defined, from ordinary years, the former are shown in italics throughout.

The resulting estimates then give one year, *1832*, which represents the immediate pre-emancipation era; *1850* marks the time when the economy had adjusted itself to the short-term effects of emancipation; *1870* represents the early years of Crown Colony government; *1890* shows the transition from sugar to banana cultivation while in *1910* this process had reached its final stages with sugar at its lowest recorded level.

B. Definition of Output

Where economic activity is carried on wholly by residents, the output is much the same whether one chooses the definition of geographical or of national income. But where a substantial part of production is in the hands of non-residents there may be a wide disparity between the two. In such cases the choice of concept depends on one's special interest. Here our main concern is with the changes in the total value of goods and services produced in the island and the pattern of the economy. If we adopt the definition of national output—that produced by Jamaicans—much of the domestic output in the early years and, to a lesser extent, towards the end of the period, would have to be deducted since most of the planters were expatriates. Further, the difference between the total output produced in Jamaica and gross national expenditure—important in the early years of the period—would not be so easily apparent. Accordingly, the concept of gross domestic product, i.e. the value of factors of production actually located in Jamaica, is adopted. This differs from the gross national product in that it includes profits sent abroad but excludes overseas earnings of Jamaicans resident or owning resources overseas. It should be noted that factors of production are here defined as those actually employed in production for exchange: i.e. the services of housewives are excluded but the value of all agricultural output, even though a considerable part of it may be consumed by the cultivator himself, is not.

C. Classification

There are three possible ways of showing output. First, output can be shown by the value added by each sector. If production becomes more specialized over the years then this will be reflected in the growth of the transport and distribution sectors. Secondly, we can separate distribution services throughout even though these were performed by the cultivator himself. This has the advantage that the production and distribution sectors are made comparable throughout the years. Thirdly, we can show output simply at final value at factor cost. This method obviously involves much loss of detail. It has, however, one advantage. Since the productive sectors include all the services rendered to the industries, the service sectors show only the value rendered to consumers directly. This enables us to trace the value of consumer services in relation to growth in total product.

It will be seen that each method has something to recommend it. In our case, however, the question of deciding the relative merits never arose because the available data were in fact only suitable for the third method—i.e. showing output at final value at factor cost. The first two are not possible here because we lack any reliable information about the value added by distribution services where rendered by outside agents, much less are we able to impute the value where producers performed all marketing operations themselves.

The method of showing output by final value has been used by Dr. F. Benham in his several studies of national income in West Indian territories[1] and, with some modifications, has been followed here. Briefly, this sets out the output of the chief sectors of the economy by final value. Imported materials used in production are deducted to show the value of domestic production only and the value of local products used in subsequent processes is included once only. The plan followed here departs from Benham's in some minor details. The contents of some of the sectors have been re-arranged. It was considered desirable to show separately passenger transport and communications. For historical reasons professional services have also been separated from other personal services. Furthermore,

[1] *The National Income of Jamaica, 1942*, Bulletins Nos. 5, 8 and 9.

no attempt was, or indeed could be, made to show separately the value of intermediate local products, but the definition of final value was consistently adhered to. Thus the value of raw tobacco and logwood sold to local manufacturing industry is included in the output of the tobacco and dyewoods industries. It will also be noted that the entry for the livestock industry includes production for human consumption only. The reason, again, is that animals used for draft purposes are included in the final product of agriculture.

It will be seen that the several sectors, as here defined, differ from the usual concepts in national income usage. Manufactures, for domestic consumption and for export, include the output of primary producers as well as the cost of marketing them. Compared with conventional estimates their value is thus overstated. On the other hand, entries under transport and communications cover consumer services only, and those under distribution the value added to imported consumer goods only. These two sectors will thus be relatively small when compared with estimates prepared on the basis of value added. A further consequence of our method of presentation is that the estimates do not show the growth of specialization. It is, however, doubtful whether this is a serious drawback. It is not likely that there was any appreciable development in specialization. The reason for this is that most agricultural production remained vertically integrated: peasants continued to combine production for the local market with transport and distribution; most estates retained responsibility for conveying output to the points of embarkation and for dealing with overseas agents.

There is another point: the output of the various sectors showing output at final value do not correspond to the incomes of the various classes. For example, distribution, as defined in the output table, does not correspond to the earnings of merchants and labour engaged in distribution. In estimating the income table we have actually attempted to distinguish between the various incomes arising out of each sector. This enabled us to prepare an output table on the basis of value added, by deducting the incomes arising out of, say, distribution services rendered to the agricultural industry from agriculture and adding them to distribution. But the estimates made for income distribution rest on rather arbitrary assumptions. The resultant table of output on the basis of value added is thus much less reliable than that showing output at final value. For this reason it is not used in the text and the definition of final value is adhered to throughout. The estimates of output by value added for the years *1832*, *1850*, *1890* and *1930* are summarized in Table III in Chapter 8.

A further departure from convention in national income accounting is made in the case of income distribution. In order to explain the process of growth in Jamaica we are interested not so much in the types of income earned as in the recipients of these incomes. From this point of view it is less important to know the changing relationship between wages, profits and rent than the distribution of these various incomes among the different classes of the population. When seeking an explanation for the level of investment, for example, it is not sufficient to know the total share of profits in output. Different classes of the community have different attitudes to enterprise and the willingness to invest can be understood only if we know the shares of profit earned by the various entrepreneurial classes, e.g. planters, peasants, etc. Moreover, in Jamaica the division between different income earners was probably less clear-cut than elsewhere. About three-quarters of houses were owner-occupied: to put the value of imputed rents into a separate category would therefore considerably understate the total income of those who were mainly wage, salary and independent workers. Instead of classifying by type of income, the criterion adopted here is the employment status of the recipient. The main classes so defined are planters, small settlers, agricultural wage earners, other wage and salary earners, merchants, independent and professional workers. 'Planters' are defined as those engaging mainly in agricultural enterprise, employing labour and capital, and small-settlers as those who generally employ no labour outside the home and little capital. 'Merchants' is a very general category which comprises, apart from petty traders, all non-agricultural enterprises which employ labour and capital. The name is misleading if it is thought to include only those engaged in the distributive services. In fact, this class includes, in addition to distribution, all manufacturing industries—except those traditionally associated with the planting class, i.e. sugar and rum—privately operated transport and communications and the hotel industry. The employment of capital and labour by this class, with the exception of petty traders, distinguishes it from other self-employed skilled workers. 'Professional workers' include the clergy, all lawyers in private practice and all doctors in private practice as well as those engaged part-time in the Public Medical Service.

Expenditure is shown at factor cost: i.e. all subsidies have to be added and indirect taxes deducted. But although practically all imported consumer goods, all domestically consumed rum and a few other locally manufactured commodities were subject to customs and excise taxes, the method adopted of estimating expenditure made these calculations necessary only in the case of the railway, post office and public utilities where surpluses are regarded as indirect taxes and deficits as subsidies.

There is one further point that needs to be mentioned with regard to the expenditure table: total expenditure in Jamaica is not equal to output as we have defined it—gross domestic product—because the two concepts refer to different groups of people. National expenditure refers to the expenditure of all persons resident in the island while domestic output refers to all people working or owning productive resources in the island. If, for example, in one year receipts from emigrants abroad are substantial then total expenditure in Jamaica will be raised correspondingly and exceed domestic output by an equal amount. This divergence does not arise with the alternative classification of national output because in that case the value of remittances from abroad would also appear in the output table. One way of dealing with this difficulty would be to deduct from national expenditure that part which is paid for out of incomes received from abroad. Even if this were possible it would have the drawback of making necessary similar adjustments to the balance of payments which are not customary, i.e. deducting that part of imports which is paid for out of earnings received from abroad. Instead we make the necessary adjustment at the foot of the expenditure table; that is, we show national expenditure first and then deduct (in total) the amount received from abroad before adding the profits sent abroad and taking account of the surplus or deficit on the balance of payments (see Ch. 1, I).

The set of tables for each year is completed with a summary table showing the relationship between output, income and expenditure. In this table the value of output of each sector is broken down into the incomes to which it gives rise. Two further columns take account of goods entering into the external trade so that the subsequent columns exhibit the value of goods available domestically and the amounts consumed and invested.

Lack of statistical data about economic activities serving domestic needs inevitably gives rise to a number of problems. These are agricultural production for home consumption, the question of pricing, investment, distribution and the balance of payments. A somewhat different problem is presented by government accounts in so far as the questions which they pose are not merely statistical but also methodological. As these six subjects apply to the whole of the period under review they will be dealt with here, whereas special problems arising in particular years are referred to in each year's estimate. However, we make one exception to this rule. Because of the special interest which attaches to slaves' incomes it was decided to include a general methodological note on this question here.

D. Ground Provisions

Ground Provisions are 'breadstuffs', chiefly yams, cocoes, and sweet potatoes, which formed the staple diet. Having a fairly short growing season and needing only infrequent attention they could be grown in small plots for personal consumption or in larger quantities for sale. Yields varied according to soil or situation but, on the whole, wherever peasants settled, ground provisions formed part of their output. Unlike other domestic foods consumed in the island, such as export crops retained for home consumption—e.g. sugar, rum and coffee—meat and fish, which can be estimated for most of the years in question, no useful information about the quantities of ground provisions in the form of yields or acreage cultivated is available except for 1884. This makes it necessary to devise some method of filling this important gap.

First, we have assumed that the average per capita demand for starch food is constant. This is because it was usually possible for the cultivator to grow other crops when the demand for ground provisions was satisfied, and also because there is no evidence of shortage except in dry seasons which did not occur in any of the years under consideration. The assumption of constant starch consumption is justified as long as there were no significant changes in the standard of living. The evidence, as revealed by the estimates given in Chapters 2 to 8, suggests that there were only slight changes in the standard of living for most of the period. Only in *1930* was there a significant rise in the standard of living. However, the demand for ground provisions was also dependent on the amount of imported starches such as bread and biscuits, flour, cornmeal and rice which tended to replace domestic produce in the higher income groups and among the peasantry when settlers' exports increased.

This brings us to our second assumption: namely, that a unit of money spent on imported food gives the same degree of satisfaction as if the same amount were spent on home produced food. In short, that a £1 spent on imported flour or rice has roughly the same food value as £1 spent on ground provisions.

The problem of estimating the total value of ground provisions thus reduces to calculating a basic standard of starchfood requirements that applies to all years from *1832* to *1930* with appropriate adjustments for population, price and import changes: that is, we make the basic assumption

$$(q_0p_1 + Q_0P_1)\frac{x_1}{x_0} = (q_1p_1 + Q_1P_1)$$

whence
$$q_1p_1 = q_0p_1\frac{x_1}{x_0} + P_1\left(Q_0\frac{x_1}{x_0} - Q_1\right)$$

where q_0 is the quantity of ground provisions in the base year,
Q_0 is the quantity of imports in the base year,
q_1 is the quantity of ground provisions in the selected year,
Q_1 is the quantity of imports in the selected year,
p_1 is the market price of ground provisions in the selected year,
P_1 is the market price of imports in the selected year,
x_1 is the population in the selected year,
x_0 is the population in the base year.

Before giving the results of this equation a few words are needed about the statistics used. Market prices of imported foodstuffs are calculated by adding the specific import duties to factor prices.[1] Prices of ground provisions have been found in a variety of sources and are assumed to be retail.[2] Population statistics used here are to be found in Chapter 9. The number for 1884 has been calculated on the assumption that growth between the census years 1881 and 1891 was even. For the quantities of ground provisions in the base year we have used the evidence of the Royal Commission on Public Revenues of 1884 which prints a number of examples of gross profit earned in provision planting.[3] From these £30 per acre is

[1] See Ch. 1, E.

[2] Correspondence between CO and Governors of Colonies, BPP, 1859 (31), p. 237; Harvey, T. and Brewin, W., *Jamaica in 1866*, London, 1867; Royal Commission on Public Revenues, etc., BPP, 1884 (C 3840) Pt. I, App. N; STC, BPP, 1895 (C 7527); HBJ for 1910 and 1932.

[3] BPP, 1884 (C 3840).

selected as the most representative yield—equal to nearly 4.3 tons per acre. The total acreage returned as under ground provisions in that year is 66,854,[1] thus giving an estimated total production of 286,617 tons. It might be thought that a simpler way of calculating the quantity of ground provisions would be to apply the 1884 acreage yields to acreage statistics in other years. But there are two difficulties: first, acreage statistics begin only in 1869, and second, the classifications change over the years. From 1910 onwards acreage under rootcrops is variously entered under ground provisions, mixed cultivation and possibly elsewhere. Before then acreage returns also show an inexplicably sharp increase. To make use of them for one year (1884) and to dismiss them as useless for others is, of course, inconsistent. The only excuse that can be offered is that the method adopted here gives reasonable answers.

Applying the equation we obtain the value of ground provisions at current prices in the several years as follows:

Year	Value of Ground Provisions £'000
1830	847·1
1850	854·1
1870	1,656·5
1890	2,601·2
1910	3,170·0
1930	4,961·9

and per capita values and quantities as:

Year	Annual Value £ current prices	Weekly Consumption Weight (lb.)
1830	2·3	21·9
1850	2·1	20·4
1870	3·3	21·0
1890	4·1	20·2
1910	3·8	19·3
1930	4·9	19·1

It will be seen that per capita consumption of ground provisions is estimated to have ranged between 21·9 lb. per week in *1832* and 19·1 lb. in *1930*. These quantities may, at first sight, appear to be rather high. But it must be remembered that ground provisions are a very bulky food with a low calorific value. In fact, these estimates represent a daily intake of between about 1,400 and 1,230 calories per day.[2] Furthermore, no estimates of pulses or other vegetables

[1] STC, BPP, 1888 (C 5508).

[2] 1 lb. ground provisions = 450 calories. *Nutrition in Jamaica*, J. Govt. Printer, 1945, p. 31.

have been included in our national income tables. No means of calculating these have been discovered and they have, therefore, been treated as substitutes for ground provisions. What lends confidence in these results, however, is that they are supported by the findings of two other investigations. First, Dr. Benham estimated the quantity of ground provisions alone at 14 lb., and that of pulses, other vegetables and fruit such as mangoes, ackees and avocadoes at 3 lb. per capita per week in 1942 which together gives a total 2 lb. below our *1930* estimate. Dr. Benham encountered a similar gap in the statistics and in presenting his estimate added that it might be 'much too low' or somewhat too high.[1] Second, that the estimates are not excessive is supported by data on food production in Nigeria. According to the report of the International Bank for Reconstruction and Development production of yams and cassava alone was equivalent to a per capita consumption of 26·8 lb. per week and that of rice, millet, maize and guinea corn added a further 4·9 lb. to the weekly diet.[2] This compares with our estimates of a weekly per capita consumption of ground provisions of 19·1 lb. and of imported cereals of 1·8 lb. in *1930*.

E. Prices

According to the method of classification adopted, all output is shown at final value. No problem, therefore, arises as to what prices to choose to show output produced for exchange. The question how to evaluate that part of output which is consumed by the cultivator himself remains, since, in that case, much of the effort involved in bringing the produce to market is not required. Strictly, we should show all subsistence production at ex-farm prices plus any costs that may be incurred in taking it from the farm to the home. Unfortunately, we do not know either the proportion of ground provisions actually marketed or the costs involved. It is, therefore, on the grounds of expediency that we use retail prices for the whole output of ground provisions. It should be noted that this problem has attracted a great deal of attention and different solutions have been advocated.[3]

[1] Benham, *op. cit.*, p. 8.

[2] *The Economic Development of Nigeria*. London, 1953. Population, p. 10; Production of Crops, pp. 243–51.

[3] E.g. Prest, A. R. and Stewart, I. G., *The National Income of Nigeria 1950–1*,

A more general problem of price statistics arises in connection with the evaluation of some domestic production, the entrepôt trade and in calculating quantity indices. Very few price series are available. There are a few runs of c.i.f. London prices of West Indian exports published in the *Economist* and elsewhere.[1] In later years the BBJ also give f.o.b. export prices and c.i.f. import prices for the more important commodities. Price statistics had therefore to be compiled for the whole period. This was done for all commodities entering into external trade by dividing the average of the declared values in three successive years by the average of the quantities. For example, the price of sugar in *1850* is calculated by dividing the average value of sugar exports in the years 1849, 1850 and 1851 by the average quantity of sugar exports in these three years. For later years these can, of course, be checked against BBJ statistics. From these, factor prices of imports were obtained by adding the estimated distribution cost to c.i.f. prices. Exports retained for home consumption are valued at the ruling f.o.b. prices on the assumption that the costs involved in marketing them were the same as conveying them on board ship. In the case of goods and services not entering into external trade the problem was much more difficult. Often, only isolated prices, usually for Kingston, and wage quotations were found which had to be used on the assumption that they were representative for the particular commodity or service involved.

The final task in Part I was to make the estimates comparable over the years. For both output and consumption the revaluation in constant prices again presented fresh problems. Chief among these were the changing importance of different commodities, the introduction of new products and services which were not definable on a unit basis. To overcome the first, weighted averages were used to obtain price relatives. This was done for meat production, construction and rent. The method of revaluing exports falls into a special class and is dealt with separately in Appendix I. For the second and third, where no comparable prices were available, the products were revalued by splitting the final value into wages and materials used and calculating the price changes in each. This was done for public utilities, transport and communications and some manufactures. For

H.M.S.O. 1953 (Col. Res. Studies No. 12.) pp. 12–15, for argument in favour of retail prices on the grounds of the equality of satisfaction of the subsistence producer and the urban purchaser.

[1] See Ch. 5, I.

government services no information about the numbers engaged and their respective incomes is available. We have, therefore, used the cost of living index.[1] This method is far from ideal, since it implies a constant standard of living of civil servants, but it seemed preferable to the alternative predial wages index.

F. Investment

From the point of view of economic analysis perhaps the most serious weakness in the estimates is that relating to investment. The value of public works carried out is available in more or less complete form for most of the years and is assumed to be fairly reliable. It is in those items that carry most weight in the total, however, that the calculations are most likely to be in error. No useful information was found about either annual additions to the stock of durable producer goods or the value of commercial and residential construction.

In the case of durable producer goods it was assumed that all goods were imported and no estimates were made of any value that might have been added locally in installing equipment or for domestically produced capital goods. This assumption is obviously not justified because there was some domestic manufacture of carriages, coastal ships and fashioning of imported metals, but lack of information made it necessary. However, the omission does not appear to be very significant because—with the exception of metals—all durable producer goods were imported in finished form and also because even the simplest and most easily produced implements and other aids to production appear to have been imported. Spades, hoes, ploughs and even agricultural carriages figure in the import lists. Secondly, as shown in Chapter 14, C, the estimates of durable goods appear reasonable in relation to total investment and also to Gross Domestic Product.

The value of producer goods was accordingly obtained by selecting from the CR all those items which appeared likely to be capital goods rather than consumer goods. This was simple enough in most cases though inevitably some borderline cases were met. Included under producer goods generally are all types of machinery, pumps, engines, commercial vehicles, carts, wagons, railway trucks, locomotives and fixtures, metals (except those used expressly for public

[1] Appendix II.

works), printing presses, public utility fixtures and fittings, tools, instruments and livestock.

The data about commercial and residential construction are still weaker. We do not know the number of shops, warehouses and other business premises in existence at any time and even for private housing this information is not available for all years. It was, therefore, necessary to compute the value of construction according to what may be expected to have taken place. In the case of residential construction, the CP give the total number of houses, with some details, for most years, but for *1832* and *1850* both population and the number of houses had to be estimated. The method adopted here was to estimate separately the number of houses built for additional population and rising housing standards and the number built to replace old houses. Since the standard of housing ranged from the planter's residence to the shanty it was considered advisable to group all houses broadly according to quality. Each group was assigned a life span ranging from forty years for the most expensive houses to ten years for the single-roomed hut. These periods may seem rather short in view of the longer life of houses found to hold elsewhere:[1] but it should be remembered that, as most wooden houses were not protected by paint or other preservatives against termites, they deteriorated more rapidly, and, also, that Jamaica was subject to regular storm damage and floods and in Kingston fires appear to have been frequent. Values for each group were obtained from newspaper advertisements and other contemporary sources or, failing such information, from property taxes.

For additional houses the average annual increase during the ten years preceding the national income years was calculated and allocated to the different groups of houses according to what was appropriate for each year.

Replacements were calculated by dividing the number of houses in each group in existence at the beginning of the estimated life span by their average life. Thus, for example, in *1930* replacements of the group with a ten-year life were calculated by dividing the number in existence in 1921 (census year) by ten; the group with a twenty-year life by dividing the number in existence in 1911 (census year) by twenty; and so on. This method gives us the average number likely to have been replaced provided that our assumptions about the

[1] In the U.S. it averages 50 years or more. Kuznets, S. *Income and Wealth of the U.S.*, Series I, Cambridge, 1952, p. 180.

durability of houses are reasonable, that the increase in houses was fairly even and that worn-out houses had actually been replaced. Where the last assumption did not appear justified, as for instance, in 1850, when a visitor to Kingston remarked on the dilapidated condition and age of the houses in the city,[1] adjustments were made in the estimates. Full details of the calculations and sources will be found in the notes for each year. It should be noted that, in order to avoid repetition, all the information about the classification of houses is given under the head Residential Construction, leaving, in the main, only the detailed table of rental value under the head Ownership of Houses.

Commercial construction falls into two parts—business premises and factories. For the former, the estimates are based on the number of merchants and shop-keepers operating from fixed premises. The average value and life of their premises is assumed to be comparable to that of the most expensive group of houses in each year. As for residential buildings the distinction between new constructions and replacements is attempted. In the case of sugar factories there is a rough guide to the relationship between the value of the factory and its contents in the evidence submitted to the RWIC of 1897.[2] According to this the value of buildings and machinery were in the ratio of 91·5 : 100. It is assumed here that when new imported equipment was installed or replaced new factories were erected or existing ones repaired at the same time. The difficulty is that the character of plant and machinery in sugar factories changed radically during the century. During the early years equipment consisted mainly of sheet metal, pipes and copper pans. In order to calculate the value of building we have to include these in our estimates of plant. From the turn of the century a thorough reorganization of the industry took place. Often several sugar plantations were amalgamated. In some cases new factories were built to house the more elaborate machinery needed for the larger output; in others, existing factories were extended. But in view of the new type of equipment it is unlikely that the ratio of building to contents was as high as previously. Unfortunately no data comparable to that of 1897 are available. It is assumed that the ratio was 40 : 100 in *1930*[3] and that between 1897

[1] Bigelow, J. *Jamaica in 1850*, New York, 1851.

[2] BPP, 1897 (C 8669) Pt. XIII. No. 756.

[3] In the United Kingdom investment in buildings in manufacturing industries averaged 38 per cent of that in plant and machinery during the years 1948–54. *National Income and Expenditure*, HMSO, 1955, pp. 49 and 51.

and 1930 the trend to relatively more costly plant was even, thus giving a ratio of 71·2 : 100 in *1910*.

The final item which needs to be included here is investment in new land. This is important because, where techniques do not change, growth of agricultural output is possible only by extending the acreage under cultivation. However, the cost of bringing in new land was not as staggering as might be supposed from a glance at the acreage statistics, available from 1869 onwards;[1] Jamaica was cultivated far more extensively at the beginning of the nineteenth century than for a large part of the period under review. In 1823 the total acreage of the major estates was 1·1 million.[2] Even if we deduct a third of the total customarily left in woodland we are still left with a figure which was not again approached until the first decade of the twentieth century. The significance of this early extent of cultivation is that most of the virgin forests had been cleared and that the subsequent expansion had to contend only with the secondary growth. In order to arrive at a reasonable evaluation of investment in new land it is useful to distinguish between the two kinds of expansion involved: that of small-settlers and that of estates. For the greater part of the period—certainly up to the end of the century—the former accounts for most of the expansion. Small-settlers took up abandoned land or went into the interior. In neither case, however, is investment likely to have been considerable; the peasant did not usually have the capital to undertake thorough land clearance. He cleared his land by burning the bush, cutting down the trees, or, when this proved too difficult, left the trunks standing. On the other hand, the growth of banana estates from the nineties onwards was brought about partly by reclaiming abandoned sugar properties and partly by expanding into pasture land. Apparently this, too, was not a formidable task because such estimates as we have of the cost of clearing land are extremely low. In 1884, for example, the cost was given as 24*s*.[3] per acre and thirteen years later at between 10*s*. and 20*s*.[4] The value of agricultural investment is therefore calculated by taking the average annual increase in cultivated acreage over two years—e.g. that for 1910 is based on the increase between 1909 and 1911—and the labour costs given for 1884, adjusted for wage changes.

[1] BBJ and HBJ.

[2] Ragatz, L. J. *Statistics for the Study of British Caribbean Economic History*, New York, 1928.

[3] Royal Commission on Public Revenues, etc., *op. cit.*

[4] RWIC, No. 756.

It will be noticed that no estimates are prepared for changes in inventories. No information is available about stocks in the island. However, these were unlikely to be large. For the most part production consisted of highly perishable commodities. As for imports, capital goods were usually bought as required. Only in the case of consumer durables and semi-durables are stocks likely to have been important.

These five items—public works, residential and commercial construction, durable producer goods and agricultural investment—make up our estimates of gross domestic investment. Apart from the estimates of residential houses and business premises no attempt is made to calculate the value of net investment in any sector.

G. Distribution (see Ch. 1, C)

This item includes only the cost of distributing imported consumer goods and the value added in the entrepôt trade. Distribution costs of domestic produce and of imported production materials are, according to our method of classification, included in the output of each sector. In the absence of any direct information about distribution margins it was again necessary to devise a method of estimating values. In the case of the entrepôt trade profits were estimated by first calculating import and re-export prices[1] and then multiplying re-export quantities by import prices. The excess of re-export values over import values thus calculated gives us the value added by Jamaican merchants. For those years in which a sufficient coverage of the goods involved was possible, margins showed a surprisingly wide range; in *1832* the average value added amounted to 15 per cent of c.i.f. import cost but in *1850* it was nearly twice as high. In later years, when the entrepôt trade in commodities had shrunk to negligible proportions, the detailed calculations were not practicable, instead a margin of 25 per cent of import value has been assumed.

For the cost of distributing consumer goods to the domestic market no satisfactory method of calculating the value added was found. Margins have, therefore, been estimated at 25 per cent of c.i.f. value of imports throughout the period.

As owner-occupation was fairly general in Jamaica it is assumed that all merchants and shop-keepers owned their business premises.

[1] Ch. 1, E.

Employment of assistants does not appear to have been very extensive: the number of store-servers enumerated in the CP amounts to only about one-third of the total number of traders. It is, therefore, assumed that the gross profit from distribution is divided between traders and wage labour in the ratio of three to one.

H. Public Accounts

Public authorities are here defined as public collective providers. Accordingly we exclude all services performed for which specific charges were made: i.e. the trading activities of the post office, irrigation, railway and public utility undertakings.

Annual accounts of the central government are available from 1832 onwards. Generally they show revenue and expenditure in broad groups and, though they lack further detail, on the whole proved sufficient for our purpose. The returns furnished by the parochial boards, however, remained poor for the whole period. With the exception of the Kingston and St. Andrew Corporation in 1930, for which estimates of expenditure were published, usually total amounts only are shown and even this information was often missing in the days of representative government. In such cases crude estimates had to be made to fill the gap. The total amounts of local authorities' income and expenditure given in our estimates are therefore highly suspect for *1832* and *1850* and this applies even more so to the allocation of different types of expenditure.

In order to bring the accounts into line with our definition of net services rendered by public authorities some general rules were followed. These are as follows:

(*a*) All trading services were deducted from both sides of the accounts. Profits or losses on trading services are shown either as indirect taxes or as subsidies.

(*b*) Reimbursements for expenditure incurred were also deducted from both sides on the assumption that sales were priced at cost. This item includes prison and industrial school sales, hospital fees, lunatic asylum receipts from paying patients and printing office sales. On the other hand, where taxes were imposed to meet the cost of specific services and only the net tax or net expenditure was shown in the accounts, it was necessary to add the amount deducted to obtain total expenditure and total revenue. This applies to the accounts of the central authority in *1850*.

(*c*) Sales and purchases of land, buildings and the railway have been deducted.

(*d*) Grants to schools are shown as transfer payments and only the salaries of the inspectorate are included with government services. The reason for regarding education as an independent service is historical. Education in Jamaica was started by private charities and religious bodies. Public aid began in the form of grants to existing schools; the policy of founding government schools was adopted only in 1885. The treatment of all education thereafter as an outside service is not entirely justified but no information is available to separate the services rendered by government from those of the denominational schools. Even if it were, a case could be made out for combining the two.

All other services rendered by public authorities are assumed to be performed by government employees. Strictly, deductions should be made for goods and services purchased from other sectors of the economy. The accounts, however, are not detailed enough to make the necessary distinction. Deductions have been made only of the amount assumed to have been spent on imported materials.

I. The Balance of Payments

We have already dealt with the reason for presenting the balance of payments in the conventional form—that is to account for the difference between gross national product and gross national income—rather than bringing it into line with the concept of output adopted in this study (see Ch. 1, B). It remains to deal with the problems raised in estimating the various components of the balance of payments.

As far as the trade in commodities is concerned, the statistics are available in official returns and are assumed to be reliable. Where no specific statements were made, as in the early years, imports are treated as c.i.f. and exports f.o.b. In the years, *1832*, *1850* and *1870*, however, the entrepôt trade was not shown separately. In order to present domestic exports and imports for home consumption only, re-exports had to be deducted from the former and the import value of re-exports from total imports. This was easy enough for exports, but for imports involved first the calculation of the import value of each commodity exported and then the deduction of this value from the total import value of each commodity.[1]

[1] For method of estimating import values, see Ch. 1, G.

The balance of trade thus obtained was considerable, both at the beginning and at the end of our period. It is, therefore, particularly unfortunate that the information about invisible items is very poor. On the incoming side of the accounts we have been able to estimate the earning of traders engaged in the entrepôt trade and the receipts of religious societies from abroad in the early years. However, both items are relatively small. For later years, attempts were made to estimate receipts from emigrants, from tourists and earnings from resources owned abroad by individuals and institutions. All these items are highly speculative. On the outgoing side we have included only debt charges which are assumed to have been paid to persons resident abroad, as most of the government guaranteed stock was floated in London. There is no information about profits sent abroad.

It will be seen that the list of invisible items is incomplete and probably subject to considerable errors. It is for this reason that we have decided to call the residual balance 'foreign balance' rather than 'foreign investment' which would have implied greater accuracy than is justified. There are, however, some checks that can be applied to this residual balance. In *1832*, for example, the positive foreign balance of £1,090,400 is not inconsistent with the profits earned by planters if account is taken of the low amount of domestic capital formation and the extent of absenteeism. In later years the size and sign of the balance can similarly be checked against what we have been able to discover about domestic investment and the profits of the various classes of entrepreneurs: i.e. the change to the small negative balance is consistent with the decline of estate cultivation and the subsequent increase in the negative balance with overseas borrowing by the government and the recovery of the large estates.

K. Income of Slaves

Slaves generally received all their income in kind: i.e. owners provided goods and services for, and, with the exception of non-predial slaves, assigned land to, their slaves on which to grow their staple foods. Our problem is, therefore, first, to evaluate these goods and services and, second, how to show them in the national income tables.

A guide to slaves' incomes is contained in the Slave Acts[1] which regulated the amount of clothing to be supplied to each slave, made

[1] 1827 and 1831.

medical attention obligatory and laid down that where no provision grounds were available, 3*s.* 4*d.* currency should be paid weekly to cover the cost of food. Slaves' incomes can thus be calculated by totalling the value of provisions grown (or the weekly payment in lieu), of fish and clothing, medical services and drugs and medicines used for the slave population. We can also estimate the rental value of slave huts and their cost of construction.

Income received in kind has slight pecularities of presentation. First, if one class (e.g. doctors) is paid by a second class (planters) to give free service to a third (slaves), the cost of the service has to be entered *twice* in the income table, as part of the income of doctors and as part of the income of slaves. Whereas if agricultural labourers buy medical services out of their wages, one makes only one entry in respect of medical service.

Secondly, when slaves perform services for themselves (grow food, build houses) one has the option of treating this as part of the income of slave owners, matched by corresponding payments from owners to slaves, or merely as part of the income of slaves, without reference to slave owners. The former method has the law on its side, but it is unnecessarily cumbersome for accounting purposes. Accordingly we have opted to treat slaves as if they were owner-occupiers of their provision grounds and huts, and show the value of ground provisions, construction and rent under predial slaves' incomes in the relevant rows. The income of predial slaves arising out of agriculture shown in row 1 is, therefore, confined to the transactions that involved planters in actual, as distinct from nominal, costs. It should be noted that the final result is not affected: total income of agricultural workers and total gross profit of planters is the same in both methods. The method used here also has the advantage in that it makes the table comparable with later years when provisions were grown mainly by independent settlers and owner-occupation was more general.

L. Accuracy

Finally a word about the reliability of the estimates. The most complete data available relate to external trade and the central government accounts. For the rest, information had to be sought from a variety of sources—Parliamentary Papers and contemporary literature. On the whole, such data were most suitable for the output approach. The expenditure table is derived from the output table with the help of import and government revenue statistics. The second approach, that of income distribution, presented the greatest difficulty. For independent estimates, the usual method is to make use of income tax returns and add an estimate of incomes below the exemption limit. This was not possible here. Income tax was first imposed in 1920, and in 1930 only 4,385 persons were assessed, involving a total of £3,946,086[1] compared with an estimated gross domestic product of £19,951,600. Alternatively, if the numbers engaged in wage and salaried occupations are accurately known and the average earnings of each group are recorded, estimates can be prepared by multiplying the two. This, unfortunately, also proved largely useless because of the different classifications of working population adopted by the census, varying duration of employment as well as the fact that a large proportion of the population was not engaged in contract work at all but was independent. The only way of tackling the problem was to allocate Domestic Product for each sector to the different factors of production contributing to output. But this, too, involved much supplementary information available only for those years subject to special commissions which, in their enquiries, called for details of costs of production. For the *1832* estimate, for example, there was the select committee inquiring into the state of trade in the West Indies which gave rise to the West India Committee's *Statement to the Board of Trade*, and which included details of expenditure for the sugar industry. Similar information was found for *1850*, *1890* and *1930*. On the other hand, absence of such enquiries made estimates impossible for *1870* and *1910*.

It will be seen then, that both income and expenditure are ultimately dependent on the output table and that the conventional checks, through independent estimates, were not possible. Furthermore, even in the case of output it is not possible to state any margins of error. Often, only single references to prices and wages were available and data had to be selected according to their 'reasonableness'. However, there are a number of ways in which we can check detailed estimates: income distribution can be compared with the pattern of expenditure; individual items can be compared with totals; and such comparisons have proved invaluable in checking estimates for different years. In this task Table VI, showing output, income and expenditure in each year, has been especially useful. On the whole,

[1] Jamaica Departmental Reports, 1930, CO 140/274, vol. 70.

it is considered that no important items have been omitted. Most of the major items which were obtained from official sources, e.g. goods entering into external trade, public administration, public works and (for some years) education, public utilities, transport and communications, are fairly reliable, their accuracy generally improving after the inception of Crown Colony government in 1866. The only weighty item which throughout may be open to doubt is food production for local consumption—though for reasons given in Ch. 1, D, this may not be too wide of the margin. Doubt arises chiefly over the quantitatively less important items.

CHAPTER 2

THE NATIONAL INCOME IN *1832*

TABLE 2.I

Output in 1832

		£'000
1. Exports	2,193·4	
Less imported materials	106·6	
		2,086·8
2. Food Production for Local Consumption		
a. Ground Provisions	847·1	
b. Animal Products	39·0	
c. Other	14·0	
		900·1
3. Building and Construction		
a. Public	43·7	
b. Residential	129·6	
c. Commercial	38·0	
	211·3	
Less imported materials	31·3	
		180·0
4. Manufacturing for Local Consumptions		
a. Factories	63·2	
b. Independent Workers	260·0	
	323·2	
Less imported materials	3·1	
		320·1
5. Passenger Transport and Communications		—
6. Distribution		
a. Entrepôt	57·7	
b. Retail	228·7	
		286·4
7. Public Administration		
a. Central	226·4	
b. Local	96·5	
		322·9
8. Ownership of Houses		552·9
9. Professional Services		
a. Legal	52·0	
b. Medical	121·8	
c. Educational, *d.* Religious	43·7	
		217·5
10. Domestic Services		175·2
Total Gross Domestic Product		£5,041·9

TABLE 2.II

Income in 1832

		£'000
1. Incomes from Agriculture:		
a. Labourers' Wages	644·7	
b. Small-Settlers' Profits	847·1	
c. Planters' Profits	1,303·2	
d. Plantation Staffs' Salaries	461·5	3,256·5
2. Other Wages and Salaries:		
a. Domestic	174·0	
b. Construction	107·5	
c. Manufacturing	—	
d. Distribution	106·9	
e. Public Administration	255·5	
f. Education	10·7	
g. Other	10·4	665·0
3. Other Profits:		
a. Trade	560·9	
b. Professions	204·5	
c. Independent Work	355·0	1,120·4
Total (Gross Domestic Products)		£5,041·9

TABLE 2.III

Expenditure in 1832

		£'000
1. Food, Drink and Tobacco:		
Imported	522·9	
Home-produced	963·3	1,486·2
2. Clothing:		
Imported	453·9	
Home-produced	195·0	648·9
3. Other Consumer Goods:		
Imported	234·0	
Home-produced	65·0	299·0
4. Personal Services:		
Professional	188·0	
Domestic	175·2	363·2
5. Passenger Transport and Communications		—
6. Rent		552·9
Total Personal Expenditure		£3,350·2
7. Government Expenditure on Goods and Services		337·5
8. Domestic Investment		263·8
9. Payments Abroad		—
10. Income from Abroad		—
11. Foreign Balance		1,090·4
Total (Gross Domestic Product)		£5,041·9

TABLE 2.IV

Revenue and Expenditure Accounts of Public Authorities

1. Central Authority

Receipts	£'000	Expenditure	£'000
Direct Taxes:		Wages and Salaries / Goods and Services	249·0
On income	—	Transfer Payments:	
On property	59·8	To persons	4·5
Indirect Taxes:		Subventions	4·7
Customs	69·7		
Excise	17·3		
Stamp duty	8·1		
Licences, fees, fines, etc	35·9	Interest	15·2
Deficit	82·6		
	£273·4		£273·4

2. Local Authorities

Receipts	£'000	Expenditure	£'000
Direct Taxes on property	146·5	Wages and Salaries / Goods and Services	132·3
		Transfer Payments:	
		To persons	7·7
		Subventions	2·2
		Surplus	4·3
	£146·5		£146·5

TABLE 2.V

The Balance of Payments

Income from Abroad	£'000	Expenditure Abroad	£'000
Total Value of Domestic Exports	2,193·4	Total Value of Retained Imports	1,175·6
Earnings from Entrepôt Trade	57·7		
Receipts from Religious Societies abroad	14·9	Balance	1,090·4
	£2,266·0		£2,266·0

TABLE 2.VI

Output, Income and Expenditure in 1832

£'000

	1	2	3	4	5	6	7	8	9	10	11	12	13	14
	Gross Domestic Output	Agricultural Labourers	Small-Settlers	Planters	Plantation Staff	Other Wages and Salaries	Merchants	Professional Workers	Independent Workers	Imports	Exports	Goods and Services Available Domestically	Consumed	Invested
1. Exports*	2,086·8	458·4	—	1,206·6	381·6	24·9	89·4	—	—	106·6	2,193·4	—	—	—
2. Food Production*	900·1	—	847·1	—	—	—	—	—	39·0	422·2	—	1,322·3	1,322·3	—
3. Building and Construction	180·0	62·2	—	—	—	88·4	29·4	—	—	31·3	—	211·3	—	211·3
4. Manufacturing for Local Consumption*	320·1	—	—	—	—	—	—	—	260·0	615·5	—	935·6	883·1	52·5
5. Passenger Transport and Communications	—	—	—	—	—	—	—	—	—	—	—	—	—	—
6. Distribution	286·4	—	—	50·4	—	71·6	164·4	—	—	—	57·7	228·7	228·7	—
7. Public Administration	322·9	—	—	10·9	10·3	253·4	17·0	2·1	29·2	—	—	322·9	322·9	—
8. Ownership of Houses	552·9	124·1	—	35·3	69·6	41·4	250·4	5·3	26·8	—	—	552·9	552·9	—
9. Professional Services	217·5	—	—	—	—	20·4	—	197·1	—	—	—	217·5	217·5	—
10. Domestic Services	175·2	—	—	—	—	164·8	10·4	—	—	—	—	175·2	175·2	—
Totals	5,041·9	644·7	847·1	1,303·2	461·5	664·9	561·0	204·5	355·0	1,175·6	2,251·1	3,966·4	3,702·6	263·8
11. Less Income from Abroad	—	—	—	—	—	—	—	—	—	−14·9	—	−14·9	−14·9	—
12. Plus Payments Abroad	—	—	—	—	—	—	—	—	—	—	—	—	—	—
13. Foreign Balance	—	—	—	—	—	—	—	—	—	1,090·4	—	1,090·4	—	1,090·4
	5,041·9	644·7	847·1	1,303·2	461·5	664·9	561·0	204·5	355·0	2,251·1	2,251·1	5,041·9	3,687·7	1,354·2

* Incomes shown in columns numbers 2 to 7, row 1, include incomes arising out of the production of retained exports as well as exports, hence columns numbers 2 to 9, row 2, show only incomes arising out of the production of ground provisions and animal products and columns numbers 2 to 9, row 4, only those arising out of the manufacture of non-export crops and public utilities. The incomes in these three rows thus do not add up individually to give the total under Gross Domestic Product. See notes under II, numbers 1, 2 and 4.

I. Output

All values shown in the estimates are expressed in sterling. Until the 1839 Act,[1] providing for the adoption of United Kingdom currency, was passed, Jamaican legal tender, known as island currency, circulated at rates often considerably below that of sterling. Wherever statistics were quoted in island currency they have been converted into sterling at the ruling rate of exchange of £140 currency = £100 sterling.[2] References to all conversions will be found in the text.

1. *Exports*

External trade statistics are given in the CR.[3] After deduction of re-exports the average value of domestic exports for the years 1832 and 1833 is £2,193,400. But net output should show only the value produced in Jamaica: a deduction must therefore be made of imported materials used in the manufacture of export crops. The value of these—£109,700, consisting chiefly of timber for containers, cordage and coal—was also taken from CR[4] and deducted from plantation crops proportionately to amounts exported and amounts—shown under Ch. 2, I, 4*a*—retained for home consumption.

2. *Food Production for Local Consumption*

(*a*) *Ground Provisions.* See Ch. 1, D.

(*b*) *Animal Products.* This item includes an estimate of fish production only. The 1844 CP returned 1,484 fishermen. Their number here has been taken as 1,500 and their average net earnings assumed to be £26 p.a. each (Ch. 2, I, 4*b*).

(*c*) *Other.* Included here are the remaining foodstuffs mainly or wholly un-manufactured. In this year it includes only coffee. Coffee was never listed in estate distributions to slaves. It may be assumed therefore that its consumption was confined to the free population. For these it has been put at 7½ lbs. p.a. each.[5]

3. *Building and Construction*

(*a*) *Public.* Expenditure on public works directly undertaken by the central government is available in the House of Assembly returns

[1] 3 Vic. cap. 39.
[2] Martin, R. M. *History of Colonies of the British Empire*, London, 1843, p. 19.
[3] Customs 12/1 and 2. [4] Customs 6/1 and 2. [5] Ch. 3, I, 2.

included in the BBJ for 1832 and 1833.[1] But roads and bridges which were the responsibility of the parochial authorities are listed only in fragmentary returns. The gaps have been filled by applying the average expenditure of the complete returns.

(*b*) *Residential.* As pointed out in Ch. 1, F, no data are available about housing for these years. The number of houses in 1832 is here calculated on the basis of population estimates for 1834 and the population census of 1844. Three broad categories of houses are distinguished: those occupied by planters, estate managers, overseers, professional people, traders, those occupied by the remainder of the free population and, thirdly, the huts built by slaves for their own use. The numbers in the first two are estimated on the basis of the occupational distribution in 1844, at 6,000 and 18,000 respectively, and the last, on the assumption that there was one hut for every six slaves, at 51,800. The average life of houses in the first two groups is taken at forty years and that of slave huts at ten years. Values are based on advertisements found in the *Kingston Chronicle and Advertiser* in 1835 adjusted for currency.[2] The cost of a slave hut for a family of six is given as £12 in 1831.[3]

No estimates are made for new houses to allow for population

Value of Residential Building

	Number built during Year	Cost £	Annual Value of Building £'000
(i) Additional Houses:	Nil.		
(ii) Replacements:	75	214	16·1
	450	114	51·3
	5,180	12	62·2
	5,705		£129·6

growth for these years. Population began to decline after the abolition of the slave trade in 1808 and continued to decline until the 1840's. The possibility of rising housing standards in the conditions prevailing immediately before emancipation must also be excluded.

[1] CO 142/45 and 46.

[2] 2nd September and 16th November, 1835. Quoted at £300 and £160 respectively.

[3] Statement to the Board of Trade re State of Colonies, BPP, 1830/1 (120), p. 36.

Because population was declining the rule of basing replacements on the number of houses in existence at the beginning of the life period for each group was not followed for these years. Instead it was decided to base the computations on the number of houses estimated for 1832, and since the white population had been reduced so drastically in the preceding years, to assume that only half of the most expensive houses due for renewal were actually replaced.

(*c*) *Commercial.* (i) *Shops, Warehouses, etc.* The 1844 census enumerates 433 merchants and 2,216 shopkeepers. Undoubtedly their numbers were even larger in 1832, but since many merchants left the island during the twenties and thirties and continued to leave until the sixties it seems reasonable to assume that not all of them were interested in maintaining or improving their business premises. The value of business premises built during the year is, therefore, calculated on the assumption that only half of those due for replacement were actually built and that the cost and life of shops and warehouses were comparable with those of the larger houses. The value of construction is thus calculated at £7,100.

(ii) *Sugar Factories.* For basis of calculation see Ch. 1, F. In the years 1832–3 no machinery was actually imported but the value of metals—brass, copper and lead—used extensively in sugar factories for conveying liquids and other purposes amounted to £33,800. The value of factory buildings has accordingly been estimated at £30,900.

4. *Manufacturing for Local Consumption*

(*a*) *Factories.* Rum was subject to an excise duty of 1*s.* 6*d.* per gallon. The amount consumed—224,493—is calculated from the tax yield given in the House of Assembly returns in the BBJ for 1832 and 1833.[1] For sugar, the per capita consumption in the United Kingdom during the years 1832–3—18 lbs.—has been taken as the basis for calculating the amount of sugar retained in the island.[2]

	£'000
Rum . . .	17·8
Sugar . . .	45·4
	£63·2

(*b*) *Independent Workers.* An attempt is made here to account for the remainder of the free population. The white population is

[1] *Op. cit.* [2] Customs Tariffs of the United Kingdom, BPP 1898 (C 8706).

included under agriculture above and under professional and government services and distribution below. The total free coloured and black population numbered 45,000[1] of whom the numbers employed are estimated at 20,300.[2] Of these about half are included under fishing, animal products, construction above and under distribution, lodging-house keeping, and as assistants to professional workers below, leaving about 10,000 to be accounted for here as tailors, dressmakers, cabinet-makers, etc. No wage quotations have been found for free labour for these years. However, earnings are not likely to have been very appreciable as the market for the output of these workers was small. Estates supplied all their needs from abroad or from their own estates. Nor is it likely that slaves could afford to buy many services from the free population. Average net earnings have accordingly been estimated at 10*s*. per week.

5. *Passenger Transport and Communications*

There is no information about passenger transport. As far as is known there were no passenger vehicles for regular hire. Postal Services were, until 1860, run by the Imperial government. No information is available about the value of these services but apparently it was negligible.

6. *Distribution* (see also Ch. 1, G)

(*a*) *Entrepôt*. The total value of the entrepôt trade for the years 1832–3 averaged £450,900. For 90·4 per cent of this trade it was possible to calculate import and re-export prices. For the remainder the margin general among the calculated commodities was used. The estimated value added by Jamaican merchants averages about 15 per cent of the c.i.f. value of imports.

(*b*) *Retail*. As explained in Chapter 1, the cost of distributing imported goods is assumed to be 25 per cent of the c.i.f. value of imports. This margin, however, applies only to those goods that passed through the hands of local merchants. It was customary for estates to obtain the goods needed for their slaves directly from abroad without using local intermediaries. Since such supplies were bought by the owners when needed, and hence the cost of carrying stocks was negligible, we have calculated the value added as 20 per cent of the c.i.f. value compared with 25 per cent in the case of goods

[1] HBJ, e.g. for 1895.

[2] Ch. 9, E.

sold by local merchants. For the method of estimating the value of imported slave supplies see Ch. 2, II, 1*a*.

7. *Public Authorities*

(*a*) *Central.* The House of Assembly returns included in the BBJ were given in sufficient detail for this purpose. Average expenditure on public buildings, etc., is deducted and shown under 3*a*, stipends of clergy are included under 9*d*, while debt charges and other transfer payments are excluded altogether.

(*b*) *Local.* Similar adjustments were made to the expenditure of parochial authorities after, first, filling the gaps in the data on the basis of complete returns and, second, converting values into sterling. (For details see Chs. 2, IV, and 1*b*.)

8. *Ownership of Houses*

This follows from the assumptions made under Ch. 2, I, 3*b*. No suitable examples of rents were found in the newspaper advertisements. Rental values have therefore been estimated at 12½ per cent for the more expensive houses. In the case of slave huts there are naturally no examples of rent since none was ever charged. Immediately after emancipation rents charged by estates for the same hut were 1*s*. per week or more.[1] The sum of 1*s*. has been used here but it should be borne in mind that the conditions under which these rents were charged were substantially different from the pre-emancipation era and may therefore exaggerate the importance of rental values in 1832.

Rental Value of Houses

Number of Houses '000	Average Rent £	Total Rental Value £'000
6·0	26·8	160·8
18·0	14·3	257·4
51·8	2·6	134·7
75·8		552·9

9. *Professional Services*

(*a*) *Legal.* The JA for 1832 lists seven barristers and ninety-seven attorneys-at-law. Their earnings have been assumed at £500 p.a. each.

[1] Gardner, W. J. *A History of Jamaica*, London, 1873, p. 398.

(*b*) *Medical*. Medical attention for slaves was provided by the proprietor. It was usually done on the basis of weekly visits to estates at 6*s*. p.a. for each slave.[1] The same sum is allowed for attendance on the free coloured population but charges for the white population were rather higher and have been put here at £1 each.

(*c*) and (*d*) *Educational and Religious*. The stipends of the ministers of the established church—the Church of England—were paid from House of Assembly votes, but were also supplemented by fees. The amount of fees was £200 in St. Ann.[2] For twenty-one parishes the total fees may be taken as £4,200. The various missionary societies were dependent for their income on their parent societies and such sums as could be raised in the island. 149 missionaries and preachers[3] are estimated to have received £100 each from abroad. Education was provided in part by the parishes but chiefly by charitable endowments and the missionary societies. Here Martin's estimate of £10,000 p.a. has been used.[4]

10. *Domestic Services*

The Slave Compensation lists return 31,966 slaves as domestics.[5] This is undoubtedly an overestimate of the actual number of 'effective' slaves. If we reduce this figure by one-third we get 21,311 which brings the number more in line with the 20,571 enumerated in the 1844 CP (see Ch. 10, A). The majority of slaves were employed on plantations and this raises the question of whether they were employed mainly to provide services for predial slaves or for their owners directly. In the former case, the value of domestics should not be entered separately but regarded as part of estates' costs of production just as canteen facilities are in modern factories; in the latter case, domestic service should be treated as if purchased out of planters' income. Contemporary evidence does not suggest that domestics were primarily engaged to relieve predial slaves but rather to provide services in planters' residences and the total value of domestic service is, accordingly, entered here. The value of the services rendered by domestics is taken to be equal to the cost of providing medical attention and imported goods and the sum of 3*s*. 4*d*.

[1] Ragatz, L. J. *The Fall of the Planter Class in the British Caribbean, 1763–1833*, New York, 1929.

[2] Martin. *History of the British Colonies*, 1834, p. 208.

[3] JA for 1840.

[4] *Op. cit.*, p. 207.

[5] BPP (215), 1837–8.

currency (2*s*. 4½*d*. sterling)[1] stipulated under the Slave Consolidation Act to be paid weekly in lieu of provision grounds. Domestic slaves' share in services and imported goods amounts to £32,800 (see Ch. 2, II, 1*a*). Cash payments bring the total income of domestic slaves up to £164,800.

Included in this item as well is the output of tavern and lodging-house keepers. The 1844 CP returns 200 persons engaged in running such establishments. This number has been used here and the net income assumed to be £1 per week each.

II. Income

As mentioned in Chapter 1, income distribution is derived by allocating domestic output to the different factors of production. The incomes arising out of each economic sector have, therefore, to be considered separately before distribution for the whole economy can be obtained.

1. *Exports*

The Statement to the Board of Trade includes a detailed account of the expenditure of a sugar estate relating to the years 1825–7.[2] This, unfortunately, is only partially useful for the present purpose because it gives no indication of the difference between costs and value of output. The method used here to obtain the various incomes arising out of estate cultivation is to estimate, first, slaves' incomes by calculating the cost of the goods and services provided for them, secondly, the salaries of plantation staff and, thirdly, the costs of other services rendered by outside factors. Finally, plantation profits are derived after deduction of all these incomes from the value of domestic output.

(*a*) *Incomes of Slaves* (see Ch. 1, K). It appears to have been usual to assign plots of land to predial slaves and to allow them time to grow their own food. The land was usually unsuitable for plantation crops and the time allowed—every alternate Saturday—probably did not affect estate production. The cost of this part of slaves' maintenance was therefore purely nominal. The supplies chargeable to plantation output are various articles of clothing and fish. The value of these are assumed to be three-quarters of retained imports of

[1] Law of 1827. [2] *Op. cit.*, p. 56.

each of these articles valued at c.i.f. prices plus 20 per cent for distribution. (Ch. 2, I, 6). To this have to be added the cost of medical attention (Ch. 2, I, 9 *b*) and the estimated cost of drugs and medicines used.

Cash Expenditure on Predial Slave Labour

		£'000
Imported Supplies	403·3	
Medical Attendance	93·0	
Cash Expenditure on Total Slave Population		496·3
Less Share of: Domestic Slaves included under 10 a.	32·8	
Wharf Labour paid to Merchants	5·1	37·9
Cash Expenditure on Predial Slaves		£458·4

(*b*) *Income of Plantation Staff.* The staff of a sugar plantation consisted generally of a proprietor or, if absent, an attorney, a manager and/or overseer, two or three book-keepers and sometimes one or two other white people. On coffee estates and pens the number of white employees was usually rather less. All were paid in cash

Salaries of Plantation Staff

	Book-keepers £'000	Overseers £'000	Attorneys £'000
Sugar	67·0	86·4	85·6
Coffee	17·2	44·2	14·8
Pens	15·3	39·3	11·8
	£99·5	£169·9	£112·2

and provided with rent-free accommodation. In 1836 there were 670 sugar estates.[1] They are assumed to have employed one overseer and two book-keepers each. Nothing is known about the number of attorneys employed. In 1852 55 per cent of the sugar estates were owned by absentees[2] but this proportion was higher in 1832 and has been put here at 60 per cent. There were in addition 343 coffee estates and 305 pens.[3] Their white staff is assumed to have consisted of one overseer and one book-keeper each. The number of attorneys has again been based on the 1852 rate of absenteeism which was 20

[1] Papers on Abolition of Slavery, BPP, 1836 (166), Pt. III, 1, p. 24.
[2] PAIJ, BPP, 1854 (1848), p. 55.
[3] Papers on Abolition of Slavery, *op. cit.*

per cent for coffee estates and 18 per cent for pens. Salaries of book-keepers were £50,[1] those of overseers £129[2] and of attorneys £214.[3] As in the case of slaves' incomes we include here only those incomes that involved planters in actual cash transactions. For this reason we do not include the rental value of houses occupied here but show it under the income of plantation staff from houseownership.

(*c*) *Other Incomes*. There remains to be added the cost of wharfage. The sugar estate, quoted in the Statement to the Board of Trade,[4] spent an average of £159 currency p.a., equal to £113, sterling on wharfage. This cost is assumed to have been incurred by each sugar and coffee estate and to have been paid to merchants. Merchants employed about 3,200 slaves[5] on dock work to whom they paid 2*s*. 4½*d*. per week for food which together with their share of slave supplies brings the total income of wharf labour up to £24,900.

Deducting these various items from the total domestic plantation output—i.e. exports, retained exports and manufactured sugar and rum less imported materials—we get planter's gross profit as a residual item.

Planters' Gross Profit

		£'000
Total Domestic Plantation Output		2,160·9
Less Slave Supplies	458·4	
Plantation Staff	381·6	
Merchants	89·4	
Wharf Labour	24·9	954·3
Planters' Gross Profit		£1,206·6

2. *Food Production for Local Consumption*

Considered here are only ground provisions and animal products since retained plantation output has already been dealt with under Ch. 2, I. Ground provisions are assumed to have been grown exclusively by slaves on the provision grounds and are treated as profits from agriculture accruing to slaves in their capacity as independent cultivators comparable to the small-settlers in later years. Part of their output was sold to other slaves, mainly non-predial slaves living

[1] Statement to the Board of Trade, *op. cit.*, p. 35. £70 currency.
[2] *Ibid.*, £180 currency. [3] *Ibid.*, p. 56. £300 currency. [4] *Op. cit.*
[5] Slave Compensation Claims, *op. cit*. This figure is equal to two-thirds of the non-predial group excluding domestics.

in the towns, and to the free population. The marketing of produce, however, appears to have been usually performed by the cultivator himself and we therefore make no deduction for the earnings of intermediaries.

The earnings of fishermen are shown under the income of independent workers.

3. *Building and Construction*

Slave huts were built by their occupants and the value of output is, as explained in Ch. 1, F, entered under income of slaves. For the rest, output is allocated to free labour and merchants in the ratio of three to one.

4. *Manufacturing for Local Consumption*

Manufactured sugar and rum have already been dealt with under 1 above. The value of output of independent workers was estimated on a net basis and, therefore, accrues wholly to independent workers.

6. *Distribution*

For method of estimating incomes arising out of the distribution of imported goods sold by local merchants see Ch. 1, B. In the case of slave supplies it is assumed that three-quarters of the value added accrued to planters and one-quarter to wages.

7. *Public Administration*

(*a*) *Central.* Incomes are taken from the BBJ. These show payments to the following occupational groups:

	£'000
Administrative Public Servants	47·9
Lawyers	7·1
Militia	72·4
Military	99·0
	£226·4

The BBJ for 1833 shows the strength of the Militia as 10,581. The average per capita cost of pay and rations for militia troops, amounting to £6·8, is allocated to planters, overseers, lawyers, doctors, attorneys, traders, government servants and other free people.

(*b*) *Local.* The data for local authorities are insufficient to distinguish the various income earners. Apart from public works and transfer payments all expenditure has been assumed to accrue to public servants.

8. *Ownership of Houses* (see Ch. 1, F)

Houses inhabited by plantation staffs were provided on the estates as part of income. The same applies to the huts inhabited by slaves. Estate owners were, of course, owner-occupiers. The houses occupied by the remainder of the free population have been assumed to be partly owned and partly rented from merchants.

9. *Professional Services*

Of lawyers' gross earnings one-fifth is assumed to have been spent on clerical assistance. Medicines were provided in estate hospitals so that doctors' incomes are identical with output of medical services. The earnings of teachers and clergy were explained in Ch. 2, I.

10. *Domestic Services*

This item is self-explanatory: incomes accruing from domestic service are entered under wages and from hotel-keeping under profits of merchants.

III. Expenditure

The method followed here is roughly that of rearranging the output table: imports are substituted for exports and account is taken of the net balance of payments.

1. *Food, Drink and Tobacco*

The value of imported food, drink and tobacco is taken from the CR from which the estimated cost of re-exports has been deducted. To this is added the island costs of distribution. The amount spent on home-grown food is equal to the total value of output: i.e. including the value of imported materials used in producing the manufactured rum and sugar.

2. *Clothing*

All articles of clothing and materials used for clothing were imported. The amount spent on clothing is thus calculated by adding distribution costs to c.i.f. value of imports. Included also are the services rendered by dressmakers, tailors, shoemakers, etc., in making up imported materials.

3. *Other Consumer Goods*

These two items are derived from the output table 1 in Ch. 2, I.

4. *Personal Services*

Under professional services is entered only the amount spent by the inhabitants of the island. £14,900 was estimated to have been contributed by missionary societies abroad and £14,600 by the government and have, therefore, been deducted from the total shown in the output table under religious and educational services.

6. *Rent*

This is identical with output.

7. *Government Expenditure on Goods and Services*

Included here is the total current expenditure on goods and services by the central and local authorities. Capital formation is shown under investment.

8. *Domestic Investment*

This consists of building and construction and the value of durable producer goods added during the year.

	£'000
Building and Construction .	211·3
Durable Producer Goods . .	52·5
	£263·8

No estimates are made of investment in new land for this year. Since estates were faced with emancipation it is unlikely that any extension in cultivated acreage took place. Investment in building and construction is identical to the gross value shown under 3 in the output table. For method of estimating durable producer goods see Ch. 1, F.

IV. Public Authorities

1. *Central Government*

(*a*) *Receipts.* Direct taxes on property consist of taxes levied on slaves, livestock, wheels and carriages. Customs duties were imposed on imports from non-British territories and the excise duty was levied on locally consumed rum. Licences, fees and fines include tonnage duties, traders' licences, the Deficiency tax, etc.

(*b*) *Expenditure.* The share of goods and services is high this year because of the extraordinary expenditure on military and militia services. In 1832 the island was relieved of the duty of contributing towards the upkeep of the West India Regiment. In the same year, however, the Slave Rebellion necessitated additional expenditure which was paid for by the island authority. This has been included here on the grounds that, in the absence of a local police force, the services of the West India Regiment were rendered to restore internal peace. Transfer payments to persons includes annuities paid to widows of Anglican clergymen which, unlike pensions paid to government employees, are not regarded as payments for services rendered in the past. This item also includes a number of miscellaneous payments to individuals, e.g. premiums on natural increase of slaves, on stock, etc.

2. *Local Government*

(*a*) *Receipts.* Local revenue appears to have been obtained mainly from direct taxation on property. The fragmentary accounts available, however, are insufficient to attempt analysis.

(*b*) *Expenditure.* The slightly more detailed information in the case of expenditure makes it possible to separate transfer payments from expenditure on goods and services. Apart from general administration, local authorities were responsible for road maintenance, for poor relief—shown under transfers to persons—and made a small contribution to education—included under subventions.

V. The Balance of Payments

As explained under item 1 of output table, no. 2.I, the value of domestic exports had to be separated from re-exports. Similarly the import cost of re-exports had to be deducted from total imports. Invisible items included in the table are the 'value added' by traders in the entrepôt trade and receipts from religious societies abroad. No further data about external payments are available to account for the huge excess of income over expenditure. It is, however, well known that it was customary for planters to transfer their profits abroad. Some used their surplus income over current expenses to invest in real estate in the United Kingdom, others were committed to repayments on debts incurred in developing the estate or on mortgages raised for other purposes. According to our estimates only £52,500 was invested in the island in durable producer goods out of a gross profit of £1,257,000 during these years. The large balance of £1,090,400 on the external account is therefore quite consistent with the transfer of profits arising out of estate cultivation.

CHAPTER 3

THE NATIONAL INCOME IN *1850*

TABLE 3.I

Output in 1850

		£'000
1. Exports	923·6	
Less imported materials	52·1	871·5
2. Food Production for Local Consumption:		
a. Ground Provisions	854·1	
b. Animal Products	146·6	
c. Other	45·0	1,045·7
3. Building and Construction:		
a. Public	28·7	
b. Residential	122·5	
c. Commercial	50·3	
	201·5	
Less imported materials	37·5	164·0
4. Manufacturing for Local Consumption:		
a. Factories	120·7	
b. Independent Workers	229·7	
	350·4	
Less imported materials	6·8	343·6
5. Passenger Transport and Communications		—
6. Distribution:		
a. Entrepôt	43·3	
b. Retail	229·0	272·3
7. Public Administration:		
a. Central	146·6	
b. Local	28·1	174·7
8. Ownership of Houses		416·2
9. Professional Services:		
a. Legal	49·0	
b. Medical	34·5	
c. Educational, *d.* Religious	79·9	163·4
10. Domestic Services		273·0
Total Gross Domestic Product		£3,724·4

TABLE 3.II

Income in 1850

		£'000
1. Incomes from Agriculture:		
a. Labourers' wages	651·9	
b. Small-Settlers' profits	999·1	
c. Planters' profits	204·4	
d. Plantation staffs' salaries	218·6	2,074·0
2. Other Wages and Salaries:		
a. Domestic	267·4	
b. Construction	130·0	
c. Manufacturing	—	
d. Distribution	96·8	
e. Public Administration	144·5	
f. Education	16·7	
g. Other	18·2	673·6
3. Other Profits:		
a. Trade	488·0	
b. Professions	172·8	
c. Independent Work	316·0	976·8
Total (Gross Domestic Product)		£3,724·4

TABLE 3.III

Expenditure in 1850

		£'000
1. Food, Drink and Tobacco:		
Imported	491·4	
Home-produced	1,164·0	1,655·4
2. Clothing:		
Imported	467·4	
Home-produced	135·7	603·1
3. Other Consumer Goods:		
Imported	186·2	
Home-produced	94·0	280·2
4. Personal Services:		
Professional	120·4	
Domestic	273·0	393·4
5. Passenger Transport and Communications		—
6. Rent		416·2
Total Personal Expenditure		3,348·3
7. Government Expenditure on Goods and Services		211·8
8. Domestic Investment		257·4
9. Payments Abroad		—
10. Income from Abroad		—
11. Foreign Balance		– 93·1
Total (Gross Domestic Product)		£3,724·4

TABLE 3.IV

Revenue and Expenditure of Public Authorities

1. Central Authority

Receipts	£'000	Expenditure	£'000
Direct Taxes:		Wages and Salaries / Goods and Services	180·2
On income	—	Transfer Payments:	
On property	12·1	Subventions	5·5
Indirect Taxes:		Interest	17·9
Customs	136·5		
Excise	17·3		
Stamp Duty	7·7		
Licences, fees, fines, etc.	22·5		
Deficit	7·5		
	£203·6		£203·6

2. Local Authorities

Receipts	£'000	Expenditure	£'000
Taxes	67·8	Wages and Salaries / Goods and Services	51·5
Deficit	0·1	Transfer Payments:	
		To Persons	15·1
		Subventions	1·3
	£67·9		£67·9

TABLE 3.V

Balance of Payments

Income from Abroad	£'000	Expenditure Abroad	£'000
Total Value of Domestic Exports	923·6	Total Value of Retained Imports	1,065·9
Earnings from Entrepôt Trade	43·3		
Receipts from Religious Societies	5·9		
Balance	93·1		
	£1,065·9		£1,065·9

TABLE 3.VI

Output, Income and Expenditure in 1850

(£'000)

	1	2	3	4	5	6	7	8	9	10	11	12	13	14
	Gross Domestic Product	Agricultural Labourers	Small-Settlers	Planters	Plantation Staff	Other Wages and Salaries	Merchants	Professional Workers	Independent Workers	Imports	Exports	Goods and Services Available Domestically	Consumed	Invested
1. Exports*	871·5	566·1	85·1	160·5	177·7	16·5	24·5	—	—	52·1	923·6	—	—	—
2. Food Production*	1,045·7	17·6	842·0	26·4	—	7·3	78·1	—	29·3	393·0	—	1,438·7	1,436·3	2·4
3. Building and Construction	164·0	—	—	—	—	123·0	41·0	—	—	37·5	—	201·5	—	201·5
4. Manufacturing for Local Consumption and P.U.*	343·6	—	—	—	—	—	—	—	229·7	583·3	—	926·9	873·4	53·5
5. Passenger Transport and Communications	—	—	—	—	—	—	—	—	—	—	—	—	—	—
6. Distribution	272·3	—	—	—	—	68·1	204·2	—	—	—	43·3	229·0	229·0	—
7. Public Administration	174·7	—	—	—	—	141·6	—	33·1	—	—	—	174·7	174·7	—
8. Ownership of Houses	416·2	68·2	72·0	17·5	40·9	21·4	134·6	4·6	57·0	—	—	416·2	416·2	—
9. Professional Services	163·4	—	—	—	—	28·3	—	135·1	—	—	—	163·4	163·4	—
10. Other Services	273·0	—	—	—	—	267·4	5·6	—	—	—	—	273·0	273·0	—
Totals	3,724·4	651·9	999·1	204·4	218·6	673·6	488·0	172·8	316·0	1,065·9	966·9	3,823·4	3,566·0	257·4
11. Less Income from Abroad	—	—	—	—	—	—	—	—	—	−5·9	—	−5·9	−5·9	—
12. Plus Payments Abroad	—	—	—	—	—	—	—	—	—	—	—	—	—	—
13. Foreign Balance	—	—	—	—	—	—	—	—	—	−93·1	—	−93·1	—	−93·1
Total Gross Domestic Product	£3,724·4	651·9	999·1	204·4	218·6	673·6	488·0	172·8	316·0	966·9	966·9	3,724·4	3,560·1	164·3

* Incomes shown in columns numbers 2 to 7, row 1, include incomes arising out of the production of retained exports as well as exports, hence columns numbers 2 to 9, row 2, show only incomes arising out of the production of ground provisions and animal products and columns numbers 2 to 9, row 4, only those arising out of the manufacture of non-export crops and public utilities. The incomes in these three rows thus do not add up individually to give the total under Gross Domestic Product. See notes under II, numbers 1, 2 and 4.

I. Output

1. *Exports*

Total exports for the years 1849, 1850 and 1851 are listed in the BBJ.[1] But in the case of imports only those from foreign countries are given; for details of British imports the CR had again to be consulted.[2] After deducting the entrepôt trade the average value of Jamaica-produced exports amounts to £923,566 for these years. Production materials, valued at £58,900, are deducted proportionately to amounts exported and amounts of processed crops retained in the island.

2. *Food Production for Local Consumption*

(*a*) *Ground Provisions* (see Ch. 1, D).

(*b*) *Animal Products.* Meat production is based on computations made for *1870* on the assumption that per capita consumption remained unchanged during this period. The *1870* data are therefore adjusted to allow for price and population changes. There is no information about local fishing. The net earnings of 1,500 fishermen[3] are estimated at 2*s*. 6*d*. per day for 156 days in the year.[4]

Output of Animal Products

	£'000
Meat	117·3
Fish	29·3
	£146·6

(*c*) *Other.* Coffee consumption is estimated at 6 lb. per person per annum. Average per capita consumption in the United States is available for the first time in 1866 when it amounted to 4·96lb.[5] But since one of the effects of emancipation was the more widespread domestic consumption of traditional export crops a higher figure has been used.

3. *Building and Construction*

(*a*) *Public.* This item comprises the expenditure on roads and bridges by the central as well as by the parochial authorities. It also

[1] CO 142/63, 64 and 65.
[2] Customs 6/18, 19 and 20.
[3] CP, 1844. BPP, 1845 (426).
[4] PAIJ, 1854. BPP (1848), p. 25.
[5] Ukers, W. H. *All about Coffee*, New York, 1922, p. 289.

includes the average cash expenditure and nominal value of convict labour in building a general penitentiary and lunatic asylum.

(*b*) *Residential.* The 1844 CP lists only 34,624 houses for the whole population of 377,433; that is about one house for every eleven persons. Probably the definition of house adopted accounts for the omission of a large number of peasants' and labourers' huts. To fill in this gap the 1861 housing ratio of 5·1 persons per dwelling is adopted. On the assumption that there were 400,000 people in 1850 the number is thus 78,431. These houses are divided into three types: those inhabited by planters, managers, overseers, professional persons, ministers of religion, lodging-housekeepers and half of all traders; those inhabited by teachers, clerks, book-keepers, policemen etc., and, thirdly, those occupied by the peasantry and estate labour numbering 5,000, 15,000 and 58,431 respectively. The value of the first two are estimated at £240[1] and £100[2] with an average life of forty years. With regard to the third E. B. Underhill estimated the value of a peasant's hut and contents at £16.[3] Assuming that the value of the furniture was one-quarter of the total, the building cost of the hut was £12. The average life of these huts is estimated at ten years.

The average annual increase in the number of houses between 1832 and 1850 was thus 144. Since the exodus of planters, merchants and

Value of Residential Building

	Number built during Year	Cost £	Annual Value of Building £'000
(i) Additional Houses:			
	144	12	1·7
(ii) Replacements:			
	62	240	14·9
	375	100	37·5
	5,699	12	68·4
	6,136		120·8
Total Value of Residential Building			£122·5

professional people continued during these years it is assumed that the new houses belonged to the third category. To obtain the average number in existence at the beginning of the life period for this group we have to deduct ten years' additions from the 1850

[1] *Morning Journal*, 19th October 1850. CO 142/9.
[2] *Ibid.*, 9th August, 1851. CO 142/10.
[3] *The West Indies*, London, 1862, p. 420.

total. Since no increase took place in the other two groups replacements are calculated from the number in 1850 except that for the most expensive class it is again assumed that only half of those due for replacement were actually built.

(*c*) *Commercial.* (i) *Shops, Warehouses, etc.* The number of merchants and shopkeepers declined from 2,649 in 1844 to 1,316 in 1861. Assuming an even rate of decline the number in 1850 is estimated at 2,179. Since the number continued to fall in subsequent years it seems reasonable to assume that only half of the business premises due for renewal were actually replaced. On the assumption that the average value and life of shops and warehouses were comparable with the largest houses the value of construction is calculated at £6,500.

(ii) *Sugar Factories.* For the basis of estimating the value of sugar factory buildings, see Ch. 1, F. During the years 1849, 1850 and 1851 machinery valued at £9,480 was imported. To this are added imported metals which were also used inside sugar factories as part of their manufacturing equipment. The value of factory building for this year is accordingly estimated at £43,800.

4. *Manufacturing for Local Consumption and Public Utilities*

(*a*) *Factories.* The quantity of rum consumed is calculated from the yield of the rum tax. Instead of taking, as in other years, a three-year average the yield for this year has been based on 1851 only. In 1849 the rum duty was suspended and tax yields continued to be affected well into the following year. In 1851, the yield had apparently returned to normal at £30,684. At 2*s*. per gallon this is equal to a levy on 306,840 gallons. Sugar consumption is assumed to be equal to the annual rate in the United Kingdom for these years—25 lb. per capita.[1] Nothing is known about the services rendered by public utilities. There were in fact at least three water companies in existence at this time: in Kingston, Spanish Town and Falmouth. They appear to have been extremely inefficient.[2]

	£'000
Rum . .	40·9
Sugar . .	79·8
	£120·7

[1] Customs Tariffs of the United Kingdom, BPP, 1898 (C 8706).
[2] HBJ, e.g. for 1905.

(*b*) *Independent Workers.* There is no information either about the value of output of the various skilled independent workers or about the numbers engaged for these years. We therefore assumed that the increase in the 'Industrial' group returned in the CP of 1844 and 1861 was even during these years. This gives us a total of 23,200. Of these we assume that about half have already been included under the other sectors and that of the remainder about three-quarters were engaged as dressmakers while one-quarter were occupied as shoemakers, cabinet-makers etc. Since it is unlikely that dressmakers were fully occupied throughout the year and that their net earnings were as high as those of male craftsmen, their wages have been computed at 1s. 3*d.*[1] for four days per week. For the others earnings have been computed on the basis of 2*s.* 6*d.*[2] per day for a five-day week.

5. *Passenger Transport and Communications*

No estimate is included under this head. See *1832.*

6. *Distribution* (see Ch. 1, G)

(*a*) *Entrepôt.* The average total value of the entrepôt trade is calculated at £158,500. In this year it was possible to calculate import and re-export prices for the major items—cotton, linen and woollen goods—covering about 87·2 per cent of the total re-export trade. The overall percentage of value added was 28·7 per cent of import prices.

(*b*) *Retail.* The retail margin is assumed to be 25 per cent of the c.i.f. value of retained imported consumer goods which, in view of the results obtained for the entrepôt trade, should be regarded as a minimum.

7. *Public Administration*

(*a*) *Central.* The value of services rendered are calculated from the financial returns in the BBJ. In some cases, where taxes were imposed to meet the cost of special services, only net expenditure or taxes were shown. The deducted sums had to be added before a three-year average could be calculated. From this total are deducted public works, ecclesiastical salaries and transfer payments. A further exclusion is 'arrears of expenditure' on the grounds that these were belated payments for services rendered in earlier years. These pay-

[1] HBJ, e.g. for 1905, p. 25.

[2] *Ibid.*

ments occurred only in 1849 and 1850 and were apparently due to the difficulty experienced in raising revenue to meet the cost of the civil establishment following the suspension of the rum duty. This is not the same as 'arrears of revenue' which occurred more regularly and are assumed to have balanced short payments for the years in question.

(*b*) *Local.* Broad groupings of expenditure are shown in the BBJ for 18 out of 22 parishes in 1849, for 17 in 1850 and for 15 in 1851. A simple average is used to complete the returns for each year separately before calculating a three-year average for each class of expenditure. Output here consists of all expenditure except that on roads and bridges, poor relief, loan repayments and payments to the Fire Company. (For details see Chs. 3, IV, and 16).

8. *Ownership of Houses*

This follows from the assumption made about the number of houses in Ch. 3, I 3*b*. Rental values of the first two groups are based on advertisements in the *Morning Journal.* In the case of huts, rent is assumed to have been equal to twenty per cent of value.

Rental Value of Houses

Number of Houses	Average Rent £	Total Rental Values £'000
5,000	19·2	96·0
15,000	12	180·0
58,431	2·4	140·2
78,431		£416·2

9. *Professional Services*

(*a*) *Legal.* The JA for 1846 lists 98 lawyers. Regarding their earnings, reference to salaries paid to officials—for example, the six Chairmen of Quarter Sessions received £1,200 p.a. each[1]—is inappropriate since the size of judicial salaries was the subject of constant attack in the House of Assembly. Instead £500 has been assumed to be the average earnings in private practice.

(*b*) *Medical.* The number of doctors practising in the island in 1850 is unknown. In 1846 there were 139 doctors[2] but by 1861 their number had declined to 50.[3] Assuming an even rate of decline the

[1] PAIJ, BPP, 1849 (1065), p. 96. [2] JA for 1846. [3] *Jamaica, 1912*, p. 62.

number practising in 1850 is calculated at 115. Average earnings are estimated at £300 p.a. which was the value of private practice in Worthy Park in that year.[1]

(*c*) *and* (*d*) *Educational and Religious.* Again no distinction can be made between the two: teachers and preachers were frequently one and the same person and resources of missionary societies were used for both purposes. As in 1832 part of the income of the clergy of the Church of England was paid out of public funds. No estimate is attempted here for supplementary livings. The value of the services rendered by the sectarian bodies is assumed to be equal to their income received. In the case of Baptists, E. B. Underhill gave the annual contribution of the 34,000 members of the church at 7*s* 4½*d.* each.[2] A similar amount is assumed to have been raised by all other sectarian bodies. The Wesleyan Church received £4,506 from abroad[3] and the Presbyterian and Moravian Missions £1,400.[4] Education was, in addition, financed from endowments,[5] public grants,[6] and fees.[7]

Educational and Religious Services

	£'000
Clergy of the Church of England	35·3
Income raised in the Island by missionary societies	30·0
Income from abroad	5·9
Endowments	2·3
Public grants	1·8
Fees	4·6
	£79·9

10. *Domestic Services*

The CP of 1844 returned 20,571 persons as engaged in domestic service. Their earnings are taken at 5*s.* per week.[8] This item also

[1] *Morning Journal*, 14th March 1850, Advertisement.
[2] Underhill, *op. cit.*, pp. 429–30.
[3] King, Rev. D. *The State and Prospects of Jamaica*, London, 1850, p. 88.
[4] Underhill, *op. cit.*, p. 439.
[5] Papers re Legislative Proceedings, BPP, 1854 (1086), p. 135.
[6] BBJ. Average calculated from House of Assembly returns.
[7] The number of scholars in 1850 was 13,233 (BPP Statistical Abstracts for the Colonies, Pt. I, 1856) of whom the miscellaneous group was probably covered by charitable endowments. This leaves about 11,600 scholars who are assumed to have made 32 weekly payments of 3*d.* each. PAIJ, *op. cit.*, p. 39.
[8] *Ibid.*, p. 25.

includes the net earnings of 216 tavern and lodging-house keepers which are estimated at 10*s*. per week.

II. Income

1. *Exports*

As a result of emancipation there were some changes in the structure of production. The traditional staples were no longer produced exclusively on plantations. Many of the former slaves became independent settlers, and, in additon to ground provisions, took up the cultivation of export crops. Lack of specific information about the extent of production by the two systems makes certain assumptions necessary. These are first, that all exported sugar, rum and coffee were produced by estates, and secondly, that half of the retained sugar, all the retained coffee and all the minor products were produced by small-settlers.[1]

Estate output accordingly amounted to:

	£'000
Sugar exported	537·2
,, retained	39·9
Coffee, exported	95·1
Rum exported	193·6
,, retained	40·9
Pimento	48·6
Ginger	20·5
	£975·8

and small-settler output to:

	£'000
Sugar, retained	39·9
Coffee, retained	45·0
Wood: Logwood	11·1
Other	5·3
Arrowroot	3·0
Other	9·2
	£113·5

(*a*) *Estate Cultivation.* Incomes arising out of estate cultivation are derived from evidence submitted to the Committee on Sugar and

[1] Sewell, W. G. *The Ordeal of Free Labour*, New York, 1861, p. 249.

Coffee Planting.[1] An examination of 103 estates giving details, shows that wages accounted for 54·7 per cent of total 'contingencies'. But of these papers only one shows fuller details of expenditure. This refers to four estates 'admittedly favourably placed':[2]

	%
Labour	56·9
Management	14·5
Attorney	3·9
English supplies	9·9
Country supplies	7·1
Island duties	·4
Wharf account	1·3
Tradesmen's bills	1·7
Rum duties	·2
Taxes	4·1
	100·0

These expenses refer to the cost of producing sugar only; the costs of producing rum were offset against the proceeds of rum sales.

The report of the House of Assembly summarizing the submitted evidence of 138 estates found 'that after deducting proceeds of rum, averaged at £14 per puncheon, the actual cost of sugar averaged 22*s*. 7½*d*. per cwt. . . . without taking into account interest on capital and money expended, equal at the least to 4*s*. 6*d*. more per cwt.' [3] Adding freight charges the cost of one hundredweight of sugar in London was

	s.	*d.*
Average cost of production	22	7½
Interest on capital	4	6
Freight	4	6
	31	7½

The average London c.i.f. price of sugar for the years 1845–7 was 31*s*. per cwt.[4] Planters thus still had a reasonable return on their investment at this time. But in the years 1849, 1850 and 1851 price of sugar averaged only 22*s*. 8*d*.[5] In the meantime wages had been reduced from about 1*s*. 7*d*.[6] to 1*s*. 3*d*.[7] per day. It is assumed here

[1] BPP, 1847–8 (245), Appx. to 7th Report. [2] *Ibid.*, p. 203.
[3] *Ibid.*, p. 153. [4] See Ch. 5. [5] *Ibid.*
[6] Sugar and Coffee Planting, BPP, 1847–8 (167), Q. 4455.
[7] PAIJ, pp. 24, 34 etc.

that other expenses were reduced in the same ratio. In the case of production materials this seems justified since import prices were generally falling throughout these years. The cost of island supplies and services probably also fell as a result of the general depression caused by the Sugar Duties Act and the commercial crisis. With regard to taxes these, as we saw in Ch. 3, I, 7*a*, were not always taken too seriously. If all costs were reduced in the same ratio as wages production costs in 1850 were 17·88*s*. compared with the f.o.b. price of 17·98*s*.,[1] representing a catastrophic narrowing in profit margins.

No details are given in the evidence of the expenses offset against rum. Nor is there any information about the cost of producing other plantation crops. Sugar and rum together, however, accounted for about 84 per cent of total estate cultivation. Not much error, therefore, appears likely to arise from assuming that the expenditure pattern of sugar estates also holds for other estates.

Incomes arising out of estate cultivation are accordingly calculated by applying the above expenditure pattern to the computed cost of production which was found to be 99 per cent of export value: i.e. £966,000. Tradesmen's bills are added to labour costs, incomes of attorneys to management but the actual cost of imported materials,

Planters' Gross Profit

		£'000
Total value of estate production		975·8
Less income of:		
Agricultural labour	566·1	
Management	177·7	
Merchants	3·2	
Other labour	9·4	
Imported materials	58·9	
		815·3
Planters' gross profit		£160·5

taken from the customs returns, has been substituted for 'English supplies'. It is difficult to account for the high proportion of 'island supplies' if by these is meant materials used in production. Local timbers, when used for fuel or fencing, were usually collected on the estates. Possibly this item may include overseas supplies purchased

[1] Calculated from quantities and values given in the BBJ, for 1849, 1850 and 1851.

from local traders instead of directly from abroad; but if this was the case, expenditure has already been included under production materials. As in *1832* payment for wharfage is assumed to accrue to merchants and labour in the ratio of three to one. Finally, Planters' Gross Profit is the difference between the total of these incomes and gross output.

(*b*) *Small-Settler's Cultivation.* Unlike the planter who dealt directly with an English agent, the small-settler usually sold his produce to a local merchant for export or the local market. A charge of 25 per cent of total output is deducted for merchants' earnings of which one-quarter is assumed to have accrued to labour. Small-settlers did not usually employ outside labour so that the remaining output represents their gross profit.

Small-Settlers' Gross Profit from Plantation Crops

		£'000
Total value of small-settlers' production . .		113·5
Less income of: merchants	21·3	
labour	7·1	
		28·4
Small-settlers' gross profit		£85·1

2. *Food Production for Local Consumption*

(*a*) *Ground Provisions.* It is assumed here that half of the total output was marketed and that of the remainder one-half was sold by the cultivators and one-half by petty traders whose services are valued at 25 per cent of retail price. There is no information about the number of peasants renting land or about the value of rents paid. Tenancy does not appear to have been important in this year as most cultivators were either owners or squatters. (See Ch. 12, A, ii.)

(*b*) *Animal Products.* It is assumed that meat production was shared equally by pens and by small-settlers. In the case of the former, it is further assumed that labour costs accounted for 30 per cent[1] of gross output and that distribution charges took another 25 per cent of which one quarter accrued to labour. Small-settlers' output is also assumed to have been subject to a distribution charge of 25 per cent which is allocated to merchants and labour in the same way. The output of fishermen accrues to independent workers.

(*c*) *Other.* This is included under 1 above.

[1] This percentage is based on *1890* data.

3. *Building and Construction*

Of the domestic output three-quarters is allocated to labour and one-quarter to merchants.

4. *Manufacturing for Local Consumption*

Manufactured sugar and rum have been dealt with under 1 above. The value of output of independent workers was estimated on a net basis and, therefore, accrues wholly to independent workers.

6. *Distribution*

See Ch. 1, G.

7. *Public Administration*

(*a*) *Central.* The BBJ returns show payments to the following occupational groups:

	£'000
Administrative public servants	94·8
Lawyers	20·6
Doctors	30·3
Military	0·9
	£146·6

The large expenditure on medical services followed the outbreak of cholera in 1850. Not enough information is given to separate the earnings of medical practitioners from other incomes. The allocation of the whole to doctors undoubtedly overstates their prosperity. Apart from doctors all others are regarded as government employees.

(*b*) *Local.* The method of estimating expenditure from available returns has been described in the output section.

	£'000
Administrative public servants	24·0
Teachers	1·3
Doctors	2·8
	£28·1

8. *Ownership of Houses*

Houses inhabited by plantation staff and generally also those by estate labour were provided on the estates as part of income. Planters and peasants were usually owner-occupiers while the houses occupied by the rest of the population are assumed to have been partly owned and partly rented from merchants.

9. *Professional Services*

As in *1832* one-fifth of lawyers' earnings are assumed to have been spent on clerical assistance. Doctors' earnings are identical with output. In the case of educational and religious services only those sums that were expressly spent on education—endowments, public grants, school fees and £2,900 from abroad,[1] totalling £11,600—are allocated to teachers.

10. *Domestic Services*

Incomes from domestic service accrue to wage earners, and from hotel-keeping to profits of merchants.

III. Expenditure

As in *1832*, the expenditure table is derived mainly from the output table, substituting imports for exports and taking account of the balance on the external account.

Domestic capital formation consists of building and construction, durable producer goods and agricultural investment. The method of calculating the first two has already been explained elsewhere. No acreage data are available for these years. Estates were contracting the area under cultivation at this time. On the other hand, the peasantry was expanding. It is assumed that the peasants opened up new land at the rate of 2,000 acres per annum. Since predial wage rates were the same in 1850 as in 1884 the cost of clearing this land is calculated at 24*s*. per acre.[2]

	£'000
Building and construction .	201·5
Durable producer goods .	53·5
Agricultural investment .	2·4
	£257·4

IV. Public Authorities

1. *Central Government*

(*a*) *Receipts*. In these years direct taxes on property were levied on stock, carriages and house property. This item also includes an un-

[1] Underhill, *op. cit.*, p. 439.
[2] Wage rates averaged about 1*s*. 3*d*. per day. PAIJ, p. 18.

known amount of taxes levied on business and professional incomes which should actually be included under direct taxation on income.

(*b*) *Expenditure*. Again no attempt could be made to separate wages and salaries from goods and services. Subventions in these years consist of the grant to the Board of Education.

2. *Local Government*

Income of parochial authorities was obtained by taxation on property and from licences, fees and fines. Again the information available was too scanty for analysis. Transfer payments consist of poor relief and a small grant for education.

V. The Balance of Payments

The method of deriving the value of domestic exports and of imports retained for home consumption was explained under this head in *1832*. In addition to exports there were also earnings from the entrepôt trade and income from abroad received by religious societies. There is no further information available to account for the adverse balance of £93,100. This probably represents borrowing from abroad for capital formation and working capital made necessary by the tremendous fall in estates' profits.

CHAPTER 4

THE NATIONAL INCOME IN *1870*

TABLE 4.I

Output in 1870

		£'000
1. Exports	1,144·2	
Less imported materials	59·3	1,084·9
2. Food Production for Local Consumption:		
a. Ground Provisions	1,656·5	
b. Animal Products	202·2	
c. Other	85·5	1,944·2
3. Building and Construction:		
a. Public	64·1	
b. Residential	185·7	
c. Commercial	29·4	
	279·2	
Less imported materials	29·2	250·0
4. Manufacturing for Local Consumption:		
a. Factories	195·4	
b. Independent Workers	585·1	
	780·5	
Less imported materials	10·1	770·4
5. Passenger Transport and Communications . .		23·7
6. Distribution:		
a. Entrepôt.	24·2	
b. Retail	271·7	295·9
7. Public Administration:		
a. Central } *b.* Local }		238·2
8. Ownership of Houses		595·7
9. Professional Services:		
a. Legal	22·0	
b. Medical	25·2	
c. Educational	22·7	
d. Religious	62·1	132·0
10. Domestic Services		341·9
Total Gross Domestic Product		£5,676·9

TABLE 4.III

Expenditure in 1870

		£'000
1. Food, Drink and Tobacco:		
Imported	634·2	
Home-produced	2,137·3	2,771·5
2. Clothing:		
Imported	480·1	
Home-produced	312·0	792·1
3. Other Consumer Goods:		
Imported	244·1	
Home-produced	273·1	517·2
4. Personal Services:		
Professional	102·9	
Domestic	341·9	444·8
5. Passenger Transport and Communications		23·7
6. Rent		595·7
Total Personal Expenditure		£5,145·0
7. Government Expenditure on Goods and Services		267·3
8. Domestic Investment		320·1
9. Payments Abroad		54·3
10. Income from Abroad		—
11. Foreign Balance		−109·8
Total (Gross Domestic Product)		£5,676·9

TABLE 4.IV

Revenue and Expenditure of Public Authorities
(Combined Account)

Receipts	£'000	Expenditure	£'000
Direct Taxes:		Wages and Salaries	254·7
On income	—	Goods and Services	56·2
On property	58·5	Transfer Payments:	
Indirect Taxes:		To Persons	17·1
Customs	221·3	Subventions	7·0
Excise	75·9	Interest	56·8
Stamp Duty	12·0	Rent	2·1
Post Office Surplus	·4	Surplus	20·6
Licences, fees, fines, etc.	44·8		
Miscellaneous Incomes	1·6		
	£414·5		£414·5

TABLE 4.V

The Balance of Payments

Income from Abroad	£'000	Expenditure Abroad	£'000
Total Value of Domestic Exports	1,144·2	Total Value of Retained Imports	1,223·9
Earnings from Entrepôt Trade	24·2	Debt Charges	54·3
Balance	109·8		
	£1,278·2		£1,278·2

TABLE 4.VI

Output and Expenditure in 1870

	Gross Domestic Product	Imports	Exports	Goods and Services Available Domestically	Consumed	Invested
1. Exports	1,084·9	59·3	1,144·2	—	—	—
2. Food Production for Local Consumption	1,944·2	507·3	—	2,451·5	2,449·2	2·3
3. Building and Construction	250·0	29·2	—	279·2	—	279·2
4. Manufacturing for Local Consumption and P.U.	770·4	624·7	—	1,395·1	1,359·9	35·2
5. Passenger Transport and Communications	23·7	3·4	—	27·1	23·7	3·4
6. Distribution	295·9	—	24·2	271·7	271.7	—
7. Public Administration	238·2	—	—	238·2	238·2	—
8. Ownership of Houses	595·7	—	—	595·7	595·7	—
9. Professional Services	132·0	—	—	132·0	132·0	—
10. Domestic Services	341·9	—	—	341·9	341·9	—
Totals	5,676·9	1,223·9	1,168·4	5,732·4	5,412·3	320·1
11. Less Income from Abroad	—	—	—	—	—	—
12. Plus Payments Abroad	—	54·3	—	54·3	54·3	—
13. Foreign Balance	—	−109·8	—	−109·8	—	−109·8
	£5,676·9	1,168·4	1,168·4	5,676·9	5,466·6	210·3

I. Output

1. *Exports*

These are the average values of domestic produce for the years 1869, 1870 and 1871. Once again the entrepôt trade—now shown separately in the BBJ[1]—is taken out. Imported materials used in production, amounting to £69,300, are deducted here and under Section 4 as for previous years.

2. *Food Production for Local Consumption*

(*a*) *Ground Provisions* (see Ch. 1, D).

(*b*) *Animal Products.* Returns of cattle slaughtered in the island start in 1876 and between that year and 1880 fluctuate around 10,000.[2] For pigs, goats and sheep the number slaughtered is available for Kingston only and there is no guide as to the proportion this might be of the total. On the other hand, the BBJ and STC list the total stock on the island for most years. These data, being generally based on taxation returns, probably understate the numbers. For want of better information, however, they have been used here to calculate the number of pigs, goats and sheep slaughtered on the assumption that half of the total stock was slaughtered in each year. The dressed meat equivalents of these animals are assumed to be the same as those used by Miss P. Deane in *The Measurement of Colonial National Incomes*:[3] i.e. 400 lb. per head of cattle, 100 lb. per pig and 50 lb. for sheep and goats.

Value of Island Meat Production

	Number '000	Total Weight '000 lb.	Price per lb.[4]	Value £'000
Cattle	10·0	4,000·0	6*d.*	100·0
Sheep and Goats	20·0	1,000·0	1*s.*	50·0
Pigs	4·5	450·0	8*d.*	15·0
				£165·0

For local fish production the net value is estimated by assuming that the 1,683 fishermen returned in the 1871 CP had a net income of 2*s.* 10*d.*[5] per day on 156 days in the year.

(*c*) Other. Coffee consumption is based on average consumption in the United States—6·79 lb.[6]—for these years.

[1] CO 142/83, 84 and 85.
[2] HBJ, relating to these years.
[3] P. 109.
[4] BBJ for 1869, 1870 and 1871.
[5] *Ibid.* Average wages of tradesmen.
[6] Ukers, *op. cit.*, p. 289.

3. *Building and Construction*

(*a*) *Public.* The average amount spent on public buildings, roads and bridges is calculated from the BBJ returns of government expenditure.

(*b*) *Residential.* The 1871 CP gave the number of houses as 102,969. These are classified according to the tax returns given in the HBJ. The tax yield of houses rated at 1*s*. 6*d*. in the £ of annual value of £6 and upwards was £128,653 in 1871.[1] On the assumption that the average annual value was £6 10*s*. 19,793 houses were included in this group. There were a further three groups of houses subject to a flat rate tax. The fifth group is obtained by subtracting the estimated number of taxed houses from the census total. Unfortunately no newspapers containing advertisements of houses for sale or rent have been found for this period. Instead a rough method has been used to estimate rental and house values. Since the annual value of houses was certainly understated for taxation purposes it has been considered here that the average value of the first group may safely be doubled and that rents of the remaining houses could be graded upwards accordingly. Secondly, it has been assumed that the relation between rents and total value of previous years also held in 1870—that is 12½ per cent—for all except the lowest where it has been put at 20 per cent. The average life of these houses has been estimated at forty, thirty and twenty years for the first three groups and at ten years for the remaining two.

The annual increase in the number of houses between the census dates 1861 and 1871 averaged 1,680. It is assumed that this number was distributed proportionately among the four lower groups. No increase is likely to have occurred in the most expensive group because the number of those inhabiting these houses, planters, lawyers and doctors, was still declining at this date. In calculating the value of replacements we are unfortunately hampered by the difference in the classifications of dwellings in 1850 and 1871. An estimate of the number of houses in existence at the beginning of their appropriate life periods was therefore attempted by deducting the calculated increases from the number in 1871 from all except the highest group which, as pointed out above, is assumed to have remained constant.

[1] HBJ for 1881.

Value of Residential Building

	Number built during Year	Cost £	Annual Value of Building £'000
(i) Additional Houses:			
	773	48	37·1
	107	32	3·4
	163	24	3·9
	637	10	6·4
	1,680		50·8
(ii) Replacements:			
	495	104	51·5
	710	48	34·1
	185	32	5·9
	690	24	16·6
	2,680	10	26·8
	4,760		134·9
Total Value of Residential Building			£185·7

(*c*) *Commercial.* (i) *Shops, Warehouses, etc.* The average annual increase in the number of merchants and shopkeepers between 1861 and 1871 was 66. The number of premises due for replacement in 1870—33—is based on the number of merchants and shopkeepers returned in the 1861 census since their number had been declining during the previous decades. The value of new additions is calculated at £6,900 and that of replacements at £3,400 respectively.

(ii) *Sugar Factories.* For basis of calculating the value of sugar factories see Ch. 1, F. During the years 1869, 1870 and 1871 imports of sugar machinery and metals averaged £20,900. The value of factory building has accordingly been estimated at £19,100.

4. *Manufacturing for Local Consumption and Public Utilities*

(*a*) *Factories.* The quantity of rum consumed is calculated, as in previous years, from the yield of the rum tax at 303,596 gallons. Average sugar consumption in the island was estimated by the Receiver-General at 6,000 hogsheads in 1870.[1] But following the discovery during the next years of the large number of small sugar mills operated by the peasantry the Governor considered this estimate too low, stating 'that the additional amount (for home consumption) might well be doubled'.[2] It is, however, doubtful whether the peasants'

[1] Report with BBJ, BPP, 1872, (C 523)
[2] Report with the BBJ, BPP, 1873 (C 709).

average output was as high as the estimated two hogsheads for this would have required at the very least four acres devoted to cane cultivation. Probably the amount retained in the island was somewhere between these two extremes and has here been put at 162,000 cwt. which is equal to an annual per capita consumption of 32·1 lb.

	£'000
Rum . .	44·9
Sugar . .	150·5
	£195·4

(*b*) *Independent Workers*. The 1871 CP enumerated about 20,000 skilled workers apart from those included already in other sectors. About three-quarters of these were dressmakers and milliners and since it is unlikely that their average earnings were as high as those of male craftsmen it is assumed that they worked, on the average, four days per week and that their net earnings amounted to 2*s* per day.[1] For the other, the annual income of tradesmen, £54 12*s*. has been used.[2]

5. *Passenger Transport and Communications*

Railway receipts in 1868 were £10,722. In the following year a new eleven mile track was opened but did not affect revenue immediately. The next year for which revenue is given in the HBJ is 1875 when receipts amounted to £24,200. A sum of £11,000 is estimated for *1870*. To this is added the value of Postal Services.[3]

6. *Distribution* (see Ch. I, G)

(*a*) *Entrepôt*. The value of the entrepôt trade averaged £95,700 in these years. The 'value added' for 59 per cent of the total trade averaged 33·8 per cent of the c.i.f. value of imports. For the remainder, where no estimates were possible the same percentage has been used to calculate the average earnings of traders.

(*b*) *Retail*. The value added by Jamaican traders is assumed to be 25 per cent of the c.i.f. value of retained imported consumer goods.

7. *Public Administration*

The value of services rendered by the government is calculated

[1] The BBJ for 1869, 1870 and 1871 give tradesmen's daily wages ranging 1*s*. 3*d*. to 3*s*. 6*d*.

[2] BBJ for 1869.

[3] BBJ for 1869, 1870 and 1871.

from BBJ returns as for previous years. In these years all services were administered directly and hence central and local services are combined in one account. (For details, see Ch. 4, IV, and Ch. 16.)

8. *Ownership of Houses*

The methods for calculating rental value were given in Ch. 4, 3*b*.

Rental Value of Houses

Number of Houses	Average Rent £	Total Rental Value £'000
19,793	13	257·3
38,336	6	230·0
5,291	4	21·2
8,076	3	24·2
31,473	2	62·9
102,969		£595·6

9. *Professional Services*

(*a*) *Legal*. There were 44 lawyers in the island in 1871.[1] Their average earnings are assumed to be the same as the salary of the Kingston Police Magistrate—£500 p.a.[2]

(*b*) *Medical*. A new Medical Service was established in 1868. Under this medical officers were appointed on a part-time basis and encouraged to carry on private practice. The salaries paid by the government are shown under 6 above and only the income from private practice is given here. This was estimated by Sir J. P. Grant to vary between £150 and £600 p.a.[3] £300 is here taken as the average income from private practice for the 35 medical officers appointed at this date as well as for those not in the Service numbering 39. Included also are the earnings of ten dentists at the same rate of income.

(*c*) *Educational*. The BBJ for 1870 shows total income from government grants, fees and other sources of elementary schools, government model schools, endowed and normal schools as £26,135 and adds £4,000 for private schools. Part of these incomes was spent on building, equipment and board and lodging. All these are deducted.

(*d*) *Religious*. Membership of the most important denominational churches is available for the first time in 1885.[4] In that year it was

[1] CP, 1871.
[2] BBJ, 1870 and 1871, Financial Accounts.
[3] HBJ, e.g. for 1886–7.
[4] HBJ, 1885.

about 100,000. Total income of the Presbyterian Church averaged 16*s*. per member. On the assumption that half of this was spent on education and that the remaining 8*s*. was the average contribution of members of all other churches, the services of denominational churches is here valued at £40,000. To this are added the stipends of the Church of England paid from public funds.

10. *Domestic Services*

The services of the 16,287 domestics and 5,631 washer-women enumerated in the 1871 census are valued at £15 12*s*. p.a. each.[1] Included here also are the net earnings of 98 tavern and lodging-house keepers, which are estimated at £54 12*s*. p.a. each.[2]

II. Income

No estimates are prepared for this year (see Ch. 1, L).

III. Expenditure

As in previous years consumer expenditure is derived mainly from the output table. The difference between consumer expenditure on professional services and the value of output is due to the public grant towards education as well as payment of the Church of England clergy. Actual consumer expenditure on postal services exceeded the value of output by £400. This is regarded as an indirect tax and is therefore not included with consumer expenditure at factor cost.

Domestic capital formation consists of building and construction, producer durables and investment in new land. The first two are explained elsewhere. The annual increase in cultivated acreage between 1869 and 1871 was 1,600 acres. The cost of clearing land is estimated at 28*s*. 9½*d*. per acre.[3]

	£'000
Building and construction .	279·2
Durable producer goods .	38·6
Agricultural investment .	2·3
	£320·1

[1] BBJ, 1869. [2] *Ibid.*

[3] Predial wage rates averaged 1*s*. 6*d*. per day. STC, BPP 1878 (C 2029).

IV. Public Authorities

In this year all local administration was combined with that of the central government.

(*a*) *Receipts.* Revenue from direct taxes on property was derived chiefly from taxes on wheels, horsekind and house property. Customs duties, in this year, include a small amount of revenue yielded by taxes on exports.

(*b*) *Expenditure.* As far as possible wages and salaries were separated from goods and services. The latter, shown here, includes mainly expenditure on transport and 'contingencies'. Transfers to persons includes poor relief, and widows' annuities. Subventions were made in respect of education.

V. Balance of Payments

Domestic exports are now shown separately in the BBJ. The import value of re-exports, however, had still to be deducted from total imports to arrive at the value of retained imports. On the expenditure side are also entered debt charges paid by the Jamaican government on the assumption that all loans for public works, etc., were floated abroad. There is again a deficit on the balance of payments. This may be accounted for by government guaranteed borrowing from abroad for immigration, public works and public utilities.

CHAPTER 5

THE NATIONAL INCOME IN *1890*

TABLE 5.I

Output in 1890

		£'000
1. Exports	1,670·7	
Less imported materials	46·2	1,624·5
2. Food Production for Local Consumption		
a. Ground Provisions	2,601·2	
b. Animal Products	270·2	
c. Other	206·6	3,078·0
3. Building and Construction		
a. Public	220·6	
b. Residential	281·0	
c. Commercial	32·3	
	533·9	
Less imported materials	97·0	436·9
4. Manufacturing for Local Consumption		
a. Factories	241·0	
b. Independent Workers	845·1	
c. Public Utilities	26·0	
	1,112·1	
Less imported materials	28·0	1,084·1
5. Passenger Transport and Communications . .	89·7	
Less imported materials	12·9	76·8
6. Distribution		
a. Entrepôt	4·6	
b. Retail	401·1	405·7
7. Public Administration		
a. Central	320·7	
b. Local	23·9	
	344·6	
Less imported materials	10·3	334·3
8. Ownership of Houses		1,018·7
9. Professional Services		
a. Legal	42·6	
b. Medical	49·3	
c. Educational	42·7	
d. Religious	66·0	200·6
10. Domestic Services		487·0
Total Gross Domestic Product		£8,746·6

TABLE 5.II

Income in 1890

		£'000
1. Incomes from Agriculture		
a. Labourers' wages	543·5	
b. Small-Settlers' profits	3,187·6	
c. Planters' profits	682·5	
d. Plantation staffs' salaries	217·3	4,630·9
2. Other Wages and Salaries:		
a. Domestic	492·1	
b. Construction	383·7	
c. Manufacturing	44·4	
d. Distribution	323·0	
e. Public Administration	386·4	
f. Education	57·7	
g. Other	21·6	1,708·9
3. Other Profits:		
a. Trade	1,256·9	
b. Professions	167·2	
c. Independent work	982·7	2,406·8
Total (Gross Domestic Product)		£8,746·6

TABLE 5.III

Expenditure in 1890

		£'000
1. Food, Drink and Tobacco:		
Imported	978·1	
Home-produced	3,293·5	4,271·6
2. Clothing:		
Imported	646·3	
Home-produced	582·1	1,228·4
3. Other Consumer Goods:		
Imported	380·9	
Home-produced	309·0	689·9
4. Personal Services:		
Professional	159·8	
Domestic	487·0	646·8
5. Passenger Transport and Communications		89·7
6. Rent		1,018·7
Total Personal Expenditure		£7,945·1
7. Government Expenditure on Goods and Services		385·4
8. Domestic Investment		638·7
9. Payments Abroad		77·9
10. Income from Abroad		−36·5
11. Foreign Balance		−264·0
Total (Gross Domestic Product)		£8,746·6

TABLE 5.IV

Revenue and Expenditure Accounts of Public Authorities

1. Central Authority

Receipts	£'000	Expenditure	£'000
Direct Taxes:		Wages and Salaries, Goods and Services	448·7
On income	—	Transfer Payments:	
On property	17·3	subventions	41·2
Indirect Taxes:		Post Office Deficit	4·3
Customs	344·2	Railway Deficit	·9
Excise	127·3	Interest	77·9
Stamp Duty	19·2		
Public Utility surplus	10·9		
Licences, fees, fines, etc.	35·7		
Interest	20·6	Surplus	2·2
	£575·2		£575·2

2. Local Authorities

Receipts	£'000	Expenditure	£'000
Direct Taxes:		Wages and Salaries, Goods and Services	77·3
On property	117·2	Transfer Payments:	
		To persons	42·9
Deficit	3·8	Interest	·8
	£121·0		£121·0

TABLE 5.V

Balance of Payments

Income from Abroad	£'000	Expenditure Abroad	£'000
Total Value of Domestic Exports	1,670·7	Total Value of Retained Imports	1,897·9
Earnings from Entrepôt Trade	4·6	Debt Charges	77·9
Emigrants' Remittances	22·2		
Profits from Abroad	14·3		
Balance	264·0		
	£1,975·8		£1,975·8

G

Output, Income and Expenditure in 1890

£'000

	1 Gross Domestic Output	2 Agricultural Labourers	3 Small-Settlers	4 Planters	5 Plantation Staff	6 Other Wages and Salaries	7 Merchants	8 Professional Workers	9 Independent Workers	10 Imports	11 Exports	12 Goods and Services Available Domestically	13 Consumed	14 Invested
1. Exports*	1,624·5	464·6	573·5	557·1	147·3	100·2	175·3	—	—	46·2	1,670·7	—	—	—
2. Food Production for Local Consumption* .	3,078·0	28·9	2,506·3	43·4	—	12·0	203·2	—	77·6	782·5	—	3,860·5	3,855·0	5·5
3. Building and Construction	436·9	—	—	—	—	327·7	109·2	—	—	97·0	—	533·9	—	533·9
4. Manufacturing for Local Consumption and Public Utilities* . .	1,084·1	—	—	—	—	37·6	14·5	—	845·1	941·5	—	2,025·6	1,933·8	91·8
5. Passenger Transport and Communications . .	76·8	—	—	—	—	61·4	15·4	—	—	20·4	—	97·2	89·7	7·5
6. Distribution	405·7	—	—	—	—	101·4	304·3	—	—	—	4·6	401·1	401·1	—
7. Public Administration .	334·3	—	—	—	—	320·6	—	13·7	—	10·3	—	344·6	344·6	—
8. Ownership of Houses .	1,018·7	50·0	107·8	82·0	70·0	204·8	430·1	14·0	60·0	—	—	1,018·7	1,018·7	—
9. Professional Services .	200·6	—	—	—	—	61·1	—	139·5	—	—	—	200·6	200·6	—
10. Other Services . . .	487·0	—	—	—	—	482·1	4·9	—	—	—	—	487·0	487·0	—
Total	8,746·6	543·5	3,187·6	682·5	217·3	1,708·9	1,256·9	167·2	982·7	1,897·9	1,675·3	8,969·2	8,330·5	638·7
11. Less Income from Abroad	—	—	—	—	—	—	—	—	—	−36·5	—	−36·5	−36·5	—
12. Plus Payments Abroad .	—	—	—	—	—	—	—	—	—	77·9	—	77·9	77·9	—
13. Foreign Balance . . .	—	—	—	—	—	—	—	—	—	−264·0	—	−264·0	—	−264·0
Total Gross Domestic Product	£8,746·6	543·5	3,187·6	682·5	217·3	1,708·9	1,256·9	167·2	982·7	1,675·3	1,675·3	8,746·6	8,371·9	374·7

* Incomes shown in columns numbers 2 to 7, row 1, include incomes arising out of the production of retained exports as well as exports, hence columns numbers 2 to 9, row 2, show only incomes arising out of the production of ground provisions and animal products and columns numbers 2 to 9, row 4, only those arising out of the manufacture of non-export crops and public utilities. The incomes in these three rows thus do not add up individually to give the total under Gross Domestic Product. See notes under II, numbers 1, 2 and 4.

I. Output

1. *Exports*

These are again taken from the BBJ.[1] The financial year was changed in 1889 to end on 31st March instead of 30th September. The changeover, therefore, involved a gap of six months for which separate accounts were made up. The figures here represent averages calculated for 2½ years. The odd half year does not appear to have affected the distribution of exports except in the case of coffee, the greater part of which seems to have been shipped in the period September to March, and, to a lesser extent, sugar and bananas. The BBJ figures for these three crops have accordingly been replaced by those given in the HBJ for the complete year. Imported materials used in production, valued at £52,843, are deducted, as in previous years, here and under Ch. 5, 4.

2. *Food Production for Local Consumption*

(*a*) *Ground Provisions* (see Ch. 1, D).

(*b*) *Animal Products*. The average number of cattle slaughtered in the island—13,423—is calculated from returns in the HBJ for these years. The number of sheep slaughtered is calculated from the average stock in the years 1889, 1890 and 1891, but in the case of pigs and goats, data were available only for the two years 1895 and 1896. (For dressed weight equivalents see *1870*.)

Value of Island Meat Production

	Number '000	Total Weight '000	Price per lb.[2]	Value £'000
Cattle	13·4	5,369·2	6*d.*	134·2
Sheep and Goats	11·2	560·0	8*d.*	18·7
Pigs	11·2	1,120·0	8½*d.*	39·7
				£192·6

There were 1,989 fishermen in the island in 1891.[3] Their average net earnings are assumed to have been 5*s.*[4] per day for a three-day week.

(*c*) *Other*. Coffee consumed in the island is calculated on the basis

[1] CO 142/104 and 105. [2] STC, BPP, 1898 (C 7527). [3] CP, 1891.
[4] BBJ. Wage rates for tradesmen are quoted at 2*s.* 6*d.*–6*s.* per day.

of United States average annual per capita consumption in the years 1889, 1890 and 1891—8·29 lb.[1]—and retained bananas at ten per cent of export value.

3. *Building and Construction*

(*a*) *Public.* Average total expenditure on public buildings, roads and railway extension by the central government amounted to £161,600 and on local roads by parochial authorities to £59,000.[2]

(*b*) *Residential.* The 1891 CP lists 134,545 houses. These are again classified according to the data provided by the house-tax but because of a change in the tax law use is made here only of the result of the financial year 1891–2.[3] In that year there were 50,493 houses in the highest group and 37,001 in the three other groups. The number of untaxed houses is the difference between the census total and the number subject to these taxes. The average value of the rated houses according to the tax yield was £7 16*s*. This is again considered an underestimate and has been doubled and the value calculated on the

Value of Residential Building

Number built during Year	Cost £	Annual Value of Building
(i) Additional Houses:		
458	125	57·3
336	30	10·1
426	10	4·3
1,220		71·7
(ii) Replacements:		
992	125	124·0
1,415	30	42·5
4,280	10	42·8
6,687		209·3
Total Value of Residential Building		£281·0

assumption that rent was equal to 12½ per cent of total value. For the second group of houses the value is taken as £30.[4] In the case of the third no information has been found at all and the value has been put at £10. The average life of these houses is estimated at forty, twenty and ten years respectively.

[1] Ukers, *op cit.*, p. 289. [2] BBJ for these years. [3] HBJ, 1893.
[4] RWIC, BPP, 1897 (C 8669), Pt. XIII, Q. 1901.

Annual additions to the number of houses averaged 1,220 in the ten years between 1881 and 1891. It is assumed that these were distributed proportionately among all groups. In the absence of comparable classification, replacements had, as in *1870*, to be based on the estimated number of houses in existence at the appropriate dates. These were again calculated by deducting the estimated increase in each group taking into account that the most expensive group was assumed to be constant before *1870*.

(*c*) *Commercial.* (*i*) *Shops, Warehouses, etc.* The average annual increase in the number of merchants and shopkeepers between 1881 and 1891 was 82. For the reasons given in *1870* replacements are again based on the 1861 CP returns. The value of new additions and replacements is thus calculated at £10,300 and £4,100 respectively.

(ii) *Sugar Factories.* For basis of calculation see Ch. 1, F. The average value of sugar machinery imported in the years 1889, 1890 and 1891 was £19,600. The value of factory building is accordingly estimated at £17,900.

4. *Manufacturing for Local Consumption and Public Utilities*

(*a*) *Factories.* Home consumption of sugar was estimated by D. Morris at one-third of total production;[1] i.e. 187,800 cwt. for these years. The amount of rum consumed is taken as equal to the number of gallons on which excise duty was collected—427,910 gallons.[2] The total value of tobacco output it estimated, on the basis of numbers employed, average wages rates, rent and cost of materials, at £50,000.[3] The amount exported is deducted and shown under 1 above. The 1891 CP returned 201 printers and compositors and their wages were £1 per week.[4] Allowing for the cost of imported materials used in production and a margin for profits, the total value of local printing is estimated at £20,000.

(*b*) *Independent workers.* There remain about 22,000 dressmakers and milliners and 5,000 other skilled workers to be accounted for.[5] The services of the former are estimated at 10*s*. and the latter at £1 per week each.[6]

[1] *Ibid.* (C 8655), p. 137.
[2] Financial Returns in the BBJ for these years.
[3] CP, 1891; BBJ and import returns.
[4] Livingstone, W. P. *Black Jamaica*, London, 1899, p. 181.
[5] CP 1891.
[6] BBJ. For the former the lowest rate and for the latter the highest rate quoted for tradesmen are taken. Both are assumed to work an average of four days per week.

(*c*) *Public Utilities*. Included under Public Utilities are all the Kingston municipal undertakings as well as the Old Harbour and Spanish Town waterworks and the Rio Cobre irrigation canal.[1]

Manufacturing for Local Consumption and Public Utilities

	£'000
Sugar	120·8
Rum	57·1
Tobacco	43·1
Printing	20·0
Independent Workers .	845·1
Public Utilities. . .	26·0
	£1,112·1

5. *Passenger Transport and Communications*

Railway receipts from passengers averaged £23,726 between 1888 and 1892.[2] No information is available about total income and expenditure of the Jamaica Street Car Company. The value of services is computed on the basis of average number of passengers and fares listed in the HBJ. 1,520,236 passengers were carried at fares ranging between 2*d.* and 1*s*. The mean fare is taken as 6*d.* Services rendered by the Post Office averaged £27,971.[3]

6. *Distribution* (see Ch. 1, G)

(*a*) *Entrepôt*. The total value of this trade averaged only £22,800. The commodities involved were numerous and a detailed estimation of value added was not possible. The earnings of traders are taken as 25 per cent of the c.i.f. value which, in view of the higher rates obtained in previous years, may be an underestimate.

(*b*) *Retail*. The value added has been estimated at 25 per cent of the c.i.f. cost of imported consumer goods.

7. *Public Administration*

The value of services rendered by public authorities is obtained from the BBJ after deduction of transfer payments, public works, education, ecclesiastical salaries and the railway.

Materials deducted include the value of medicines estimated to

[1] BBJ and HBJ for these years.

[2] Col. Rep., BPP, 1890 (C 6221–1); 1892 (C 6563–19) 4/5 of stated receipts and 1893 (C 6857–15).

[3] BBJ for these years.

have been used in public hospitals. (For details see Chs. 5, IV, and 16.)

8. *Ownership of Houses*

This follows from the assumptions made under Ch. 5, I, 3*b*. Rental value of the first group was estimated at £15. 12*s*. For the second group rent is similarly estimated at 12½ per cent but in the case of the third at 20 per cent.

Rental Value of Houses

Number of Houses	Average Rent £	Total Rental Value £'000
50,493	15·6	787·7
37,001	3·7	136·9
47,051	2·0	94·1
134,545		£1,018·7

9. *Professional Services*

(*a*) *Legal.* The census of 1891 lists 80 barristers and attorneys. Of these nine held official appointments and seventy-one were in private practice. The earnings of the latter are estimated at £600 p.a. each.[1]

(*b*) *Medical.* There were 93 doctors practising in the island in 1891. Their income is estimated at £600 p.a. from all sources. This is the average salary paid to those engaged wholly in the Public Service.[2] The earnings of doctors in the Medical Service—£13,700—are deducted because they have already been included under 7 above. The income of the twelve dentists[3] is assumed to be the same.

(*c*) *Education.* The contribution of education to total output is taken to be equal to annual expenditure on education less amounts spent on buildings, board and lodging and equipment, which are included in other sections of the output table. Elementary and secondary schools received £34,800 from the government. The former also collected £8,400 in fees while the income of the latter and other schools from fees, trust funds, etc., amounted to a further £9,300.[4] The total income of all educational establishments is thus estimated at £52,400 of which about £9,700 was spent on buildings and boarding expenses.

[1] HBJ, 1892. Salary paid to Registrar of the Supreme Court of Judicature.
[2] BBJ. [3] CP, 1891. [4] BBJ.

(*d*) *Religion.* The returns of church livings in the BBJ show clergy of the Church of England to number 94 of whom 24 received their stipends from public funds—£5,975—and 70 from other sources. The various other denominations appear to have relied mainly on the contributions by their members, which varied between 14*s.* 9*d.* for Presbyterians and 6*s.*—12*s.* p.a. in the Anglican Church.[1] The total membership of all denominations listed in the HBJ adds up to about 120,000. The average annual offering is taken at 10*s.* each.

10. *Domestic Services*

The 1891 census returns 26,686 persons as domestic servants and a further 10,400 washerwomen. Average wages were 2*s.*–3*s.* per week plus food or 4*s.*–6*s.* per week for those who 'found for themselves'.[2] Here 5*s.* is taken as the average weekly wage.

The earnings of 94[3] hotel, tavern and lodging-house keepers are estimated at £52 p.a. each.

II. Income

1. *Exports*

The shares of estates and small-holdings in agricultural output are computed on the basis of evidence submitted to the RWIC and the HBJ. The former tabulates acreages under different crops according to the size of holding.[4] Defining small-settlers as those cultivating less than twenty acres each, the difference between the tabulations of twenty acres and over and total acreage is taken to be the share of small-settlers. Assuming the same ratio to hold for *1890* as in 1896, acreage distribution of the major crops for estates and small-settlers is as follows:

Acreage cultivated by Estates and Small-Settlers

	Estates' Acreage	Small-Settlers' Acreage	Total Acreage[5]
Sugar	26,937	5,439	32,376
Coffee	5,287	15,365	20,652
Bananas	8,254	7,420	(15,674)*
Coconuts	4,886	4,095	(8,981)*
Cocoa	584	540	1,124

* refers to 1892.

[1] Livingstone, *op. cit.*, p. 161. [2] *Ibid.*, p. 176. [3] CP, 1891.
[4] RWIC (C 8669), Pt. XIII (756). [5] HBJ, 1892 and 1895.

The next step is to allocate production according to acreage. Productivity per acre was usually considerably lower for small-settlers than for estates, but no information about respective yields is available. In the case of sugar it is assumed that the additional value of rum represents the higher cane yields obtained by estates. For bananas it is assumed that small-settlers' yields were about three-quarters of those obtained by estates. This rather high ratio is justified by the fact that banana acreage was expanding rapidly during these years and that small-settlers were benefiting from virgin soil as much as estates. Coffee lands were much older and here the superior equipment employed by estates is the reason for estimating yields at double those of small-settlers. The estimated growers' value of tobacco leaf supplied to local factories is assumed to accrue to estates. Lime juice is also assumed to be the produce of estates, but logwood, pimento, oranges, and ginger are divided equally between small-settler and estate production. The respective values of output are thus:

Share in Total Agricultural Output

	Estates £'000	Small-Settlers' £'000	Total £'000
Coffee	196·2	282·4	478·6
Sugar	304·6	61·5	366·1
Logwood	176·8	176·7	353·5
Bananas	210·7	141·0	351·7
Rum	265·4	—	265·4
Pimento	33·2	33·3	66·5
Oranges	23·3	23·2	46·5
Ginger	15·2	15·3	30·5
Coconuts	14·5	12·2	26·7
Cocoa	6·4	5·8	12·2
Lime Juice	3·2	—	3·2
Other	—	47·4	47·4
Total Value	£1,249·5	£798·8	£2,048·3
Value of Produce supplied to Local Manufacturing Industries (tobacco)	22·5	—	22·5
	£1,272·0	£798·8	£2,070·8

(*a*) *Estate Cultivation.* (i) *Wages.* Labour costs per acre under cul-

[1] *Op. cit.* (C 8669), Pt. XIII (756).

tivation for the major crops are listed in the RWIC.[1] Applying these to total estate acreage we get the following wages bill:

Estates' Wages Bill

		£'000
Sugar:	cultivation £5·5 per acre	148·2
	reaping and manufacture £3 10*s*. per Hhd.	97·4
Rum:	distilling 25*s*. per puncheon	24·8
Coffee:	cultivation—average for 5 years £5·7	30·1
	reaping, milling, packing, etc. 20*s*. per cwt.	33·2
Bananas:	cultivation and reaping £7·5 per acre	61·9
Logwood:	16*s*. per ton	42·1
Other commodities estimated at		26·9
Total Wages Bill		£464·6

(ii) *Salaries*. Salaries of plantation staff are calculated on the assumption that estates employed one overseer and one book-keeper each except for sugar estates which employed two book-keepers each. In 1890 there were 164 sugar estates, 112 banana estates, 29 coffee estates and about 400 pens.[1] Of these 77 employed attorneys.[2] The salary of overseers was £150 p.a., of book-keepers £30 p.a.[3] and that of attorneys is assumed at £200 each.

Salaries of Plantation Staff

	£'000
Attorneys	15·4
Overseers	105·8
Book-keepers	26·1
Total Salaries	£147·3

(iii) *Other Charges*. Imported materials are deducted from estates and small-settlers proportionately to output. The distribution cost of the estates' share is calculated at £8,100 of which three-quarters are allocated to merchants and the rest to labour. The cost of wharfage and cartage done by outside factors is estimated at five per cent of total output—£62,600—of which three-quarters are assumed to have been earned by labour and one-quarter by traders. Finally

[1] HBJ. Lists of properties in cultivation.

[2] About 30 per cent of sugar estates were owned by absentees. RWIC (C 8669), Pt. XIII (752); for banana and coffee estates the number is estimated at 21 and 7. HBJ, 1891 and 1895.

[3] RWIC (C 8669), Pt. XIII, Q. 1112.

planters' gross profit is the amount remaining after deducting these various incomes from domestic output.

Planters' Gross Profit

		£'000
Total value of Domestic output .		1,239·7
Less income of Agricultural labour .	464·6	
,, ,, ,, Management . .	147·3	
,, ,, ,, Merchants . .	21·7	
,, ,, ,, Other labour . .	49·0	
		682·6
		£557·1

(*b*) *Small-Settlers' Cultivation.* Apart from the total cost of imported materials, small-settlers' output is charged with the earnings of traders in marketing their crops. This is assumed to have taken 25 per cent of total output of which one-quarter accrues to labour.

Small-Settlers' Gross Profit

		£'000
Total value of Domestic output . .		778·3
Less income of Merchants . .	153·6	
,, ,, ,, Other labour . .	51·2	
		204·8
		£573·5

2. *Food Production for Local Consumption*

(*a*) *Ground Provisions.* It is assumed that only one-quarter of the output of ground provisions was sold by petty traders. The value of their services is estimated at 25 per cent of the retail value of ground provisions. Again we make no deduction for rents paid by peasants. Squatting had by this time practically disappeared but in the main its place appears to have been taken by land-ownership and not tenancy.

(*b*) *Animal Products.* The value of meat production is assumed to have been shared equally between the pen-keepers and small-settlers. Of the pen-keepers' share 30 per cent was paid to agricultural labour,[1] and it is assumed that distribution costs took a further 25 per cent of which one-quarter accrued to labour. Small-settlers employed no labour in stock-rearing but they are also charged with distribution

[1] Royal Commission on Public Revenues, etc., BPP, 1884 (C 3840), p. 114. Calculated from income and expenditure of Pen A.

costs of 25 per cent which are allocated to traders and labour in the same way.

(*c*) *Other*. This is included under 1 above.

3. *Building and Construction*

The net value is allocated to traders and labour in the ratio of one to three.

4. *Manufacturing for Local Consumption and Public Utilities*

Sugar and rum have already been dealt with under section 1. There remain tobacco, printing and public utilities. In the case of tobacco produced for home consumption and for export it is assumed that half of the value of the finished product accrues to estates and that the remainder is shared equally by labour and merchants. The value of printing was estimated on the basis of net earnings and is allocated to labour and traders accordingly. After deducting imported materials from the gross value of public utility services the remainder is allocated to salaries and wages.

5. *Passenger Transport and Communications*

Receipts from all railway operations show an average surplus of £20,436 over current expenses for these years. Applying the same proportion to passenger services we get a surplus of £7,750. The surplus on the operation of the Jamaica Street Car Company is estimated at 20 per cent—£7,600. After deducting the cost of imported materials the remainder is allocated to wages and salaries. The same method is followed in allocating postal services.

6. *Distribution*

See Ch. 1, G.

7. *Public Administration*

(*a*) Central. The BBJ show payments to the following occupational groups:

	£'000
Administrative public servants .	171·7
Judicial	38·6
Medical.	51·6
Military	8·3
Constabulary	50·5
	£320·7

Doctors' earnings are listed in the BBJ. The remainder of expenditure on medical services less cost of imported drugs and medicines is assumed to have been paid to matrons and nurses and is allocated to wages and salaries.

In the case of local authorities it is assumed that all services were rendered by administrative public servants.

8. *Ownership of Houses*

The distinction between owner-occupied and rented houses was made in respect of houses subject to the flat-rate tax, i.e. the intermediate group only. In the year 1891–2 only 29 per cent of these were rented. The proportion was even lower—25 per cent—in the previous year when this group comprised a larger share of the more expensive houses. It appears, therefore, that house-ownership was slightly more common in the case of the more expensive houses. We shall assume here that in the first group only 25 per cent of houses were rented from traders, 29 per cent in the second group but 25 per cent in the third. Owner-occupied houses in the first group include all planters and plantation staff, most of the professional workers, government servants, other salary earners and some independent workers; in the second, some of the peasantry; and in the third, some peasants and agricultural wage labour.

9. *Professional Services*

Again one-fifth of lawyers' gross earnings is allocated to clerical workers and for this year the same proportion is deducted for assistance by nurses and clerical staff to doctors and dentists.

10. *Domestic Services*

Output is allocated to wages and profits as in previous years.

III. Expenditure

Again consumer expenditure is largely taken from the output table. In this year there were deficits on the railway and postal services and a surplus on the working of the public utilities. The first two are regarded as subsidies to consumers and have to be added and the last as an indirect tax which has to be deducted to obtain consumer expenditure at factor cost. Domestic investment again consists of building and construction, durable producer goods and investment in new land. The annual increase in cultivated acreage between 1889 and 1891 was 4,600 acres. Costs are taken at 24*s*. per acre. This figure actually refers to 1884 but in that year and the two preceding years wage rates show such wide variations that no definite trend in the intervening period can be discerned.[1] Cost of clearance is therefore estimated at 24*s*. per acre in *1890* and average predial wage rate of 1*s*. 3*d*. in 1890.[2] is used as basis for computing costs in other years. (See also Ch. 1, F.)

	£'000
Building and construction	533·9
Durable producer goods	99·3
Agricultural investment	5·5
	£638·7

IV. Public Authorities

1. *Central Government*

(*a*) *Receipts*. Direct taxes were levied on stock and on agricultural holdings. Customs duties again include a small amount of revenue obtained from export taxes—£4,625.

(*b*) *Expenditure*. Subventions include grants to education, the Jamaica Institute and subsidies paid to the Telegraph Company and for steam communications with Halifax.

2. *Local Government*

All revenue appears to have been obtained from direct taxes on property. Transfer payments to persons were all made in respect of poor relief.

V. Balance of Payments

On the income side of the balance of payments are shown the value of domestic exports and earnings from the entrepôt trade—now shown separately in the BBJ for both imports and exports. Under profits from abroad are entered the earnings of the Government Savings Bank since all the Bank's funds were invested abroad.

[1] STC, BPP, 1888 (C 5508).

[2] BBJ, 1889, 1890 and 1891.

Remittances from abroad are estimated on the assumption that each emigrant sent home only £1 p.a. This is half the average amount given for later years but then this period was one of reduced opportunities abroad when many emigrants were actually returning. The numbers living abroad at this time are calculated at 22,200.[1]

There are again no data to account for the remaining balance. In view of the increased imports of durable producer goods, the considerable loans raised for railway extensions and public works and also American investment in the banana industry this balance may be assumed to represent capital imports.

[1] This is roughly the excess of the numbers leaving over those returning in the years between 1881 and 1889. See Ch. 9, C, iv.

CHAPTER 6

THE NATIONAL INCOME IN *1910*

TABLE 6.I

Output in 1910

		£'000
1. Exports	2,568·1	
Less imported materials	137·8	2,430·3
2. Food Production for Local Consumption		
a. Ground Provisions	3,170·0	
b. Animal Products	350·4	
c. Other	284·9	3,805·3
3. Building and Construction		
a. Public	249·4	
b. Residential	428·7	
c. Commercial	55·5	
	733·6	
Less imported materials	244·2	489·4
4. Manufacturing for Local Consumption		
a. Factories	388·9	
b. Independent Workers	998·4	
c. Public Utilities	73·1	
	1,460·4	
Less imported materials	57·1	1,403·3
5. Passenger Transport and Communications	165·3	
Less imported materials	17·0	148·3
6. Distribution		
a. Entrepôt	7·4	
b. Retail	504·9	512·3
7. Public Administration		
a. Central	386·8	
b. Local	58·0	
	444·8	
Less imported materials	10·3	434·5
8. Ownership of Houses		1,215·7
9. Professional Services		
a. Legal	57·6	
b. Medical	97·2	
c. Educational	75·8	
d. Religious	61·8	292·4
10. Domestic Services		630·4
Total Gross Domestic Product		£11,361·9

TABLE 6.III

Expenditure in 1910

		£'000
1. Food, Drink and Tobacco:		
Imported	1,243·9	
Home-produced	4,138·3	
		5,382·2
2. Clothing:		
Imported	866·9	
Home-produced	738·4	
		1,605·3
3. Other Consumer Goods:		
Imported	413·5	
Home-produced	373·9	
		787·4
4. Personal Services:		
Professional	228·9	
Domestic	630·4	
		859·3
5. Passenger Transport and Communications		165·3
6. Rent		1,215·7
Total Personal Expenditure		£10,015·2
7. Government Expenditure on Goods and Services		508·3
8. Domestic Investment		908·3
9. Payments Abroad		238·8
10. Income from Abroad		−232·8
11. Foreign Balance		−75·9
Total (Gross Domestic Product)		£11,361·9

TABLE 6.IV

Revenue and Expenditure Accounts of Public Authorities

1. Central Authority

Receipts	£'000	Expenditure	£'000
Direct Taxes:		Wages and Salaries / Goods and Services	498·7
On income	—	Transfer Payments:	
On property	35·9	Subventions	81·7
Indirect Taxes:		Interest	224·5
Customs	469·3		
Excise	122·9		
Stamps	24·6		
Railway Surplus	62·8		
Post Office Surplus	6·2		
Public Utilities Surplus	·3		
Licences, fees, fines, etc.	55·8		
Interest	16·9		
Miscellaneous incomes	4·5		
Deficit	5·7		
	£804·9		£804·9

2. Local Authorities

Receipts	£'000	Expenditure	£'000
Taxes	161·6	Expenditure	165·8
Deficit	4·2		
	£165·8		£165·8

TABLE 6.V

The Balance of Payments

Income from Abroad	£'000	Expenditure Abroad	£'000
Total Value of Domestic Exports	2,568·1	Total Value of Retailed Imports	2,645·4
Earnings from Entrepôt Trade	7·4	Debt Charges	224·5
Emigrants' Remittances	120·0	Sundry Payments Abroad	14·3
Profits from Abroad	12·8		
Receipts from Tourists	100·0		
Balance	75·9		
	£2,884·2		£2,884·2

TABLE 6.VI

Output and Expenditure in 1910

£'000

	Gross Domestic Output	Imports	Exports	Goods and Services Available Domestically	Consumed	Invested
1. Exports . . .	2,430·3	137·8	2,568·1	—	—	—
2. Food Production for Local Consumption	3,805·3	995·1	—	4,800·4	4,785·3	15·1
3. Building and Construction	489·4	244·2	—	733·6	—	733·6
4. Manufacturing for Local Consumption and P.U. . .	1,403·3	1,221·7	—	2,625·0	2,484·7	140·3
5. Passenger Transport and Communications . . .	148·3	36·3	—	184·6	165·3	19·3
6. Distribution .	512·3	—	7·4	504·9	504·9	—
7. Public Administration . .	434·5	10·3	—	444·8	444·8	—
8. Ownership of Houses . .	1,215·7	—	—	1,215·7	1,215·7	—
9. Professional Services . .	292·4	—	—	292·4	292.4	—
10. Domestic Services . .	630·4	—	—	630·4	630·4	—
Totals . . .	11,361·9	2,645·4	2,575·5	11,431·8	10,523·5	908·3
11. Less Income from Abroad	—	−232·8	—	−232·8	−232·8	—
12. Plus Payments Abroad . .	—	238·8	—	238·8	238·8	—
13. Foreign Balance	—	−75·9	—	−75·9	—	−75·9
	£11,361·9	2,575·5	2,575·5	11,361·9	10,529·5	832·4

I. Output

1. *Exports*

The average value of domestic exports, as shown in the BBJ, was £2,568,100 for the years 1909, 1910 and 1911.[1] Imported materials

[1] CO 142/123, 124 and 125.

used in production, consisting chiefly of manure, coal and packing materials, such as bags and sacks and cordage—totalling £151,200—are deducted, as in previous years, from exports and under 4 below.

2. *Food Production for Local Consumption*

(*a*) *Ground Provisions*. See Ch. 1, D.

(*b*) *Animal Products*. The average number of cattle slaughtered in the island is given in the HBJ for these years. The average number of sheep, goats and pigs slaughtered is calculated from returns in the BBJ and STC for the years. (For dressed weight equivalents see *1870*.)

Value of Island Meat Production

	Number '000	Total Weight '000lb.	Price per[1] lb.	Values £'000
Cattle	17·0	6,815·2	6*d.*	170·4
Sheep and Goats	15·0	750·0	1*s.*	37·5
Pigs	15·6	1,560·0	8*d.*	52·0
				£259·9

The 1911 CP returns 2,900 fishermen. It is assumed that their average net earnings were equal to those of tradesmen at 4*s.*[2] per day and that they went fishing on 156 days in the year.

(*c*) *Other*. For coffee the average per capita consumption in the United States—10·01 lb.[3]—has again been used. Retained bananas are estimated at 10 per cent of export value.

3. *Building and Construction*

(*a*) *Public*. Expenditure on public buildings, roads and bridges and railway extensions by the central government averaged £198,000 during these years and on local roads by parochial authorities is estimated at £51,400.

(*b*) *Residential*. The 1911 CP tabulates all houses according to the number of rooms. Some advertisements were found in the *Jamaica Daily Gleaner* which gave the total or rental value of houses. The accompanying descriptions seemed to cover only the largest two groups. Here value was calculated on the assumption that rent was

[1] STC BPP, 1914–16 (Cd. 7667).
[2] BBJ for these years. Daily wage rates of tradesmen are quoted at 2*s.* 6*d.*–6*s.*
[3] Ukers, *op. cit.*, p. 289.

equal to 12½ per cent of value (see Ch. 6, I, 8). For the two other groups no information was found and value had to be estimated. The average life of these houses was assumed to be forty years for the first two groups and twenty and ten years for the remainder. The number 'not stated' in the census returns has been included with one-roomed dwellings.

As no census was taken in 1901 the annual increase in the number of houses had to be calculated for the intercensal increase 1891 and 1911. It is assumed that the growth of 2,470 houses per annum was proportionate to all classes. To obtain the number due for replacement it was again necessary to deduct the estimated increase from each class.

Value of Residential Building

Number built during Year	Cost £	Annual Value of Building £'000
(i) Additional Houses:		
83	288	23·9
291	144	41·9
978	48	46·9
1,118	10	11·2
2,470		123·9
(ii) Replacements:		
95	288	27·4
540	144	77·8
2,655	48	127·4
7,220	10	72·2
10,510		304·8
Total Value of Residential Building		£428·7

(*c*) *Commercial.* (i) *Shops, Warehouses, etc.* The average annual increase in the number of merchants and shopkeepers between 1891 and 1911 was 31. The number of premises due for replacement is based on the 1871 CP returns. The value of new constructions and replacements is thus calculated at £8,900 and £14,100 respectively.

(ii) *Sugar Factories.* For basis of estimating the value of sugar factory buildings, see Ch. 1, F. The average value of imported sugar machinery, pans and stills was £45,685. The value of factories built or repaired during the year has accordingly been calculated at £32,500.

4. *Manufacturing for Local Consumption and Public Utilities*

(*a*) *Factories*. Domestic rum consumption is calculated from the yield of the rum tax—455,976 gallons. Estate sugar production retained in the island averaged only 89,814 cwt. for these years.[1] The reliability of these returns, however, is open to doubt. Allowing for understatements and for small-settler production it does not seem unreasonable to suppose that home consumption was equal to the quantity exported—322,906 cwt.—which is equal to an annual per capita consumption of 44·8 lb.

Although industrial establishments are now listed in the BBJ the details furnished are insufficient to compute output. Where local manufactures were subject to excise duties quantities produced could be estimated and evaluated, involving assumptions only about retail prices. This was done for tobacco for local consumption, beer and matches. For printing we again have only information about the numbers employed.[2] On the assumption that the average income of the 273 printers and compositors was £65[3] p.a. and allowing for costs of imported materials and profits, the value of printing is estimated at £25,000.

(*b*) *Independent Workers*. Included here are 28,400 dressmakers, tailors, milliners and shoemakers whose net average earnings are assumed to have amounted to 10*s*. per week.[4] There remain about 5,000 employed as cabinet-makers, butchers, bakers, etc., whose average earnings are assumed to have been £1 per week.

(*c*) *Public Utilities*. Public utilities include the undertakings of the Kingston General Commissioners and the two irrigation systems.[5]

Manufactures for Local Consumption and Public Utilities

	£'000
Rum	42·7
Sugar	209·2
Tobacco	91·6
Beer	4·6
Matches	15·8
Printing	25·0
Independent Workers	998·4
Public Utilities	73·1
	£1,460·4

[1] HBJ, 1910, 1911 and 1912. [2] CP, 1911. [3] BBJ. Wage rates of tradesmen.
[4] *Ibid.* This is equivalent to four days' work at the lowest daily rate quoted for tradesmen. [5] *Ibid.*

5. *Passenger Transport and Communications*

Receipts from passengers carried on the railway averaged £49,836 for these years.[1] The value of services rendered by the West India Electric Company—formerly the Jamaica Street Car Company—is assumed to have been double that of *1890* because the extent of operations since the change of ownership in 1897 had been considerably increased. Third, average expenditure on telephone and telegraph services amounted to £39,547 in these years.[2]

6. *Distribution* (see Ch. 1, G)

(*a*) *Entrepôt*. The total value of the entrepôt trade was £37,100 for these years. The commodities involved were too numerous and small to make detailed estimation of distribution margins possible. Earnings of traders are, therefore, again calculated at 25 per cent of the c.i.f. value of imports.

(*b*) *Retail*. The value added by Jamaican traders is calculated at 25 per cent of the c.i.f. value of imported consumer goods.

7. *Public Administration*

(*a*) *Central*. This item again excludes public works, grants to education, ecclesiastical stipends and transfer payments.

(*b*) *Local*. No details are available about the expenditure of parochial authorities. Average expenditure in the years 1909, 1910 and 1911—excluding the Kingston Public General Commissioners—amounted to £165,840. From this have to be deducted expenditure on roads and transfer payments. The latter accounted for 34 per cent in 1890 and in 1930. The same proportion has accordingly been used here. But in the case of public works, the share was only about 15·6 per cent in 1930 compared with 46·6 per cent in 1890. For 1910 the share is assumed to have been 31 per cent. Deducting these two items the sum of £58,000 is left for general administrative services. (For details see Chs. 6, IV, and 16.)

8. *Ownership of Houses*

This follows from 3*b* above. Rental values for the two first groups were £36 and £18 and for the third and fourth were estimated at £6 and £2.

[1] BBJ. Wage rates of tradesmen. [2] *Ibid.*

Rental Value of Houses

Size of House	Number of Houses	Average Rent £	Total Rental Value £'000
5 rooms and over	6,207	36[1]	223·5
3–4 rooms	21,627	18[1]	389·3
2 ,,	72,671	6	436·0
1 ,,	83,429	2	166·9
	183,934		£1,215·7

9. *Professional Services*

(*a*) *Legal.* The HBJ lists 11 barristers and 85 solicitors in private practice. Their average earnings are estimated at £600 p.a.[2]

(*b*) *Medical.* Of the 134 medical practitioners listed in the HBJ about one-third were in the Public Medical Service. The average income of doctors is estimated at £600 p.a.[3] but from this are deducted the emoluments derived from the Public Service. Included also are the earnings of 47 dentists which are similarly estimated at £600 p.a.

(*c*) *Educational.* Elementary schools were financed by government grants while other educational establishments received the greater part of their income from fees and endowments. Public grants, excluding administrative expenses, amounted to £62,300 in these years. The income of secondary schools is listed incompletely and in filling in the gaps use was made of details in the HBJ. The total so calculated together with that of training colleges is £23,500. From this has to be deducted the amount—estimated at £10,000—spent on board and lodging and equipment.

(*d*) *Religious.* In these years the stipends of the remaining Church of England clergy paid from public funds amounted to only £1,200. According to fragmentary returns in the HBJ the membership of all denominations was about 142,000. Total income is given for the Church of England and the Presbyterian Church only. The last shows an average contribution for religious purposes of 5·7*s*. per member. This is taken as representative of the other denominations.

[1] *Jamaica Daily Gleaner*, 18th March, 1910.

[2] This, the salary paid to the Registrar of the Supreme Court of Judicature, is the lowest salary paid to legal office holders and has been selected because it is considered unlikely that average earnings in private practice were as high as the salaries in the senior appointments. HBJ, 1911.

[3] This, the salary paid to Senior Medical Office at the Public Hospital, is the lowest quoted for full-time officers in the Medical Service. HBJ, 1912.

10. *Domestic Services*

The 1911 CP enumerated 35,701 domestic servants and 11,715 washerwomen. Their weekly wages are given as 3*s*.–12*s*. in the BBJ for these years. Five shillings is taken as the average here.

The net earnings of 270 hotel, tavern and lodging-house keepers are estimated at £52 per annum.

II. Income

No estimates are prepared for this year. See Ch. 1, L.

III. Expenditure

Consumer expenditure on professional services is again shown net of the public contribution to education. In this year there were surpluses on the working of the railway, post office and public utilities which are again deducted from expenditure and shown as indirect taxes. Domestic investment consists of building and construction, durable producer goods and investment in land. The first two items have already been discussed. It remains to be added here that the annual increase in cultivated acreage between 1909 and 1911 amounted to 15,700 acres. Costs are estimated at 19·2*s*. per acre.[1]

	£'000
Building and construction . .	733·6
Durable producer goods . .	159·6
Agricultural investment . .	15·1
	£908·3

IV. Public Authorities

1. *Central Government*

(*a*) *Receipts*. In this year direct taxes on property consist entirely of taxes on house property and land. Customs revenue consists only of import duties. Excise taxes in these years include levies on locally manufactured and consumed beer, matches, tobacco as well as rum.

[1] Average predial wage rate in 1910 was 1*s*. per day. BBJ, 1909, 1910 and 1911.

(*b*) *Expenditure*. Subventions include the grant to education, the Jamaica Institute and the Direct Cable and Direct Steamship subsidies.

2. *Local Government*

No details of income and expenditure of parochial boards have been found.

V. Balance of Payments

Emigrants' remittances are calculated on the assumption that each of the estimated 60,000 Jamaicans living abroad[1] sent £2 p.a. to relatives in the island.[2] Profits from abroad include the earnings of the Savings Bank[3] which at this date still invested all funds abroad. Tourist expenditure is assumed to be about one-third of that in *1930*. On the expenditure side are again included debt charges as well as imports. Sundry payments abroad consist of subsidies paid to the Direct Cable and Steamship subsidies. A further item which ought to be shown here is profits earned by foreign companies, notably the American fruit companies, in the island. No information is available to prepare an estimate nor the extent to which such payments were offset by profits earned abroad from Jamaican investments. On the whole, it seems likely that the balance shown here understates the extent of foreign investment in the island.

[1] Col. Rep., BPP, 1912 (Cd. 6007–39), p. 32.

[2] The average total value of remittances was estimated at £125,000 p.a. by the Unemployment Bureau. Quoted in Labour Conditions in the West Indies, BBP, 1938–9 (Cmd. 6070), p. 78.

[3] BBJ for these years.

CHAPTER 7

THE NATIONAL INCOME IN *1930*

TABLE 7.I

Output in 1930

		£'000
1. Exports	3,957·8	
Less imported materials	490·7	3,467·1
2. Food Production for Local Consumption		
a. Ground Provisions	4,961·9	
b. Animal Products	970·4	
c. Other	322·2	6,254·5
3. Building and Construction		
a. Public	512·2	
b. Residential	912·4	
c. Commercial	82·9	
	1,507·5	
Less imported materials	324·2	1,183·3
4. Manufacturing for Local Consumption		
a. Factories	667·6	
b. Independent Workers	1,462·2	
c. Public Utilities	91·9	
	2,221·7	
Less imported materials	160·4	2,061·3
5. Passenger Transport and Communications	386·5	
Less imported materials	50·3	336·2
6. Distribution		
a. Entrepôt	11·5	
b. Retail	1,029·6	1,041·1
7. Public Administration		
a. Central	1,018·3	
b. Local	174·1	
	1,192·4	
Less imported materials	79·3	1,113·1
8. Ownership of Houses		2,546·5
9. Professional Services		
a. Legal	122·4	
b. Medical	124·4	
c. Educational	236·5	
d. Religious	95·9	579·2
10. Domestic Services		1,369·3
Total Gross Domestic Product		£19,951·6

TABLE 7.II

Income in 1930

		£'000
1. Incomes from Agriculture		
a. Labourers' wages	1,439·2	
b. Small-Settlers' profits	6,945·2	
c. Planters' profits	1,331·7	
d. Plantation staffs' salaries	422·5	10,138·6
2. Other Wages and Salaries:		
a. Domestic	1,392·1	
b. Construction	910·6	
c. Manufacturing	163·2	
d. Distribution	856·8	
e. Public Administration	1,124·4	
f. Education	286·7	
g. Other	54·7	4,788·5
3. Other Profits:		
a. Trade	2,948·1	
b. Professions	335·7	
c. Independent Work	1,740·7	5,024·5
Total (Gross Domestic Product)		£19,951·6

TABLE 7.III

Expenditure in 1930

		£'000
1. Food, Drink and Tobacco:		
Imported	2,292·3	
Home-produced	6,751·7	9,044·0
2. Clothing:		
Imported	1,282·9	
Home-produced	942·2	2,225·1
3. Other Consumer Goods:		
Imported	1,572·7	
Home-produced	782·3	2,355·0
4. Personal Services:		
Professional	396·1	
Domestic	1,369·3	1,765·4
5. Passenger Transport and Communications		386·5
6. Rent		2,546·5
Total Personal Expenditure		£18,322·5
7. Government Expenditure on Goods and Services		1,375·5
8. Domestic Investment		2,049·4
9. Payments Abroad		295.3
10. Receipts from Abroad		−550·5
11. Foreign Balance		−1,540·6
Total (Gross Domestic Product)		£19,951·6

TABLE 7.IV

Revenue and Expenditure of Public Authorities

1. Central Authority

Receipts	£'000	Expenditure	£'000
Direct Taxes:		Wages and Salaries	544·8
On income	98·2	Goods and Services	809·7
On property	77·9	Transfer Payments:	
Indirect Taxes:		Subventions	281·9
Customs	1,102·2	Railway Deficit	99·9
Excise	268·4	Interest	295·3
Stamps	75·9		
Post Office Surplus	8·5		
Public Utilities Surplus	·8		
Licences, fees, fines, etc.	125·7		
Interest	26·9		
Miscellaneous	5·7		
Deficit	241·4		
	£2,031·6		£2,031·6

2. Local Authorities

Receipts	£'000	Expenditure	£'000
Direct Taxes:		Expenditure	409·1
On property	445·9	Surplus	36·8
	£445·9		£445·9

TABLE 7.V

The Balance of Payments

Income from Abroad	£'000	Expenditure Abroad	£'000
Total Value of Domestic Exports	3,957·8	Total Value of Retained Imports	5,765·1
Earnings from Entrepôt Trade	11·5	Debt Charges	295·3
Emigrants' Remittances	114·7		
Receipts from Tourists	307·0		
Profits from Abroad	126·8		
Sundry Receipts	2·0		
Balance	1,540·6		
	£6,060·4		£6,060·4

TABLE 7.VI

Output, Income and Expenditure in 1930

£'000

	1	2	3	4	5	6	7	8	9	10	11	12	13	14
	Gross Domestic Output	Agricultural Labourers	Small-Settlers	Planters	Plantation Staff	Other Wages and Salaries	Merchants	Professional Workers	Independent Workers	Imports	Exports	Goods and Services Available Domestically	Consumed	Invested
1. Exports*	3,467·1	1,181·6	1,179·1	835·9	204·3	257·8	498·5	—	—	490·7	3,957·8	—	—	—
2. Food Production for Local Consumption*	6,254·5	174·9	4,865·8	327·8	75·4	19·0	381·6	—	87·8	1,833·8	—	8,088·3	8,088·3	—
3. Building and Construction . . .	1,183·3	—	—	—	—	887·5	295·8	—	—	327·7	—	1,511·0	—	1,511·0
4. Manufacturing for Local Consumption and Public Utilities* . .	2,061·3	—	—	—	—	163·2	68·0	—	1,462·2	2,852·7	—	4,914·0	4,506·2	407·8
5. Passenger Transport and Communications . .	336·2	—	—	—	—	286·1	50·1	—	—	180·9	—	517·1	386·5	130·6
6. Distribution	1,041·1	—	—	—	—	260·3	780·8	—	—	—	11·5	1,029·6	1,029·6	—
7. Public Administration .	1,113·1	—	—	—	—	1,096·1	—	17·0	—	79·3	—	1,192·4	1,192·4	—
8. Ownership of Houses .	2,546·5	82·7	900·3	168·0	142·8	230·5	806·1	25·4	190·7	—	—	2,546·5	2,546·5	—
9. Professional Services .	579·2	—	—	—	—	285·9	—	293·3	—	—	—	579·2	579·2	—
10. Other Services . . .	1,369·3	—	—	—	—	1,302·1	67·2	—	—	—	—	1,369·3	1,369·3	—
	19,951·6	1,439·2	6,945·2	1,331·7	422·5	4,788·5	2,948·1	335·7	1,740·7	5,765·1	3,969·3	21,747·4	19,698·0	2,049·4
11. Less Income from Abroad										−550·5	—	−550·5	−550·5	
12. Plus Payments Abroad										295·3	—	295·3	295·3	
13. Foreign Balance . .										−1,540·6	—	−1,540·6	—	−1,540·6
Total Gross Domestic Product . . .	£19,951·6	1,439·2	6,945·2	1,331·7	422·5	4,788·5	2,948·1	335·7	1,740·7	3,969·3	3,969·3	19,951·6	19,442·8	508·8

* Incomes shown in columns numbers 2 to 7, row 1, include incomes arising out of the production of retained exports as well as exports, hence columns numbers 2 to 9, row 2, show only incomes arising out of the production of ground provisions and animal products and columns numbers 2 to 9, row 4, only those arising out of the manufacture of non-export crops and public utilities. The incomes in three rows thus do not add up individually to give the total under Gross Domestic Product. See notes under II, 1, 2 and 4.

I. Output

1. *Exports*

The average value of domestic exports was £3,957,800 for the years 1929, 1930 and 1931.[1] Imported production materials, valued at £534,500, are deducted here and under 4 below.

2. *Food Production for Local Consumption*

(*a*) *Ground Provisions*. See Ch. 1, D.

(*b*) *Animal Products*. The number of cattle slaughtered in the island was given as 32,559 for 1934.[2] The total number of other stock in the island for the years 1929, 1930 and 1931 is available for sheep only; for pigs the number has been based on data for the 1910's and in the case of goats it is assumed that the number slaughtered was equal to the number of hides exported. (For the dressed meat equivalents of these animals see *1870*).

Value of Island Meat Production

	Number '000	Total Weight '000 lb.	Price per[3] lb.	Value £'000
Cattle . . .	32·6	13,040·0	7·75*d*.	421·1
Sheep and Goats .	192·8	9,640·0	9*d*.	361·5
Pigs . . .	16·0	1,600·0	1*s*. 3*d*.	100·0
				£882·6

The quantity of fish caught was estimated in the BBJ at 2,808,000 lb. with a landed value of £87,750.

(*c*) *Other*. Home consumption of non-manufactured export crops is estimated at 10 per cent of export value. The most important item included here is bananas. The rather low value assigned to these is explained by the fact that locally consumed bananas were usually below the quality standards exacted for export and hence commanded lower prices. If banana consumption was greater than this, then it may be argued that this fruit replaced other starch and vegetable products included under ground provisions and the under-estimate in retained exports is balanced by an excess in group *a*.

[1] BBJ, 1929, 1930 and 1931. CO 142/143, 144 and 145.
[2] *Beef Cattle Industry in Jamaica*. J. Govt. Printer, 1935. [3] BBJ, *op. cit*.

3. *Building and Construction*

(*a*) *Public*. Expenditure by the central government averaged £458,600 for these years and that of parochial authorities is estimated at £53,600. (See section 7*b*.)

(*b*) *Residential.* The housing ratio was 4·48 in 1921 and 3·83 in 1943.[1] It is assumed here that the ratio in 1930 was four persons per dwelling and further that the increase in each class in the years was proportionate to the increase in the inter-census years 1921 and 1943. The houses are again grouped according to size and the unspecified included with one-roomed dwellings. The average value of the first two groups is based on advertisements found in the *Jamaica Daily Gleaner* for 1930. In each case, however, the lowest price was taken

Value of Residential Building

	Number built during Year	Cost £	Annual Value of Building £'000
(i) Additional Houses			
	422	400[2]	168·8
	900	220[3]	198·0
	2,200	50	110·0
	3,444	10	34·4
	6,966		511·2
(ii) Replacements			
	110	400	44·0
	415	220	91·3
	3,635	50	181·8
	8,410	10	84·1
	12,570		401·2
Total Value of Residential Building .		.	£912·4

to allow for the fact that most advertisements related to houses situated in Kingston and these obviously commanded a higher price than comparable houses in rural areas. For two-roomed and single-roomed dwellings the values of £50 and £10 have been entered. The average life of houses is estimated at forty years for the first two groups, twenty for the third and ten for the last.

[1] CP. [2] *Jamaica Daily Gleaner*, 7th March, 1930.
[3] *Ibid.*, 2nd January, 1930.

Annual additions thus averaged 6,966 between 1921 and 1930. These are allocated to the different groups according to their respective rates of growth over these years. To calculate replacements in the first two groups we have deducted the calculated increase between 1911–30 and the estimated increase in the preceding twenty years (see 1910); for the third group the 1911 census was used and for the last the 1921 census.

(*c*) *Commercial.* (i) *Shops, Warehouses etc.* The 1921 CP enumerated 3,963 merchants and shopkeepers but by 1943 the number of traders employing labour and working on their own account from fixed premises had risen to 6,045. Assuming a steady rate of growth new additions numbered 95 in 1930. Replacements of existing premises are based on the 1891 census. The value of new constructions and replacements is thus calculated at £38,000 and £34,000 respectively.

(ii) *Sugar Factories.* For basis of estimating sugar factory buildings see Ch. 1, F. The average value of imported sugar machinery was £27,300 during these years. The value of factory buildings has accordingly been calculated at £10,900.

4. *Manufacturing for Local Consumption and Public Utilities*

(*a*) *Factories.* Domestic rum consumption, as in previous years, is calculated from the yield of the excise tax on rum—923,636 gallons. Per capita sugar consumption is estimated at 50 lbs.: that is about 22,700 tons.

The output of other industrial establishments is based on returns in the BBJ for 1929, 1930 and 1931. Where information was incomplete for some factories the gaps were filled in on the basis of returns for others. In the case of the dyewoods factory it was assumed that all output was exported. For the tobacco factory the value of home consumption had to be added to exports. Retained tobacco output was estimated with the help of excise revenue. By taking the median duty of 1*s.* per 100 on cigars selling at 5–10*s.*, the excise revenue of £19,326 is equal to 36,652,000 cigars with a retail value of £144,945. This assumes that the incidence of the tax was equal for all types of manufactured tobacco. Periodicals are calculated from the publications showing both price and circulation listed in the BBJ.

(*b*) *Independent Workers.* This category again comprises the output of all the remaining workers not accounted for in other sections. Chief among them are dressmakers, tailors, milliners and shoemakers whose number is estimated at 30,200 for 1930. Net earnings are calculated at 12*s*. per week.[1] There remain a further 10,000 workers employed as bakers, butchers, cabinet-makers, etc. Their weekly earnings are assumed to have been £1.[2]

(*c*) *Public Utilities*. Public utilities include only those undertakings operated by the Kingston Public General Commissioners.[3]

Value of Manufactures for Local Consumption and Public Utilities

	£'000
Rum	102·5
Sugar	249·8
Tobacco	144·9
Other Manufactures	98·1
Printing	72·3
Independent Workers	1,462·2
Public Utilities	91·9
	£2,221·7

5. *Passenger Transport and Communications*

(*a*) *Transport*. Receipts from passengers carried by the railway averaged £58,885.[4] Road transport consisted of tramways operated by the Jamaica Public Service Company Ltd., and motor cars and buses used for passenger transport. No information is available about the number of passengers carried on Kingston trams. For road transport the number of motor cars used for passengers—1,579—given by the Collector-General[5] is multiplied by the average income of tradesmen—26*s*. per week.[6] To this amount have to be added the estimated earnings of owners of vehicles—£35,500—and the cost of imported materials—£35,600.

Passenger Transport

	£'000
Rail	58·9
Road	177·8
	236·7

[1] BBJ, *op. cit*. Wage rates in manufacturing industries are quoted at 12*s*.–26*s*. per week.
[2] *Ibid*.
[3] Estimates of the Kingston and St. Andrew Corporation, 1931–2. J. Council Minutes.
[4] BBJ, *op. cit*.
[5] Report for 1930–1. J. Council Minutes.
[6] BBJ, *op cit*.

(*b*) *Communications.* Average expenditure on telephone and telegraph services by the Post Office, less maintenance and construction, amounted to £99,879.[1] Half as much is added to this amount to allow for the services rendered by the four private companies operating in the island.

6. *Distribution*

(*a*) *Entrepôt.* The total value of the re-export trade amounted to only £57,575. The commodities involved were too numerous and often too ill-defined to make detailed estimation of the value added by Jamaican traders possible. Twenty-five per cent of the c.i.f. value of imports has again been taken as the entrepôt earnings.

(*b*) *Retail.* See Ch. 1, G.

7. *Public Administration*

(*a*) *Central.* This item again shows the average value of services rendered by the central government, as shown in the BBJ, after deduction of public works, education, transfer payments and trading services, which are shown elsewhere.

(*b*) *Local.* The BBJ show only total income and expenditure for parochial authorities. More detailed information is available in the estimates for the Kingston and St. Andrew Corporation for the financial year 1931–2.[2] After deducting trading services, transfer payments and public works took 33·8 and 15·6 per cent of the remaining expenditure. Applying these percentages to the average total parochial expenditure given in the BBJ, after deducting trading services, the value of services rendered by the local authorities is calculated at £174,100.

Imported materials used by public authorities include government stores, instruments and medicines. (For details see Chs. 7, IV, and 16.)

8. *Ownership of Houses*

Rental value of dwellings is calculated on the basis of estimates prepared for 3*b* above. Some advertisements found in the *Jamaica Gleaner* gave both selling price and rental value. These invariably show extremely high rents in relation to price: many are around 16·5 per cent and one was found at 18·7 per cent. This is probably due to the fact that most of them refer to houses in Kingston where

[1] BBJ, *op. cit.*

[2] *Op. cit.*

the large influx of people raised the demand for accommodation. To allow for the rather lower rents in rural areas, rental value here has been calculated at 14 per cent for all except the smallest houses for which it was put at 20 per cent.

Rental Value of Houses

Size of House	Number of Houses '000	Average Rent £	Total Rental Value £'000
5 Rooms and over	11·4	56	638·4
3–4 Rooms	33·0	30·8	1,016·4
2 rooms	94·5	7	661·5
1 room	115·1	2	230·2
	254·0		2,546·5

9. *Professional Services*

(*a*) *Legal.* The 1932 HBJ lists 15 barristers and 138 solicitors practising in the island. Their gross earnings are estimated at £800 p.a. which was the salary paid to Magistrates.[1]

(*b*) *Medical.* Of the 126 doctors listed in the HBJ twelve were full-time officers in the Public Medical Service and a further forty were employed part-time. The gross income of doctors is assumed to be equal to that of District Medical Officers without private practice—£700 p.a. including £100 house allowance.[2] Excluding the doctors wholly engaged in government service and deducting the income of those employed part-time—salary and vaccination fees amounting to £16,991—which is included under public authorities' expenditure in 7*a* above, total income from private practice is estimated at £62,800.

In addition, the HBJ lists 88 dentists whose gross earnings are assumed to be £700 p.a.

(*c*) *Educational.* Elementary and industrial schools were wholly financed from government grants. Most of the secondary schools received small grants from the government but relied mainly on fees and other sources for their income. Average government expenditure on education, excluding administrative expenses, amounted to £183,100 for these years. The income of secondary schools, other than from public funds, was estimated on the basis of incomplete returns given in the BBJ. By applying average income from fees and other sources per pupil to all schools a total of £67,500 is obtained.

[1] HBJ, 1932.

[2] *Ibid.*

From this have to be deducted boarding expenses for 9 out of 25 schools which are calculated from the BBJ returns at £14,100.

(*d*) *Religious*. The HBJ lists the religious bodies of Jamaica. For two of them, the Church of England and the Presbyterian Church, income amounted to £31,832 but no membership was given. For other churches only membership was given and their average annual contribution is assumed at 10*s*. per member.

10. *Domestic Services*

Assuming an even rate of growth in the number employed in domestic service between 1921 and 1943[1] it is estimated that there were 62,600 with an income of 8*s*. per week.[2]

Similarly hotel, lodging-house and bar keepers are estimated to have numbered 646. Their average net earnings are assumed to have amounted to £2 per week.[3]

II. Income

1. *Exports*

The total value of domestic exports plus the value of produce estimated to have been retained for home consumption amounts to £4,507,900. As in previous years, when income distribution was attempted, the next step is to discover the shares of estates and of small-settlers in total output.

Acreage statistics are available for the major commodities. But in the case of bananas the information in the HBJ is obviously incomplete. In 1930 81,848 acres were returned as under banana cultivation compared with 63,168 acres in 1920 while exports had risen from 9 million stems to 24·5 million stems in the ten years. More useful information is available in the JBC Report. The average number of stems handled by the major buying agencies was as follows:

Average Number of Stems handled in the Years 1929, 1930 and 1931[4]

	'000
By the United Fruit Company	11,221·5
JBPA	7,170·6
Atlantic Fruit Company	4,619·9
Miscellaneous Companies	14·7
Number of Stems exported	23,026·7

[1] CP, 1921 and 1943. [2] BBJ, *op. cit*. Wage rates quoted at 8*s*.–10*s*. per week.
[3] *Ibid*. This is the highest rate quoted for skilled workers.
[4] JBC., J. Govt. Printer, 1936, Jamaica, App. C.

The JBPA purchased all their fruit by contract. Taking average deliveries for the years 1929, 1930 and 1931 total deliveries by the under 20-acre groups amounted to 3,791,700 stems.[1] The United Fruit Company and the Atlantic Fruit Company obtained supplies from their own properties, by contract and by open market purchases. Of the total acreage contracted to these two companies 16,064 were of less than twenty acres each.[2] At eighty stems per acre[3] deliveries by contract growers in this group amounted to 1,285,120 stems. Open market purchases by the United Fruit Company in 1930 amounted to 4,160,000 stems.[4] The bulk of these came from small-settlers.[5] Allowing for open market purchases by the Atlantic Fruit Company, total accepted deliveries for export by small-settlers are estimated as follows:

Number of Stems delivered by Small-Settlers

	'000 Stems
To: JBPA	3,791·7
Contractual deliveries to the two companies	1,285·1
Open market deliveries to the two companies	5,000·0
	10,076·8

and by the larger properties on contract or by the Companies' own estates is estimated as follows:

Number of Stems delivered by Large Properties

	'000 Stems
To: JBPA	3,378·9
United Fruit Company	6,740·5
Atlantic Fruit Company	2,816·0
Miscellaneous Companies	14·7
	12,950·1

There remains the estimated amount of fruit sold in the home market. Large proprietors were liable to rejection of their fruit on account of low grading as much as small-scale cultivators. In spite of the wide range of yields obtained by the different cultivation groups, the percentage of count bunches per stems varied only between 62 and 66.[6] Domestic consumption is therefore allocated in

[1] *Ibid.*, Appx. J.
[2] *Ibid.* p. 9.
[3] *Ibid.*, p. 6. Average yield of the 5–20 acres group.
[4] *Ibid.*, Table XXIX, p. 39.
[5] *Ibid.*, p. 10.
[6] *Ibid.*, p. 6.

proportion to export deliveries: i.e. 1,008 thousand to small settlers and 1,295 thousand to estates.

Total sugar output was estimated at 66,700 tons. According to the returns in the HBJ 61,300 tons were manufactured by estates[1] and the remaining 5,400 tons by small-settlers. Not all the canes processed in estate factories, however, were grown on estate lands. According to the SSIJ estates purchased one-third of their cane requirements from outside growers.[2] But this information was based on a number of years during the 1920's when contractual cane growing was declining. To allow for some decline the slightly lower ratio of 30 per cent

*Shares in Total Agricultural Output**

£'000

	Estates	Small-Settlers	Total
Bananas	1,404·4	1,090·1	2,494·4
Sugar	562·6	171·6	734·2
Rum	173·0	—	173·0
Coffee	75·3	143·6	219·0
Pimento	119·0	119·0	238·1
Logwood, raw	28·1	28·1	56·1
Coconuts	79·6	79·6	159·1
Cocoa	45·5	45·5	91·1
Grapefruit	30·3	30·3	60·6
Ginger	25·0	25·0	50·1
Nuts and kernels	32·3	32·3	64·6
Oils, essential	16·5	16·5	33·1
Other	67·3	67·3	134·5
	2,658·9	1·848·9	4,507·9
Value of produce supplied to local manufacturing industries	91·9	91·9	183·7
	£2,750·8	£1,940·8	£4,691·6

* Not all the cross totals balance owing to rounding off.

is adopted. At 11·0965 tons of cane per ton of refining sugar[3] total production of canes manufactured in factories was 680,215 tons and the quantity produced by outside growers 204,065 tons. The usual basis of payment to cane farmers was 5 per cent of the selling price

[1] HBJ, 1930 and 1932. List of sugar estates in cultivation.
[2] SSIJ, J. Govt. Printer, 1929, p. 88.
[3] *Ibid.*, pp. 88–9. Average of 22 estates.

of sugar[1] which for these years was £11·006 per ton.[2] The value of cane farmers' output is thus calculated at £112,200. Most of this was produced by farmers cultivating less than 5 acres each and the whole is therefore allocated to small-settlers.[3] Adding the additional tonnage marketed or consumed by small-settlers directly we get small-settlers' share as £171,600. The value of estates' output of sugar is accordingly £562,600.

Rum was generally manufactured by the estates. For coffee the acreages listed in the HBJ are used and output allocated on the assumption that settlers' yields were only half of those obtained by estates. There is no information about the remaining commodities. These amounted to about 20 per cent of the total and are assumed to have been shared equally by the two types of production systems. Included here also is the estimated growers' value of logwood, tobacco, copra, etc., supplied to local manufacturing industries.

(*a*) *Estate Cultivation.* Cultivation expenses in the banana industry consisted chiefly of wages and salaries. Wage employment is estimated for 1930 by assuming an even rate of growth between 1921 and 1943. This gives the number of men employed as 16,590 and women as 7,660. This method is, of course, highly suspect because census returns of gainfully employed are rather unreliable. If, however, we assume that the average working week was only four days then the estimated number engaged appears more reasonable. Wages of banana workers were between 1*s.* 6*d.* and 2*s.* 6*d.* for men and between 1*s.* and 1*s.* 6*d.* for women in 1937.[4] Assuming that the decline in these wages had been of the same order as that of the general wage level,[5] the wages of banana workers in 1930 were 2*s.* 5·4*d.* for men and 1*s.* 3*d.* for women. The total wages bill for the banana industry is thus calculated at £522,600. In addition staff costs are estimated at ten per cent of output.

The cost of cane grown on estates averaged 14*s.* 6*d.* per ton.[6] Total cultivation costs for estates are accordingly calculated at £345,209. In addition, the cost of manufacture, excluding capital charges, were £4·8 per ton.[7] Total estate costs were therefore £639,400.

[1] WISC, BPP, 1930 (Cmd. 3517), p. 117.

[2] f.o.b. price Jamaica, calculated from values and quantities given in the export returns.

[3] SIC, 1945, J. Govt. Printer, p. 25.

[4] Labour Conditions in the West Indies. Report by Major G. St. J. Orde Browne, BPP, 1938–9 (Cmd. 6070), p. 94.

[5] *Ibid.*, p. 97.

[6] WISC, *op. cit.*, p. 43.

[7] SSIJ, *op. cit.*, p. 77. Average of 18 estates.

Of this about 55·3 per cent was spent on wages and a further 10 per cent on staff.

No information is available about production costs of other commodities. It has been assumed that wages accounted for 50 per cent of total output. Imported materials are allocated to estates and small-settlers proportionately to total output. To this are added distribution costs which are again estimated at 25 per cent and allocated to merchants and wage labour in the ratio of one to three.

As in *1890* we estimate the cost of wharfage done by outside factors at 5 per cent of total output which is allocated to merchants and to wages in the ratio of one to three.

Planters' gross profit is obtained by deducting these various incomes from domestic plantation output:

Planters' Gross Profits

		£'000
Total value of domestic plantation output		2,437·6
Less incomes of: Agricultural labour	1,181·6	
Plantation staff	204·3	
Merchants	93·1	
Other labour	122·7	1,601·7
		£835·9

(*b*) *Small-Settler Cultivation.* Apart from the total cost of imported materials used in production, small-settler cultivation is also charged with the cost of marketing their output, estimated at 25 per cent of which one-quarter is allocated to labour.

Small-Settlers' Gross Profits

		£'000
Total value of small-settlers' output		1,719·6
Less incomes of: Merchants	405·4	
Other labour	135·1	
		540·5
		£1,179·1

2. *Food Production for Local Consumption*

(*a*) *Ground Provisions.* Again we assume that only one-quarter of peasants' output was marketed by petty traders whose services are estimated at 25 per cent of the final value of output. The assumption that peasants paid no rent is no longer valid. According to the 1943 CP about 15 per cent of the holdings of less than fifty acres each were rented. We have not found any data about rental values and are thus unable to make any deductions for rental value. The resultant estimate is thus a slight overstatement of peasants' gross profits.

(*b*) *Animal Products*. In the case of meat production it was estimated in 1933 that while there were about 131,135 head of cattle in breeding pens the total number in the island was about 200,000 and that the difference was accounted for by small-settlers' stock.[1] Assuming that this ratio held for all livestock the value of output of pens was £578,100 and that of small-settlers £304,500. Costs of production are available for pens in St. Ann's parish in 1935. Average expenditure by seven pens—which are assumed to be representative of the industry—on wages was 52 per cent and on salaries was 28 per cent of the total cost in 1935.[2] In that year total costs amounted to 28*s*. ¾*d*. per 100 lb.[3] compared with the contract price of beef supplied to public institutions of 28*s*.[4] But in the years 1929, 1930 and 1931 the contract price of beef averaged 60*s*. 4*d*. per 100 lb. On the assumption that pen-keepers had managed to reduce wages by 20 per cent during these years—as had been done in other wage employment—the percentage shares are recalculated and the difference between the new expenditure and the average *1930* price allocated to pen-keepers' gross profit. Small-settlers' share in meat production is again charged with a distribution margin of 25 per cent accruing to traders and wages in the ratio of three to one.

3. *Building and Construction*

As in previous years the domestic value of building is allocated to wages and merchants in the ratio of three to one.

4. *Manufacturing for Local Consumption and Public Utilities*

Sugar and rum have already been dealt with under 1 above. There remain the value added by the manufacturing industry to the raw materials supplied by the agricultural industry—estimated at £183,700—printing and public utilities. For the first two, the wages bill is estimated from employment statistics included with the returns of manufacturing establishments in the BBJ and the number of printers and compositors enumerated in the 1921 CP. Together they

[1] Cattle and Dairy Industry of the Colony, J. Govt. Printer, 1933, p. 1.
[2] Beef Cattle Industry, *op. cit.* [3] *Ibid.* [4] *Ibid.*

number 1,730. Wages are taken at £52 p.a.[1] After deduction of wages and imported materials the remainder is allocated to merchants' gross profit. The net income arising out of public utility services is allocated to wages and salaries.

5. *Passenger Transport and Communications*

Total railway receipts exceeded current expenditure by £28,526. Allocating this surplus proportionately to passenger and goods receipts we get a surplus of £4,600 over current expenditure on passenger transport. The remainder is allocated to wages and salaries. The value of road transport was estimated on the basis of wages £106,700 and gross profit £35,000. The expenditure of the post office, after deduction of imported materials, is allocated to wages and salaries. In the case of the private companies it is assumed that profits accounted for 20 per cent of expenditure and the remainder was spent on wages and salaries.

6. *Distribution*

See Ch. 1, G.

7. *Public Administration*

As in previous years the net income arising out of government expenditure is assumed to accrue to government employees except for those doctors who were employed on a part-time basis.

8. *Ownership of Houses*

It is assumed that three-quarters of all houses were owner-occupied and that the remainder were rented from merchants. Owner-occupiers in the first two groups of houses include planters, professional workers, plantation staff, government employees and some traders; in the third, the remaining traders, teachers, clerical workers, some peasants and some other independent workers; in the fourth, other clerical workers, shop assistants, some peasants and some independent workers; and in the fifth agricultural wage labour and some domestics.

9. *Professional Services*

One-fifth of lawyers' and doctors' gross earnings are allocated to wages and salaries for administrative and other assistance. In the case

[1] BBJ, *op. cit.* Wage rates in manufacturing industry.

of education services rendered were estimated net of boarding expenses. The whole amount shown in the output table is therefore assumed to have been spent on teachers' salaries. The same applies to religious services.

10. *Domestic Services*

Output is allocated to wages and profits as in previous years.

III. Expenditure

The same procedure for obtaining expenditure from the output table was again followed for this year. Domestic investment in this year consists only of building and construction and durable producer goods. No estimate is included for investment in new land because the area under cultivation actually contracted during these years.

	£'000
Building and construction .	1,507·5
Durable producer goods .	541·9
	£2,049·4

IV. Public Authorities

1. *Central Government*

(*a*) *Receipts.* In this year direct taxes on income appear for the first time. The bulk of excise duty is still derived from rum consumed in the island while tobacco and beer make up most of the remainder. Licences, fees, fines etc. include motor car registrations, firearms, agricultural produce dealers' licences in addition to a number of other manufacturers' and traders' licences.

(*b*) *Expenditure.* Wages and salaries as stated here are equal to the 'Personal Emoluments' listed in the Blue Books. Transfer payments include the education grant, subventions and the excess of Colonial Development Fund issues over receipts.

2. *Local Government*

All revenue of Parochial Boards appears to be derived from direct taxes on property.

V. Balance of Payments

Just as in *1832* there was the difficulty of accounting for the huge excess of receipts over expenditure abroad so in this year there is the problem of accounting for a large surplus of expenditure over receipts. The *West Indies Year Book* for 1930 referring to the figures for 1928 stated that 'the excess of imports over exports is explained partly by the tourist trade and by the fact that many Jamaican labourers abroad remit money to their dependants in the Island'. But it is difficult to account for this. The average value of emigrants' remittances during these years was calculated by Miss P. Deane to amount to £114,700.[1] The Tourist Trade Development Board recorded an average of 4,462 long-term visitors and 18,988 cruise tourists for the years 1929–31.[2] The value of their expenditure during these years was estimated at £307,000.[3] Profits from abroad include the amount of profits assessed for income tax in 1930[4] as well as the earnings of the Government Savings Bank from overseas investments.[5] This item may be considerably below the real total: first, because the number of incomes falling below the exemption limit may be appreciable and, second, because the efficiency of the tax authorities in collecting information is open to doubt. On the expenditure side, all debt charges paid by the government are again assumed to have been paid to overseas creditors. There is no information about the extent to which Jamaicans may have subscribed to public loans. Nor is there any means of estimating the amount of profits paid to foreign shareholders. The resulting balance therefore may be slightly above or considerably below the real total of foreign investment.

[1] Deane, *op. cit.*, p. 140.
[2] Council Mins. CO 140/278, 1932, App. XXVII, Vol. 73.
[3] Deane, *op. cit.*, p. 140.
[4] Departmental Reports, 1930. CO 140/274, Vol. 70.
[5] Total earnings of the Savings Bank averaged £30,100 (BBJ). The proportion received from abroad is estimated from details of invested funds given in the HBJ for these years.

CHAPTER 8

SUMMARY TABLES

WITH the exception of Table III, all the following tables summarize the estimates prepared in Chapters 2 to 7. Thus Tables 8.I and 8.II show gross domestic product at final value at current and at *1910* prices; Tables 8.IV and 8.V show total incomes and total expenditure at current prices and Table 8.VI gives personal expenditure at *1910* prices. All information on sources and methods will be found in the appropriate chapters.

Table 8.III, on the other hand, shows gross domestic product classified according to the value added by each sector. This is the only place where this table appears: a few explanatory words about its construction are, therefore, included here. To derive gross domestic product according to value added from gross domestic product at final value we have to make three adjustments. First, we have to deduct the value of distribution services from the productive sectors and add it to 'Transport and Distribution'. Secondly, we have to deduct the value of manufacturing processes from agriculture and add it to 'Manufacturing'. Thirdly, the value of raw materials supplied to manufacturing industry has to be taken out of 'Manufacturing' and entered under 'Agriculture'. For the first, we have used the detailed tables of income distribution: i.e. the incomes accruing to merchants and to transport and distributive workers in the agricultural and manufacturing industries. The second adjustment affects mainly sugar and rum. In *1930*, according to our calculations in Chapter 7, manufacturing costs accounted for about 40 per cent of the total value of sugar and rum. We have applied this ratio to the total value of sugar and rum produced by estates in the years *1832* and *1850*. For *1890*, the detailed production costs, given in Chapter 5 have been used to calculate manufacturing costs.

TABLE 8.I

Gross Domestic Product at Current Prices

	1832		1850		1870		1890		1910		1930	
	£'000	%	£'000	%	£'000	%	£'000	%	£'000	%	£'000	%
1. Exports	2,086·8	41·4	871·5	23·4	1,084·9	19·1	1,624·5	18·6	2,430·3	21·4	3,467·1	17·4
2. Food Production for Local Consumption	900·1	17·8	1,045·7	28·1	1,944·2	34·3	3,078·0	35·2	3,805·3	33·5	6,254·5	31·3
3. Building and Construction	180·0	3·6	164·0	4·4	250·0	4·4	436·9	5·0	489·4	4·3	1,183·3	5·9
4. Manufacturing for Local Consumption and P.U.	320·1	6·3	343·6	9·2	770·4	13·6	1,084·1	12·4	1,403·3	12·4	2,061·3	10·3
5. Passenger Transport and Communications	—	—	—	—	23·7	0·4	76·8	0·9	148·3	1·3	336·2	1·7
6. Distribution	286·4	5·7	272·3	7·3	295·9	5·2	405·7	4·6	512·3	4·5	1,041·1	5·2
7. Public Administration	322·9	6·4	174·7	4·7	238·2	4·2	334·3	3·8	434·5	3·8	1,113·1	5·6
8. Ownership of Houses	552·9	11·0	416·2	11·2	595·7	10·5	1,018·7	11·6	1,215·7	10·7	2,546·5	12·8
9. Professional Services	217·5	4·3	163·4	4·4	132·0	2·3	200·6	2·3	292·4	2·6	579·2	2·9
10. Domestic Services	175·2	3·5	273·0	7·3	341·9	6·0	487·0	5·6	630·4	5·5	1,369·3	6·9
Total Gross Domestic Product at current Prices	5,041·9	100·0	3,724·4	100·0	5,676·9	100·0	8,746·6	100·0	11,361·9	100·0	19,951·6	100·0

TABLE 8.II

Gross Domestic Product at 1910 Prices

	1832		*1850*		*1870*		*1890*		*1910*		*1930*	
	£'000	%	£'000	%	£'000	%	£'000	%	£'000	%	£'000	%
1. Exports	1,828·6	31·7	770·9	15·8	928·1	15·5	1,279·9	16·1	2,430·3	21·4	3,288·9	20·6
2. Food Production for Local Consumption:												
a. Ground Provisions	1,598·3	27·7	1,611·5	33·0	2,096·9	34·9	2,550·2	32·2	3,170·0	27·9	3,846·4	24·1
b. Animal Products	46·8	0·8	169·7	3·5	208·2	3·5	263·5	3·3	350·4	3·1	759·7	4·8
c. Other	8·1	0·1	43·2	0·9	60·2	1·0	98·6	1·2	284·9	2·5	279·4	1·8
3. Building and Construction	278·9	4·8	277·4	5·7	296·7	4·9	355·4	4·5	489·4	4·3	798·1	5·0
4. Manufacturing for Local Consumption	375·4	6·5	457·8	9·4	775·5	12·9	1,068·1	13·5	1,403·3	12·4	2,147·4	13·4
5. Passenger Transport and Communications	—	—	—	—	28·2	0·5	96·0	1·2	148·3	1·3	323·3	2·0
6. Distribution	275·2	4·8	320·1	6·5	247·1	4·1	426·5	5·4	512·3	4·5	672·6	4·2
7. Public Administration	346·1	6·0	231·1	4·7	236·3	3·9	321·0	4·1	434·5	3·8	846·4	5·3
8. Ownership of Houses	501·3	8·7	518·3	10·6	681·6	11·3	889·7	11·2	1,215·7	10·7	1,677·5	10·5
9. Professional Services	226·4	3·9	207·9	4·2	161·7	2·7	200·6	2·5	292·4	2·6	482·4	3·0
10. Domestic Services	287·4	5·0	278·6	5·7	285·5	4·8	375·8	4·8	630·4	5·5	847·4	5·3
	5,772·5	100·0	4,886·5	100·0	6,006·0	100·0	7,925·3	100·0	11,361·9	100·0	15,969·5	100·0

Sources: Chapters *2–7*. For method of Revaluation at *1910* prices see Ch. I, E, and Appendix I.

TABLE 8.III

Gross Domestic Product Classified According to Value Added

	1832		*1850*		*1890*		*1930*	
	£'000	%	£'000	%	£'000	%	£'000	%
1. Agriculture	2,205·7	43·7	1,462·2	39·3	4,105·2	47·0	8,279·7	41·5
2. Building and Construction	180·0	3·6	164·0	4·4	436·9	5·0	1,183·3	5·9
3. Manufacturing	987·0	19·6	672·2	18·0	1,190·7	13·6	2,346·3	11·7
4. Transport and Distribution	400·7	7·9	398·7	10·7	973·2	11·1	2,534·2	12·7
5. Public Administration	322·9	6·4	174·7	4·7	334·3	3·8	1,113·1	5·6
6. Ownership of Houses	552·9	11·0	416·2	11·2	1,018·7	11·6	2,546·5	12·8
7. Professional Services	217·5	4·3	163·4	4·4	200·6	2·3	579·2	2·9
8. Domestic Services	175·2	3·5	273·0	7·3	487·0	5·6	1,369·3	6·9
	5,041·9	100·0	3,724·4	100·0	8,746·6	100·0	19,951·6	100·0

K

	1832		1850		1890		1930	
	£'000	%	£'000	%	£'000	%	£'000	%
1. Incomes from Agriculture and Manufactured Exports:								
a. Labourers' Wages	644·7	12·8	651·9	17·5	543·5	6·2	1,439·2	7·2
b. Small-Settlers' Profits	847·1	16·8	999·1	26·8	3,187·6	36·5	6,945·2	34·8
c. Planters' Profits	1,303·2	25·8	204·4	5·5	682·5	7·8	1,331·7	6·7
d. Plantation Staff's Salaries	461·5	9·2	218·6	5·9	217·3	2·5	422·5	2·1
Total Income from Agriculture and Manufactured Exports	3,256·5	64·6	2,074·0	55·7	4,630·9	53·0	10,138·6	50·8
2. Other Wages and Salaries:								
a. Domestic	174·0	3·5	267·4	7·2	492·1	5·6	1,392·1	7·0
b. Construction	107·5	2·1	130·0	3·5	383·7	4·4	910·6	4·6
c. Manufacturing	—	—	—	—	44·4	0·5	163·2	0·8
d. Distribution	106·9	2·1	96·8	2·6	323·0	3·7	856·8	4·3
e. Public Administration	255·5	5·1	144·5	3·9	386·4	4·4	1,124·4	5·6
f. Education	10·7	0·2	16·7	0·4	57·7	0·7	286·7	1·4
g. Other	10·4	0·2	18·2	0·5	21·6	0·2	54·7	0·3
Total Other Wages and Salaries	665·0	13·2	673·6	18·1	1,708·9	19·5	4,788·5	24·0
3. Other Profits:								
a. Trade, etc.	560·9	11·1	488·0	13·1	1,256·9	14·4	2,948·1	14·8
b. Professions	204·5	4·1	172·8	4·6	167·2	1·9	335·7	1·7
c. Independent Workers	355·0	7·0	316·0	8·5	982·7	11·2	1,740·7	8·7
Total Other Profits	1,120·4	22·2	976·8	26·2	2,406·8	27·5	5,024·5	25·2
Total Income (Gross Domestic Product)	5,041·9	100·0	3,724·4	100·0	8,746·6	100·0	19,951·6	100·0

TABLE 8.V

Expenditure at Current Prices

	1832		1850		1870		1890		1910		1930	
	£'000	%	£'000	%	£'000	%	£'000	%	£'000	%	£'000	%
1. Food	1,486·2	29·5	1,655·4	44·4	2,771·5	48·8	4,271·6	48·8	5,382·2	47·4	9,044·0	45·3
2. Clothing	648·9	12·9	603·1	16·2	792·1	14·0	1,228·4	14·0	1,605·3	14·1	2,225·1	11·2
3. Other Consumer Goods	299·0	5·9	280·2	7·5	517·2	9·1	689·9	7·9	787·4	6·9	2,355·0	11·8
4. Personal Services	363·2	7·2	393·4	10·6	444·8	7·8	646·8	7·4	859·3	7·5	1,765·4	8·8
5. Passenger Transport	—	—	—	—	23·7	0·4	89·7	1·0	165·3	1·5	386·5	1·9
6. Rent	552·9	11·0	416·2	11·2	595·7	10·5	1,018·7	11·7	1,215·7	10·7	2,546·5	12·8
Total Personal Expenditure	3,350·2	66·5	3,348·3	89·9	5,145·0	90·6	7,945·1	90·8	10,015·2	88·1	18,322·5	91·8
7. Government Expenditure on Goods and Services	337·5	6·7	211·8	5·7	267·3	4·7	385·4	4·4	508·3	4·5	1,375·5	6·9
8. Domestic Investment	263·8	5·2	257·4	6·9	320·1	5·6	638·7	7·3	908·3	8·0	2,049·4	10·3
9. Net Payments abroad	—	—	—	—	54·3	1·0	41·4	0·5	6·0	0·1	−255·2	−1·3
10. Foreign Balance	1,090·4	21·6	−93·1	−2·5	−109·8	−1·9	−264·0	−3·0	−75·9	−·7	−1,540·6	−7·7
Total Expenditure (Gross Domestic Product)	5,041·9	100·0	3,724·4	100·0	5,676·9	100·0	8,746·6	100·0	11,361·9	100·0	19,951·6	100·0

TABLE 8.VI

Personal Expenditure at 1910 Prices

	1832		*1850*		*1870*		*1890*		*1910*		*1930*	
	£'000	%	£'000	%	£'000	%	£'000	%	£'000	%	£'000	%
1. Food, Drink and Tobacco:												
Imported	579·0	14·0	690·8	15·0	546·9	10·1	988·5	13·0	1,243·9	12·4	1,694·9	12·4
Home-Produced . . .	1,705·4	41·1	1,910·3	41·6	2,497·0	46·2	3,115·8	40·9	4,153·4	41·5	5,462·3	39·9
2. Clothing:												
Imported	437·2	10·5	543·6	11·8	461·7	8·5	793·4	10·4	866·9	8·6	822·2	6·0
Home-Produced . . .	195·0	4·7	226·2	4·9	390·0	7·2	582·1	7·7	738·4	7·4	942·2	6·9
3. Other Consumer Goods:												
Imported	116·4	2·8	111·7	2·4	126·5	2·3	326·7	4·3	413·5	4·1	808·6	5·9
Home-Produced . . .	130·0	3·1	150·4	3·3	260·1	4·8	263·0	3·5	358·8	3·6	707·1	5·2
4. Personal Services:												
Professional	196·9	4·8	164·9	3·6	132·6	2·5	159·8	2·1	228·9	2·3	325·9	2·4
Domestic	287·4	6·9	278·6	6·1	285·5	5·3	375·8	4·9	630·4	6·3	847·4	6·2
5. Passenger Transport . .	—	—	—	—	28·2	·5	113·9	1·5	165·3	1·7	378·8	2·8
6. Rent	501·3	12·1	518·3	11·3	681·6	12·6	889·7	11·7	1,215·7	12·1	1,677·5	12·3
Total Personal Expenditure at 1910 Prices	4,148·6	100·0	4,594·8	100·0	5,410·1	100·0	7,608·7	100·0	10,015·2	100·0	13,666·9	100·0

PART II

COMMENTARY

CHAPTER 9

POPULATION

In this chapter we examine the growth of the population and its effect on the number of people available for work. Because the rate of growth changed so dramatically at about the time of emancipation we deal separately with growth before and after 1834. The third section deals with external migration. This leads us to consider the rates of growth of the different races and, finally, the changes in the working population.

A. Population Growth up to 1834

The population of Jamaica at the time of emancipation consisted of Europeans, Africans and people of mixed descent. Except for the slave population no official returns of numbers are available. The most widely accepted estimate, however, puts the total population in 1834 at 371,070, of whom 15,000 were whites, 45,000 were free coloureds and blacks while the remaining 311,070 were slaves.[1] Of these three groups only one—the free coloureds and blacks—had increased during the previous years.

The white population had declined rapidly during the previous decade. It had never been very large and even at its highest, in 1824, numbered only 34,152.[2] Unlike the emigrants to the North American continent, the Europeans who began to arrive in the island from the beginning of the eighteenth century onwards did not usually intend to make their home there. They came to make a fortune in sugar planting and its ancillary occupations and, whether successful or not, often left after a few years. Frequently they came alone but, where they brought their families, thought it advisable to send them back to the United Kingdom as soon as possible. The white population was thus transient and predominantly male. Moreover, mortality was high. They were much more susceptible to tropical diseases than the Africans and generally found it more difficult to acclimatize themselves: a difficulty to which an unsuitable way of life contributed in

[1] HBJ, e.g. for 1895, p. 40.

[2] Burns, W. L. *Emancipation and Apprenticeship*, London, 1937, p. 27.

no small degree. *Lady Nugent's Journal*[1] speaks frequently of sickness and deaths as a result of riotous living. Among the white military the death rate averaged 121·3 per thousand between 1817 and 1836.[2] But this cannot be taken as representative because, apart from their habitual mode of life, the health of troops was also jeopardized by the malarial areas in which they were often stationed.[3]

As a result of the shortness of their average stay, the adverse sex ratio[4] and the high death-rate, the actual increase in the number of whites during the eighteenth century was insignificant compared with that of the slaves. Because of the ever-present danger of slave insurrections, this growing numerical difference between the white and slave populations caused considerable concern and led the island government to introduce the Deficiency Laws to compel planters to maintain a certain ratio between the two races. This ratio was changed from time to time but usually amounted to about one white person to every fifty slaves on the estates. The fine imposed for failure to comply with the law, however, failed to encourage emigration from Europe and came to be regarded as merely another form of tax. This, in fact, was inevitable. Except for the chance of making a fortune in planting there was little to attract Europeans to the island. Hence immigration of men without capital was limited to the numbers needed for supervising slaves. But a sugar plantation employing 200–300 slaves required only about half a dozen whites and often even this small number was difficult to maintain since their chance of advancement was virtually non-existent. Thus inevitably, white immigration was small and during the 1820's even failed to compensate for the numbers leaving the island.

There was another reason for the sharp decline during these years. The revolt of the Spanish colonies on the American continent destroyed the pre-eminent position of Jamaica in the entrepôt trade. Henceforward the independent republics in Latin America increasingly traded with the United Kingdom direct. As a result many Jamaican merchants left for Colombia and Mexico and in 1825 'an invasion of Mexico by British and French merchants had taken place'.[5]

The free coloureds were the offspring of white men and slave

[1] Edited by F. Cundall, London, 1939.
[2] Statistics of the Health of Troops since 1803, BPP, 1837–8 (138), p. 70.
[3] *Ibid.* [4] Ch. 9, D.
[5] Armytage, F. *The Free Port System in the British West Indies*, London, 1953.

women who had been freed by their fathers. They are first enumerated separately in 1775 when their number was returned as 4,093.[1] By 1834 they had increased to 40,000—though to what extent this was due to continued miscegenation and manumission or to self-reproduction is not known. It was always said that public opinion compelled slave owners to free their coloured children. Nevertheless, this does not appear to have been heeded universally for the free coloured population in 1834 is considerably below the coloured population returned in the 1844 CP (Table XII). There were in addition a number of blacks who bought themselves free with savings or were freed by the liberality of their owners. Manumissions, however, as judged by the number of free blacks appear to have been very infrequent. Indeed this is hardly surprising as the purchase price was difficult to raise, in spite of the frequent references found in literature to slave affluence. The *Anti-Slavery Reporter* quotes the market value of slaves in Jamaica in 1824 as £45 sterling but slaves purchasing their freedom were said to have been charged between £100 and £200.[2] Between 1817 and 1826 only 4,782 slaves were manumitted.[3] Of these only 1,951 had been paid for. A second return[4] gives the numbers manumitted between 1825 and 1830 as 2,804 but the details for the overlapping years do not agree. Since free blacks were estimated to have numbered only 5,000 in 1834 it seems probable that a greater part of the gratuitous manumissions referred to coloured slaves.

Like the white population, the slave population had been declining for some years. The decline, however, began much earlier and probably dates from the abolition of the slave trade in 1808. Table I shows the number of slaves registered between 1800 and 1832. Unfortunately these statistics are not very satisfactory. Between 1816 and 1817 the number registered increased by over 32,000 as a result of the stricter supervision enforced under the Slave Registration Act of 1817. As these statistics had previously been collected as a basis for the poll tax, under-registration was presumably general and persistent. Again, between 1829 and 1832 the number returned falls sharply from 322,421 to 302,666. This decline is improbable because

[1] HBJ, e.g. for 1895, p. 40.

[2] Quoted by Mathieson, W. L., *British Slavery and its Abolition*, London, 1926, p. 40.

[3] Slave Manumissions (Jamaica), BPP, 1830–1 (302).

[4] Jamaica: Manumissions Granted, 1825–30, BPP, 1831–2 (365).

only two years later the Slave Compensation Claims,[1] which are presumably accurate, show the slave population to have numbered 311,070. The decrease in the 1832 data may be due to the insurrection which began during the Christmas holiday in 1831. The number of slaves killed during the rebellion, and of those executed subsequently, is estimated at only 400,[2] but it took some time after order was restored before all slaves returned to the plantations. It is absence from the plantations rather than deaths which seems to account for the difference between what the population may be expected to have been in 1832, following previous population trends, and the numbers actually returned. This is shown by the smooth downward trend

TABLE I

Returns of Slave Population 1800–1832

Year	Number	Year	Number,
1800	300,939	1812	319,912
1	307,940	3	317,424
2	307,199	4	315,385
3	308,668	5	313,814
4	308,542	6	314,038
5	308,775	7	346,150
6	312,341	1820	342,382
7	319,351	3	336,253
8	323,827	6	331,119
9	323,704	9	322,421
1810	313,683	1832	302,666
1	326,830		

Source: Martin, R. M. *History of the Colonies of the British Empire*, London, 1843, p. 7.

between 1817 and 1834 which one gets if one ignores the 1832 returns and substitutes those of 1834. We conclude, therefore, that the slave population began to decline in 1808 by an unknown extent and that the decline between 1817 and 1834 was 35,100.

The Slave Registration Act of 1817 also required owners to account for the difference in the number of slaves returned at successive registrations. Thus between 1817 and 1829 we have details of births, deaths and manumissions (Table II). Using the mortality statistics, A. M. Tulloch and H. Marshall calculated the average death rate between 1817 and 1829 at 25 per thousand.[3] The cor-

[1] BPP, 1837–8 (215).
[2] Sel. Com. on Slavery, BPP, 1831–2 (721), Q. 4195.
[3] Statistics of the Health of Troops since 1803, *op. cit.*, App. III.

responding birth-rate to account for the decline in the slave population, less manumissions, would thus be 20 per thousand. The birth-rate as calculated from Table II, however, amounts to 22·7 per thousand. Since the number of births is not likely to be overstated we must conclude that the number of deaths or manumissions recorded are understated. Manumissions (Table II) numbered only 3,981 for the twelve years from 1817 to 1829, but according to the two other sources noted above,[1] they were 6,251 during these years. Thus if we allow for this number of manumissions and add the remaining difference between the figures in Table II and the total decline given in Table I to the mortality statistics, the death-rate becomes 27 per thousand compared with the birth rate of 22·7 per thousand.

TABLE II

Comparison of Returns of Increases by Birth and Decreases due to Deaths and Manumissions with Total Changes in Slave Population

Year	Increases by Birth	Decreases by		Net Change	Actual Change in Population
		Deaths	Manu-missions		
1817–20 . .	24,346	25,104	1,016	−1,774	−3,768
1820–23 . .	23,249	26,351	921	−4,023	−6,129
1823–26 . .	23,026	25,170	927	−3,071	−5,134
1826–29 . .	21,728	25,137	1,117	−4,526	−8,698

Source: Slave Registrations: Jamaica. BPP, 1833 (539).

But as pointed out by G. W. Roberts, the Slave Registers omitted to record the number of infants who were born and died in the interval between successive registrations: that is children who died before reaching the age of three. Something must therefore be added to both rates to allow for this omission. We can obtain a rough estimate of this gap in the data by assuming that infantile mortality during these years was comparable with that of the worst period for which records are available. The highest average infantile death-rate on record occurred during the quinquennium 1906–10 when it amounted to 192 per 1,000 live births. If we raise this to 200 per 1,000 live births, to allow for those that died between the ages of

[1] See fn. 3 and 4, p. 129.

one and one-and-a-half years, the mortality of children in the inter-registration periods averaged 5,680. Adding this number to the registration data, the birth- and death-rates of the slave population during the years 1817 and 1929 are raised to 28·4 and 32·7 per 1,000 respectively.

Death-rates of 32·7 per 1,000 among slaves are quite consistent with what is known about population trends from other sources. By 1817 the slave population in Jamaica was already old. In that year

TABLE III

Sex Ratio and Place of Birth of the Slave Population in 1817

Place of Birth	Men	Women	Total	Sex Ratio
Africa	68,631	58,272	126,903	45·9
Jamaica	104,688	114,559	219,247	52·3
Total	173,319	172,831	346,150	49·9

Source: Sel. Com. on Slavery, BPP, 1831–2 (721), Q. 7937.

the number of slaves born in Africa accounted for 37 per cent of the total slave population (Table III). These slaves were already of working age on introduction to the island and must have reached middle or old age already by 1817. Mortality was, therefore, bound to be high during the ensuing years as these older slaves died off. In the absence of further information it is, of course, dangerous to be too categorical about causes of mortality. But it seems unlikely that harsh treatment or disease were responsible for the high death-rate. After the abolition of the slave trade, owners had every reason to maintain their labour force. For this reason, slaves generally appear to have had enough food and adequate clothing and shelter. Doctors were employed to visit estates regularly and most estates also maintained a hospital. Medical attention for the slaves was thus probably as good as might be expected at that time.

Nor could the number of births be large enough to compensate for deaths. Most of the slaves imported into the island were already adults at the time of introduction. If we add to this the period necessary for acclimatization, it will be seen that their reproductive life in the island was considerably reduced. Thus inevitably the birth-rate was low among African-born slaves. It is commonly supposed that before the abolition of the slave trade planters deliberately discouraged procreation among their slaves by importing more males than females and by preventing the slaves from living together. But the statistics do not bear this out. As seen from Table III, the sex ratio in 1817 was quite favourable: for the African-born population it was almost 46, thus indicating a fairly high proportion of women among the newly enslaved even if allowance is made for the greater mortality among male slaves. Furthermore, the fact that by 1817 the Jamaica-born population already accounted for nearly two-thirds of the total number of slaves suggests that planters cannot have been too successful—if such was indeed their intention—in preventing co-habitation among their slaves.

As a result of the low birth-rate among the Africa-born slaves the first generation of island-born slaves was much smaller than that of their parents. Thus, even if the Jamaica-born slaves had enough children to replace themselves, the birth-rate would still have been below the death-rate. It follows that the death-rate was bound to exceed the birth-rate until the high proportion of aged had been reduced by deaths. In 1834 children under six years of age accounted for only 12·5 per cent of the total slave population[1] compared with a proportion of between thirteen and fourteen of children aged less than five years later in the century.

B. Population Growth 1834–1930

During the ten years following emancipation the population appears to have been constant. The 1844 census actually records an increase of about 6,000 over the estimated number in 1834, but this cannot be taken as evidence of natural population growth because it may have been due partly to an understatement of the free coloured population at the earlier date and partly to immigration in the intervening years (see Ch. 9, C). In fact, an interval during which the population is stationary is to be expected between a prolonged decline and an increase. The arrest of the downward trend appears to have been due to a rise in the birth-rate and probably also to a fall in the death-rate. In 1844 the number of children born during the preceding decade accounted for 26·2 per cent of the total population which corresponds to the proportion of those under ten years of age subsequently (Table IV).

[1] Slave Compensation Claims, *op. cit.*

TABLE IV

Census Population and Age Structure

Age	1844		1861		1871		1881		1891		1911		1921	
	'000	%	'000	%	'000	%	'000	%	'000	%	'000	%	'000	%
Under 5 years	51·7	13·7	61·1	13·8	71·0	14·0	75·7	13·0	83·1	13·0	114·8	13·8	111·7	13·0
5– 9 years	47·2	12·5	54·8	12·4	63·1	12·5	75·4	13·0	78·7	12·3	118·2	14·2	120·9	14.1
10–14 ,,	62·7	16·6	55·8	12·6	60·7	12·0	71·5	12·3	85·7	13·4	98·2	11·8	105·1	12·3
15–19 ,,			48·8	11·1	49·3	9·7	55·8	9·6	66·5	10·4	80·0	9·6	87·6	10·2
20–29 ,,	121·3	32·2	74·4	16·9	99·9	19·7	109·5	18·9	116·4	18·2	153·5	18·5	151·1	17·6
30–39 ,,			50·1	11·4	58·6	11·6	73·0	12·6	77·8	12·1	100·0	12·0	97·5	11·4
40–49 ,,	68·5	18·1	41·2	9·3	41·4	8·2	47·5	8·2	60·8	9·5	71·0	8·5	82·5	9·6
50–59 ,,			24·6	5·6	27·8	5·5	26·6	4·6	32·5	5·1	46·4	5·6	48·7	5·7
60 years and over	26·0	6·9	30·5	6·9	33·0	6·5	37·8	6·5	36·9	5·8	48·8	5·9	52·6	6·1
Unknown					1·3	0·3	8·0	1·3	1·1	0·2	0·5	0·1	0·4	0·0
Total	377·4	100·0	441·3	100·0	506·1	100·0	580·8	100·0	639·5	100·0	831·4	100·0	858·1	100·0

From 1844 onwards population growth was rapid. During the first fifty years the population doubled itself and by 1943 the 1844 figure had been trebled. Table V shows the inter-censal rates of growth for the years between 1844 and 1943. The earlier enumerations shown here were invariably criticized on the grounds of incompleteness but the evidence supporting these assertions is conflicting. In 1844, for example, doubts about completeness were based on the fact that since 'it was the first enumeration of the inhabitants of the colony which has been made during freedom it may be presumed that the returns are not altogether to be depended on'.[1] In 1871 the census commissioner thought omissions still likely but considered that of the two preceding enumerations that of 1844 was probably the more accurate 'as at that time there was a smaller proportion of the population in the remoter parts of the island, than there has been of late times'.[2] Since the rates of population growth revealed by these censuses seem to be consistent with each other and with what is otherwise known, it seems unlikely that any of them were significantly in error and, so far as total growth is concerned, may therefore be assumed to be reliable. Such confidence, unfortunately, is not inspired by the detailed classifications used in the various reports—but these criticisms belong to later parts of this chapter.

TABLE V

Population Growth 1844–1943

Year	Inter-censal Increase '000	Inter-censal Rate of Growth p.a %
1844–61	63·7	0·9
1861–71	65·0	1·4
1871–81	74·7	1·4
1881–91	58·7	0·9
1891–1911	191·9	1·4
1911–21	26·7	0·3
1921–43	378·9	1·6

Sources: CP.

According to Table V, population growth averaged 1·4 per cent p.a. or more for all except three inter-censal periods. Between 1844

[1] CP, 1844. [2] Report accompanying the BBJ, BPP (C 709), p. 37.

and 1861 and between 1881 and 1891, it was only 0·9 per cent, and during the decade spanning World War I, it fell to its minimum 0·3 per cent p.a. The relatively small growth during these years, however, was the result of exceptional causes without which population growth would have been considerably higher and the average rate of growth not far off 1·4 per cent for the whole period.

The low rate of growth in the years between 1844 and 1861 was due to the high death rate caused by unusually severe epidemics. In October 1850 cholera broke out and swiftly swept over the whole island. The epidemic lasted eighteen months and was estimated to have taken a toll of between 25,000–30,000 lives.[1] No sooner had it ceased when smallpox appeared, to be followed by yet another outbreak of cholera in 1854. The official estimates of deaths during the first and more severe cholera epidemic suggest that, but for it, the average rate of growth would have been 1·4 per cent p.a. We can verify this by calculating what the population was in 1850, assuming first a rate of growth of 1·4 per cent from 1844 onwards and, secondly, by subtracting eleven years' growth, at the same rate, from the 1861 census total. These two calculations give us 410,100 and 378,800 respectively. The difference between these, 31,300, is the approximate number of deaths due to the cholera epidemics—i.e. nearly 8 per cent of the estimated population in 1850.

From 1881 onwards population growth was affected by external migration. This subject will be dealt with more fully in section C. Here we have to establish only the extent to which migration affected the annual rate of growth. The available annual migration statistics are practically worthless for this purpose. But we can estimate what population growth would have been without migration by taking the natural increase in population—that is the excess of births over deaths (Table XI). Accordingly the population in 1891 would have been 664,300, as compared with 639,500 recorded in the census, and hence the annual rate of growth would have been 1·4 per cent, instead of the actual 0·9 per cent. Similarly between the years 1891 and 1911 the rate of growth would have been 1·6 per cent p.a. and during the following decade 1·2 per cent (Table XI). Between 1921 and 1930 the rate of natural increase is calculated on the basis of the Registrar-General's report for 1930[2] as 1,015,700, which gives an annual rate of growth for these years of 1·7 per cent.

[1] Past and Present State of H.M. Colonies, BPP, 1852 (1539), p. 30.
[2] BBJ, 1930.

Thus, population growth would have been constant in the second half of the nineteenth century but for the heavy emigration of the 1880's. This brings us to consider separately the birth- and death-rates.

Until 1878, unfortunately, vital statistics are even more scanty than before 1834. An attempt to obtain annual registrations was actually made as early as 1844 but only a few registrations were made and after a few years the attempt appears to have been abandoned completely.[1] A second, and more successful, attempt was made in 1878. The results of these registrations are summarized in Table VI. They have been shown to be reasonably accurate by G. W. Roberts[2] from 1891 onwards.

TABLE VI

Vital Statistics, 1881–1935

(5-Year Averages)

Year	Deaths per 1,000	Births per 1,000	% Illegitimate Births	Infant Mortality per 1,000 Live Births	Number of Marriages per 1,000
1881–85	22·89	37·42	58·9	158·4	4·53
1886–90	24·03	36·91	60·4	174·4	5·04
1891–95	21·89	38·40	60·6	171·1	5·18
1896–1900	22·02	38·80	62·6	174·8	4·41
1901–05	22·70	40·72	64·5	174·1	4·17
1906–10	24·36	38·32	62·4	192·0	5·43
1911–15	22·75	37·93	65·3	179·2	3·50
1916–20	26·89	36·36	69·2	174·2	3·76
1921–25	23·51	36·50	71·6	176·1	3·75
1926–30	19·56	36·43	72·1	160·0	4·43
1931–35	18·26	33·44	71·9	142·7	3·77

Source: Historical Supplement to the Registrar-General's Annual Report of 1945, J. Govt. Printer.

It was suggested above that the death-rate during the seventeen years preceding emancipation was about 33 per 1,000 and, further, that the rate began to fall somewhere around the middle thirties. In

[1] Cholera (Jamaica), *op. cit.*, p. 90.

[2] 'A Note on Mortality in Jamaica', *Population Studies*, 1950, vol. IV, no. 1, p. 67.

1844 those aged forty years and over still accounted for a relatively large number of the population. The death-rate must accordingly have continued to be influenced—though to a diminishing extent—by the old age structure subsequently. Taking this into account it seems probable that during the years between 1844 and 1861 the death-rate had been reduced to about 26 per 1,000 except for the few years of exceptionally heavy mortality during the cholera epidemics. Dr. Milroy, after visiting the island in 1852, suggested that the standard of health of the population was lower during the post-emancipation period than previously and that, as a result, the death-rate was likely to be higher.[1] That the deterioration in general health standards made people more susceptible to infectious diseases seems to be borne out by the high mortality during the cholera epidemics. But it is difficult to see how the average death-rate could have been higher more generally unless the mortality during the epidemic was substantially overstated.

By the 1880's the death-rate had dropped to about 23–24 per 1,000 and remained around this level until the early 1920's. Stricter enforcement of quarantine regulations and vaccination prevented the recurrence of serious outbreaks of yellow fever, smallpox and cholera. There were, however, climatic factors which occasionally raised the death-rate. Hurricanes, for example, are invariably followed by flooding which in turn leads to pollution of water supplies and the contamination of food. Unless prompt steps are taken diseases break out and spread swiftly. The hurricanes of 1903 and 1912 were indirectly responsible for the higher death-rates recorded in these years. The Kingston earthquake of 1907, for similar reasons, resulted in higher mortality. It will also be noted that Jamaica did not escape the influenza pandemic of 1918: the death-rate in this year—33 per thousand—is the highest on record.

Once the basic steps to prevent the spread of diseases had been taken further advances in reducing the death-rate were both more difficult and more costly. Some attempts had already been made during the latter part of the nineteenth century to ensure pure water supplies, control sewage disposal and supervise food markets: but these affected only urban areas. The reduction in the death-rate beginning in the 1920's was the result of more widespread and concerted efforts to improve public health (see Ch. 15, C).

Infantile mortality, like the total death-rate, did not begin to fall

[1] *Op. cit.*, p. 91.

definitely until the 1920's. It remained at around 174 per 1,000 live births in the twenty years from 1886 to 1905 (Table VI). During the quinquennium 1906–10 the rate increased sharply to 192 per 1,000—that is proportionately a little more than deaths at all ages—but, in contrast to the rise in the total death-rate during the years between 1916 and 1920, that of infants actually declined. By the second half of the twenties infantile mortality had been reduced to 160 per 1,000 but even then it accounted for nearly 30 per cent of deaths at all ages.

High infantile mortality is, of course, typical of poor countries. But in Jamaica the reason for the slow progress made in reducing it was usually sought not so much in poverty as in the high proportion of illegitimate births. The percentage of illegitimate births (Table VI) rose from about sixty in the 1880's to over seventy in the 1920's. Furthermore, the death-rate was persistently higher among illegitimate than among legitimate children—usually exceeding it by one-half. But it is doubtful whether illegitimacy by itself is a sufficient explanation. Social observers[1] agree that illegitimate children generally do not lack in maternal care and affection. Where the unmarried mother has to work her child or children are usually cared for by the grandmother or other relative. The difference between legitimate and illegitimate children, as far as physical well-being is concerned, is thus only one of income. As illegitimacy occurs mainly among the poorer classes, a higher death-rate among their children is, therefore, to be expected.

The birth-rate began to rise during the 1830's and by about the middle forties is estimated to have approached 40 per thousand. This estimate is based on our assumption that the rate of population growth was 1·4 per cent and that the death-rate, apart from epidemics, was falling to about 26 per thousand. The birth-rate remained at nearly 40 per thousand until about 1910. It began to fall earlier than the death-rate, thus slowing down population growth during the second decade of the twentieth century (Table VI). During the subsequent decades, however, the birth-rate fell less rapidly thus bringing about the higher growth rates recorded in these years.

The small fluctuations in the birth-rate up to 1905, if accurate, seem to reflect the departure of young men abroad and their return home. Thus the birth-rate in the eighties was below but during the nineties and early 1900's above the average trend. This explanation,

[1] E.g., Simey, T. S. *Welfare and Planning in the West Indies*, Oxford, 1946.

however, does not apply to subsequent years because emigration practically came to an end in 1920 while the birth-rate continued to fall. In fact, most of the reduction in the birth-rate was due to a fall in legitimate births, which are not likely to be affected by migration because emigrants were drawn mostly from among the lower income groups among whom marriage was not usual. Legitimate births began to fall from 15 per thousand in the years 1906–10 to 10 per thousand in 1926–30.[1] On the other hand, the illegitimate birth-rate fluctuated between 24 and 26 per thousand, being low in the quinquennium 1906–10 when emigration was heavy and high in the 1920's when there was a net inflow of migrants. The reduction in the size of family of married women began at the time of decreasing infantile mortality and thus seems to follow the experience of other countries, such as the United Kingdom during the middle of the nineteenth century, in that the better chance of survival induced people to have fewer children. Even so the fertility of married women was still higher than that of single women. The Census of 1943, for example, shows that the average number of children born to married mothers was 6·5 compared with 4·90 to single and common-law mothers.[2] Thus, in spite of the reduction in the legitimate rate, Jamaica had not reached the position where the average number of children born to upper and middle class mothers—as defined by marital status—was actually less than that in the poorer classes.

C. Immigration and Emigration

Apart from changes in birth- and death-rates, population growth in Jamaica, as already noted, was also determined by external migration. Altogether there were four distinct migratory movements: the three inward flows of Europeans, liberated Africans and indentured labour from the Far East and, fourthly, the outward flow of Jamaicans. The first three were organized in response to a wide-felt need for estate labour but from 1880 onwards there was the paradoxical situation of costly immigration continuing simultaneously with a remarkable exodus of native labour. Moreover, though each stream of migration was followed by a return flow, the net gains and losses resulting from the two-way movement did not compensate each

[1] Historical Supplement to the Registrar-General's Annual Report of 1945, J. Govt. Printer.

[2] Pp. 57–8.

other. As will be seen below the migratory movement affecting population growth most was that of emigrating Jamaicans.

(i) *Immigrants from Europe*

Although efforts to secure immigration of Europeans dates back as far as the conquest of the island, the attempt to obtain white immigrants for manual employment began only at the time of emancipation. Declining population and apprehensions about the effect of freedom on the supply of native labour induced some planters to seek labour in Europe. The greater attraction of the temperate zones left few sources of supply. Between 1834 and 1845 only 2,698 immigrants from Great Britain, 1,038 from Germany and 91 from Madeira arrived in the island (Table VII). But even this limited immigration was not a success: of the total number of Madeirans brought to the island only half remained in 1847;[1] of the 500–600 Germans settled in Seaford Town, Westmoreland, only 150 remained at the same date;[2] of one group of 21 British immigrants in Trelawny only 8 were left at the end of the first year and of another 150 brought to the island in 1835 only one still remained six years later.[3] Mortality among them was high but emigration to the United States or return to their native countries also accounted for a considerable portion of the loss. Part of the reason for these disappointing results is to be found in the inadequate preparations made for the immigrants. Employers failed to recognize the importance of providing adequate food, shelter and medical facilities in smoothing over the initial period of acclimatization. Much of the hardship suffered by immigrants, particularly from diseases, could have been avoided with more foresight. Where employers took greater trouble over welfare immigration was more successful. Freeman's Hall in Trelawny, for example, had been working with English and German labour only and by the end of the first four years not one of them had died.[4] Partly responsible for the general failure of European immigration too, was the unwillingness of white immigrants to take up work previously done by slaves and now despised by the freed men—an unwillingness which became all the greater when the immigrants were expected to work side by side with the ex-slaves. No doubt this

[1] SCP, BPP, 1847–8 (206), Q. 12,946.
[2] *Ibid.* (167), Q. 4,519.
[3] Sel. Com. on Employers and Labourers, BPP, 1842 (479), Q. 6079.
[4] PWI, Part II, Jamaica, BPP, 1841 (344), p. 5.

also explains why the introduction of immigrants in Freeman's Hall was more successful.

TABLE VII

Number of Immigrants from Europe

Year	Country of Origin		
	Great Britain	Germany	Madeira
1834 . . .	2	—	—
5 . . .	358	506	24
6 . . .	613	532	67
7 . . .	360	—	—
8 . . .	—	—	—
9 . . .	—	—	—
1840 . . .	—	—	—
1 . . .	1,333	—	—
2 . . .	19	—	—
3 . . .	—	—	—
4 . . .	—	—	—
5 . . .	13	—	—
Total . . .	2,698	1,038	91

Source: SCP, BPP, 1846–7 (167), p. 383.

(ii) *Liberated Africans*

The abolition of the slave trade in the British Empire demanded, for the sake of consistency with the principles that had motivated it and in fairness to the West Indian planters, similar action in the rest of the world. Foreign powers, however, were slow to concur. Consequently British ships were despatched to patrol the trading routes and slavers were, from time to time, intercepted. If captured in the Western Atlantic, the liberated slaves were landed in the West Indies, but most of the interceptions took place off the African coast and in such cases Africans were taken to Sierra Leone or St. Helena. Faced with the demand for labour the British government permitted their transfer, and the recruitment of other Africans, for work in the West Indies in 1840. Three years later private schemes were replaced by a government plan regularizing conditions of work and repatriation. Immigrants were to be bound by no contract, they were to be left free to find their own employment and they were to be entitled to repatriation after five years. Even this did not result in a large increase. The response of voluntary labour was poor. For them 'a calm survey of the whole matter induced a general idea that the comforts and advantages of Sierra Leone were not out-weighed by the prospects held out by emigration'.[1] Most of the immigrants were thus liberated slaves but their number depended chiefly on the level of the slave trade. The largest number of immigrants arrived in the years 1845–9 when the Brazilian slave trade was flourishing (Table VIII). Its abolition in 1852 reduced the number subsequently and, after a small recovery in the early sixties due to the Cuban and American slave trade, the movement came to a complete standstill with abolition in those countries. Altogether Jamaica received over 11,000 Africans—that is about 28 per cent of all Africans who landed in the British West Indies.[2]

TABLE VIII

Immigration of Liberated and Other Africans

Years	Numbers
1834–39	1,388
1840–44	2,533
1845–49	3,936
1850–54	1,324
1855–59	362
1860–64	1,837
1865–67	11
	11,391

Source: Roberts, G. W. *Population Studies*, vol. VII, no. 3, pp. 259–61.

(iii) *Indentured Labour from the Far East*

Permission to recruit labour under indenture in the Far East was obtained in 1845. The influx of labourers, however, was not as great or as even as might have been expected from the clamour that had led to its inception. In 1842 the Select Committee on Relations between Employers and Labourers had estimated the labour requirements of sugar estates at 24,600 and that of coffee estates at 9,600.[3] In fact, between 1845 and 1847 (Table IX) only 4,550

[1] *Trinidad Standard*, 11th August, 1842. Quoted by G. W. Roberts, *Population Studies*, 1954, vol. VII, no. 3, p. 247.

[2] Roberts, G. W., *op. cit.*, p. 254.

[3] *Op. cit.*, p. 481.

indentured East Indians arrived in the island compared with 8,800 in British Guiana and 4,431 in Trinidad,[1] and, with the exception of the arrival of 472 Chinese in 1854, immigration ceased altogether until 1860.

TABLE IX

Immigration and Return Home of Indentured Labour

Year	Arrivals	Returns
1845–49	4,550	—
1850–54	472	1,547
1855–59	—	126
1860–64	4,635	—
1865–69	3,018	—
1870–74	6,322	1,345
1875–79	3,564	1,576
1880–84	2,327	1,720
1885–89	601	1,205
1890–94	2,620	942
1895–99	1,782	348
1900–04	1,317	1,444
1905–09	2,649	790
1910–14	4,209	502
1915–17	615	414
Total	38,681	11,959

Sources: 1845–49. SCP, BPP, 1847–8 (167), p. 383.
1850–93. HBJ, 1895.
1894–1917. *Ibid.*, 1920.

What had caused this change of attitude in the intervening years? One reason was that the native labour supply had been temporarily eased. A severe drought in 1844 forced many people back to wage employment and their competition with estate labour had made possible a reduction in wages of as much as 25 per cent.[2] Then in 1846 came the news of sugar duty equalization, and, in the following year, the failure of several important West India merchant houses reduced even further the already meagre supply of working capital. As a result planters temporarily lost interest in immigration schemes. Moreover, immigration was a costly business. The cost of introducing the initial 4,550 immigrants alone had been £75,363[3] and employers were in addition liable for the return trip. An indenture

[1] SCP, BPP (167), pp. 383–4. [2] *Ibid.*, Q. 4455. [3] *Ibid.*, p. 406.

period of only five years was hardly worth while so long as some labour was still available locally (see Ch. 11, B). In the end, despite continuing complaints of labour shortage, the scheme had only a lukewarm reception. And this accounted for the half-hearted way the whole business was conducted.

For immigration to be successful several conditions have to be fulfilled. In the first place, much depends on the selection of the immigrants. Naturally only the poorest section of the Indian community were willing to contract for work abroad but even among these selection was badly carried out. Many of them were too old and in bad health: of the first group of immigrants 185 had died on passage and a further 190 were dead by June 1847.[1] Secondly, the condition of immigrants while in the island required careful attention. Wages had to be adequate to assure to the immigrant a minimum standard of subsistence and housing, and medical attention had to be provided. Laws regulating these did not begin to be passed until 1869. Finally, the immigrants had to be repatriated at the expiry of their indenture. This obligation, planters were slow to honour. As late as 1852 those immigrants who had arrived in 1845 were still in the island[2] and in 1853 an export tax had to be levied to send back time-expired immigrants.

Attempts to reopen the flow of indentured immigration to the island were made from time to time during the 1850's but it was not until 1859 that the Assembly's bill received the Royal Assent. This and subsequent legislation was intended to regulate the length of indentures, working conditions, remuneration and welfare. Generally indentures were for five years with a further period of five years' residence before the labourer was entitled to a return passage. Provisions were made to protect the immigrant from capricious employers. A Protector of Immigrants was appointed to ensure that legislation was enforced and to keep records of all immigrants including vital statistics.

Immigration was resumed in 1860 but even then the numbers brought to the island were small compared with those introduced into Trinidad and British Guiana. The decline in sugar output in the intervening years had reduced the demand for labour and the banana which began to replace sugar needed much less labour. Arrivals were most regular between 1861 and 1881, but subsequently, until its

[1] *Ibid.*

[2] Sugar Growing Colonies, Pt. II, Jamaica, BPP, 1852–3 (76), pp. 148–9.

cessation in 1917, immigration was intermittent and involved only small numbers except in the years 1891, 1895, 1910 and 1913. The immediate reasons for this were mismanagement by recruiting officers in India, failure of funds or changes in the facilities for financing immigration. But, more generally, planters were none too anxious to incur the costs of introduction which, at £15 10*s*. cash per immigrant or £17 10*s*. in instalments, remained prohibitively high.[1] On the whole, they preferred native labourers when they could get them. The Jamaican was stronger, he was used to the work and he was acclimatized. The East Indian was a reliable labourer, but this advantage outweighed his shortcomings in other respects only where local supplies of labour failed completely such as in the sugar estates in Westmoreland, Clarendon and St. Thomas in the 1870's[2] and on the banana estates in St. Mary and St. Thomas in the 1890's.[3]

Sickness and mortality among the East Indians remained high. The death-rate was always high in the year following arrival in the island and in 1868 actually was 121·1 per thousand.[4] Indeed the lowest rate for the four years 1867–70 was as much as 62·2 per thousand.[5] Nor did the birth-rate compensate for these losses. For the first fifteen years for which records are available, 1869–83, the birth-rate averaged only 16·8 per thousand. It exceeded the death rate only in 1884 and then fell back again until 1893.[6] The low birth-rate is hardly surprising because more men were introduced than women. Men were better workers and, as indentured contracts were for only a few years, employers saw no advantage in introducing women for whom they would be liable and to the labour of whose offspring they had no claim. In 1867, for example, of the new arrivals women numbered only 498 against 1,091 men.[7] Although this lack of balance had obvious drawbacks—the relatively high incidence of crime, suicide and mental disorders was attributed to it—men continued to predominate among new arrivals. The higher death-rate among men tended to reduce the adverse sex ratio to some extent but even in 1911 women accounted for only 43 per cent of the total East Indian population.[8]

Attempts were made to encourage immigrants to settle in the island after the expiry of their indenture by offering cash payments

[1] Col. Rep., BPP, 1893 (C 6857–15). [2] BBJ, 1871.
[3] BBJ, 1892. [4] HBJ, e.g. for 1895, p. 216.
[5] *Ibid.* [6] *Ibid.* [7] Report with the BBJ, BPP, 1869 (C 1456).
[8] CP, 1911.

or land. Even so a high proportion left the island. Up to 1917, of the total number introduced during the past 72 years, about 31 per cent had been repatriated or left for work in Central America. If we also take into account the high death-rate among the indentured immigrants it is not surprising that by 1921 East Indians, including those born in the island, numbered only 18,600 and accounted for only 2·2 per cent of the total population.[1]

(iv) *Emigration of Jamaicans*

The last stream of migration to be traced here is that of Jamaican labour to other West Indian islands and to the American continent. Although the movement became significant numerically only in the 1880's it should be noted that Jamaicans had responded to overseas

TABLE X

Emigration and Return Home of Jamaican Labour According to the Annual Migration Statistics During the Years 1881 and 1934

Years	Total Departures	Total Returns	Net Departures	Net Returns
1881–84*	54,539	26,676	27,863	—
1885–89	29,624	35,349	—	5,725
1890–94	2,082	3,920	—	1,838
1895–99*	3,591	3,069	522	—
1900–04*	3,257	3,212	45	—
1905–09*	32,839	24,255	8,584	—
1910–14	49,841	39,733	10,108	—
1915–19*	43,909	24,958	18,951	—
1920–24	58,337	58,453	—	116
1925–29	22,064	27,540	—	5,476
1930–34	5,899	28,459	—	22,560

* Incomplete Returns.
Sources: Col. Rep.

recruitment long before this date. In 1853 between 1,500 and 2,000 left for work on railway construction in Panama.[2] In the following year 'emigration to Navy Bay continued with even greater eagerness,

[1] *Ibid.*, 1921.
[2] Past and Present State of H.M. Colonies, BPP, 1854–5, Pt. II (1909).

though possibly the number who have returned since the railway was finished has equalled that which went'.[1]

Regular returns of the numbers leaving and returning begin in 1883 and continue until 1899. From that year until 1911 checks on migration apparently ceased except for four years. Thereafter returns are available annually except for 1915. All these returns are included in Table X. It must be stressed, however, that they are worthless except for indicating migration trends because, apart from the gaps in the data, there is reason to believe that they understate the actual volume of migration.

An alternative method of estimating the volume of migration of Jamaican labour is to take, as was done in Section B, the difference between population growth by natural growth and the actual census enumerations. This method gives more plausible results of the total volume than the annual migration statistics, first, because annual registrations of births and deaths were fairly reliable and, secondly, because the net flow of migrants, other than Jamaican labour, was comparatively unimportant. On the other hand, it is less informative as it yields only net figures for each inter-censal period and thus obscures the several migratory movements. The Census Commissioner for 1891 actually reported a net outflow of Jamaican labour of 27,682 between the years 1883 and 1887, and a net inflow of 9,777 during the following four years. But these figures still leave a net outflow of 5,886 persons unaccounted for (Table XI).

TABLE XI

Migration of Jamaican Labour According to the Census Estimates During the Years 1881 and 1920

Years	Net Departures
1881–1890	23,791*
1891–1910	43,438
1911–1920	77,071

* Excludes departure of 1,048 East Indians.
Sources: CP, 1891, 1911 and 1921.

Apart from the short-lived exodus to Panama in the years 1853 and 1854, we can distinguish three main waves of emigration. The first occurred during the 1880's, the second after the turn of the century—both to Panama and Costa Rica—and the third, between 1916 and 1920, to Cuba. Emigration throughout these years also took

[1] Past and Present State of H.M. Colonies, BPP, 1856 (2050).

place to a number of other countries. Haiti, Colombia, British Guiana, British Honduras and the United States all received Jamaicans. The numbers recorded as leaving directly for these places, however, were relatively small.

The first attempt to cut a canal across the Isthmus of Panama was made by a French company in 1880. Labour for this was recruited in Jamaica as well as other West Indian islands. The numbers leaving from Jamaica reached a peak with 24,301 in 1883.[1] Many of the emigrants returned for a holiday and then went back to earn more. But two years later it was reported that Colon 'no longer exercised so great an attraction . . . as formerly, many recognizing that they can obtain regular work in Jamaica, the cheaper living, the better climate, home associations and other local advantages are more than equal to the higher and somewhat nominal rate of wages earned at the Isthmus'.[2] In the same year railway construction was begun in Costa Rica. This to some extent compensated for the partial suspension of the Canal project. But in 1887–8 fewer labourers left for either country in spite of the continuing efforts by recruiting agents.[3] The failure of the Canal company in the following year caused much hardship and the Jamaican government took steps to repatriate emigrants. When repatriation ceased over 6,000 Jamaicans were reported to be still living on the Isthmus.[4]

The net loss to the island, however, was much greater. According to the migration statistics over 84,000 left the island while only 62,000 returned, thus leaving a deficit of about 22,000. This compares with a net outflow of Jamaican labour given by the census method, of nearly 24,000.

Apart from the hardship caused by the sudden cessation of work, the situation of emigrants even while work was in progress was often bad. In 1886 reports were received in Jamaica about the distressed condition of emigrants. It was alleged that many had been engaged to work on the Costa Rica railway under false pretences. Subsequent investigations carried out by a representative of the Jamaican government verified these complaints.[5] Both in Costa Rica and in Panama there were far too many labourers for the available employment. Even among the employed conditions 'amounted in many cases to destitution leading to sickness, distress and mortality'. The canal

[1] Col. Rep., BPP, 1885 (C 4583), p. 19.
[2] *Ibid.*, 1887 (C 5239), p. 43.
[3] *Ibid.*, 1889 (C 5620-14).
[4] *Ibid.*, 1890 (C 6221-1).
[5] Quoted in Col. Rep., BPP, 1888 (C 5249-10), p. 20.

project was also accompanied by much civil disorder. The burning down of Colon in 1885 was followed by insurrection and, in the same year, an unprovoked attack on Jamaicans by Colombian troops resulted in the death of eighteen and the wounding of a further twenty.[1]

As a result the Jamaican government began in 1893 to enact a series of laws aimed at protecting the emigrants and of minimizing the risk of burdening the colony with the cost of repatriation. Under Law 23 of 1902, consolidating the previous Acts of 1893, 1894 and 1899, the Governor had the power to proclaim any country to which the law should apply. No labourers were allowed to leave for such a country without a permit. This permit could be obtained on a deposit of 25*s*. in the Treasury, this covering the cost of repatriation in case of need. The registration of all recruiting agents was also required. In 1925 the scope of this legislation was widened to include penalties for persons who permitted labourers to leave without a permit, including shipping agents, for unregistered agents and for persons who attempted to induce labourers to emigrate by 'means of intoxication, coercion or fraud'. Enforcement of these laws does not, however, appear to have been very stringent as a considerable volume of emigration remained unrecorded.

Emigration virtually ceased until the Panama project was revived by the United States in 1904. At the same time, banana planting in Cost Rica was being rapidly extended. Once more, labour was recruited in the West Indies. In 1911–12 of the 13,109 emigrants from Jamaica as many as 10,829 left for Central America.[2] By that time, the total number of Jamaicans resident or employed in Central America was estimated at 60,000.[3] This agrees fairly well with the census estimates of net loss by emigration—43,438 between 1891 and 1911—taking into account those who had remained after the first canal project—about 24,000—and mortality throughout these years. It is, however, far in excess of the net loss shown by the migration statistics in Table X thus suggesting a considerable volume of unrecorded emigration. The outbreak of Panama Disease in the Costa Rican banana and the completion of the Panama Canal in 1914 reduced the demand for labour. In the year 1916–17 only 1,494 labourers left for Central America.[4]

Although departures for Cuba had been recorded as early as 1898 it was not until the boom of the sugar industry after World War I

[1] Col. Rep., BPP, 1886 (C 4904), p. 169.
[2] *Ibid.*, 1912 (Cd. 6007–39).
[3] *Ibid.*
[5] *Ibid.*, 1899 (Cd. 3–6).

that the island became the most attractive destination for emigrating Jamaicans. According to the annual migration statistics 7,351 out of 8,773 persons left for Cuba in 1918.[1] The great increase in the total to 23,618 in the following year[2] was also due to departures to Cuba. These statistics do not appear to be complete, first, because the total loss due to migration in the decade between 1911 and 1921, according to the census, was 77,071—most of which took place after 1914, i.e. after the completion of the Panama Canal—and, secondly, because the number of Jamaicans living in Cuba in the early 1930's was estimated at between 60,000[3] and 63,800.[4] We conclude, therefore, that the annual statistics seriously understate the volume of emigration immediately after the end of the war and possibly also during the twenties.

Migration to Cuba received its first set-back with the sudden fall in sugar prices in 1920. Again, those already in the island experienced much hardship. The slump left many of them unemployed and, following the declaration of a local moratorium, outstanding wages were left unpaid.[5] Even so not many of them wished to return to Jamaica but preferred to stay in the hope of a better turn of events. Only about 400 people were repatriated by the Jamaican government.[6]

The exodus to Cuba was also remarkable for the large proportion of women who were now seeking employment abroad. The evidence for this is, unfortunately, only indirect. Whereas formerly labour migrated mainly for agricultural and constructional work—offering little opportunity for female employment—now substantial numbers took up personal service, dressmaking and laundry work. Of the total estimated number in Cuba in 1930—60,000—as many as 25,000 were domestic servants.[7]

D. Racial Composition

Table XII shows the estimated racial composition of the population in 1834 and the census classifications for the years 1844 to 1921. The censuses distinguish three groups—white, coloured and black—until 1881, and subsequently the Eastern races as well. The classifications for the European and Oriental races are probably accurate,

[1] *Ibid.*, 1920 (Cmd. 508–8). [2] *Ibid.*, HMSO, 1923 (Col. no. 1143), p. 7.

[3] Report of the Secretary for Immigration in Cuba. J. Council Mins., 1930, vol. 71, App. XXVIII. [4] *Ibid.*, 1934, 75, App. XXIV.

[5] Col. Rep., HMSO, 1923 (Col. no. 1143), p. 7. [6] *Ibid.*

[7] Report of the Secretary for Immigration in Cuba for 1930, *op. cit.*

but those for the coloured and black are rather doubtful. Distinction between coloured and black must obviously be arbitrary and actual classification probably depended as much on family tradition as on actual pigmentation.

As seen in Table XII the share of the white population declined persistently from 1834 onwards. The coloured and black populations, on the other hand, show only small variations after 1844. Broadly, of these the former shows some slight tendency to rise while the latter tended to decline until 1911. It will be noticed that the proportion of the coloureds rose from 10·8 per cent in 1834 to 18·1 per cent ten years later. As only a negligible part of this increase can possibly be due to under-estimation of the free coloured population in 1834 (Ch. 9, B) this rapid growth confirms the view that not all coloured children had been freed before emancipation. We conclude, therefore, that the 1834 total was not far different from 1844 and that at least 23,000 coloureds were still enslaved in 1834. Table XII also brings out the negligible effect of the introduction of East Indian and Chinese indentured labour, from 1845 onwards, on the racial composition. From 1·9 per cent in 1881 their share in the total increased only slowly to 2·4 per cent in 1921.

The great reduction in the number of whites during the 1820's appears to have been arrested in the following decade. Between 1844 and 1871 the white population declined further from 15,800 to 13,100 but thereafter began to increase again slowly. The loss up to 1871 was the result of the continued decline in estate activity. Many planters, unable to make their properties pay, simply abandoned them and returned to the United Kingdom. Most of those leaving appear to have been people who still had roots in the United Kingdom, while those with families in the island tended to remain, thus bringing about a gradual change in the white population from an expatriate to a resident community. We can see this from Table XIII which shows that the sex structure became increasingly more favourable after emancipation until in 1921 it was almost even. Even the very low female to male ratio in 1844 of 41·1 represents a considerable improvement on 1834 when, according to partial returns,[1] women accounted for only 34 per cent. In spite of the more favourable sex

[1] Partial population returns are available in the earlier BBJ. The BBJ for 1830 lists the population for nine parishes and a further three are given in that for 1828. Combined, they show a total white population, for the twelve out of twenty-one parishes, of 8,738 of whom 2,988 were women.

TABLE XII

Racial Composition of the Population

	1834		1844		1861		1871		1881		1891		1911		1921	
	'000	%	'000	%	'000	%	'000	%	'000	%	'000	%	'000	%	'000	%
White	15·0	4·0	15·8	4·2	13·8	3·1	13·1	2·6	14·4	2·5	14·7	2·3	15·6	1·9	14·5	1·7
Coloured	40·0	10·8	68·5	18·1	81·1	18·4	100·3	19·8	110·0	18·9	122·0	19·0	163·2	19·6	157·2	18·3
Black—Free	5·0	1·3	293·1	77·7	346·4	78·5	392·7	77·6	444·2	76·5	488·6	76·4	630·2	75·8	660·4	77·0
Slaves	311·1	83·9														
East Indian									11·0	1·9	10·1	1·6	17·4	2·1	18·6	2·2
Chinese									0·1	0·0	0·5	0·1	2·1	0·3	3·7	0·4
Other									1·1	0·2	3·6	0·6	2·9	0·3	3·7	0·4
Total	371·1	100·0	377·4	100·0	441·3	100·0	506·1	100·0	580·8	100·0	639·5	100·0	831·4	100·0	858·1	100·0

Sources: 1834, HBJ, e.g. 1895, p. 40.
1844–1921, CP.

ratio, however, the number of whites did not increase appreciably. This may have been the result of a relatively low birth-rate or, more probably, of emigration.

The intercensal growth rates of the coloured population show remarkable deviations from the total growth rates in some years. In the decade 1861 to 1871 the rate of growth of the coloured population was 2·1 per cent, compared with 1·4 per cent for the total

TABLE XIII

Sex Ratio of the White Population

Year	Males	Females.
1844	58·9	41·1
1861	52·8	47·2
1871	52·7	47·3
1881	53·0	47·0
1891	53·2	46·8
1911	52·5	47·5
1921	50·6	49·4

population; between 1871 and 1881 it was only 0·9 per cent, compared with 1·4 per cent, and between 1911 and 1921 the coloured population actually declined by about 6,000 while total population increased at an annual rate of 0·3 per cent. There is no reason why these rates should have diverged so greatly. Birth- and death-rates of the coloured population are not likely to have differed very greatly from total rates. If anything, they might have been slightly more favourable because, generally, the coloured enjoyed higher living standards than the black population. Nor can these changes be attributed to increasing or decreasing miscegenation. Apart from the improbability of such rapid changes, there is reason to believe that intercourse between races actually declined after emancipation. For one thing, fewer whites remained in the island and these increasingly had their own families with them. Secondly, after emancipation fewer labourers remained resident on estates; this reduced contact between female labourers and planters. Thirdly, the pre-emancipation structure was perpetuated in economic stratifications thus creating a wide gap between the whites at one level and the blacks at the other.

These extraordinary changes in the growth rates of the coloured population therefore point to obvious inconsistencies in the classifications over the years. It is well known that women have a greater tendency than men to describe themselves as coloured rather than black. But although this is borne out in Table XIV it does not account for the divergences between the growth rates of coloured and total population; rises in the female to male ratio do not coincide with years of rapid growth. The conclusion then must be that changes in classification were arbitrary.

Since the classification of the coloured population is so very unreliable that of the black population must also be suspect. Hence,

TABLE XIV

Sex Ratio of the Coloured Population

Year	Males	Females
1844	46·2	53·8
1861	47·3	52·7
1871	47·8	52·2
1881	46·6	53·4
1891	45·5	54·5
1911	47·2	52·8
1921	44·4	55·6

TABLE XV

Sex Ratio of the Black Population

Year	Males	Females
1844	48·0	52·0
1861	48·3	51·7
1871	48·8	51·2
1881	48·8	51·2
1891	48·3	51·7
1911	47·9	52·1
1921	47·0	53·0

all that can be done is to point out that the growth rates of the black population, according to the census returns, were generally below total growth rates until 1911 but above them subsequently. As this change coincided with a reduction in the number of the coloured population any linking between growth rates and falling death-rates, suggesting that public health measures benefited the black population relatively more than others, cannot be justified.

E. The Working Population

Finally we turn to the size of the working population. From 1844 onwards we have the census returns of the numbers occupied. Before then data are limited to the bald classifications used in the Slave Compensation Claims of 1834.[1] Both sets of data are shown in Table XVI, column 2. Compared with total population these returns show extraordinary variations over the years.

TABLE XVI

Census Returns of Occupied Population

(1) Year	(2) Working Population '000	(3) Working Population as % of Total Population	(4) Population aged 10 years and over as % of Total Population
1834 . .	255·3*	82·1*	n.a.
1844 . .	234·6	62·2	73·8
1861 . .	240·7	54·5	73·7
1871 . .	216·4	42·8	73·5
1881 . .	282·8	48·7	74·0
1891 . .	373·5	58·4	74·7
1911 . .	410·9	49·4	72·0
1921 . .	443·9	51·7	72·9

* Slave Population only.

In 1834 as much as 82 per cent of the slave population were returned as occupied and in 1844 the proportion for the total population was 62 per cent. The ratio fell subsequently to 42·8 per cent in 1871 but thereafter rose again until in 1891 it reached 58·4 per cent. Thus only in 1871 was the ratio at all comparable with that found in other countries. In 1834 everyone except children under six years of age and the 'aged, sick and runaways' were included in the working population. The resultant high ratio may be due to the organization of work under slavery which, by arranging tasks according to age and sex, resulted in an occupation for practically everyone able to stand on his feet. With compensation money being scaled to the productive value of each slave, this tendency to classify people as occupied may well have been encouraged. The improbability of the statistics of the working population from 1844 is brought out even more clearly if we compare the ratios of the occupied with the ratios of those of working age—that is the proportion of those aged ten years and over

[1] *Op. cit.*

—shown in column 4. It will be seen that while the former ranges between about 43 and 63 per cent the latter remains fairly constant at about 73 per cent. These statistics in effect mean that in 1844 and 1891 eight out of a possible ten persons were occupied; in 1861, 1881, 1911 and 1921 seven out of ten were occupied and only in 1871 was the number as low as six out of ten.

Beginning in 1891 the censuses classify occupations by sex. While the ratio of male employment to total males of working age fell by only three points from 81·6 per cent in 1891 to 78.6 per cent in 1911, at which it remained in 1921, that of females declined steeply from 75·4 per cent in 1891 to 60 per cent in 1911 but rose again to

TABLE XVII

Census Classification of Working Population According to Sex 1891–1921

	Males		Females	
	Nos. '000	Nos. as % of Working Age	Nos. '000	Nos. as % of Working Age
1891	183·4	81·6	190·2	75·4
1911	220·6	78·4	190·3	60·0
1921	224·3	78·5	219·6	64·6

64·6 per cent ten years later (Table XVII). Since neither age nor sex structure can account for such large fluctuations we conclude that changing census definitions were responsible. Indeed, the 1911 Census Commissioner pointed out that 'wives and children were returned as engaged in agriculture in 1891 in a greater proportion than was done either in 1881 or in 1911'.[1] It is, however, doubtful whether even the 1911 census conformed to the usual definition of gainful employment—that is including only those engaged in economic activity and excluding all housewives, even though they may have contributed to agricultural output, on the grounds that they were primarily engaged in domestic tasks. According to this definition we would expect between 32 and 37 per cent of all women

[1] P. 8.

of working age to be occupied[1]— hence the number returned in 1911 still appears to include a considerable number of wives.

Because the census classifications of female employment are useless as they stand and a more meaningful estimate of the working population is needed in later chapters, our next task is to eliminate the variations arising from changing classifications. We can do this by assuming that the 1871 returns were correct because that year shows the most reasonable ratio of occupied to total population. Our problem then is to discover the ratio of females occupied to the total number of females of working age in 1871 and to apply this ratio to all other years on the assumption that the number of women available for work remained a constant proportion of all women aged ten years and over. As we have no sex classification for 1871 we calculate female employment by assuming that the male ratio in 1871 was the same as in 1891—that is 81·6 per cent of all men of working age. This gives us the number of occupied males in 1871 as 146,900. Deducting this from the total occupied population, the number of occupied women is thus estimated at 69,500 or 36·2 per cent of all women of working age which compares with 37·3 per cent in Great Britain in 1851.[2] From this we can calculate the numbers occupied in all years by taking 36·2 per cent as the standard proportion for women throughout but for men 81·6 per cent up to 1891 and actual census figures for 1891 and subsequent years. Adding the calculated numbers of occupied men and women together we get a revised total working population which is much more in line with that of other countries and also compares well with the proportion of 40·8 per cent occupied in Jamaica in 1943 (Table XVIII, column 7).

For 1834 no comparable age statistics are available. However, we know that in that year the slave population was relatively old and that the white population was predominantly male. For both reasons the proportion occupied is likely to have been somewhat higher in 1834 than subsequently and has here been estimated at 45 per cent.

[1] The Census of Great Britain for 1851 returns 37·3 per cent of the women of working age as occupied (deducting farmers' wives, etc., not included in later years) and the censuses of England and Wales for 1901 and 1911 return the proportions as 31·6 and 32·5 respectively. Census of Great Britain for 1851, BPP (5355), 1854, pp. cxl–cxlix, and Census of England and Wales for 1911, General Report, BPP, 1917 (Cd. 8491), p. 157.

[2] *Ibid.*

Such variations as are evident in the revised estimates are, by definition, the result of changes in the age and sex structure of the population. As seen in Table XVI, column 4, the proportion of those aged ten years and over remained remarkably stable at around

TABLE XVIII

Calculated Working Population

Year	Males		Females		Total	
(1)	(2) Nos. '000	(3) Nos. as % of Total Population	(4) Nos. '000	(5) Nos as % of Total Population	(6) Nos. '000	(7) Nos. as % of Total Population
1834 .	—	—	—	—	167·0	45·0
1844 .	110·4	29·3	51·9	13·8	162·3	43·1
1861 .	128·5	29·1	60·8	13·8	189·3	42·9
1871 .	146·9	29·0	69·5	13·7	216·4	42·7
1881 .	169·7	29·2	80·3	13·8	250·0	43·0
1891 .	183·4	28·7	91·3	14·3	274·7	43·0
1911 .	220·6	26·5	114·8	13·8	335·4	40·3
1921 .	224·3	26·1	123·0	14·3	347·3	40·4

74 per cent until 1881. By 1891 the proportion had risen slightly but the effect of this on the numbers occupied was offset by an accompanying rise in the female to male ratio. On the other hand, in 1911 the proportion of people of working age had declined thus reducing the numbers occupied while in 1921 the effect of a slightly older population was to a small extent offset by a further increase in the proportion of women.

As these calculations depend on the census age classifications a comment is needed here about their accuracy. Calculations carried out by G. W. Roberts[1] to test the accuracy of vital statistics revealed inaccuracy of the census classifications in the under ten years age groups: those between 0–4 years tending to be lower, and those between 5–9 years higher, than the numbers calculated from the annual registrations suggested. On the whole, however, it appeared that the total for children below ten years of age was reasonably accurate. A further calculation carried out to test the accuracy of later age groups—by comparing survival rates for the several age

[1] A Note on Mortality in Jamaica, *op. cit.*

groups as far as possible over the period—also revealed some variations; none of these appear unreasonable, once account is taken of the effect of migration, except for the youngest age groups.

To complete our revisions we must deduct the excess of the census enumerations over the calculated totals from the detailed census returns. This is done by taking the excess out of agriculture throughout. The reasons for this are, first, that the census commissioner in 1911 suggested that over-enumeration occurred in this industry and, secondly, that women assisting in agriculture are more likely to think of this as employment than they are of, for example, domestic service when they are primarily housewives in urban areas.

So much for the revision of the size of the total working population. But some further problems arise out of the detailed classifications used in the censuses. In the early years, descriptions of occupations were not uniform. In 1844 only twenty-nine occupations were distinguished; in 1861 the number was nearly four hundred, some of which were merely duplicates but others vague and difficult to classify. From 1881 onwards the censuses classify occupations according to five main industrial categories—agriculture, industry and construction, commerce, professional services and domestic service. We have used the classification for the earlier years. It should also be noted that the later censuses were not always consistent: some occupations were variously classified in different censuses; thus washerwomen and hoteliers, in the revised estimates, are included under domestic service and fishermen appear under agriculture. A further alteration occurs in the industrial employment category in 1881. In the census for this year, unlike in those for other years, no entries were made for coopers, sawyers and joiners. Since the only place where they could have been entered was agriculture we have deducted 3,000—a number slightly below that returned in 1891—from agriculture and added it to industry.

Having made these adjustments to the classifications we find that two implausible figures remain: one is the steep rise in the number included in the industrial group between 1861 and 1871; the other is the relatively low number returned under domestic service in 1881. The share of the industrial group in total employment, according to our revised classifications as detailed above, rose from 16·9 per cent in 1861 to 18·5 per cent in 1871 and then fell back to 16·8 per cent in 1881 and 17·2 per cent in 1891. Looking at the detailed table of industrial employment (Table XXIX, Ch. 10) we see that there was a sudden jump in the number of dressmakers from about 9,700 in 1861 to about 17,000 ten years later. There is no reason why the number of dressmakers should have increased so sharply during these years. It is more likely to have been the result of changing classifications used in the censuses. Accordingly we have reduced the 1871 figure for industrial employment from 18·5 per cent to 16·9 per cent by deducting 3,340 from the number of dressmakers. The movement in the proportion of those returned under domestic service likewise is improbable. According to our revised estimates, the share of domestic employment in total employment was 10 per cent in 1861, 10·2 per cent in 1871 but fell to 9·2 per cent in 1881, rising sharply thereafter to 13·5 per cent in 1891. The fall between 1871 and 1881 was due to the number of domestic servants having fallen by over 1,000. (Table XXI, Ch. 10.) This is improbable, even if we allow for the increase in the number of washerwomen. Again some adjustment must be made. In the absence of other information, we have assumed that the number of domestic servants rose proportionately to the population between 1871 and 1881: i.e. by 15 per cent or by 2,440. This increases the number of domestic servants by 3,820 to 18,727 and increases the share of domestic service in total employment to 10·8 per cent. The corresponding adjustments are made in agriculture: i.e. we add 3,340 to agriculture in 1871 and deduct 3,820 from agriculture in 1881. The revised estimates are shown in Part B of Table XIX.

It will also be noted that an attempt has been made to classify the pre-emancipation working population according to agricultural and non-agricultural employment. In Table XVII we estimated the total working population in 1834 at 167,000. If we assume that half of the free population was occupied we get the number of slaves occupied as 137,000. This total enables us to make proportionate adjustments to the details of occupations given in the Slave Compensation Claims. Accordingly, the number of slaves engaged in agriculture becomes 112,500. Allowing for the number of free people engaged as planters and salaried staff we estimate the total number at 116,000—as for 1844—or a proportion of the total number occupied slightly below that estimated ten years later. This calculation is, of course, highly speculative and it should be noted that no use is made of it except in Ch. 14, A, where per capita output in the agricultural and non-agricultural sectors is compared.

Part A. Census Classification

Industry	1844		1861		1871		1881		1891		1911		1921	
	'000	%	'000	%	'000	%	'000	%	'000	%	'000	%	'000	%
1. Agriculture* . . .	188·4	80·3	183·1	76·0	143·7	66·4	208·6	73·8	271·3	72·6	271·5	66·1	285·7	64·3
2. Industry and Construction . .	18·5	7·9	34·6	14·5	45·5	21·1	47·1	16·6	57·6	15·4	72·4	17·6	73·6	16·6
3. Commerce	4·9	2·1	4·1	1·7	6·3	2·9	7·4	2·6	10·9	2·9	19·8	4·8	20·6	4·6
4. Professions . . .	2·0	0·9	2·5	1·0	4·4	2·0	4·7	1·7	7·0	1·9	9·2	2·2	11·4	2·6
5. Domestic Service . .	20·8	8·8	16·4	6·8	16·5	7·6	15·0	5·3	26·7	7·2	38·0	9·3	52·6	11·9
	234·6	100·0	240·7	100·0	216·4	100·0	282·8	100·0	373·5	100·0	410·9	100·0	443·9	100·0

Part B. Revised Classification

Industry	1834		1844		1861		1871		1881		1891		1911		1921	
	'000	%	'000	%	'000	%	'000	%	'000	%	'000	%	'000	%	'000	%
1. Agriculture* . . .	116·0	69·5	116·0	71·5	131·6	69·6	147·0	68·0	168·9	67·5	172·5	62·8	196·0	58·5	192·0	55·3
2. Industry and Construction . .			18·5	11·4	32·0	16·9	36·6	16·9	42·0	16·8	47·2	17·2	60·7	18·1	61.1	17·6
3. Commerce . . .	51·0	30·5	4·9	3·0	4·1	2·2	6·3	2·9	7·4	3·0	10·9	4·0	19·8	5·9	20·6	5·9
4. Professions . . .			2·0	1·3	2·5	1·3	4·4	2·0	4·7	1·9	7·0	2·5	9·2	2·7	11·4	3·3
5. Domestic Service .			20·8	12·8	19·0	10·0	22·1	10·2	27·0	10·8	37·1	13·5	49·7	14·8	62·2	17·9
	167·0	100·0	162·2	100·0	189·2	100·0	216·4	100·0	250·0	100·0	274·7	100·0	335·4	100·0	347·3	100·0

* Includes sugar factory workers.

CHAPTER 10

THE PATTERN OF PRODUCTION

IN this chapter we trace the changes in the pattern of production. This is done in three parts: first, we examine the relative importance of the major industries; secondly, changes within the sectors, and finally, the effects of these inter- and intra-industrial shifts on the geographical pattern of production.

A. THE RELATIVE IMPORTANCE OF SECTORS

In Table XX we show the percentage shares of the occupied population engaged in the major industries in the years between 1844 and 1921. The table shows two outstanding trends: one, the rapid fall in the share of agricultural employment after 1881; the other, the sharp relative rise in the numbers employed in domestic service. Compared with these two striking movements, other changes were relatively unimportant: the shares of professional and of commercial employment rose only slightly while those of industrial employment remained virtually unchanged.

TABLE XX

Percentage Distribution of Labour Classified According to Industry

	1844	1861	1871	1881	1891	1911	1921
	%	%	%	%	%	%	%
1. Agriculture .	71·5	69·6	68·0	67·5	62·8	58·5	55·3
2. Industry and Construction .	11·4	16·9	16·9	16·8	17·2	18·1	17·6
3. Commerce . .	3·0	2·2	2·9	3·0	4·0	5·9	5·9
4. Professions . .	1·3	1·3	2·0	1·9	2·5	2·7	3·3
5. Domestic Service	12·8	10·0	10·2	10·8	13·5	14·8	17·9
	100·0	100·0	100·0	100·0	100·0	100·0	100·0

Source: Table XIX, Pt. B.

Until the 1880's, agriculture accounted for around 70 per cent of the total labour force. Emancipation thus appears to have had no effect on the proportion of those in this occupation. In Table XIX we estimated the proportion in 1834 at about 70 per cent. According to our revised census estimates the share was 71·5 per cent in 1844 and in 1881 still accounted for 67·5 per cent. But thereafter the share began to drop rapidly. By 1891 it had already declined to 63 per cent and continued to fall subsequently until in 1921 it accounted for only 55 per cent.

As a general rule a decline in the proportion of agricultural employment is the result of rising living standards. But this clearly was not the case in Jamaica. Rising living standards usually reduce not only the number of those working on the land but also those entering domestic service. The big fall in the agricultural proportion during the 1880's was accompanied by a considerable rise in the number of domestic servants (Table XX). The share of domestic servants, after being stable at around 10 per cent, rose sharply to 13·5 per cent in 1891 and continued to increase thereafter until in 1921 it accounted for nearly 18 per cent.

TABLE XXI

Numbers in Domestic Employment

	1844	1861	1871	1881	1891	1911	1921
1. Domestic Servants . .	20,571	16,253	16,287	18,727*	26,503	35,701	49,965
2. Washerwomen .	—	2,586	5,631	8,104	10,400	11,715	9,580
3. Hotel-keepers, etc. . . .	216	48	98	123	94	270	551
4. Other . . .	—	126	68	18	89	2,025	2,061
	20,787	19,013	22,084	26,972	37,086	49,711	62,157

* The Census of 1881 actually returns the number of domestic servants as 14,907. For reasons given in Ch. 9, E, we have increased this number by 3,820.

A high proportion of the labour force in domestic service is characteristic of lack of employment opportunities. The decline in the share of agricultural employment, beginning in the 1880's, while that of domestic service increased, thus suggests that population growth was beginning to outstrip cultivable land, and that, as a result, surplus workers entered domestic service. (See Ch. 15, D.)

Had the relative decline in agricultural employment been the result of rising living standards, then we should have expected a comparable expansion in industry and construction. But, as seen from Table XX, the proportion of those engaged in industry and construction remained fairly stable at around 17 per cent until the end of the century and rose only slightly to 18 per cent in 1911.

The proportion of those engaged in commerce, on the other hand, began to rise after 1861. It rose slowly to 3 per cent in 1881 and then relatively rapidly to 6 per cent in 1921. The doubling of the share during the last forty years is, again, a clear index of lack of employment opportunities. It was the result mainly of an increase in the numbers engaged in shop-keeping and petty-trading (Table XXII).

TABLE XXII

Numbers in Commercial Employment

	1844	1861	1871	1881	1891	1911	1921
1. Merchants . . .	433	150	203	216	239	332	376
2. Shop-keepers . .	2,216	1,166	1,774	2,339	3,131	3,649	3,587
3. Petty-traders* . .		437	1,594	1,175	1,667	3,573	4,164
4. Clerks	1,555	636	1,132	1,812	2,242	3,212	3,694
5. Transport Workers	687	1,105	1,263	1,282	2,074	4,193	3,792
6. Other	—	620	342	565	1,587	4,795	5,013
	4,891	4,114	6,308	7,389	10,940	19,754	20,626

* Includes itinerant traders.

Finally, the steady increase in professional employment from 1·3 per cent in 1844 to 3·3 per cent in 1921 was the result of a major change in the composition of this group. After emancipation the number of doctors and lawyers declined sharply. Compared with the 200 doctors practising in the island in 1830,[1] the 1861 CP returned only 87 medical practitioners of all descriptions of whom only 50 were said to be qualified.[2] After the establishment of the Government Medical Service the number of doctors began to increase again but even in 1921 had not reached the 1830 total. The ranks of the legal profession were similarly depleted but in their case the decline was not arrested until 1881. The cause of the increase in the

[1] Jamaica in 1912, p. 62.

[2] *Ibid.*

number of professional workers, however, is the spectacular growth in the number of teachers and civil servants. Between 1861 and 1871 both groups had doubled their numbers and continued to increase subsequently. The increase in these two groups was, in fact, greater than the growth of the total working population and accounts for the fact that the professional group's share did not fall as a result of the reduced number of other professional workers.

TABLE XXIII

Numbers in Professional Employment

	1844	1861	1871	1881	1891	1911	1921
1. Doctors and Dentists . .	N.S.	87	84	89	107	182	197
2. Lawyers . . .	N.S.	60	44	37	80	113	93
3. Clergy . . .	267	278	255	261	329	344	327
4. Public Servants*	N.S.	624	1,203	1,481	1,501	2,241	2,521
5. Teachers . . .	640	448	871	1,270	1,733	2,207	2,178
6. Others† . . .	1,127	992	1,911	1,520	3,229	4,124	6,107
Total	2,034	2,489	4,368	4,658	6,979	9,211	11,423

* Includes constabulary, prison and reformatory superintendents, parochial officers, official inspectors and post officer engineers.

† Includes mainly military and naval staff in early years but in later years includes also engineers, dispensers, journalists and stenographers.

We can also assess the relative importance of sectors according to their share in output. Table XXIV shows the shares of agriculture, construction, manufacturing and services at final value between *1832* and *1930*. These years are not strictly comparable with those of the census returns. Nevertheless, we can see that a very different picture from that of the employment statistics emerges.

First, the share of agricultural output declined sharply from 60·4 per cent in *1832* to 54·5 per cent in *1850* in contrast to the constant proportion of agricultural employment. This discrepancy was the result of a general substitution of the less valuable products grown for the home market for the more valuable export crops during these years.

Secondly, the share of agricultural output remained fairly stable between *1870* and *1890*. This, again, contrasts with the employment statistics which show a rapid decline after 1881. The share of services, likewise, remained constant during these years, in spite of the sharp increase in the proportion of domestic servants.

One reason for this divergence between output and employment after 1881 is to be found in the changing composition of agriculture. Beginning in the seventies the banana increasingly supplanted sugar

TABLE XXIV

*Shares in Output of the Major Industries**

	1832	*1850*	*1870*	*1890*	*1910*	*1930*
	%	%	%	%	%	%
1. Agriculture and Exports†	60·4	54·5	56·7	56·2	57·8	50·8
2. Building and Construction	3·6	4·4	4·4	5·0	4·3	5·9
3. Manufacturing . . .	5·1	6·2	10·3	10·0	9·5	8·2
4. Services	30·9	34·9	28·6	28·8	28·4	35·1
	100·0	100·0	100·0	100·0	100·0	100·0

* The definitions of agriculture and manufacturing used in this table do not follow conventional usage. Agriculture here includes the value of manufactured sugar and rum exports and also the value of distribution services. Manufacturing includes the value of raw materials supplied by the agricultural industry and the value added by distribution services. For further details see Ch. 1, B.

† Includes manufactured sugar, rum and tobacco retained for domestic consumption.

Source: Ch. 8.

as the major export crop until in *1910* it accounted for half of the total value of exports. Since the banana is a much less labour-intensive crop it was possible to expand output without a proportionate increase in employment.

But there is another reason for this divergence. Those unable to find employment in agriculture, because of the lower labour requirements of the new crop and the failure of total activity to make up for this reduction and also to keep pace with population growth, were increasingly driven to domestic service. The relevance of this increase is that the per capita value of domestic servants was considerably below that of agricultural workers so that increasing employment was not matched by a proportionate increase in output.

We conclude that there were two important shifts in the pattern of production. The first, as revealed by the output table, occurred immediately after emancipation and was caused by a decline in exports. The second, as revealed by the employment statistics, began during the eighties and was the result of population growth beginning to outstrip the supply of cultivable land.

B. Agriculture

Before emancipation the agricultural industry—indeed the whole Jamaican economy—was dominated by the production of export crops. As long as suitable land was available and planters had control over their labour supply, it was more profitable to produce export crops and to buy imports than to divert some of the resources to the production of food for the domestic market. The only excep-

TABLE XXV

*The Pattern of Agricultural Output**

	1832	*1850*	*1870*	*1890*	*1910*	*1930*
	%	%	%	%	%	%
1. Ground Provisions . .	27	43	54	55	50	49
2. Animal Products . . .	1	8	6	6	6	9
3. Retained Exports . . .	1	2	3	4	4	3
4. Exports	71	47	37	35	40	39
	100	100	100	100	100	100

* Agricultural output is shown at final value. Thus it includes the value of manufactured sugar and rum and of distribution services but it excludes the value of agricultural products supplied to manufacturing industry.
Sources: Chs. 2–7.

tions were root crops—yams, cocoes and sweet potatoes—known as ground provisions. As practically any land was suitable for this cultivation, ground provisions did not compete with the staple export crops for land. Nor did it involve much diversion of labour as the crop, once planted, required only little attention. In fact, under the Slave Acts[1] only one day per fortnight was set aside for the cultivation of ground provisions and this apparently was quite sufficient

[1] 1827 and 1831.

to produce enough food for the bulk of the population. A small part of export crops was retained for consumption on the plantations or sold in the towns. But quantitatively, this cannot have been very important considering that the bulk of the population—the slaves—received sugar and rum only on special occasions and coffee, apparently, not at all. Stock-rearing in the island was primarily designed to supply estates with draft animals. The demand for meat and fish was largely met by imports—though contemporary literature suggests that slaves sometimes reared pigs, goats and poultry in their 'gardens'.[1] Production for the home market accounted for only 29 per cent of total agricultural output and of this as much as 27 per cent was taken up by ground provisions (Table XXV).

Emancipation of the slaves, however, caused a dramatic change in the pattern of agricultural output. The 1830's and 1840's saw a widespread abandonment of plantations and, with it, a sharp fall in exports. Most of the slaves who left the plantations became independent settlers. The change from slave worker to peasant thus had little effect on the total agricultural labour force. But it did have important consequences for the pattern of output. Whereas formerly as slaves, the peasants had produced exports as well as their own subsistence, now they grew mainly ground provisions. Their attempts to cultivate the traditional exports—with the partial exception of coffee—were, for reasons to be dealt with in Ch. 12, not very successful. The peasants were rather more successful with the production of coffee and semi-manufactured sugar for the local market. They also took up stock-rearing for human consumption more extensively than they had done as slaves. But what expansion there was in production for the home market was negligible compared with the steep fall in plantation output. Hence the total value of agricultural output declined from £2,986,900 in *1832* by over one-third to £1,917,200 in *1850*, and with it the share of exports from nearly three-quarters to less than one-half of total agricultural output.

The total agricultural labour force began to grow during the 1840's. The increase, however, took place in independent small-scale cultivation. The numbers working on plantations continued to fall. We do not know how many people were actually engaged in sugar and coffee planting before emancipation but, allowing for the number of ineffectives among the enumerated predial slave population in 1834,

[1] E.g. A. Barclay, *A Practical View of the Present State of Slavery in the West Indies*, London, 1827, p. 315.

the total number employed cannot have been very far below 100,000. In 1860, the numbers working on sugar estates was estimated at only 20,000.[1] According to the CP of 1891 the number of male workers, including those employed in the factories, was 19,000 while the number of coffee workers was only about 4,000. Thus by the 1860's, the majority of labour must have been engaged in small-scale cultivation. This change is also evident in the increasing importance of ground provisions in total agricultural output as well as in the continuing relative decline in exports. Production for the local market, after *1850*, in fact just about kept pace with population growth. The share of ground provisions continued to increase until in *1890*

TABLE XXVI

Ratios of Exports, Retained Exports and Animal Products to Ground Provisions

	1832	*1850*	*1870*	*1890*	*1910*	*1930*
1. Exports	259	108	69	64	81	80
2. Retained Exports . . .	5	17	12	10	11	20
3. Animal Products . . .	2	5	5	8	9	7
Total 1–3	266	130	86	82	101	107

Source: Table XXV.

it accounted for 55 per cent of total agricultural output (Table XXV). As the output of ground provisions has been estimated on a basis of constant per capita consumption—allowing only for changes in the level of imported food substitutes, which were relatively unimportant—its increasing share in total agricultural output means, in fact, a smaller per capita agricultural product. Hence it is only when the share of ground provisions falls that total agricultural output increases. Such a fall occurred only after the 1890's. The ratio of exports to ground provisions rose from 64 in *1890* to 81 in *1910* (Table XXVI).

The growth in exports towards the end of the century was the result of the rapid expansion in banana cultivation. Banana exports actually began in 1869 but it was during the 1890's and 1900's that

[1] Sewell, *op. cit.*, p. 264.

the biggest rate of increase occurred. Exports fell steeply during World War I but recovered again with the return of peace. The war and post-war period also saw a recovery in sugar exports.

The increase in exports, however, was not accompanied by an increase in employment. In fact, total agricultural employment declined from 196,000 in 1911 to 192,000 in 1921. The fall in the numbers engaged in export production appears to have been relatively even greater. Male employment in the production of export crops fell from 43,000 in 1891 to 40,000 in 1921 (Table XXVII).

This decline in employment in the export industry was the direct consequence of the substitution of the banana, with its lower labour requirements, for sugar. The available employment statistics, unfortunately, do not help us to trace this shift in the demand for labour in detail. For reasons given in Ch. 9, E, we are limited to the use of the statistics for male employment. But even these are not very satisfactory for this purpose.

TABLE XXVII

Number of Men Engaged in Agriculture and Fisheries Classified According to Product

(Employers and Employees)

	1891	1911	1921
1. Bananas	3,787	23,255	15,462
2. Sugar*	19,206	13,153	19,929
3. Provisions†	90,615	104,610	112,567
4. Pen-keeping	15,825	3,579	3,432
5. Coffee	4,444	2,171	1,462
6. Others‡	3,723	11,583	10,302
	137,600	158,351	163,154

* Includes cane farmers.
† Includes 'general', 'persons assisting in cultivation' and 'cassava planters'.
‡ Includes fishermen.
Sources: CP.

There was a steep rise in banana employment from nearly 4,000 in 1891 to 23,000 in 1911 (Table XXVII). This rise, however, was greater than the increase in exports, which was only fourfold. By

1921 the numbers had declined by one-third. This was partly due to the attenuation of the banana industry during the 1914–18 war following the conversion of some banana estates to sugar. The fact that banana exports had, at this time, almost recovered their pre-war level suggests, however, that the 1921 enumeration was not very reliable.

The decline shown in sugar employment to 13,000 in 1911 and the subsequent recovery to nearly 20,000 in 1921 follows the trend in exports. It is interesting to note here that most of the recovery in the numbers was due to a growth in the number of cane farmers, that is independent farmers supplying sugar canes to factories under contract, and not to labour employed directly by the estates.

The reduction in sugar output up to the war also affected pen-keeping in so far as it reduced the demand for draft animals. Some of the fall from 15,825 in 1891 to 3,579 in 1911 was also due to the falling value of logwood and pimento, the collection of which was usually combined with stock-rearing. Even so, the decline in employment appears rather greater than can be explained by the reduction in output.

The returns of male employment thus do not seem to reflect accurately the actual shift in production. Possibly some banana workers were returned under other heads in 1891 and in 1921. But these shortcomings in the classifications were probably inevitable because throughout these years considerable changes were taking place in estate cultivation. There was a great amount of conversion first from sugar to banana planting and then back to sugar. Many estates also planted both crops simultaneously (see Ch. 11 I).

C. Industry

Manufacturing industry in Jamaica lacked the natural stimulus of raw materials and cheap power. From time to time hopes were raised by the discovery of mineral deposits but, on further investigation, these proved insufficient to make mining economic until the extensive bauxite deposits were discovered during World War II. The mining boom of the 1850's, for example, produced only negligible quantities of copper, lead and zinc. Even if deposits had proved more profitable it is doubtful whether any local industry could have developed around them as the other pre-requisite to manufacturing —cheap power—was not available. Jamaica has no coal deposits and the development of hydro-electric power was generally considered to be impracticable owing to the uneconomic cost of harnessing the highly irregular water supplies of the island. Up to 1930 the only company developing hydro-electricity was the West India Electric Co. Ltd., which used water power to operate the tramway and supply electric light to Kingston and Lower St. Andrew.[1]

Hence the first manufacturing industries which developed in Jamaica were those using agricultural raw materials. In the main, such manufacturing was limited to the processing necessary to ensure good condition for overseas markets. Cane juice, for example, has to be expressed and crystallized a day or two after reaping, otherwise the sugar becomes invert. Similarly rum distillation has to be done locally. The sugar industry, moreover, has the advantage of producing its own fuel from the expressed cane. Processing, though on a less extensive scale, was also involved in a number of other agricultural crops such as coffee which has to be cleaned and dried locally.

TABLE XXVIII

Number of Factories Classified According to Product

	1890[1]	*1910*[1]	*1929*[2]
Tobacco	2	17	1
Tannery	2	17	2
Beer and Ale . . .	1	7	7
Mineral Waters . .	—	8	4
Soap	—	—	4
Copra	—	—	11
Sisal and Rope . .	—	—	6
Other	3	13	17
Total	8*	62	52

* Number of factories surviving in 1910.
Sources: (1) BBJ, 1910.
(2) *Ibid.*, 1929.

The rise of new manufacturing industries towards the end of the century was, in part, the logical development of this processing of agricultural materials. Tobacco and dyewoods factories were all users

[1] Col. Rep., BPP, 1921 (Cmd. 1103–10), p. 20.

of local raw materials. A second development taking place at the same time was the substitution of home produce for bulky imports such as beer, ale and mineral waters.

Before 1890 a few factories had been set up to manufacture beer, tobacco and matches but between the years 1890 and 1910 the opening up of new enterprises proceeded at an impressive rate. In 1910, as shown in Table XXVIII, there were 62 factories in operation and probably the number that had been set up in the intervening years was much greater. Of the 62 factories, tobacco and tanneries accounted for 17 each, factories producing mineral waters 8, beer and ale 7 and the remainder consisted of match, dyewood, banana and cassava starch factories.

The information about output given in the BBJ is, unfortunately, too improbable to be taken seriously. It appears, however, that many of these factories were uneconomically small. We can see this from their rate of survival. Between 1910 and 1929 the number of tanneries was reduced from seventeen to four and that of tobacco factories even more sharply from seventeen to one. Since this reduction was not accompanied by a loss in total output—which is actually estimated to have increased, in the case of tobacco, from £130,100 in *1910* to £187,100 in *1930*—we conclude that it must have been due to the amalgamation of factories. Scale of operation appears to have been less important in the case of factories producing beer and ale and mineral waters because in their case the number was reduced by only four from fifteen in 1910 to eleven in 1929.

What happened to these superfluous enterprises may be illustrated by the experience of the dyewood extract industry. The West India Chemical Works in Spanish Town were started in 1893[1] to extract dyes from logwood locally to save the heavy freight charges on the raw product when world prices began to fall. A few years later a rival firm began operations in Lacovia, St. Elizabeth.[2] It was sufficiently successful to increase investment in its equipment in 1909.[3] But a year later its interests were taken over by the West India Chemical Works, putting an end to 'competition in the purchase of logwood'.[4]

While competition and amalgamation reduced the number of existing establishments new enterprises were started. In 1929 there were four soap, eleven copra and six sisal and rope factories. Again the

[1] Col. Rep., BPP, 1896 (C 7944-13).
[2] *Ibid.*, 1907 (Cd. 3729-13).
[3] *Ibid.*, 1911 (Cd. 4964-13).
[4] *Ibid.*, 1912 (Cd. 6007-3).

local supply of raw materials was important. Where neither local supplies nor heavy freight charges on imports provided inducements to local enterprise no development took place. The presence of an abundant labour supply, by itself, was not sufficient. Most of the industries established drew on only a negligible number of workers. Even the industry with the largest labour force—the tobacco factory—employed only 400 workers in 1931. The next largest was the dye-wood factory, employing 200, and the third, a copra factory, with 150 workers. The remainder employed, on the average, only 21 workers.

TABLE XXIX

Numbers Employed in Industry and Construction

	1844	1861	1871	1881	1891	1911	1921
1. Dressmakers, Tailors, etc.	N.S.	9,714	13,650*	17,607	22,331	25,139	28,366
2. Shoemakers	—	808	1,710	1,830	1,768	3,147	3,015
3. Butchers	—	151	368	430	611	1,033	1,038
4. Carpenters, etc.	—	5,793	7,922	10,852	9,181	9,263	8,226
5. Blacksmiths	—	818	1,432	1,377	1,185	1,122	1,051
6. Bricklayers, etc.	—	1,767	2,417	2,527	2,502	2,860	2,042
7. Other	—	12,941	9,073	7,339	9,642	18,163	17,393
Total	18,485	31,992	36,572	41,962	47,220	60,727	61,131

* The CP of 1871 actually returns the number of dressmakers, etc., as 16,990. For reasons given in Ch. 9, E, we have reduced this number by 3,340.

This small development of manufacturing industry is in contrast to the continuing importance of craftsmen working on their own account. The number of these increased sharply after emancipation until about the 1860's but thereafter continued to increase only proportionately to population growth. The initial increase followed the breaking down of the isolation of estates which gave rise to more opportunities for production for exchange. Table XXIX shows that the number of dressmakers, shoemakers and other craftsmen serving consumers directly continued to rise relatively to total industrial employment. The number of butchers also increased but in their case the provision of public slaughterhouses and the closer supervision of the marketing of meat were responsible for the substantial rise thereafter. On the other hand, the decline in plantation activity and the shift in export crops reduced the demand for craftsmen concerned with the earlier stages of production. The number of carpenters and blacksmiths, for example, began to fall after 1881 as a result of declining demand for wooden containers following the contraction of the sugar and coffee industries and the increasing substitution of bags and sacks as packing materials.

One result of the decline in carpenters and blacksmiths, and the relative rise in dressmakers and other workers producing consumer goods, was that the industrial group became predominantly female. Indeed the ratio of women to men in this group is exceeded only by that in the domestic group. This change also had the further effect in that the value of output declined relative to the numbers employed. This can be seen by comparing the combined shares of construction and manufacturing output with the proportion of the labour force engaged in industrial and constructional employment shown in Table XXX. This comparison brings out two trends.

TABLE XXX

Shares of Industry and Construction in Total Output and Employment

	1870	*1890*	*1910*	*1930*
Output of Manufactures and Construction as Percentage of Total Output*	14·7	15·3	15·3	14·3
Employment in Industry and Construction as Percentage of Total Employment†	16·9	17·2	18·1	17·6

* It should be noted that in constructing this table we have altered the shares in output given in Table XXIV to bring them into line with the census returns shown in Table XX above: i.e. we have included the manufactured value of tobacco and logwood extract exports and deducted the estimated value of agricultural materials supplied to the manufacturing industry.

† Census years 1871, 1891, 1911 and 1921.

First, the share of employment was consistently higher than output and, secondly, after about 1871 the gap between the shares in output and in employment tended to widen.

D. Transport

(i) *Road Communications*

The provision of an adequate network of roads and bridges in an island like Jamaica is a formidable task. The island is long and narrow and traversed by mountain chains. These rise steeply from narrow coastal plains and are separated by valleys which are considerably above sea level. Areas that are flat occupy only 14·5 per cent of the total.[1] The presence of many rivers, whose volume increases many times during the rainy seasons, posed yet another problem. Added to the inherent topographical difficulties was the damage caused to bridges and roads by recurrent hurricanes.

Until 1865, however, little attempt was made to cope with the problem of providing internal communications. A few roads were maintained in an indifferent condition to connect the most important centres of trade with the ports. Conveyance of output from estates situated further inland was a costly and often hazardous undertaking at the best of times while during the rainy season all internal traffic, even on horseback, was brought to a standstill. Because of the lack of roads prices of produce varied greatly from place to place and in some contiguous areas by as much as 100 per cent.[2] It was, in fact, usually cheaper to transport produce by boat from one extremity of the island to the other than to send it by road into the neighbouring parish. In the towns conditions were no better. In 1860 Kingston had not a 'street that can exhibit a square yard of pavement'.[3] Stable manure was used to repair road surfaces[4] and any Kingstonian abroad at night risked life and limb.[5] The effects of poor communications are obvious. Transport costs were high, the quality of the produce suffered and in some areas producers had no possibility of increasing output above subsistence because they had no access to markets.

It was only after the change in government in 1865, that effective steps began to be taken to improve and extend roads and to link them with an adequate number of bridges. At first the work was concentrated mainly on improving existing roads—that is those serving the sugar industry—but during the nineties this policy was

[1] HBJ, e.g. for 1928, p. 23.
[2] King, D. *State and Prospect of Jamaica*, London, 1850.
[3] Sewell, *op. cit.*, p. 174.
[4] RWIC, BPP, 1897 (C 8669), Pt. XIII, Q. 1172.
[5] Gardner, *op. cit.*, p. 421.

abandoned in favour of providing access to the fruit-growing areas.[1] By 1882 there were 764 miles of main roads and about 3,000 miles of parochial roads.[2] During the nineties a further 1,000 miles of new roads were added and the length of bridges constructed by that time measured 22½ miles.[3] In 1909 there was one mile of metalled surface to every 2·18 square miles of area.[4]

Until 1865, the usual means of conveying produce was necessarily coastal transport. But with the construction of new roads and the improvement of existing ones, sea communications became less important. It is difficult to trace the growth of road transport as neither employment nor output data are satisfactory. The censuses do not distinguish between transport workers and others employed in the agricultural industry so that the number in Table XXII includes only those specializing in transport services. According to the censuses the number of chauffeurs rose from 114 in 1911 to 1,085 ten years later. Considerable expansion appears to have taken place in mechanical transport during the 1920's for by 1930 the number of motor cars registered was 6,825 and that of trucks 1,702.[5] But these figures do not reflect the volume of road transport as a considerable portion of output continued to be conveyed to the markets in carts, on mules and even on foot by the peasants themselves.

The introduction of mechanical transport created new problems. The existing roads served the light-wheeled traffic well enough but, since most of them had been constructed without foundations, they were not adequate for heavier transport. Marl was used to cover the surface but only two or three roads were rolled mechanically; the remainder relied on slow-moving traffic to roll it in.[6] With the increased use of motor traffic after the war this method of surfacing was no longer satisfactory. The heavier and faster moving vehicles caused 'grooving' and made frequent remetalling necessary.[7] Average maintenance costs had risen from £32 per mile in 1916[8] to £116 per mile in 1925.[9] After the war work was begun on new road construction.

[1] Further Correspondence re Finances, BPP, 1900 (Cd. 125).

[2] Royal Commission on Public Revenues, etc., BPP, 1884, Pt. I (C 3840), p. 20.

[3] Further Correspondence re Finances, *op. cit*.

[4] Papers re Mechanical Transport, BPP, 1909 (Cd. 4589).

[5] Collector-General's Report for 1930–1. J. Dept. Reports, 1933, p. 198.

[6] *Transport Problems in Jamaica*, Crown Agents for the Colonies, 1923, p. 10.

[7] *Ibid.* [8] Col. Rep., BPP, 1917 (Cd. 8434–16), p. 24.

[9] *Ibid.*, HMSO, 1927 (Col. no. 1327), p. 24.

A new programme was launched in 1925 with the object of improving through-traffic but progress was slow and in 1930 the import of motor vehicles weighing more than 2½ tons unladen had to be prohibited again.[1]

The condition of Kingston's streets had also been attracting attention for some time. Considerable improvements were made between 1897 and 1905[2] but, again, the roads proved totally inadequate for the new traffic after the war. Work on reconstructing the city's streets was begun in 1925[3] and three years later nearly all had been surfaced with asphalt.[4]

(ii) *Rail Communications*

The history of the Jamaica railway dates back to 1843 when the Jamaica Railway Company was incorporated. The original estimates were for a main line from Kingston to Spanish Town with branches to the Angels, Port Henderson and Caymanas but the cost of construction was underestimated and the company began operations on a single track, 14 miles long, from Kingston to the Angels.[5] In 1859 a loan for an extension to Old Harbour was guaranteed by the island government but the issue was not successful[6] and it was not until 1869 that this was completed. The traffic on this short line was too small to do much more than cover the running charges and rolling stock and tracks were not efficiently maintained. In 1879 the Jamaican government took over the railway and began reconstructions. Six years later the track was extended to Porus in the west and Ewarton in the north and the railway subsequently proved to be a 'sound and advantageous investment'.[7]

The fruit trade was growing rapidly at this time, and as transport of bananas by rail was much more satisfactory than by road, because it decreased the likelihood of bruising, demands were voiced for further railway extensions. Plans for connecting Ewarton with Port Antonio and Porus with Montego Bay were submitted in 1888.[8] A few months earlier Messrs. Henderson and Batten had been asked to report on the prospects of such extensions. They were unfavourably impressed and reported that there was 'no reasonable prospect

[1] *Ibid.*, H.M.S.O., 1931 (Col. no. 1550).
[2] HBJ, 1905.
[3] Col. Rep., HMSO, 1927 (Col. no. 1327), p. 26.
[4] *Ibid.*, HMSO, 1928 (Col. no. 1458), p. 25.
[5] HBJ, 1895, p. 477.
[6] Sewell, *op. cit.*, p. 181.
[7] Col. Rep., BPP, 1902 (Cd. 788–43).
[8] HBJ, 1895, p. 479.

of obtaining from traffic such a sum sufficient, or nearly adequate, to meet the interest and the cost of management and maintenance'.[1] Despite this warning there was considerable interest in these extensions and an offer from some American capitalists to buy the railway and extend its operations was received with enthusiasm by the elected members of the Legislative Council.[2] Under the subsequent contract of sale the American company was bound to extend the existing tracks at the rate of 12½ miles within the first 18 months and at the rate of 12½ miles per annum thereafter until the two lines between Kingston and Port Antonio on the one hand and Montego Bay on the other were completed.[3]

The work was duly carried out and in 1894 the line to Montego Bay was opened and two years later that to Port Antonio. Both lines, however, proved unprofitable. In the case of the Montego Bay line it was found that the receipts did not even cover the running charges nor was there any prospect of increasing traffic. The Port Antonio line was also failing to meet the interest charges.[4] Consequently the company was unable to meet the debt charges and in 1898 the trustees on behalf of the bondholders applied to the government to take over the management of the railway. In August 1900 the railway became once more the property of the government. Money had to be spent immediately to bring the railway into working order. But even then receipts covered debt charges only partially and after the war they failed to do even that.

Working expenses were, of course, extremely high because of the mountainous nature of the country. Apart from this inevitable disadvantage it was also found that the routes chosen were not the best. In the case of the Montego Bay line the 47 mile track between Porus and Catadupa had very little traffic to draw on. More traffic was available in the River Minho valley and it was later found necessary to build extensions as far as Frankfield to serve this area. A direct route through Trelawny would have reduced the running charges and also avoided the need to use motor transport to bring freight to the Frankfield terminus. In the north-east the whole of the line between Annotto Bay and Port Antonio had to compete with coastal transport and after the war the railway had to compete with road

[1] Quoted in Report on the Finances of Jamaica, BPP, 1899 (C 9412), p. 6.
[2] *Ibid.* [3] HBJ, 1895, p. 479.
[4] Correspondence re Public Finances and Resources, BPP, 1899 (C 9177), p. 12.

transport as well. It now no longer had any area of unrestricted monopoly. The average haul was only 33 miles and the traffic was not sufficiently dense to make up for this short distance and the high running costs.[1]

In contrast to the railway the construction of the Kingston tramway proved an immediate financial success. The first four miles of rails were laid and opened to traffic in 1876. Two years later the line was extended bringing the total length up to 12¼ miles. Further extensions were made in the years 1884 and 1885 to May Pen Cemetery and to Constant Spring. During the first year of operation one-third of a million passengers were carried and the number increased rapidly until in 1884 it exceeded one million.[2] Ownership was transferred from the Jamaica Street Car Company to the West India Electric Company in 1897, which immediately began to develop the water power of the Rio Cobre River.[3] The plant was completed two years later and from that time onwards Kingston trams were run on hydro-electric power. Subsequently further extensions were made to Papine and Rockfort Gardens bringing the total length of track up to twenty-six miles.[4]

E. The Geographical Pattern of Production

The expansion and decline of various crops resulted in differential regional development because the wide variations in climate, soil and elevation in Jamaica make some areas more suitable for particular crops than others. Changes in the regional distribution of economic activity are best measured by the changes in the geographical distribution of the population to which they gave rise. Table XXXI shows the parochial distribution of population at census dates from 1844 onwards and of the slave population in 1832. Before passing on to comment on these statistics two warnings are necessary.

First, the total for the slave population in 1832 is, as pointed out in Ch. 9, A, slightly below the number of slaves returned for compensation claims in 1834, but this probably does not affect the geographical distribution to any important extent. What does introduce a bias, however, is the omission of the white and free coloured population. The free non-planting community was largely urbanized and its omission in 1832 explains the large increase in Kingston in 1844.

[1] *Transport Problems of Jamaica*, p. 7. [2] HBJ, 1895. [3] *Ibid.*, 1910.
[4] *Ibid.*, 1928.

The effect on the relative rate of growth of the other parishes is not likely to be so great because from the few returns available for 1828 and 1830 it appears that the free population was roughly proportional to the slave population.[1] The first complete check is available only in 1861 when the white and coloured population accounted for

TABLE XXXI

Distribution of Population by Parishes

'000

Parish	1832*	1844	1861	1871	1881	1891	1911	1921	1943
1. Kingston .	5·3	32·9	27·4	34·3	38·6	48·5	59·7	63·7	110·1
2. St. Andrew .	13·5	19·0	23·5	31·7	35·0	37·9	52·8	54·6	128·2
3. Port Royal .	6·0	6·9	7·9						
4. St. Thomas in the East	23·3	25·3	26·2	32·7	33·9	32·2	39·3	42·5	60·7
5. St. David .	7·4	6·6	6·5						
6. Portland .	7·3	8·5	8·5	25·3	28·9	32·0	49·4	49·0	60·7
7. St. George .	11·5	8·8	9·1						
8. St. Mary .	23·5	15·7	17·1	36·5	39·7	42·9	73·0	71·4	90·9
9. Metcalfe .	—	13·8	15·8						
10. St. Ann . .	24·8	25·8	36·3	39·6	46·6	54·1	70·6	70·9	96·2
11. Trelawny .	25·3	27·0	27·1	28·8	32·1	31·0	35·5	34·6	47·5
12. St. James .	22·0	25·5	26·9	29·3	33·6	35·0	41·4	41·9	63·5
13. Hanover .	21·8	21·6	23·5	26·3	29·6	32·1	37·4	38·4	51·7
14. Westmoreland	19·6	24·6	33·8	40·8	49·0	53·4	66·4	68·9	90·1
15. St. Elizabeth	18·4	25·4	37·8	45·2	54·4	62·3	78·7	79·3	100·2
16. Manchester .	19·3	22·1	32·7	38·9	48·5	55·5	65·2	63·9	92·8
17. Clarendon .	16·2	17·4	24·7	42·8	49·8	57·1	73·9	82·6	123·5
18. Vere . . .	8·0	8·5	10·1						
19. St. Catherine	7·5	12·8	12·7	54·0	61·1	65·5	88·1	96·6	121·0
20. St. John . .	6·0	8·2	9·3						
21. St. Dorothy	5·1	5·3	5·4						
22. St. Thomas in the Vale .	10·8	15·7	19·0						
Total . .	302·6	377·4	441·3	506·2	580·8	639·5	831·4	858·1	1,237·1

* Slaves only. Sources: Chapter 9, A and B.

about 20 per cent in eighteen out of twenty-two parishes; for about 13 per cent in St. David, St. George and St. Thomas in the East; while in St. Catherine and Kingston they were above the average with 30 and 50 per cent.[2] It is difficult to decide what changes in the geographical distribution may have occurred in the intervening years. On balance, it seems more likely that urban growth, particularly of whites, declined relatively to rural. But in the absence of reliable

[1] BBJ, 1828 and 1830.

[2] CP, 1861.

TABLE XXXII

Parochial Increase of Population as Percentage of Island Increase

Parish	1832–44	1844–61	1861–71	1871–81	1881–91	1891–1911	1911–21	1921–43
	%	%	%	%	%	%	%	%
EAST								
Kingston	—	71·3	109·2	98·1	114·1	94·7	103·4	119·9
St. Andrew	114·6	103·7	88·1	96·3	98·4	107·2	100·2	162·8
St. Thomas	89·6	87·7	87·2	90·4	86·3	93·8	104·7	99·1
Portland	79·4	87·0	125·4	99·6	100·6	118·8	96·1	86·0
St. Mary	108·3	95·4	96·7	94·9	98·2	130·9	94·9	88·3
CENTRE								
St. Catherine	123·3	94·5	101·5	98·6	97·4	103·5	106·2	87·0
Clarendon	92·3	115·0	107·2	101·5	104·2	99·5	108·3	103·7
Manchester	98·8	126·6	103·7	108·6	103·9	90·4	95·0	100·7
St. Elizabeth	119·1	127·4	104·3	105·0	104·0	97·2	97·7	87·7
St. Ann	89·7	120·4	95·1	102·6	105·4	100·4	97·3	94·2
Trelawny	92·1	85·9	92·7	97·2	87·7	88·1	94·5	95·3
WEST								
Westmoreland	108·3	117·5	105·2	104·7	99·0	95·6	100·6	90·8
Hanover	85·5	93·1	97·6	98·1	98·5	89·5	98·9	93·9
St. James	100·0	90·2	94·9	100·0	94·6	91·0	98·1	105·2

Source: Table XXXI.

information it seems best to omit Kingston altogether and allow for an error in the case of St. Catherine in comparing the changes between 1832 and 1844.

Secondly, it is important to note that parish boundaries changed. In 1867 the number of parishes was reduced from twenty-two to fifteen. This affected only the eastern half of the island where the existing fifteen parishes were reduced to seven. The new groupings (Table XXXI), do not correspond exactly to the former parishes; in some cases boundaries were actually altered but, since most of these affected the less densely populated areas, it may be assumed that not much error arises from ignoring them. (See Ch. 16, D.)

Table XXXI shows that population growth was not uniform for all parishes. We can express this more concisely by calculating the increase of each parish as a percentage of the island increase. Thus

TABLE XXXIII

Internal Migration

Years	Inter-censal Increase in Total Population	Mean Deviation of Parochial Increases from Total Increase
	%	%
1832–44	15·9*	15·8
1844–61	16·9	14·8
1861–71	14·7	8·5
1871–81	14·7	4·1
1881–91	10·1	5·7
1891–1911	30·0	11·2
1911–21	3·2	3.8
1921–43	44·1	17·5

* Excludes Kingston.
Source: Table XXXI.

parishes with a rate above 100 increased more than the island average and those with a rate of less than 100 correspondingly less. Differences between the relatively increasing and relatively decreasing parishes were much greater in some years than in others (Table XXXII); this suggests relatively more migration in some periods than in others. We can measure these differences in migration by taking the size of dispersion from the mean rate of increase. This method is only approximate because it ignores regional differences in birth- and death-rates. However, such differences are not sufficient to explain the very considerable dispersion shown in Table XXXIII.

Three periods are particularly outstanding for the size of their dispersion: 1832–61, 1891–1911 and 1921–43.

During the first period, lasting from 1832 to 1861, the direction of migration was largely from the extremities of the island towards the centre. In the initial twelve years, people moved from the eastern parishes of St. George, St. David and St. Dorothy chiefly to the interior parishes of St. Thomas in the Vale, St. Andrew and St. John and, in the west, from Hanover to St. Elizabeth and, to a lesser extent, also to Westmoreland. The parish of St. Catherine (old boundaries) also shows a large increase in its population from 7,500 to 12,800, but this was probably the result of the omission of the free population residing in Spanish Town in 1832.

The interesting aspect of these movements is that abandonment of estates does not appear to have been immediately relevant either in attracting people or in driving them away. Sugar and coffee cultivation declined in parishes that showed relative population losses as well as in those showing gains, while in other declining areas relative population changes were slight. The largest relative losses in sugar estates occurred in St. Elizabeth, St. George, St. Catherine, St. Dorothy, St. Thomas in the Vale, St. Andrew, St. David, St. Thomas in the East and in Portland.[1] For the coffee industry the data are less reliable but apparently estates were abandoned mostly in St. John, St. Andrew, St. Thomas in the Vale, Metcalfe and St. George.[2] According to this evidence, population movements were determined not so much by the decline of estates as by the availability of undeveloped land. The parishes which attracted people were poorly endowed in cultivable land and because of this they were not only marginal to estate production but also contained much land which had hitherto been neglected completely.

According to a return of properties for 1844 landholdings of less than ten acres each—mostly those established since 1838—were most numerous in Manchester, St. Ann, St. Thomas in the Vale, Clarendon and St. Elizabeth.[3] Of these only two—St. Thomas in the Vale and St. Elizabeth—correspond with parishes with the largest relative population gains. This discrepancy cannot be accounted for by the omission of the free population in 1832 because we have already excluded the two parishes of Kingston and St. Catherine where the

[1] Table LVII, Ch. 14.

[2] Papers re Abolition of Slavery, BPP, 1836 (166), Pt. III, p. 24, and PAJ, BPP, 1854 (1848), p. 55.

[3] JA, 1845.

free population was most numerous. It is more probable that these returns of landholdings included only the legally held and registered holdings and excluded those of doubtful tenure. This is difficult to verify since the data for landholdings even in later years are not reliable. However, as will be seen in Ch. 12, A, (ii), there are grounds for thinking that squatting may, at that time, have been extensive.

In the years from 1844 to 1861 the movement was continued further into the interior of the island. St. Elizabeth, Manchester, Clarendon and St. Ann became the most important gainers while the eastern and western parishes, with the exception of St. Andrew and Westmoreland, continued to gain less than the island average.

In the following years migration continued to follow the same pattern. The central areas and Westmoreland continued to gain at the expense of the other western parishes and St. Thomas in the East. Noteworthy is the temporary increase in Portland during the years from 1861 to 1871. But, on the whole, the volume of migration was much less. Abandonment of sugar cultivation was no longer confined to marginal estates: now size of estate became the determining factor in survival, and this meant that smaller properties were abandoned as well. Squatting was widespread during these years, but with the more general neglect of abandoned land people no longer had to seek it in the remoter regions.

The second period of increased migration—between 1891 and 1911—witnessed a complete change in direction. The eastern parishes of St. Mary and Portland now had the maximum rates of growth, while all the western parishes and Manchester gained less than the island average. In the early years banana cultivation was largely carried on by the resident peasantry in the north-east, but with its adoption as an estate crop in the 1890's the demand for labour encouraged the new eastward migration. This labour came largely from the west, where the sugar industry was going through its bleakest period. But not all the relative losses in the western parishes and in Manchester can be attributed to the eastward movement, since emigration was once more becoming important after the turn of the century.

Between 1911 and 1921 recruitment for wage labour and the military abroad reduced internal migration to its lowest level. The years are notable chiefly for movements away from Trelawny, Manchester and Portland to Clarendon, which was becoming the most important sugar-producing parish.

Dominating all internal migration in the years 1921–43 was the movement towards Kingston. Not only the city but also the suburban parts of St. Andrew grew at a phenomenal rate. While the island increase in population was 44·2 per cent Kingston gained 72·8 and St. Andrew 134·7 per cent. This was due not to a higher birth-rate, which was actually considerably below the island average, but entirely to migration. In fact of the total resident population of the city in 1943 only 43·5 per cent had been born there, and in St. Andrew the proportion was not much higher with 49 per cent.[1]

The city had not always been so attractive to migrants. In the years up to 1861 the decline of the mercantile and professional community had caused an absolute fall in numbers. The population began to increase subsequently with the expansion of government services, though part of the large increase between 1861 and 1871 may have been due to changing boundaries. During the eighties, however, the population of Kingston grew rapidly. During these years workers were already coming in search of employment. The number of domestic servants grew, as did that of the self-employed. No doubt returning emigrants in these years also helped to swell the numbers. With the expansion of banana cultivation in the north-east and renewed opportunities abroad during the following thirty years, however, the attraction of Kingston waned once more. But during the years 1921–43, when both of these had ceased, the trend was again reversed.

Compared with the flow to Kingston and St. Andrew movements to other parts of the island during these years were small. Among them the largest was to Clarendon and, further west, to St. James where sugar production was recovering rapidly. On the other hand, Portland showed the smallest increase of all—only 24 per cent. Banana cultivation in this parish began to be affected by Panama Disease in 1912 and the consequent reduction in acreage reduced employment.

The years 1921 to 1943, therefore, saw a complete change in the pattern of internal migration. Whereas in the first movement, between 1832 and 1861, people left sugar and coffee estates for independent settlement, and in the second, between 1891 and 1911, sugar planting for wage employment on banana estates, they now tended to leave the independent settlement areas to try their luck in Kingston or, to a lesser extent, for wage employment on sugar estates. Of the

[1] CP, 1943.

migrant population of Kingston the greatest number had come from St. Catherine, St. Ann, St. Elizabeth, St. Mary and Manchester. People from these parishes also contributed to the growth of western parishes and Clarendon, while the declining banana planting in Portland encouraged a move to St. Thomas. That the centres of small-settler cultivation were no longer a magnet to migrants is evident in that as many as 95·5 per cent of the population of St. Elizabeth in 1943 had been born in that parish. The proportions for Manchester and St. Ann were also high.

The interesting point about this movement to Kingston and its suburbs is that it was not matched by a similar growth of other urban areas. In 1871 the population of Kingston was 28,847 while the average size of the next thirteen towns was 4,187, of which Annotto Bay was the largest with 10,369 inhabitants. During the following fifty years the gap between the capital and the average size of other towns widened continuously until in 1921 Kingston and Halfway Tree had a population of 88,044 compared with an average of only 3,099 of the next thirteen towns of which the largest, Spanish Town, had only 8,694 inhabitants. Moreover, while Kingston continued to grow the proportion of people living in all other urban areas tended to decline. In 1871 16·4 per cent of the total population lived in the fourteen largest towns; in 1891 this had declined to 12·9 per cent, and although it recovered subsequently it was still only 14·9 per cent in 1921.

We conclude, therefore, that growth of Kingston and suburban St. Andrew was not part of a general trend towards greater urbanization but simply an isolated movement. The movement, moreover, was not in response to real employment opportunities because, as we saw above, there was little development in the city to correspond to the magnitude of the influx. Instead, most of the immigrating labourers found openings in petty trade and domestic service or none at all—but this raises the problem of unemployment to which we return in Ch. 15, D.

CHAPTER 11

THE PLANTATION ECONOMY

THE plantation economy was general in all sugar-growing colonies before emancipation. The freeing of the slaves, however, altered one fundamental part of its structure. In this chapter we shall describe, first, the impact of emancipation on this system, secondly, how it adjusted itself, and then go on to trace its subsequent development.

A. THE PLANTATION ECONOMY IN 1830

The plantation economy became the predominant production system in all the sugar-growing colonies of the British West Indies for three reasons. First, planters could draw on an unlimited supply of unskilled cheap labour, secondly, sugar enjoyed a virtual monopoly in the British market for most of the period and, finally, all consumption and production goods could be obtained cheaply from abroad. Given all these the system was free to acquire characteristic features. A typical sugar estate employed about 200 to 300 slaves in unskilled or semi-skilled work, supervised by a white staff numbering only about five or six. The slaves were divided into gangs, according to age and sex, for various tasks suited to their ability, led by a negro slave-driver. These several gangs were supervised by white book-keepers—a job in which accountancy was the last requirement—who in turn were responsible to overseers or managers. At the top of the hierarchy was the owner or, if absent, his attorney—not usually a lawyer—who was charged with full responsibility for running the estate.

Slaves were paid in kind with imported food and clothing and usually assigned a plot of ground on which to grow their own staple foods. All imported supplies were obtained by planters direct from their British factors, or on credit granted by them, in return for the sole right to dispose of the year's output. Planters were apt to complain about the prices obtained and the commissions charged but, on the whole, the system worked well. The merchants performed a valuable service in providing suitable ships at the time when they were wanted, by advancing duties payable on their produce and selling it in the United Kingdom.

By 1830 severe inroads had already been made into this system. The process of deterioration has been fully described by L. J. Ragatz.[1] Here a résumé will suffice as a background to our account of the impact of emancipation on this system. The first event to affect the plantation economy adversely was the War of Independence which brought the United States within the prohibited clauses of the Navigation Laws. Henceforth the West Indies had to rely on the much more costly supplies from Europe. In Jamaica this does not appear to have had the disastrous consequences it had elsewhere in the Caribbean; in fact the last quarter of the eighteenth century actually saw the most rapid expansion of the Jamaican sugar industry. On the other hand, the abolition of the slave trade affected Jamaica more seriously in that, as we shall see in Ch. 13, A, (i) and (ii), the consequent decrease in the labour force was one of the causes contributing to the decline in output. Even so this did not bring about any fundamental changes. A smaller labour force did not mean increasing real wages because labourers were still tied to their masters. It was the third blow—complete emancipation—that struck at the foundations of the system: once labour was free to choose its employment the ordinary rules of the market governing supply and demand came into operation. Henceforth planters could maintain their labour force only if they offered wages high enough to prevent workers from seeking other employment.

B. The Supply of Labour after 1838

The economic argument against a system of production based on slavery rested on two grounds. First, it was argued that slave labour prevented owners from adopting cost-reducing innovations and, secondly, that slaves worked less 'hard' than free labourers would for the same real income because they had no incentive to do more than the absolute minimum they could be compelled to do. In effect, the argument of the opponents of slavery was that with freedom productivity per worker would rise more steeply than the cost to the employers; hence planters would benefit from larger output, labour from higher real income, as well as liberty, and a new era in the economic life of the island would begin.

[1] *The Fall of the Planter Class in the British Caribbean.*

The first argument has no theoretical foundation. There is no reason why slavery itself should prevent the introduction of labour-saving innovations because slaves cost money just as any other factor of production. If, during slavery, planters did not replace labour by machines the reason was either that the real cost of slaves was lower than that of machines or because the possible future returns from the soil did not warrant long-term investment. Merely to point out that output per man could have been higher with increased mechanization is not proof of the abolitionists' argument because increased output is not necessarily the same as lower production costs.

The validity of the second proposition depends on the supply of labour. If free labour had no alternative opportunities of employment then it would have had to compete for estate employment and thus force real wages down. This appears to have been the result of emancipation in Barbados and some of the other small islands which were already densely populated before 1838 and where all cultivable land was in the hands of large plantations. There, the freed slaves had no alternative but to work for estates and employers managed to keep wages low.

In Jamaica, however, the situation was different. The large estates had never covered more than a portion of the total area of the island and considerable tracts of cultivable land were still available. Thus, in order to prevent the freed slaves from leaving for these lands, estates had to offer wages that were higher than the returns to be obtained from independent cultivation.

The possibility of competing opportunities of employment had already been recognized before emancipation and had indeed been one of the arguments used by planters against emancipation. Faced with the inevitability of emancipation the obvious course for planters should have been the reorganization of the industry to make labour more productive. The estates were given four years' grace (originally six years) during the Apprenticeship instituted to smooth the transition between slavery and complete emancipation.

Unfortunately emancipation began badly in Jamaica. The Apprenticeship was hastily conceived and badly administered and insufficient provisions were made to equip the apprentice for freedom. In the end the System came to represent the remains of shackles to the apprentice and impending ruin to the planter. Its effect varied, of course, in the several islands. Jamaica was noted for its bitterness and niggardliness in interpreting the emancipation laws. One such instance was the withholding of customary 'indulgences'—fish and meal—in order to extort extra labour. The Apprenticeship thus brought estates no nearer a solution of the labour problem. Planters had missed the opportunity to establish new rules of conduct, as, for example, the definition of various responsibilities and their reward. Without such backing 1838 could not fail to be the threshold to even greater problems.

It was not inevitable that labour should have been reluctant to undertake regular work voluntarily. Indeed planters initially had much in their favour; it was widely reported that slaves often had formed deep attachments to their huts and gardens. Nor were there attractive opportunities for alternative employment since independent land settlement was bound to prove difficult. Yet the end of the Apprenticeship saw a great exodus from the estates. This is usually explained in terms of an association in the ex-slave's mind between sugar planting and slavery and the consequent literal interpretation of freedom. But this is hard to believe. Slaves had acquired standards of tastes in food and clothing that presupposed an exchange economy and which complete self-sufficiency in the mountains rendered impossible. On the contrary, had they been assured of attractive wages and conditions of employment there is no reason to suppose that they would not have remained on the estates. As it was, the failure to change production methods and the continuing shortage of cash made it impossible for planters to pay adequate wages.

What was the wage necessary to keep labour on the estates? During the Apprenticeship sugar planters had encouraged apprentices to work longer hours by offering high wages. As much as 2*s*. 6*d*. and 3*s*. 4*d*.[1] currency (1*s*. 6*d*. and 2*s*. sterling) was paid for a day's free labour and apprentices purchasing their freedom had also been valued at 2*s*. 6*d*. currency per day.[2] This rate the labourers accordingly took to be the new wage. But, in fact, such high wages had been possible only because they were for a small part of the work performed: the rest of the labour had been secured under the provisions of the emancipation laws and cost planters no more—and where they succeeded in withholding 'indulgences' even less—than under slavery. Instead, in 1839, planters offered 1*s*. 0½*d*. currency[3] (7½*d*. sterling) per day. But this was unacceptable to the workers.

Unable to secure agreement on wages planters tried other methods of coercing labour. Among them the offsetting of rents of houses

[1] Jamaica—re State of Colony, BPP, 1839 (107), p. 120. [2] *Ibid.* [3] *Ibid.*

against wages and the imposition of penalties redeemable by the labour of every person over ten years of age on the estates caused most bitterness. The result was that workers were all the more anxious to leave. On the 138 sugar estates, for which data are available, the 'resident' labour force had declined from 41,820 in 1832 to 13,973 in 1846.[1] But the actual reduction was even greater because 'resident' includes women and children whose labour was no longer as generally available as it had been formerly. The position on coffee estates was even more serious. Contrary to expectations the labourers preferred sugar to coffee cultivation. Under slavery conditions had been less harsh in coffee than in sugar planting because the former did not lend itself to ganging with its accompanying cruelty. Wages paid in the picking season were also higher than those prevailing in sugar.[2] This unexpected preference was said to be due to the 'advantages during crop-time in sugar' and to the fact that the workers were 'very fond of gathering the cane'.[3] No doubt they still regarded the custom of sucking canes in the field as one of the perquisites of the job. Another reason was the relatively more continuous employment. On sugar estates holing and planting was followed by weeding; in turn succeeded by a three to four months' season of reaping and manufacturing. When this was done the cycle was immediately repeated. In the cultivation of coffee, once the walk was established, the chief task was the picking of the fruit and its processing. Apart from these there were only pruning and weeding, so that the demand for labour during harvest time was about three times that for routine husbandry.

Those who left the estates for independent cultivation often returned for occasional work during slack periods. But, generally, peak production on estates coincided with that on the settlements, and it was at this time that labour was most needed and most difficult to obtain. But even those who remained did not prove satisfactory workers. They refused to bind themselves for regular employment and worked when and for how long they pleased. The institution of payment by task failed as an incentive to greater effort because labourers did what they considered a fair day's work—usually six hours—and no more.[4] More serious was their irregularity. The custom grew up of working only three or four days per week, generally omitting the beginning and end of the week. Both were said to be due

[1] SCP, BPP, 1847–8 (245), App., p. 234.
[2] *Ibid.*, (206), Q. 12,894.
[3] *Ibid.*, Q. 12,893.
[4] *Ibid.*, (167), Q. 4,448.

to a limited standard of living. The workers, so it was asserted, could get all they wanted for three days' work. This, however, is doubtful since workers on similar employment abroad or in other wage employment at home showed no such reluctance to work steadily. It is more probable that the small remuneration offered for extra work was not worth the effort. Undoubtedly, too, the irregularity of payments—shortage of cash was endemic among planters—and arbitrary deductions from wages were contributory factors. G. W. Sewell observed that public works contractors never experienced any difficulty in obtaining labour, which they attributed to the fact that their employees were paid regularly each week while those on estates often had to wait two or three months for their wages.[1] But, whatever the reason, planters could not continue working the estates with an uncertain labour supply. Workers were needed continuously at planting and especially harvesting time. The cane had to be cut when ripe, and once cut had to be processed immediately. With workers available only in the middle of the week they could not reap on Fridays because there were no workers in the factory at the week-end, and they could not prepare the cane for Tuesday's work because no reapers were available on Mondays.

With the failure to obtain a steady labour supply locally, proposals began to be put forward for immigration to fill the gap. Apart from securing a nucleus of dependable labour to keep the estates going it was also hoped that the presence of immigrants would induce more regular habits among the indigenous population. The source of immigrants, however, presented problems. There was no labour available for migration in the other West Indian islands at this time; European labour was neither suitable nor available in sufficient numbers, and plans put forward from time to time for introducing manumitted slaves from the United States were fruitless. Recruitment from Africa was prohibited at first because of the difficulty of ensuring good treatment in the islands and the danger that this might renew the slave trade in the continent. In 1840 permission was obtained to introduce free or liberated Africans for work in the islands. But, as we saw in Ch. 9, C, (ii), not many volunteered and the supply of liberated Africans depended on the volume of the slave trade to the United States and Brazil and the vigilance of the British Navy in the Middle Passage. In the end, West Indian planters had to go as far afield as India for their labour. Permission to recruit East Indians

[1] *Op. cit.*, p. 194.

under indenture was granted in 1845. But again results were disappointing. Mismanagement of finances and recruitment resulted in low numbers and poor selection. Indentured immigration was also an extremely expensive form of supplying labour which not many estates in Jamaica, unlike those in British Guiana and Trinidad, could afford. Unfortunately, information about comparative productivities in these colonies is only indirect. After emancipation the view appears to have become increasingly accepted that sugar planting in the West Indies was more extensive than was justified under competitive conditions[1]—that is, many estates had only been established under the shelter of protection. More specifically we have returns of comparative costs of production during three pre-emancipation years which, since the cost of slaves' maintenance was presumably comparable in these colonies, may be taken to reflect productivity. According to these returns, the cost of producing one hundredweight of sugar was 10*s*. 5½*d*. in Jamaica, 9*s*. 5*d*. in Trinidad and only 6*s*. 6½*d*. in British Guiana;[2] this suggests substantially lower yields in Jamaica than in Trinidad, and especially British Guiana.

We conclude, then, that Jamaican estates failed to get enough labour to maintain their pre-emancipation level of output, first, because they were unable to pay sufficiently high wages and offer conditions attractive enough to local labour to compete with independent settlement, and secondly, because the low productivity of many estates could not bear the burden of indentured immigration. However, once most of the uneconomic estates had been eliminated and employment opportunities outside the plantations failed to expand proportionately to population growth, labour ceased to be a problem.

C. The Problem of Finance after 1838

As long as labour had alternative employment opportunities production costs after emancipation were bound to be higher than under slavery, unless labour costs could be reduced by increased capital investment. But this raised the question of finance.

Before the abolition of slavery the capital needed by the plantations came from within the industry or private persons in the United

[1] SCP (206), Q. 13,402.
[2] *Ibid.*, (184), Q. 9815. The years are not specified.

Kingdom. Production, in spite of the wide variations in annual output, often yielded a considerable surplus above current expenditure, but usually only a small part was ploughed back while the major share was used for debt repayments or invested in the United Kingdom. In *1832* only £83,400 is estimated to have been invested in Jamaican plantations[1]—that is less than 7 per cent of plantation gross profits, most of which were earned in the sugar industry. The huge profits of the prosperous period, moreover, had encouraged a sanguine view of the future, and many proprietors recklessly borrowed money on the security of their estates for consumption or investment abroad. By the 1830's nine-tenths of the estates were said to be mortgaged far beyond their value,[2] with the result that they were already experiencing difficulty in raising even working capital. The receipt of compensation money temporarily eased the problem by providing planters with cash or, where it was swallowed up immediately in debt repayments, by improving their credit standing abroad. Prices, too, were favourable at this time. Sugar prices recovered from their depressed level of 24*s.* per cwt. (London c.i.f.) in 1830 and remained high until 1846. Coffee prices also did not begin their catastrophic decline until the middle 1840's, and rum prices remained favourable for an even longer period (Table XLIII, Ch. 13).

Nevertheless, finance was a perennial problem. The British merchants who, in the past, had been willing to advance short-term capital on the security of the year's output generally continued to do so after emancipation. The great need of estates, however, was for large-scale investment on long-term, and this type of finance merchants were neither equipped nor willing to undertake. Hence planters had to find alternative sources.

The Colonial Bank of the West Indies, with its headquarters in London, was founded in 1836 and the Planters' Bank of Jamaica three years later. Their activities were the usual ones for banking establishments: 'dealing generally in bullion, money and bills of exchange, and lending money on commercial paper and government securities'.[3] They thus performed the useful and much needed service of providing local currency. The Colonial Bank was modelled on the Scottish system of banking, i.e. the granting of credit on personal security, but as far as the planting community was concerned aid to

[1] Ch. 2. [2] Sewell, *op. cit.*, p. 236.
[3] Martin, R. M. *History of the British Empire*, London, 1843, p. 20.

them was restricted by the Bank's charter which explicitly precluded it from lending or advancing money on the security of land, houses or tenements, or upon shops, 'nor to deal in general wares or merchandise of any nature whatsoever'.[1]

This left the private investor in the United Kingdom as the only alternative. In fact, estates owned by absentees had, on the whole, less difficulty in raising capital than those of resident proprietors, thus giving the absentee a better chance of survival than the resident. With the new needs of the sugar industry, moreover, absenteeism ceased to be the great scourge of the plantations. While production relied heavily on manual labour the main requirement of managers was an ability to organize and supervise labour. Production under slavery did not require any formally trained technicians because the methods employed in sugar factories were extremely simple. There was, in fact, every advantage in having the proprietor on the estate because, however ignorant of techniques he may have been, sheer self-interest compelled him to maintain a contented labour force and to avoid waste. Thus where the proprietor chose to return to the United Kingdom the estate was not only burdened with the charges of an additional supervisor but also, because the absentee usually retained only imperfect control over affairs in the island, all sorts of malpractices were encouraged. The evil of absenteeism thus lay in the lack of interest in long-term developments and the failure to ensure that efficient and responsible persons remained in charge. Usually someone as ignorant of techniques as themselves was selected with even less interest in the preservation of the estate. With increasing mechanization in sugar manufacture, however, trained managers were needed. The amateur sugar planter—even at his best—no longer sufficed. For this reason absenteeism was no longer a disadvantage. Indeed it was the first logical step in the separation of ownership and management necessary in a highly capitalized industry.

By the 1840's it was already evident that estates owned by absentees were more efficient than those of residents.[2] The absentee proprietor had better opportunities for obtaining capital provided his property was a sound investment and he could rely on able managers. It is for this reason that British Guiana recovered so quickly during the forties. At the time of emancipation in the colony of Berbice, for example, twenty out of thirty-three estates were owned by residents.[3]

[1] *Ibid.* [2] SCP, e.g. (167), Q. 4506, 5075–81, and (206), Q. 10,845.
[3] SCP, e.g. (167), Q. 4506, 5075–81, and (206), Q. 10,845.

Many of them were unable to survive the immediate effects of emancipation and sold out to absentees, who invested in new equipment and made the property profitable. As a result they could also afford to introduce indentured labour from the Far East.

In Jamaica, too, there is evidence of the greater success of the absentee. The most enterprising of them, a Mr. Price, introduced several innovations and indeed his main difficulty in bringing them into use appears to have been not capital but the conservatism of his local representative.[1] More generally, however, conditions in Jamaica were not so favourable for the transition to greater capitalization partly because all the cane land had been cultivated for several decades, and thus did not provide as attractive an investment opportunity as the comparatively fresh soils of British Guiana, and partly because the soils of many of the estates were in any case too poor to make investment profitable. For these reasons, absentees often did not find it worth while to hang on to their property and, unable to find a willing investor, simply abandoned it. The resident, on the other hand, had no choice and tended to cling to his uneconomic property, with finance as difficult to obtain as ever.

D. The Crisis of 1847

Emancipation thus resulted in a large reduction in the number of estates. Between 1836 and 1846 some 157 sugar estates were abandoned (Table XXXIV). Many of them were uneconomic in the sense that they had been profitable only as long as labour mobility could be restricted, and hence wages controlled. During the forties the plantation economy began to adjust itself slowly to the effects of emancipation. In some cases attempts were made to reduce labour costs by increasing investment. In the two years 1845 and 1846 an average amount of £10,000 was invested in sugar machinery and millwork[2]—a type of equipment unknown in Jamaica a few years earlier. But the sugar industry was still protected from the full force of competition by one factor—market monopoly. This last prop was also to be withdrawn. In 1846 the Sugar Duties Act was passed by the Imperial government, proposing the abolition of all protective duties gradually during the next eight years. News of this blow was followed by the commercial crisis in the succeeding year. In the twelve months

[1] SCP, (167), Q. 5,048.

[2] Exports and Imports (Colonies), BPP, 1852 (144).

from August, 1847, thirteen West India houses went into liquidation,[1] and in 1848 the failure of the Planters' Bank added to the confusion. Credit was unobtainable and investment virtually came to a standstill. Between 1846 and 1850 the London c.i.f. price of sugar fell from 34*s*. 5*d*. to 26*s*. 1*d*. If profits were low before the depression they were dangerously low now. Whereas in *1832* planters' gross profits—that is, deducting prime costs only—on the average amounted to about 56 per cent of the f.o.b. value of output, by *1850* they had fallen to 16·5 per cent.[2] At this level profits were not even large enough to cover capital charges. According to the evidence submitted to the Sugar and Coffee Planting Committee capital charges amounted to 4*s*. 6*d*. per cwt. of sugar in 1846–7.[3] To meet this cost alone profits in *1850* would have had to be at least 25 per cent of gross output. Curtailment of credit and the disastrous fall in prices set off another phase of abandonment. Between 1846 and 1852 a further 86 sugar estates were abandoned. By the time the Jamaican sugar planters had to face free trade, in 1854, the most uneconomic estates had been eliminated and survival of the remainder henceforth depended on their ability to keep abreast of technical improvements.

Coffee estates also continued to be abandoned. In their case, too, protection had over-stimulated production in the past and with increasing world competition there was little incentive to hold on, let alone expand production (Ch. 13, A, (ii)). Statistics on coffee estates are rather contradictory. The Sugar and Coffee Planting Committee[4] gave the reduction in the number of estates between 1832 and 1846 as 465, and the Papers re Sugar Growing Colonies[5] between 184(?) and 1852 as 223. On the other hand, a return[6] for 1836 gave the number of coffee estates at that date as only 387, while another[7] for 1852 returned 248. Part of this discrepancy may be due to different classifications of estates that combined coffee with other cultivations such as ginger, pimento, etc.

The only representative of the large-scale entrepreneur showing signs of expansion during these years was the pen-keeper. The increased demand for draft cattle by sugar estates following the replacement of animal for human motive power after emancipation

[1] Evans, D. M. *The Commercial Crisis 1847–8*, London, 1848, App. LXIX–LXXX.
[2] Chs. 2 and 3.
[3] *Op. cit.*, (245), App., p. 153.
[4] *Op. cit.*, (245), App., p. 255.
[5] BPP, 1852–3 (76), Pt. II, p. 188.
[6] Papers re Abolition of Slavery, BPP, 1836 (166), Pt. III, p. 24.
[7] PAIJ, BPP, 1854 (1848), p. 55.

led to the establishment of new pens. The number of pens increased from 305 in 1836 to 636 in 1852 (Table XXXIV). The continuing abandonment of sugar estates, however, reduced the demand for cattle and pen-keepers subsequently turned to the ancillary products of pimento and logwood and after the 1890's began to concentrate on livestock for human consumption.

E. The Incumbered Estates Court Act

The remaining sugar estates became progressively more indebted as the value of annual output fell short of merchants' advances and, in turn, this came to have serious effects on any attempts to introduce cost-reducing machinery. Not many people were willing to risk their capital when returns on it had to take their place in the queue of a number of prior charges. Nor had the owner the alternative of sale. Because the value of mortgages often exceeded the selling value of the property it was not worth his while to look for a purchaser and creditors could get possession only after costly and lengthy legal proceedings. The result of this impasse was the existence of a large number of unprofitable estates with the eventual prospect of abandonment. To meet the situation the Imperial government passed the West India Incumbered Estates Court Act in 1854, leaving it open to each colony to adopt it. The Act was modelled on the Irish Incumbered Estates Act, which had been designed to relieve a similar situation. It broke through the complicated judicial procedure by enabling estates to be sold summarily by judicial decree on application of the owner or any of the creditors. The success of the measure had been immediate in Ireland, and it was expected to be equally beneficial to the West Indies. There, because few estates had perfect titles, tedious investigations had previously been necessary, but now the sale could be effected in a short time and special provisions were made to avoid interruption of cultivation. The purchaser got a clear title to the estate because the Act provided for the apportionment of the purchase price among the creditors.

Jamaica adopted the Act in 1861. Between December 1862 and July 1863 nine estates containing 7,944 acres had been sold for £9,570, and up to March 1864 another sixteen, comprising 26,779 acres, for £22,560 and a further seven were pending.[1] Thus up to 1865

[1] Cust, J. R. *A Treatise on the West Indian Encumbered Estates Acts*, London, 1865, pp. 312–14.

thirty-two estates had been dealt with under the Act, but since 1852 the number of sugar and coffee estates had declined from 675 to approximately 380 (Table XXXIV).

Helpful as the Incumbered Estates Court was, it could succeed only where indebtedness was the obstacle to improvement. In such a case the new owner, with a clear title, was able to invest capital—especially at this time of rising prices—thus turning the estates once more into a profitable enterprise. The difficulty, however, was finding a purchaser. The man willing to invest capital abroad, previously eager to seize opportunities in the sugar islands, now sought the shelter of corporate finance. Sugar planting was still a lottery—yields still fluctuated—but it no longer promised the rich prizes it had produced under the old Plantation System. Hence progress in the other sugar islands was achieved either with or without the Incumbered Estates Court because there sugar planting became a corporate enterprise. But in Jamaica most estates were too small and amalgamation had to precede corporate finance

F. Beet Sugar Competition

Because Jamaican estates had not been able to take advantage of the Incumbered Estates Court to extricate themselves from the morass of their debts they were all the less prepared to face the consequences of beet sugar competition. Estates which had survived the 1847 crisis and continued production until the 1870's had done so mainly because of favourable prices. There was no change in the structure of the sugar industry and little technical improvement. It was, therefore, still highly vulnerable to adverse price movements as the mortality of estates during the eighties and nineties was to show. The price of sugar began to fall in the early seventies and continued to fall almost without interruption until the turn of the century. Between 1869 and 1896 the number of estates was reduced by nearly one-half from 266 to 146. Their initially straitened financial situation, together with the world-wide loss of confidence in cane sugar, made credit all the more difficult to obtain. The rapid fall in sugar prices during the eighties and nineties, moreover, led to the failure of many West India merchanting houses. In Jamaica the firm of Hawthorn and Watson . . . 'at one time of high standing and credit, [was] not brought down by any outside speculations or undue mercantile operations, but simply by the losses incurred in finding money for carrying on sugar estates'.[1] For Jamaica, United Kingdom mercantile houses at this time still continued to be the chief source of credit. Even with the geographical shift in trade 'they found advances for the cultivation of the estates, and in many instances, block advances, mortgage advances as well and they controlled the products. If [their produce] was sold in America it was sold through their agents and they got a commission.' [2]

The Colonial Bank was at this time still precluded from advancing working capital to estates. It was still the only considerable financial institution in the West Indies and did its chief business with governments, merchants and small depositors.[3]

Temporary relief was afforded to sugar estates by an Imperial grant to the West Indies following the recommendation of the Royal West India Commission of 1897. Jamaica's share of this was £10,000 which was lent to two estates in Westmoreland and St. James for two years which, 'without the aid of advances would have been compelled to go out of cultivation'.[4]

G. Central Factories

Those estates that survived these critical years proved the need for radical reorganization. Although since the 1850's most of the losses of sugar estates had been among the smaller properties, the average size of those remaining in cultivation was still very small. In 1890 the average size was only 187 acres in cane land and the average output of estates' factories 149 tons p.a. (Table LXI, Ch. 14). In order to compete, estates had to be much bigger than this. The transformation of the industry, however, involved two problems: first, to increase the average size, and second, to obtain the capital necessary to finance this reorganization.

The obvious solution to the problem of size was the Central Factory already advocated by Lord Grey half a century earlier.[5] The principle underlying this system was that one large factory should serve a whole cane-growing area. The essential condition, however, was that the area on which the factory could draw for cane supplies should be large enough to keep the plant fully occupied. This could

[1] RWIC, BPP, 1897 (C 8656), Q. 471. [2] *Ibid.*, Q. 473. [3] *Ibid.*, Q. 505.
[4] Col. Rep., BPP, 1904 (Cd. 1768–19), p. 22.
[5] Described in *The Colonial Policy of Lord John Russell's Administration*, London, 1853, but advocated already before then. See, e.g., SCP, (137), Q. 5865.

be achieved either by the amalgamation of existing estates or by contracting with cane farmers for supplies of cane at specified times. The natural conditions for this development were not as favourable in Jamaica as they were, for example, in Cuba and British Guiana with their vast stretches of flat areas. However, such plains as there were in Jamaica were at this time still divided between a dozen or more estates. Considerable economy could thus be achieved by the establishment of one efficient factory in place of several small ones. In short, where the establishment of central factories was feasible it made possible the introduction of superior equipment and it enabled the plant to be used more intensively over a longer period of time.

TABLE XXXIV

Number and Size of Estates 1836–1930

Year	Sugar		Banana		Coffee		Pens
	No.	Size Acres	No.	Size Acres	No.	Size Acres	Number
1836[1] . .	670	n.a.	—	—	343	n.a.	305
1846[2] . .	513	n.a.	—	—	n.a.	n.a.	n.a.
1852[3] . .	427	n.a.	—	—	248	n.a.	636
1865[4] . .	300	n.a.	—	—	80	n.a.	n.a.
1869[5] . .	266	n.a.	—	—	n.a.	n.a.	n.a.
1880[6] . .	202	185	—	—	n.a.	n.a.	n.a.
1890[6] . .	162	187	113*	75*	29	103	n.a.
1900[6] . .	111	196	215	99	34	74	n.a.
1910[6] . .	74	294	435	105	26	112	383
1920[6] . .	66	368	329	123	n.a.	n.a.	354
1930[6] . .	39	661	505	103	19	132	484

* Refers to 1893.

Sources: 1. Papers re Abolition of Slavery, BPP, 1836 (166), p. 24.
2. SCP, BPP, 1847–8 (245), p. 153.
3. PAIJ, BPP, 1854 (1848), p. 55.
4. BBJ, 1865.
5. BBJ 1869.
6. HBJ relating to these years. (From 1880, the numbers shown under sugar refer to factories only.)

The capital needed for the central factory was, of course, beyond the resources of any private investor. Again the obvious solution was corporate finance. Expatriate company finance had been important in the sugar industry of British Guiana since the middle of the century, and in Trinidad had led to the establishment of a central factory as early as 1874.[1] In Jamaica, however, the majority of estates were still owned by private individuals, and as most of these appear to have been residents the problem of external finance was as difficult as ever. The first step towards centralization was, therefore, the amalgamation of adjacent estates into larger units. We do not know when amalgamations first began. The HBJ records six amalgamations in the financial year 1883–4. It seems probable, however, that amalgamations took place much earlier than this. We have already seen that sugar output remained stable for over two decades, beginning in the middle fifties. Yet during the same period the number of estates was reduced from 427 to 266. Since, as we shall see in Ch. 14, B, there is no evidence of any substantial increases in productivity we must conclude that most of the reduction in numbers was accounted for by mergers of adjacent estates.

In the first place, amalgamations involved mainly the combination of cane areas to provide a larger supply of canes for one factory. One of the factories was closed down and the other expanded either by transferring equipment from the disused factory or by adding new plant. But this process did not become general until the turn of the century when two factors gave it encouragement. First, the Brussels Treaty, abolishing all bounty systems, restored confidence in the future of cane sugar. The treaty did not result in an immediate increase in sugar prices, but producers felt that, protected from unfair competition, the prospects of the industry were sufficiently good to make investment worth while. The Jamaican government also gave encouragement to the establishment of central factories under Law 31 of 1902. This provided for government guarantee of interest on the capital of any company 'manufacturing or preparing any of the products of the island'. The law also provided for contracts with cane growers and empowered the companies to enter the lands of contracting growers on breach of contract. In the year 1909–10 two estates in Clarendon were reorganized. Amity Hall drew on Perrins, Pusey Hall, Sutton-Chesterfield and Low Ground, while Morelands estate combined with Hillside-Raymond, Holland estate in St. Elizabeth was re-equipped in the year 1910–11, and in the same year Rose Hall, in St. James, after actually being abandoned, was reclaimed. In 1909–10 there were altogether 74 operating units with an average

[1] The Madeleine Sugar Co. Ltd. Trinidad, 1951, p. 4.

size of 294 cultivated acres, representing an increase in size of more than one-half during the previous twenty years.

H. The Rise of Banana Estates

The difficulties of raising capital for sugar did not apply to banana planting. Once the banana was adopted as an estate crop expansion was rapid. In 1893 there were already 113 estates, and by 1910 the number had reached 435. The reasons for this impressive development were the large profits to be secured from banana planting and the comparatively low capital outlay required. Most of the banana land is situated in Portland and St. Mary, where sugar cultivation was abandoned as unsuitable at an early date. Thus land was cheap, no capital equipment was required and most of the current expenses went into wages which, as a result of large-scale abandonment of sugar plantations and population growth, were low.

The profitability of sugar and banana estates may be compared in the results of our national income calculations given in Part I. For *1890* we have estimated the gross returns to planters (again deducting prime costs only) from banana planting at 47 per cent of the total value of estate output compared with 31 per cent on sugar estates. Since capital charges were a much heavier burden on sugar estates it will be seen that, of the two, banana estates were much the more profitable undertaking.

As a result no difficulty was experienced in finding the necessary capital. Some was provided through corporate channels from the United States, but this was only a small portion of the total: in 1893 the Boston Fruit Company—predecessor of the United Fruit Company—owned only fifteen banana estates out of a total of 113.[1] The main supply of capital came from private internal sources and was, furthermore, usually invested by the saver himself, or in association with other individuals, without going through intermediate channels. Thus while sugar plantations continued to be abandoned for lack of capital in the eighties and nineties, profits from trades and professions began to be invested in bananas.

Most frequently, banana estates were established on land long abandoned or never cultivated. But often also existing sugar estates were turned over directly to banana planting. In the first place, conversions took place mainly in the parishes of St. Mary, Portland, St.

[1] HBJ, 1895.

Thomas, St. Ann and St. Catherine where the suitability of banana cultivation was undoubted. But by 1910 the process had continued beyond this to parts of Trelawny, St. James, Hanover, St. Elizabeth and Clarendon, where the natural conditions for bananas were less favourable, but they still brought in higher returns than the sugar they replaced.[1]

Thus from about 1890 land was no longer abandoned. Most of the subsequent reduction in the number of sugar estates appears to have been the result of either amalgamation or of conversion to banana planting. As shown in Table XXIV, between 1880 and 1910 the number of sugar estates was reduced by 128. Unfortunately, we cannot accurately assess the importance of each factor, as the lists of estates do not always indicate amalgamations and, where conversions took place on change of ownership, we cannot be sure that the property retained the same name. Attention has already been drawn to a number of amalgamations. To judge by the increase in average size, amalgamations must have been considerably more widespread than is indicated in the HBJ. As far as conversions are concerned, it seems that between 1884 and 1911 on at least 59 properties bananas replaced sugar. It appears, therefore, that amalgamations and conversions were equally important in the reduction in the number of sugar estates during the years 1890 and 1910.

In a few cases, estates combined sugar with banana planting. In 1910 there were seven such estates, and here undoubtedly the profits from banana planting had kept sugar production alive during the most difficult years of beet sugar competition and low prices.

Size of estate was not an important factor in the case of banana planting (Table XXIV). The average size of estates increased slowly from 75 acres in 1893 to 123 acres in 1920, but by 1930 it had again been reduced. There was no incentive to plough profits back into estates to increase size or efficiency and hence profits were available for investment in other enterprises.

I. The Recovery of the Sugar Estates

We have seen how the first steps towards reorganization of the sugar industry began to be taken during the depression. At first it took the more modest form of amalgamation of adjacent estates,

[1] HBJ.

but shortly before the outbreak of war the changes were more radical. This process, however, accounted for only part of the reduction in the number of operating units and estates continued to withdraw from sugar planting altogether.

But from the outbreak of World War I the sugar industry began to expand again. During the war the attraction of banana planting declined with the losses resulting from three successive hurricanes and irregular shipping services, while that of sugar increased with rising prices and the assurance of protection after the return of peace. Sugar planting was more attractive in the long run because, although subject to variations, output was never wholly destroyed by adverse weather conditions as was the banana. The relative riskiness of the two industries is, of course, reflected in the level of profits. According to our national income calculations profit margins of both cultivations were lower in *1930* than they were in *1890* at about 10 per cent in sugar and 43 per cent in banana cultivation.[1] But these figures have only very limited usefulness in indicating the relative profitability of the two industries after the war. First, by 1930 sugar prices had fallen much more than banana prices, so that the sugar industry was undoubtedly much more attractive relatively to bananas in 1920 than in 1930. On the other hand, it is not known to what extent planters actually obtained the f.o.b. value of bananas. As the industry was dominated by the United Fruit Company they probably received much less. In fact, the discontent aroused over the exercise of the Company's monopolistic power may well have encouraged the return to sugar planting (Ch. 13, D, (v)). Hence the large difference between sugar and banana profits was perhaps not so great as appears from these estimates.

Let us consider, then, how the expansion of the sugar industry proceeded. As we have seen, the foundations for an efficient industry had been laid in the immediate pre-war years. During the war and subsequently amalgamations and the establishment of central factories continued. In 1920 Frome, for example, combined a total of four former estates and amalgamations had proceeded further also in ten other estates. In the same year, too, a dozen new estate names are included in the list of properties which, together with the extension of acreage, more than balanced—for the first time in about one hundred years—the loss of abandoned estates. The average size of estates was now 368 acres. During the next ten years both

[1] See Ch. 6.

—amalgamations and new estates—account for most of the increase in the average size of estates to 661 acres.

During the early stages towards centralization cane supplies from contracting farmers were also important. Between 1911 and 1921 the number of male cane workers nearly quadrupled from 3,117 to 11,901.[1] If the census returns are to be trusted this means that in 1921 the numbers engaged in cane farming actually exceeded that of workers employed by sugar estates directly. But during the 1920's the number of cane growers, especially among the peasant producers, began to decline. For this the profitability of banana cultivation, together with the low prices paid for canes, were responsible. Payment for canes supplied to the factory was usually fixed at 5 per cent of the selling price of sugar—though in the case of one factory producing for the home market as much as 6–6¼ per cent was paid.[2] The cost of cultivating canes on estates was generally above the prices paid to outside growers, but this was usually balanced by the superior sucrose content of the estate cane.[3]

As long as estates were not large enough to keep their plant fully occupied it was clearly in their interest to continue contracting with outside growers. But in the ten years up to 1930 the average size of estates had increased by four-fifths and with it the need for external supplies declined. In 1929 only about one-third of the cane manutured by factories came from outside growers.[4]

How did the Jamaican sugar industry finance this revolution in its structure in so short a time compared with the other sugar growing colonies? In the introduction to the SSIJ, H. H. Cousins states that up to 1929, with one exception, the re-equipment of all sugar factories had been financed by local enterprise.[5] The investment took place either by combining sugar with banana planting or by going over completely to banana planting for a few years and then reverting to sugar. Of the eighteen new names among the sugar estates in 1930, five had previously planted bananas and two had been abandoned since the 1880's. No previous reference to the remaining eleven has been found. But of the other estates already cultivating sugar in 1920 many had at one time or another combined sugar with banana planting.

According to the lists given in the HBJ changes in ownership of sugar estates were frequent. But in spite of this no definite trend

[1] CP. [2] WISC, BPP, 1930 (Cmd. 3517), p. 117.
[3] SSIJ, J. Govt. Printer, 1929, p. 77. [4] *Ibid.*, p. 38. [5] *Ibid.*, p. 1.

towards corporate finance can be discerned. Most of the owners appear to have been private individuals occasionally associating in partnership with other individuals. Incorporated companies were rare. As far as can be seen from the HBJ only six of the forty factories operating in 1930 were owned by companies. Moreover, apart from the three estates owned by the United Fruit Company, all the others appear to have been owned by Jamaicans.

CHAPTER 12

THE GROWTH OF THE PEASANTRY

WITH emancipation the small-scale cultivator, who had been completely ousted by the slave-owning planters already in the early part of the eighteenth century, reappeared in the Jamaican economy. Unlike his predecessor, however, the new landowner was not European but mainly an emancipated slave. The expansion of this new peasantry proceeded unevenly. In this chapter we shall take each phase in turn and analyse the causes that determined its size and character and attempt to measure its success.

A. GROWTH OF THE PEASANTRY, 1838–65

(i) *The First Settlers*

The first settlement of small proprietors, Sligoville, was founded in 1835 by some free coloured people and those able to commute the remaining term of their Apprenticeship.[1] In 1838 there were already 2,114 persons with holdings of under forty acres each. Three years later the number had increased to 7,919[2] and by 1845 the numbers owning holdings of less than ten acres each had reached 19,397.[3]

The former slaves were able to acquire land in a number of ways. One sprang from the previous practice of planters to reserve that part of the estate which was unsuitable for cane-growing for provision planting. These 'parcels', under the changed conditions, were rented to labourers as part remuneration. But much animosity was caused by this system and planters became willing to sell in an attempt to pacify the labourers and to encourage them to remain near the property. This willingness ceased when it became evident that the independent labourer, not unnaturally, considered his own land to have prior claim on his time. There were, moreover, only few who had been able to save sufficient money during the Apprenticeship to buy land.

Another, and much more important, movement to independent

[1] Mathieson, W. L. *British Slave Emancipation*, London, 1932, p. 67.
[2] PWI, Pt. II, BPP, 1841 (344), p. 228. [3] JA for 1845.

landownership was encouraged by the missionaries. Of these the outstanding personality was the Baptist minister William Knibb. In 1838 he began a series of land purchases on which he settled the freed slaves. After reserving a portion for a chapel he divided the land into plots of between one and three acres each which he resold to the freed slaves. The years 1838–40 were relatively favourable for this policy because export prices were still high and wages had not yet been reduced. Knibb accordingly 'recommended [those wishing to become land-holders] by industry, by frugality, by an attention to their daily work; during the first two years of freedom in which we enjoyed prosperity to secure, if they possibly could, a home for themselves'.[1] Up to 1842 the amount paid for land by settlers was estimated at £70,000.[2]

Local opinion remained hostile to the peasantry. Owners once aware of Knibb's purpose refused to sell land to him, but he usually got round this difficulty by using intermediaries in his negotiations. The House of Assembly also sought to discourage small-scale settler expansion by discriminatory legislation, but most of the proposed measures were disallowed by the home government. Only one, requiring costly licences, for the sale of small quantities of manufactured sugar and coffee, was passed in 1840. According to Knibb, however, this law was 'frequently evaded'.[3]

Knibb's aim was to create complete villages—later known as the Free Village System. His original object was not the creation of a self-sufficient peasantry but rather to provide a solution to the hardship caused by planters' attempts to extort extra labour by charging exorbitant rents against wages. By providing him with a small freehold the settler could 'go to any estate he pleases to work, and to return to his home and family when he has fulfilled as an hireling his day's employ'.[4] By 1842 already the number of such villages was estimated at between 150–200 comprising a total acreage of about 100,000.[5]

The new settlers were, in effect, only part-time peasants. For the most part they continued to work for the estates for about three days during the week, reserving the remaining days for the cultivation of their own plot. On this they grew provisions, raised stock and some

[1] Hinton, J. H. *Memoir of Wm. Knibb*, London, 1849, pp. 485–6.
[2] Phillippo, J. M. *Jamaica: Its Past and Present State*, London, 1843, p. 228.
[3] Sel. Com. on West India Colonies, BPP, 1842 (479), Q. 6011.
[4] Hinton, *op. cit.*, p. 305. [5] Phillippo, J. M., *op. cit.*, p. 228.

of the traditional export crops, while the cash incomes from wage labour enabled them to vary their diet with imported food and to buy clothing and other consumer goods. This combination of wage labour with independent cultivation appears to have been eminently successful. Knibb, himself, was well satisfied with the result. In 1842 he went so far as to express his wish that 'the labouring population [in England] were half as well off as they were in my adopted country —I mean Jamaica'.[1] In the island, too, the success of the movement was acknowledged. In 1841 Sir Charles Metcalfe, the Governor, wrote of the thriving condition of the peasantry as a 'more pleasing feature in the present order of things. . . . I do not suppose that any peasantry in the world have so many comforts, or so much independence or enjoyment'.[2]

These opinions are confirmed by circumstantial evidence. Metcalfe observed that the peasantry were 'dressed in good clothes, and many of them riding on horseback'.[3] Again housing was said by Phillippo to compare favourably with those of the English agricultural labourer.[4] Up to 1842 3,000 cottages were estimated to have been erected at a total cost of £100,000[5] which, at about £33 each, also represented a considerable improvement on the average hut occupied by slaves, the value of which was given at only £12 in 1831.[6]

The village chapel gave spiritual leadership, and the ministers were always ready to take up the cudgels on behalf of their followers. In the island and abroad the Baptists voiced the grievances and hardship suffered at the hand of planters and the Assembly. In return settlers' loyalty was strong. Between 1835 and 1840 Knibb's own three congregations had raised over £11,000 for chapel buildings during the previous five or six years.[7] Two years later total membership of the Baptist Church was 34,000[8] and the contribution for the 'support of the minister, the erection and repair of the chapels, the maintenance of Divine worship and the spread of the Gospel' averaged about 12*s*.,[9] 'affording their ministers a very respectable support'.[10]

In the social sphere, too, Knibb's dream of transforming the ex-slave into a self-respecting free man accepting family obligations, appeared to be coming true. Marriage was said to be general. Phil-

[1] Hinton, *op. cit*., pp. 427–8. [2] PWI, Pt. II. p. 91. [3] *Ibid.*
[4] *Op cit*., p. 220. [5] *Op. cit*., p. 228.
[6] Statement re State of Colonies, BPP, 1830–1 (120), p. 36.
[7] Sel. Com. on West India Colonies, *op. cit*., Q. 6037.
[8] Underhill, E. B. *The West Indies*, London, 1862, p. 430. [9] *Ibid*., p. 429.
[10] PWI, p. 91.

lippo calculated that marriages were taking place at the rate of 14,840 per annum during these years.[1] The women usually stayed at home to look after the household. Neither they nor their children sought gainful employment outside the home. Connected with the churches were usually schools, and parents were most anxious to have their children literate. 'The younger branches of the peasants' family are learning rapidly, reading, writing and arithmetic.' [2] Children were certainly not regarded as a source of income. 'To see a class of children at work in the field . . . is of rare occurrence.' [3]

But prosperity was short-lived. In 1844 a severe drought reduced the yield of ground provisions and caused much hardship among the freeholders. The loss of food crops forced many of them to rely on wage labour entirely, and the resultant wage reductions also meant less opportunity to save for land purchase by the still landless. Income of the Baptist Church also declined. 'Our poor people cannot give', wrote Knibb.[4] Further land purchases by the church were thus also out of the question. In the following year Knibb died, and no other religious leader succeeded him to revive the movement and the growth of the freehold peasantry was temporarily arrested.

(ii) *Squatting*

After Knibb's death the balance of opinion was increasingly tilted against the peasantry. The planters were unanimous about the effect of independent settlement on the supply of wage labour. It reduced the numbers available for work and those that continued to work for wages did so only irregularly. If in their official capacity as legislators the planters ceased to press for measures restricting independent cultivation they also did nothing to encourage it. Roads and bridges were neglected, administration of justice was partial and the fiscal system pressed unfairly on the poorer classes. (See Ch. 16, C.)

In the Mother country the belief was generally held that independence encouraged idleness and paved the way to a return to barbarism. According to the most influential opinion, Thomas Carlyle's, 'Quashee' was naturally lazy and without the compulsion of labour lounged around all day 'sunk to his ears in pumpkin imbibing saccherine juices and much at his ease in Creation'.[5] Lord Grey,

[1] *Op. cit.*, p. 232. [2] PWI, p. 160. [3] *Ibid.*, p. 161. [4] Hinton, *op. cit.*, p. 477.
[5] *An Occasional Discourse on the Nigger Question*, London, 1869. Coll. Works, Essays, 6, vol. II.

supporting the abolition of the West India sugar monopoly, wrote that the preference had enabled planters to pay 'extravagant wages', thus encouraging idleness and hence obstructing 'progress in civilization'.[1] All were agreed that the prosperity of the island depended on the large plantations and that scarcity of labour alone was the cause of their declining profitability. Carlyle's remedy was to compel labourers to work several days per week; that of Lord Grey took the more sophisticated form of taxing the produce of provision grounds and of abolishing customs duties on foodstuffs thereby reducing the demand for peasants' output and hence compelling them to return to the estates. Neither suggestion was adopted. Politically they were impossible and economically it is doubtful whether, by themselves, they could have prolonged the life of plantations.

However, among the workers the desire for independent landholdings continued unabated. Originally only a preference over wage employment, the possession of land became, in time, also an economic necessity. The number of sugar and coffee estates, as we have seen, continued to decline. Employment was thus reduced and wages fell. This, in turn, meant that labourers had fewer opportunities to save for land which, at between £3 and £5 per acre[2] of provision land, was still expensive in relation to wages. Apart from the lack of purchase money, the opportunity for land purchase was also restricted partly because owners were often unwilling to sell land, but chiefly because they themselves no longer had a clear title. Unable to acquire land legally, the would-be peasants were forced to squat.

The attention of the SCP of 1847 was already directed to the problem of squatting. The evidence submitted, however, was confined to vague references and preoccupied with the difficulty of preventing squatting on abandoned properties.[3] From indirect evidence it would appear that the practice was by no means rare even at this early date. First, the geographical distribution of the population shows that the parishes with the largest relative increase in population between 1834 and 1844 were not those where the freehold peasantry had become most important. (See Ch. 10, E.) Secondly, we have estimated that the total numbers engaged in agriculture remained stable between 1834 and 1844 so that the reduction in estate employment must have been offset by increases in the peasantry. Reduction

[1] *The Col. Policy of Lord John Russell's Administration*, p. 60.
[2] SCP, BPP, 1847–8 (167), Q. 6602.
[3] *Ibid.*, e.g. Q. 5128–30 and 6596–9.

in estate employment proceeded from two causes: abandonment of estates and decreasing employment on those estates that remained in cultivation. Unfortunately the problem of estimating this reduction is complicated by lack of meaningful statistics. It was customary for estates to describe as labourers all those who were resident on the properties, i.e. including women and children. Thus the 'resident' labour force on estates abandoned up to 1846 was stated to have been 49,383 in 1832,[1] and on 138 of the sugar estates still in operation in 1846 it was said to have decreased by two-thirds.[2] Applying this reduction in 'residents' to all sugar estates in cultivation in 1846 and adding the numbers thrown out of work through abandonment we get a total decline in estates' 'resident' labour of 153,000. Assuming that only 43 per cent of those resident were working this represents a reduction in estates employment of at least 65,800. This figure is clearly improbable, and is to be explained by the fact that many of those who ceased to reside on estates did not stop working for wages but merely acquired a houseplot outside its boundaries.

Further evidence of the loss of estate labour may be sought in the reduction of average output. Between 1832 and 1846 average output of estates declined from 104 tons to 67 tons.[3] If this decline is typical of all plantation output it represents a decrease in manpower of about two-fifths which, if our estimates of the agricultural labour force in 1834 are accepted, indicates a loss of about 46,000. Here, again, it is difficult to know to what extent estate work was actually spread over the labour force because, as we have already seen, many labourers worked only irregularly. Possibly the decline in the estate labour force was not proportional to the decline in output.

On the whole, it would seem from these various sources that squatting was extensive already in 1846 and although we have not been able to calculate any figures it seems reasonable to assume that the peasantry at this time may have numbered at least 30,000 and probably more and, since the number of freeholds had not increased materially since 1844, squatters must have numbered about 10,000 or more.

Unfortunately we cannot use our national income estimates to check this because our calculations of peasant output include the output of wage labourers cultivating their plots of land in their spare time as well as those who were whole-time peasants—a distinction which was still important at this time but tended to disappear subsequently.

[1] *Ibid.*, (245), App., p. 225. [2] *Ibid.*, p. 234. [3] Table LXI, Ch. 14.

Squatting increased subsequently as estates continued to be abandoned. In 1860 W. G. Sewell estimated the total number of proprietors at 50,000[1] and six years later T. Harvey and W. Brewin put the number of 'freeholders' at 60,000.[2] Both estimates appear reasonable if the authors intended to convey the total number of peasants, irrespective of their title to the land they occupied. As estimates of the number of legal owners, however, they are clearly improbable. We have seen that there were barely 20,000 freeholders in 1845, and that subsequently the number of land purchases can only have been few. That the majority of peasants at this time were squatters is also confirmed by later evidence. Up to the year 1876 the government had recovered 27,000 acres from squatters and it continued to recover more subsequently.[3]

This change in land tenure is important because it also reflects the transformation of the peasant economy from part-time cultivation to self-sufficiency. During William Knibb's time the peasants, as we saw above, depended on estate employment to provide the cash for the goods they were unable to produce themselves. Since sugar prices were still high and consequently also wages, peasants were also prosperous. But by the end of the decade, sugar prices had fallen, wages had been cut and there was less wage employment. Hence the settlers had fewer opportunities to work for estates and when they did obtain employment its return was less. As a result they increasingly had to turn to their own holdings to provide all their income. As before they grew their own staple needs, but in addition they also began to produce more for the domestic market. Any surplus above subsistence needs they sold to the remaining wage labourers on estates or in the towns. In Portland, for instance, they built up a flourishing traffic in yams, cocoes and plantains to Falmouth for sale to workers on the Trelawny sugar estates.[4] But, on the whole, peasants were worse off because lower estate activity reduced not only their income from wage employment but also affected them indirectly by reducing the purchasing power of those remaining on the estates and living in the towns. It was, in fact, only when peasants turned to export crops that their living standards began to improve.

(iii) *The Emergence of the New Peasantry*

With the continuing decline in estate production, the market for

[1] *Op. cit.*, p. 248.
[2] *Op. cit.*
[3] See Section 3 A.
[4] PAIJ, BPP, 1854 (1848), p. 14.

staple foodstuffs also shrank and consequently the peasantry were increasingly driven to export crops to provide them with cash incomes. In this second change in their production pattern, however, they were faced with considerable obstacles. The traditional crops, sugar, rum and coffee, were not ideal for small scale cultivation because they required technical skills and a level of investment far beyond their resources. Because of this, peasant production of sugar was usually confined to the raw cane juice for their own needs. With coffee, on the other hand, they were more successful because although lack of investment reduced the quality of the product it did not make it unmarketable. In fact, most of the increased export of coffee during these years was due to peasant production, and by 1866 their share in total production was estimated at two-thirds.[1] By contrast, the 'minor products'—logwood, arrowroot, fustic, beeswax, honey and coconuts—offered better opportunities because they generally required little processing before sale and hence no investment in equipment. Exports of these commodities in the late fifties were considerably above those in the early 1840's—we cannot unfortunately check this as our returns of quantities begin only in 1850—and according to G. W. Sewell this increase was entirely due to peasant production.[2]

A glimpse of the peasant economy is provided by statistics compiled by the Hanover Society of Industry in 1859.[3] Peasants in that parish, according to these, had, on the average, 2¾ acres each. But nearly one-half owned five acres each. The larger peasants usually cultivated only one acre, leaving the rest fallow or in pasture. But the most interesting finding of the Society was that one acre could produce sufficient ground provisions, sugar, arrowroot, ginger, etc., to yield £30. Since only half of this was retained for domestic consumption, the settlers thus had a substantial cash income which, according to Sewell, was adequate for all their current needs and left a margin for investment in improved dwellings.[4]

B. The Rebellion of 1865

In the three years 1863 to 1865 drought reduced output. This was not the first time that peasants' harvests had been destroyed by drought: in 1844 the effect of a dry season had also been severe. What

[1] Harvey, and Brewin, *op. cit.* [2] *Op. cit.*, p. 249.
[3] Reproduced in *Past and Present State of H.M. Colonies*, BPP, 1861 (2841).
[4] *Op. cit.*, p. 251.

made the situation critical this time, however, was the concurrent higher cost of living and lack of alternative employment. Prices of food and textiles had risen with the outbreak of civil war in North America and peasants no longer had the opportunity of working for estates. Consequently, 'multitudes were suffering from want, little removed from starvation'.[1] This was also evident in the 'ragged and even naked condition of vast numbers of them, so contrary to the taste for dress they usually exhibit'.[2] Predial larceny was also increasing and legal redress was hard to obtain. The Special Magistrates appointed under the Emancipation Act to safeguard the freed slaves had long ago left the island or left office. There had never been enough of them for the work involved, and in many cases justice was partially administered by those magistrates who had been chosen and appointed from amongst the planting interest. Nor did the colonial administration of justice inspire confidence. Petitions to remove injustices received inadequate attention. The official attitude, as exemplified by the Queen's letter sent in reply to the small-holders of St. Ann, who had petitioned for access to Crown lands, was still that prosperity depended on the large plantations.[3]

Discontent caused by poverty and maladministration culminated in insurrection in 1865. It began in Morant Bay, and within a short time spread over the larger part of the eastern parishes. Order was restored quickly and harshly in the course of which 439 people were killed and executed and 1,000 houses destroyed.[4] However, this event led the Colonial Office to acknowledge, what, but for the Assembly's and the Governor's preoccupation with petty squabbles, should have been apparent for some time, that the peasantry was politically important: that in the twenty-seven years since full emancipation 'a large body of ignorant, penniless predials [were] elevated, by their own exertions, to the rank of landed proprietors, tax-payers and voters'.[5] The Governor, Eyre, was recalled, the Assembly was persuaded to surrender its constitution and Crown Colony government replaced a representative government that had never represented anything but a minority.

This change in government is a landmark in the history of the Jamaican peasants because the new government interested itself in them, and immediately set to work on measures which benefited

[1] Papers re Affairs of Jamaica, BPP, 1866 (3595), p. 1. [2] *Ibid.*
[3] *Ibid.*, p. 139. [4] Jamaica Royal Commission, BPP, 1866 (3682), p. 25.
[5] Sewell, *op. cit.*, p. 247.

them. At first it concentrated on improving communications, health and education, and tackled the question of land tenure; but later it began to take more specific steps to encourage peasant expansion, with the land settlement scheme, agricultural education, credit and co-operation.

The new government not only acknowledged the existence of the peasantry, but also the fact that it was making a greater contribution towards the prosperity of the island than the plantations. Addressing the Colonial Institute in 1879 Sir Anthony Musgrave,[1] at the time Governor of Jamaica, described the economic revolution that was taking place in the island. In his words it was 'inconsistent with the facts to suppose that the population are dependent for their present well-being . . . upon the cultivation of sugar estates'. Sugar was employing only five per cent of the population, while most of the remaining agricultural workers were peasants. Moreover, the bulk of the services provided by the government at this time was paid for by the peasants themselves.

The continued decline of sugar and the expansion of banana planting went even further in persuading official opinion that the future was with the peasant. During his administration Sir Henry Blake gave active encouragement to this development by launching the land settlement scheme, founding the Jamaica Agricultural Society and building roads and bridges specifically to give access to the fruit-growing area.

In the depressed condition of the sugar industry, moreover, the dangers of depending on a single export were all too obvious and its slender prospects of recovery, at that time, led the Royal West India Commission of 1897 to recommend further land settlement and diversification of agriculture. 'No other reform affording so good a prospect for the permanent welfare in the future of the West Indies as the settlement of the labouring population on the land as small peasant proprietors.' [2] Thus thirty years after the Queen's letter had advised Jamaicans that prosperity depended 'upon their working for wages, not uncertainly or capriciously, but steadily and continuously',[3] the commission was saying that the 'existence of a class of small proprietors among the population is a source of both economic and political strength'. [4]

[1] *Jamaica: Now and 15 Years Since*. Proceedings of the Royal Colonial Institute, 1879–80, vol. XI.
[2] BPP, 1897 (C 8655), p. 18.
[3] Papers re Affairs of Jamaica, BPP, 1866 (3595), p. 136.
[4] *Op. cit.*, p. 17.

C. The Growth of the Peasantry 1865–1930

Between 1860 and 1930 the number of small settlers increased more than threefold. The statistics of landholdings (Table XXXV) are not very satisfactory in indicating the growth of the peasantry because, being compiled from taxation returns, they show only those properties on which the holdings tax had been paid. That these tended to diverge from the actual number is evident in the considerable fluctuations in the under-five-acres group—the class most likely to have a poor tax-paying record. It was in fact the large number of

TABLE XXXV

Number of Landholdings of less than Fifty Acres each 1838–1930

Year	Under 5 Acres	5–49 Acres	Total Number of Holdings under 50 acres
1838[1]	n.a.	n.a.	2,114*
1841[1]	n.a.	n.a.	7,919*
1845[2]	n.a.	n.a.	19,397†
1860[3]	n.a.	n.a.	50,000
1866[4]	n.a.	n.a.	60,000
1880[5]	36,756	13,189	49,945
1890[5]	95,942	16,015	111,957
1895[5]	70,740	16,887	87,627
1899[5]	60,671	16,160	76,831
1902[5]	108,943	24,226	133,169
1930[5]	153,406	31,038	184,444

* Less than 40 acres each.
† Less than 10 acres each.

Sources: 1. PWI, BPP, 1841, Pt. II, Jamaica (344), p. 228.
2. JA, 1845.
3. Sewell, *op. cit.*, p. 248.
4. Harvey, and Brewin, *op. cit.*
5. HBJ for these years.

arrears in this group during the nineties that finally led to the change in the method of taxation in 1902. The new method was based on the value of the property and as a result no statistics comparable to the previous ones are available except for 1930.

Taking only those years which returned large numbers, on the assumption that the shortcomings in other years were due to nonpayment of taxes, we see that there was a fairly steady expansion in landholdings of less than fifty acres each from about 112,000 in 1890 to 133,000 in 1902 and further to 184,000 in 1930. There are two noteworthy features about this expansion. First, it was greater than population growth. Taking the number of peasants as a proportion of total population we see that the ratio rose from about 11 per cent in 1860 to 17·5 per cent in 1890 and again to 18 per cent in 1930. In terms of working population the rise was even faster—namely from about 26 per cent in 1860 to 45 per cent in 1930. Secondly, there was a relatively greater increase in the number of the large landholders. Those cultivating between five and fifty acres each increased from about 13,000 in 1880 to 16,000 in 1890 and again to 24,000 twelve years later; that is they increased their share in the total under 50-acres group in the twelve years beginning in 1890 from 14 per cent to 18 per cent. Subsequently, however, the growth in the smaller holdings was relatively greater so that by 1930 the share of the 5–49 acres group had fallen back slightly to 17 per cent.

The growing numerical importance of the peasantry was also accompanied by a spectacular rise in their share in output. The share of small-settlers in total agricultural output rose from about half in *1850* to nearly three-quarters in *1890*. During the subsequent forty years, however, it failed to keep pace with expansion in total agricultural output, mainly as a result of the relatively greater growth in estates' output of animal products, and consequently by *1930* their share had declined to 68 per cent.

We conclude that the expansion of the peasantry after 1865, in terms both of output and numbers, was rapid. We turn next to the reasons for this remarkable expansion.

(i) *Land Registration and Land Settlement*

In 1867 Sir J. P. Grant set up a Lands Department to investigate the title of all doubtful holdings and in the same year began a series of legislations designed to recover all lands in illegal possession. In many cases, however, land occupied by squatters had been abandoned for a considerable number of years and as a result it was often impossible to discover any title. The laws that were passed accordingly envisaged two approaches to the problem: one was the eviction of those unable to prove a good title to the land they were occupying and the other the declaration of forfeit land for which no quit rent or land taxes had been paid. Where no owner was apparent, the District Court Law enabled the government to take possession of the land provisionally and lease it to the squatters. A period of seven years was allowed for the rightful owner to establish his claim; if none came forward the Crown had the right to sell the land.

By 1876–7, 26,925 acres of land had already been recovered from squatters and nearly all of these lands were rented out by the government on seven-year leases.[1] The squatters were glad to exchange their precarious possession for a good lease at a fair rent. 'In no instance has the enforcement of this law given rise to any complaint. On the contrary, it seems an acceptable measure to all parties.' [2] As a result of the summary process of dealing with illegal occupation, squatting decreased. Another reason was attributed to the increased value of land following the expansion of banana planting which made landowners 'more watchful and look better after their land'.[3] In 1890 only 267¾ acres were recovered from 37 squatters.[4]

Owing to imperfections in the original law the procedure for declaring forfeit land on which no quit rent or land taxes had been paid could not be implemented until Law 5 of 1871 had been passed. But during the subsequent five years nearly 90,000 acres had reverted to the Crown.[5] Action thereafter was again slow and the law had to be amended again in 1884 and in 1888 to simplify forfeiture of land. Under the previous law 'the chances of proceedings being vitiated by errors, trivial in themselves, occurring in the preliminary stages, . . . had prevented the enforcement of forfeitures for many years, and large arrears of these cases had subsequently accumulated'.[6] The several laws were consolidated and simplified in 1896. By 1912 240,368 acres had reverted to the Crown:[7] of these 128,000 had been forfeited between 1894 and 1901 alone.[8]

Thus by the end of the 1870's considerable tracts of land had already reverted to the Crown. The government itself required only small tracts of land for specific purposes such as railway building. The renting of land was proving an undesirable policy as rent payments frequently fell into arrear. Moreover, like squatting, it discouraged good husbandry as the tenant would plant the land to exhaustion and then look for fresh land to repeat the same process. On the other hand, there were few would-be settlers who could

[1] Report in BBJ, BPP, 1879 (C 2444). [2] *Ibid.*, 1873 (C 709).
[3] BBJ, 1890. [4] *Ibid.* [5] Report in BBJ, (C BPP, 1879 2444).
[6] Col. Rep., BPP, 1890 (C 6621–1), p. 3. [7] Jamaica in 1912.
[8] Col. Rep., BPP, 1902 (Cd. 788–43).

afford to buy land outright nor were there any financial institutions to advance the purchase price. It was, therefore, left to the government to initiate a method for the disposal of Crown lands.

In 1895 Sir Henry Blake introduced a scheme under which Crown lands could be bought in lots of between 5 and 50 acres each. The purchaser had to pay one-fifth of the price but was allowed ten years in which to pay the remaining four-fifths interest free. In the interests of sound agriculture the settler was encouraged to cultivate permanent crops with an offer to remit one-fifth of the purchase price if within ten years he had brought one-fifth of his holding under permanent crops.[1] The scheme met with an immediate response. In the first year 'numerous applications were received'. But at first nothing was sold because 'applicants did not fully understand the conditions and others applied for purchase of land not yet forfeited to the Crown'.[2] Four years later 1,177 lots had been sold under the scheme and although payment of the instalments was not always prompt the point of forfeiture had been reached in only sixteen cases.[3] The price of government land, ranging between 15*s*. and 30*s*., with an average of £1 per acre, compared favourably with that of between £1 and £6 per acre for private land.[4] By 1902–3 the total number of settlers under the scheme had reached 1,889 covering 20,088½ acres. Of these 687 acres had reverted to the Crown; most of these were in the 'White Limestone districts, where low prices had affected the principal product, coffee, or in places where access was tedious or difficult'.[5] By 1909 a total of 30,751 acres had been sold under the scheme but of these only about 6,000 acres had been paid for in full by some 600 purchasers, while 9,000 acres had either been taken back for failure to pay instalments or where chronically in arrear. The Collector-General thought it best to proceed 'very slowly and cautiously in the matter of instalment sales, seeing that of the acreage now out on credit about 25 per cent is chronically in arrear or taken back'.[6] In 1909, 1910 and 1911 no more fresh lands were opened up under the scheme.

On the whole, the response to the land settlement scheme was disappointing. The number of plots sold during the first seven years of the scheme—1,889—was considerably less than the increase of

[1] Rules as to Sale of Lands by the Government of Jamaica to Small Settlers, J. Govt. Printer (no date).

[2] Col. Rep., BPP, 1897 (C 8279–14), p. 13.

[3] Col. Rep. 1902 (Cd. 788–21), p. 27.

[4] RWIC, *op. cit.* (C 8669), No. 759.

[5] Col. Rep., BPP, 1904 (Cd. 1768–19).

[6] Col. Rep., BPP, 1911 (Cd. 4964–36).

7,339 in the 5–50 acres group, shown in Table XXXV. According to these figures, it appears that the majority of the settlers bought or rented land independently. The reason for this is not far to seek. Peasants wanted to grow bananas and land suitable for this crop was not likely to be forfeited to the Crown once their owners recognized its value. Hence most of the land available under the scheme was either unsuited to banana cultivation or in remote areas without adequate access.

Sir Henry Blake had already begun to deal with the problem of building roads during his term of office. Recognizing the importance of the fruit trade he abandoned his predecessors' policy of providing roads and bridges for the sugar industry in favour of that of the banana.[1] The task, however, was formidable and the financial straits of the public treasury at the turn of the century brought public works to a temporary standstill. In 1902 the policy of opening up fresh lands had to be modified and sales were henceforth restricted to lands to which access was already provided.[2]

Subsequently, other amendments were made to the scheme. In 1916 selection of the settler was sought to be improved by requiring a recommendation from the applicant and by offering remission of part of the purchase price only if a 'suitable dwelling house' was erected in addition to the establishment of one-fifth of the area in permanent crops. In the same year the upper limit of holdings was raised from 50 to 300 acres.[3] By 1920 the total acreage sold under the scheme had risen to 40,452 and of these only 1,573 acres had been taken back for failure to pay instalments.[4]

One drawback, however, remained. Land available under the scheme came into the possession of the government only through forfeiture and this meant that it was usually poor. It was with the object of making more suitable land available that the government took two important steps after the war. The first, in 1920, was to grant powers, and lend public funds, to Agricultural Loan Banks for the purchase and resale of land to small settlers. This met with an immediate response. Between 1920 and 1926 the Loan Banks had dealt with 14,283 acres for resettlement.[5] The second step was the purchase and breaking up of large properties by the government

[1] Further Correspondence re Public Finances, BPP, 1900 (Cd. 125).
[2] Col. Rep., BPP, 1902 (Cd. 788–43), p. 42.
[3] Revised Rules. Quoted in HBJ.
[4] Col. Rep., BPP, 1920 (Cmd. 508–8), p. 4.
[5] HBJ, 1828, p. 413.

directly. In 1923 Spring Gardens in St. Thomas, containing 746 acres, was bought and resold to 236 settlers.[1] This was followed in 1929 by the purchase of Kelletts containing 5,065 acres[2] and in the following year by those of Tobolski and Monklands with 2,050 and 1,500 acres respectively.[3]

(ii) *Techniques*

The traditional method of cultivation employed by the peasantry is usually described as 'firestick agriculture'. This involves the clearing of virgin land by burning followed by continuous planting, without rotation or artificial aids, until soil exhaustion or erosion reduced yields to such an extent that land had to be abandoned. While land was freely available the consequences could be avoided by moving on to fresh land but with increasing population this became increasingly difficult.

The problem of improving peasant agriculture received official attention from time to time but the task of setting up agencies with sufficient resources to experiment with different techniques, to disseminate the results and persuade the peasant to adopt them was, as we shall see below, formidable and one for which no satisfactory solution was found. The problem of peasant cultivation is, of course, quite different from that of estates. The latter are best equipped for monoculture because they can reap the advantages of large-scale production and because they usually have sufficient resources to take the risks of cyclical harvest failures. The ideal policy for the peasant by contrast is that of mixed cultivation. Not only does this reduce the risk of harvest failure but it also needs very much less capital, an important consideration for peasants. By growing a variety of products the peasant can assure himself and his family a basic food supply all the year round and, by selling any surplus, increase his standard of living by purchasing those consumer goods and production materials which he is unable to produce himself. But this policy also has technical advantages to recommend it: the judicious combination of crops can ensure a healthy soil and by using sheltering plants which, themselves, yield economic crops—e.g. the ackee—the more tender growths such as cocoa and coffee can be protected.

However, for most of the time the peasants were left to themselves to experiment with different crops and techniques. We have already

[1] Col. Rep. HMSO, 1930 (Col. No. 1509), p. 14. [2] *Ibid.*
[3] *Ibid.*, 1931 (Col. No. 1550).

seen that there was no difficulty in persuading them to adopt new crops. With techniques, however, improvements were slow. Plantation work had prepared them for only the simplest routine husbandry and the crude techniques in use in the sugar factories in the pre-emancipation era. Technical training was introduced into the school curriculum in 1867 but, apart from the fact that the schools offered places to only a small proportion of the child population (see Ch. 15, B), the quality of the teaching of technical subjects as that of general subjects was poor. These technical schools did not prove popular with parents because they too often attempted to teach subjects which were unrelated to their needs or they merely reproduced the everyday drudgery of the small-holding in the school grounds. In 1877 the industrial schools were written off as 'entire failures'.[1]

In view of this poor background it is surprising that the peasantry succeeded so well in growing export crops. In some cases they even made a positive contribution to agricultural knowledge as when, for example, they exposed the long-held fallacy of the inevitability of soil exhaustion in coffee growing. One settler giving evidence before the RWIC in 1896 described how with manure he brought under cultivation land that had been abandoned for fifty years by its owner as 'exhausted'.[2]

Where crops required processing the peasants encountered even greater obstacles. Lack of capital and the small size of output prevented the acquisition of efficient equipment. For extracting cane juice the use of 'Jim Crow' mills was widespread. In 1870 5,615 such mills were said to be in use.[3] They were very primitive constructions—their value was estimated at only £10 each[4]—operated manually and of course very wasteful. In 1892 it was reported that an improved type of mill was being imported[5] but no further details are available. As with estates, the answer to the problem was central factories. For sugar the solution was increasingly found in concentrating on cultivation and selling the canes to the central factories. In the case of coffee, too, the advantages of selling the green beans to central factories was increasingly recognized. In 1896 two factories —one at Petersfield and one at Chesterfield—were operating on this basis.[6]

[1] Educational Systems of the Chief Colonies of the British Empire, BPP, 1901 (Cd. 416), p. 581.
[2] *Op. cit.* (C 8669), Q. 1277.
[3] Report with BBJ, BPP, 1873 (C 709).
[4] Hanover Society of Industry, *op. cit.*
[5] Col. Rep., BPP, 1894 (C 7319–1).
[6] RWIC, (C 8669), Q. 1,222.

(iii) *Agricultural Research and the Spread of Knowledge*

The first step to improve agricultural techniques among the peasantry was taken in 1893. In that year a travelling instructor was appointed to teach the peasantry improved methods of agriculture.[1] Subsequently several members of the Department of Agriculture were seconded to this work. With the inauguration of the Land Settlement scheme a more specific approach was necessary and in 1895 Sir Henry Blake established the Jamaica Agricultural Society 'to collect and disseminate useful information, encourage the improved cultivation of products and better breeds of stock; and to watch over the interests of the Agricultural Industry generally'.[2] In 1902 it became the declared policy of the government to aim at an agricultural revolution.[3] This was to be brought about by lectures, demonstrations and competitions. The responsibility for achieving this revolution was left to the Jamaica Agricultural Society which had begun field work shortly after its formation. Until 1909, in fact, both bodies—the Department of Agriculture and the Jamaica Agricultural Society—maintained separate services but in that year it was decided to delegate the whole work to the Agricultural Society.

To facilitate contact with the peasant the Society set up a system of branch societies. In 1897 six branches had already been formed. The number increased rapidly thereafter and by 1935 had reached 298.[4] It also began publishing a monthly journal in 1897 which was circulated to all members. Agricultural instruction, however, continued to suffer from lack of funds and adequately trained personnel. The Agricultural Society had been launched with only £1,000 p.a. and although this amount was raised to £4,000 two years later it was still totally inadequate for the work involved.[5] In 1910 there were only eleven instructors covering the whole island and by 1935 their number had risen to only twenty-one[6] at a time when the peasantry numbered nearly 200,000. Apart from this inadequacy in numbers, the qualifications of instructors were not always up to the standard

[1] Rep. Com. on the Department of Agriculture, J. Govt. Printer, 1914, p. 50.
[2] The Jamaica Agricultural Society, *Journal of the Jamaica Agricultural Society*, 1938, vol. XLII, p. 530.
[3] Col. Rep., BPP, 1902 (Cd. 788–43), p. 50.
[4] Girvan, D. T. M. *The Jamaican Agricultural Society 1895–1951*, typescript, p. 26.
[5] *Op. cit.*, p. 537. [6] *Op. cit.*

required. The Society had no sound basis for instructing the peasantry in their special problems because it did no research itself and what research was done by the Department of Agriculture—and most of that was not concerned with the problems of small-scale cultivation—was not easily accessible to them. The blurred division of responsibility between the two bodies, moreover, caused some overlapping of services and in the 1930's it began to be felt that so important a service should be part of the government and not left to an outside agency. There was also the difficulty that actual membership of the Society fell far short of the potential. Though total membership had risen relatively rapidly during the early years to 4,000 in 1910 it failed to increase sufficiently thereafter.[1] By 1935 there were still only 7,568 members.[2] Accordingly in 1932 the first of a series of steps was taken to secure closer co-ordination culminating finally in the transfer of the extension service to the Department of Agriculture in 1951.

The most valuable aspect of the Society's work was its encouragement of a spirit of independence and self-help among the peasantry. Through the organization of branch societies it laid the basis for co-operation and taught its members useful crafts such as improved methods of housebuilding, higher standards of housekeeping and domestic crafts. In fact the strength of the Society lay in 'those attributes which made for good citizenship'.[3]

(iv) *The Co-operative Movement*

We have already seen that co-operation began to play an important part in land settlement during the 1920's. The formation of People's Co-operative Loan Banks was first facilitated by the Industrial and Providential Societies Law of 1902.[4] The main stimulus, however, came with the enactment of Law 6 of 1912[5] under which public funds were made available to Loan Banks for lending to their members. According to the HBJ twenty-four societies were registered in the years between 1912 and 1914 and the number continued to increase subsequently until in 1928 there were forty with a paid-up capital of £38,674.[6]

The scope of the Loan Banks included the advance of money for co-operative, agricultural and industrial purposes. There is, unfor-

[1] *Op. cit.* [2] *Ibid.* [3] *Op. cit.*, p. 541. [4] Law 33 of 1902.
[5] The Agricultural Loan Societies Law. [6] HBJ, 1928, pp. 412–13.

tunately, little information about their activities. It was said that several societies were well managed and that they performed a useful service in assisting peasants with cheap credit.[1] Generally, however, the demand for short-term credit does not appear to have been very great owing to the widespread cultivation of bananas which kept peasants supplied with funds all the year round.[2] Among those societies borrowing money from the government, the purchase of land for resale thus became the predominant activity.

The formation of co-operatives for the marketing of crops, on the other hand, did not gather strength until after the war. The need for it had been apparent among banana producers since the 1890's when the United Fruit Company had virtually become the sole buyer of fruit in the island. Various attempts were made to protect the producer from exploitation but these took the form of providing alternative shipping and marketing outlets and not the organization of producers. (See Ch. 13, D, (v).)

The movement towards co-operative marketing first received encouragement from the experiment of the DiGiorgi Fruit Corporation. This company introduced the novel scheme of guaranteeing a fixed price for all fruit supplied by contracting growers together with an additional payment of 50 per cent of all profits realized by the Corporation from the sale of fruit.[3] The fact that the DiGiorgi Fruit Corporation succeeded in retaining the loyalty of its contracting growers in the face of the United Fruit Company's competition gave encouragement to those favouring co-operative marketing among small producers.

In 1925 the Imperial Economic Committee recommended the establishment of a Jamaica Co-operative Association and of a Direct Line between Jamaica and Great Britain and granted £1,200 for two years to help in the formation of the Association.[4] Two years later the Jamaica Banana Producers Association was formed and within six months contracts for fruit were signed with over 7,000 growers covering more than 36,000 acres of banana cultivation.[5] In order to aid the establishment of the Direct Line the Jamaican government guaranteed the issue of £200,000 and the Colonial Development Fund advanced £50,000 in 1931.[6] In 1929 the Jamaica Direct Fruit

[1] WISC, Pt. IV, HMSO, 1930 (Col. No. 49), p. 78.
[2] WISC, BPP, 1930 (Cmd. 3517), p. 118.
[3] Petition of the JBPA, mimeograph, 1935, p. 16.
[4] Rept. of the JBC, J. Govt. Printer, 1936, p. 66.
[5] Petition of the JBPA, p. 20.
[6] Rept. of the JBC, p. 66.

Line, Ltd., established by the Jamaica Banana Producers Association in association with the DiGiorgi Fruit Corporation, came into existence. The disastrous experience of the first Direct Line also led the Jamaican government to pass the Jamaica Co-operative Marketing Association Protection Law[1] which, apart from making provisions for dealing with disloyal contractors, also made the local manager of competing fruit companies personally liable if his company persistently purchased and exported produce subject to co-operative marketing contract. In the first year of operation the JBPA handled nearly 24 per cent of exports and two years later, in 1931, this had risen to 34 per cent.[2]

It soon became apparent that the United Fruit Company was not going to tolerate the growth of such a powerful competitor. The Company set about discrediting the Association with its customers in the United Kingdom and it also resorted to its former tactics of diverting supplies from the Association's ships by raising prices temporarily and by destroying the confidence of contractual growers in the financial integrity of the Association. In practice the protective legislation proved a dead letter as in no case was it possible to establish a case against the manager where his agents or sub-agents had bought supplies from the Association's contractual growers.[3] As a result, supplies to the Association began to fall off and, after the 1933 hurricane, difficulties were again experienced in filling the Association's ships. The conflict was finally resolved with an agreement between the Association and the United Fruit Company under which the Association was to be reformed as an ordinary trading company. This agreement was followed by an undertaking by the fruit companies to contribute towards a fund which eventually led to the establishment of Jamaica Welfare, Ltd.

The initial success of the JBPA encouraged the formation of co-operative marketing associations for other crops. In 1929, four associations were established dealing with fruit and vegetables, citrus, dairy products and pimento.

(v) *Predial Larceny*

The problem of predial larceny, like that of illegitimacy, is a recurrent subject in the literature of Jamaica. Both are said to have their origin in slavery and both have been held responsible for

[1] Law 5 of 1928.
[2] Rept. of the JBC, App. C.
[2] Petition of the JBPA, p. 48.

poverty and its attendant evils thereafter. According to the RWIC of 1897, for example, predial larceny was ranked equally important with technical inefficiency as the 'drawback to the system of peasant proprietorship'.[1] The subject, therefore, deserves examination.

Predial larceny means the stealing of growing crops and small stock. It is reported to have been increasing since the 1850's but statistics of convictions were considered to be an imperfect guide to its prevalence because 'detections bear no proportion to commissions'.[2] The penalty of proved larceny, flogging for a second conviction, had been imposed by Governor Eyre, but since offenders were seldom caught its imposition was rare. In 1869 a new approach was made by appointing resident householders as rural headmen of police. 'It was thought that the creation of some system whereby a body of detectives could be formed who would be of the people and living among the people, was likely to be of some use in the repression of this inveterate evil.'[3] In spite of this the number of offences continued to grow. The Produce Protection Law 37 of 1896 represented an attempt to check the offence from the receiving end. It restricted the sale of produce to certain hours of the day, and required each person carrying on the business of buying and selling, or of buying and exporting, agricultural produce to take out a licence. It also required that certain produce when in transit be accompanied by a form giving particulars as well as the name of the owner of the property from which the produce was dispatched. With only a third of the population literate this must certainly have been a difficult law to enforce. A second measure passed together with the Produce Protection Law gave power to anyone to detain any person found in possession of any article under suspicious circumstances, and enabled a judge to inflict the punishment of flogging on habitual stealers of produce. This, not surprisingly, was disallowed. The casual roadside buying and selling of produce had already been prohibited under Act 32 of 1889 but had to be repealed because, instead of fulfilling its purpose, it tended to restrict legitimate trade.[4]

In 1883 it was claimed that only one-twentieth of all cases were brought into court,[5] and in spite of the various measures adopted the number of convictions for larceny continued to fall short of the

[1] *Op. cit.* (C 8655), p. 18. [2] PAIJ, BPP, 1854 (1848), p. 34.
[3] Col. Rep., BPP, 1870 (C 151).
[4] Col. Rep., BPP, 1895 (C 7629–17), p. 105.
[5] Royal Commission on Public Expenditure, etc., BPP, 1884 (C 3840).

incidence. In 1901 there were 1,137 convictions but in the following year only 651.[1] The decline was attributed to 'the better condition of the peasantry, increased severity of magistrates, greater activity of the rural police and more plentiful employment on estates'.[2] But in 1907 the number had again risen to 2,542.[3] In 1908 it was 2,510 but in the following year had again dropped to 1,303.[4] Once more the decline was due 'to the improved economic conditions generally prevailing throughout the island'.

Evidence of the damage caused by this type of theft is very conflicting. Evidence before the RWIC in 1897 ranged between accounts of complete stripping of grounds and an occasional theft by a starving man. Mr. Gossett, a coffee planter, complained that grapefruit he was cultivating was being stolen 'so much that I can hardly keep them on the trees. I have some very good ones, but it is extremely difficult to prevent them being stolen.' And further that stealing was 'for sale. Before there was a market they would not touch them. Now they sweep off most of the crop in one night.'[5] The same hazard was said to be encountered by peasants growing oranges for export. 'The fruit is green . . . because if they leave fruit on the trees it is stolen.'[6]

Other witnesses held different opinions. The Rev. S. C. Morris did 'not think that there is really very much reason for the hue and cry against petty larceny in this country. That there are petty thieves I do not all deny . . . but considering all the circumstances surrounding the lower classes, the wonder is, that this evil is not more widespread. Careful observation will show that the evil is more observable in those districts where the people are placed in the most unfavourable and disadvantageous circumstances, and it is very often just to relieve present crushing want. That our people are *thieves* as is commonly said, is by no means true. Take for instance the unprotected way in which cultivations of all classes or sorts are kept in this country. Large acreages of canes, bananas and coconuts, left unprotected in all parts of the island, a great temptation to the poor people, and yet how seldom do they trouble them.'[7]

If theft was confined to small quantities it is understandable that peasants did not co-operate in catching the culprit. In that case, however, the crime cannot have deterred them from taking

[1] Col. Rep., BPP, 1904 (Cd. 1768–19), p. 68. [2] *Ibid.*
[3] Col. Rep., BPP, 1911 (Cd. 4964–36), p. 27. [4] *Ibid.*
[5] *Op. cit.* (C 8669), Q. 1241–2. [6] *Ibid.*, Q. 2413. [7] *Ibid.*, No. 774.

advantage of the land settlement scheme or other facilities open to them to improve their cultivation. In fact the average value assigned to the stolen property in 2,349 cases brought into court in 1905 amounted to only 1·03*s.*[1] The argument that larceny was an important factor in discouraging land settlement is finally robbed of all conviction by the fact that settlement was made so easy. Such a scheme should have eliminated all necessity to steal because of want. The fact that larceny continued in spite of the land policy suggests that there was something about the scheme itself that prevented it from being the panacea that had been intended.

(vi) *Gross Profits and the Pattern of Production*

In Table XXXVI we have estimated the gross return to peasants from cultivation for export and for domestic market. It should be

TABLE XXXVI

Total and Per Capita Gross Profits from Peasant Cultivation

Year	Total Gross Profits Current Prices £'000	No. of Peasants* '000	Per Capita Current Prices £	Gross Profits *1910* Prices £
1850	927·1	n.a.	—	—
1890	3,079·8	112·0	27·5	26·0
1930	6,044·9	184·4	32·8	26·2

* Number cultivating less than 50 acres each.
Sources: Chs. 3, 7 and 9, and Table XXXV.

noted that the estimates of gross profit include the value of output produced by agricultural labourers in their spare time. They are thus not strictly comparable with the number of peasants. However, this difference between output and employment became less important after the middle of the century and is not likely to affect the results for *1890* and *1930* appreciably. Gross profits are estimated to have increased more than three-fold between *1850* and *1890* and, again, nearly doubled during the following forty years (Table XXXVI). Per capita gross profits increased from nearly £28 to £33 between *1890* and *1930* but most of this increase appears to have been the result of rising prices.

[1] Col. Rep., BPP, 1907 (Cd. 3285–11), p. 28.

This increase in gross profits was mainly the result of the larger share of exports in peasants' output. The peasants' share in exports increased nearly four-fold between *1850* and *1890* and continued to

TABLE XXXVII

The Share of the Peasantry in Export Crops

Year	Total Value of Export Crops*	Value of Peasants' Exports	Share of the Peasantry in Exports
	£'000	£'000	%
1850 . . .	1,089·3	113·5	10·4
1890 . . .	2,048·3	798·8	39·0
1930 . . .	4,691·6	1,940·8	41·4

* Includes value of export crops retained for domestic consumption.
Sources: Chs. 3, 5 and 7.

increase slightly subsequently (Table XXXVII). The years between *1850* and *1890* thus saw a dramatic change in the pattern of peasant production. In *1850*, 83 per cent of their output consisted of subsistence food—ground provisions—and only 11 per cent of exports (Table XXXVIII); in *1890* the share of subsistence food had dropped to 74 per cent and that of exports risen to 23 per cent. Subsequently the trend towards greater diversification continued but at a reduced rate so that by *1930* the share of ground provisions had dropped only slightly further to 69 per cent and that of exports had risen to 27 per cent.

In Chs. 3, 5 and 7, we have attempted to separate the shares of peasants and of estates in the several export crops. From this it emerges that the total value of peasants' output increased at first mainly as a result of expansion in coffee, logwood and banana production and to a lesser extent due to increases in the 'minor' crops. By *1890*, in fact, the share of peasant production was greater than that of estates in the case of coffee, about equal in the case of logwood and about one-third in the case of bananas. Only in sugar production did the peasant output lag considerably behind that of estates. For *1930* the peasants' share is again estimated at about half for the minor products and considerably below estate production in sugar, but the gap between the respective shares in banana output had been narrowed with peasant production accounting for nearly 44 per cent of the total.

Increasing prosperity of the peasantry is thus seen to be mainly due to their growing share in export crops. This was made possible by the introduction of crops suited to their scale of production and to their techniques rather than by improvements in techniques or

TABLE XXXVIII

The Pattern of Peasant Production

	1850 %	*1890* %	*1930* %
1. Ground Provisions	83	74	69
2. Export Crops*	11	23	27
3. Animal Products	6	3	4
	100	100	100

* Includes export crops retained for domestic consumption.
Source: Chs. 3, 5 and 7.

by the institution of the government land settlement scheme. As we have seen there is little evidence of higher productivity as a result of improved methods of cultivation or equipment, and only relatively few peasants took advantage of the land settlement scheme. The importance of the new constitution lay in the government's attitude in the wider sense: its encouragement of peasant expansion, protection of their interests—as in their struggle with the banana monopoly—the formation of the Jamaica Agricultural Society and the provision of public works.

CHAPTER 13

EXTERNAL TRADE

IN Ch. 10 we saw that there was little change in the importance of the major sectors of the economy but that there were some important changes within some of these sectors. These intra-industrial shifts were, as shown in Chs. 11 and 12, linked to changes in the structure of production. Our next task is to relate these changes to the level of external trade in commodities and the balance of payments. In the first section we shall show how much of total output was devoted to exports and account for changes in this ratio by tracing the histories of the different export crops. The second section deals with the terms of trade and the third with changes in the level and composition of imports. As external trade also depends on treaties and tariffs we devote the following section to changes in the geographical pattern of trade. The chapter concludes with an account of capital movements.

A. EXPORTS

Before emancipation the Jamaican economy was dominated by the export trade. The total value of domestic exports accounted for about 44 per cent of total output in *1832* (Table XXXIX). The ratio of exports to Gross Domestic Product was probably even higher at the beginning of the century because quantities of sugar and coffee exports during the 1830's were below those of the second and third decade and there is, at the same time, no evidence that production for the home market had expanded in the intervening years.

After 1838, however, the importance of the export trade declined sharply. Abolition of slavery caused a reduction in the labour force on the plantations and this resulted in a huge fall in estate production affecting all the major export crops. Taking three-year averages to eliminate seasonal fluctuations, we see from Table XLII that sugar exports declined by about two-fifths between 1838 and 1840, coffee by about one-quarter and rum exports by about one-third.

Adjustment to the effects of emancipation had hardly begun when the estate economy was further affected, first by news of the ending of the sugar monopoly and secondly by the commercial crisis of 1847. As a result exports of sugar and coffee continued to decline while that of rum was merely halted. By *1850* the value of exports had reached its depth with £923,600, accounting for only 24 per cent of total output.

Exports began to recover again only during the early 1850's. Prices of sugar, coffee and rum started to rise in 1853 and continued to be favourable for about two decades thereafter. As a result estate

TABLE XXXIX

Exports and National Income

Year	(1) Total Value of Domestic Exports* at Current Prices £'000	(2) Total Value of Domestic Exports* at *1910* Prices† £'000	(3) Exports as Percentage of G.D.P. at Current Prices %
1832	2,193·4	1,889·2	43·5
1850	923·6	806·6	24·3
1870	1,144·2	965·6	20·2
1890	1,670·7	1,323·9	19·1
1910	2,568·1	2,568·1	22·6
1930	3,957·8	3,565·6	19·8

* Includes the value of imported production materials.
† For method of computing exports at *1910* prices see Appendix I.
Sources: Chs. 2–7.

production ceased to decline. The increase in exports that took place during the 1850's and 1860's, however, was due to expansion of peasant production of coffee and some of the minor products. In the twenty years beginning 1851, again taking three-year averages, pimento and ginger exports increased by about two-fifths, coffee by about two-thirds and logwood, most of all, about twenty-fold. Recovery was thus brought about only by a change in the composition of exports. The share of sugar in exports had fallen to less than 45 per cent in *1870* from nearly 60 per cent in *1832* (Table XLI). Coffee exports, on the other hand, had risen to over 14 per cent after their sharp decline to 10 per cent in *1850* but the biggest increase had taken place in the share of the minor products which had more than

TABLE XL

Composition of Domestic Exports

(current value) £'000

	1832	1850	1870	1890	1910	1930
Sugar . .	1,304·3	537·2	509·2	245·3	209·2	484·4
Coffee . .	403·7	95·1	172·8	304·0	149·6	199·1
Rum . . .	299·7	193·6	221·7	208·3	152·9	70·5
Pimento . .	90·1	48·6	30·5	66·5	75·1	216·4
Logwood .	37·9	11·1	170·0	353·5	72·5	56·1
Ginger . .	18·5	20·5	13·7	30·5	46·8	45·5
Bananas . .			0·9	319·7	1,334·0	2,267·7
Oranges . .			0·6	46·5	43·9	11·7
Coconuts .			3·0	26·7	77·4	144·6
Cocoa . .				12·2	91·5	82·8
Logwood Extract .					147·6	82·2
Grapefruit .						55·1
Other. . .	39·2	17·5	21·8	57·5	167·5	241·7
Total . . .	2,193·4	923·6	1,144·2	1,670·7	2,568·0	3,957·8

Sources: Chs. 2–7.

TABLE XLI

The Shares of the Major Exports in Total Domestic Exports

	1832	*1850*	*1870*	*1890*	*1910*	*1930*
	%	%	%	%	%	%
Sugar . . .	59·5	58·2	44·5	14·7	8·1	12·2
Coffee . . .	18·4	10·3	15·1	18·2	5·8	5·0
Rum . . .	13·7	20·9	19·3	12·5	6·0	1·8
Bananas . .	—	—	0·1	19·1	52·0	57·3
Miscellaneous	8·4	10·6	21·0	35·5	28·1	23·7
	100·0	100·0	100·0	100·0	100·0	100·0

Source: Table XL.

doubled in the years between *1850* and *1870*. All the same, the expansion of exports of coffee and the minor products was not as rapid as population growth and hence the ratio of exports to total output continued to decline and by *1870* had fallen to about 20 per cent.

During the 1870's the export trade received another blow from beet-sugar competition. The price of sugar began to fall rapidly in 1873 and continued to fall until the turn of the century and as a result sugar production began to decline once more. The quantity of sugar exports fell by about 43 per cent during the thirty years beginning in 1871—again taking three-year averages. Coffee and rum exports, on the other hand, remained at around the same level. That the total value of exports continued to grow during these years was due in part to the continued growth in logwood exports, but even more so to the banana trade. From its first appearance in the export list in 1869, the export of bananas grew rapidly so that by *1890* already it accounted for over 19 per cent of total exports; its share, in fact, being exceeded only by that of logwood.

It was, however, only after *1890* that exports began to rise faster than total output. This was almost entirely the result of an even greater rate of increase in banana exports. There were also small increases in pimento and ginger exports. But all other exports declined: sugar continued to fall until 1913 and rum and coffee exports also began to decline with the deterioration of the market during the 1890's.

After World War I banana exports continued to expand relative to total exports until in *1930* they accounted for over 57 per cent of the total. There were also increases in exports of sugar, cocoa and ginger but exports of logwood declined while those of coffee remained stable.

We conclude then that the share of exports in total output declined until *1890*, first because of the huge fall in sugar, coffee and rum exports, and, after *1850*, because the recovery in coffee and the expansion in other crops was not sufficient to keep pace with population growth. The increase in the ratio after *1890*, on the other hand, was the result mainly of the rapid expansion of banana exports.

If we eliminate price changes, as shown in column 2, Table XXXIX, we see that the quantities of exports rose more slowly than values between *1870* and *1890* but more quickly thereafter. This suggests that after *1870* changes in prices were not completely offset by changes in composition. But this question will be taken up in Section B. Our next task here is to trace the histories of the major export crops.

TABLE XLII

Quantities of Major Commodities Exported in the Years 1814 to 1931

Year	Sugar '000 cwt.	Coffee '000 cwt.	Rum '000 glns.	Logwood '000 tons	Pimento '000 lb.	Ginger '000 lb.	Bananas '000 stems	Oranges No. million	Coconuts '000	Cocoa '000 cwt.
1814 . .	1,448	304·0	—	—	—	—	—	—	—	—
5 . .	1,593	244·3	—	—	—	—	—	—	—	—
6 . .	1,389	154·4	—	—	—	—	—	—	—	—
7 . .	1,717	132·1	—	—	—	—	—	—	—	—
8 . .	1,653	226·2	—	—	—	—	—	—	—	—
9 . .	1,614	125·8	—	—	—	—	—	—	—	—
1820 . .	1,769	197·6	—	—	—	—	—	—	—	—
1 . .	1,680	150·2	—	—	—	—	—	—	—	—
2 . .	1,414	176·6	—	—	—	—	—	—	—	—
3 . .	1,418	181·5	—	—	—	—	—	—	—	—
4 . .	1,451	247·1	—	—	—	—	—	—	—	—
5 . .	1,115	189·8	—	—	—	—	—	—	—	—
6 . .	1,501	181·7	—	—	—	—	—	—	—	—
7 . .	1,211	229·8	—	—	—	—	—	—	—	—
8 . .	1,364	198·4	—	—	—	—	—	—	—	—
9 . .	1,386	198·6	—	—	—	—	—	—	—	—
1830 . .	1,379	198·7	3,214	—	—	—	—	—	—	—
1 . .	1,396	125·5	3,523	—	—	—	—	—	—	—
2 . .	1,432	176·9	2,757	—	—	—	—	—	—	—
3 . .	1,257	88·1	3,220	—	—	—	—	—	—	—
4 . .	1,256	158·3	2,924	—	—	—	—	—	—	—
5 . .	1,149	94·6	2,450	—	—	—	—	—	—	—
6 . .	1,054	120·1	2,117	—	—	—	—	—	—	—
7 . .	904	86·3	2,050	—	—	—	—	—	—	—

1838 . .	1,053	111·5	2,304	—	—	—	—	—	—	—
9 . .	765	84·1	1,654	—	—	—	—	—	—	—
1840 . .	517	76·9	1,294	—	—	—	—	—	—	—
1 . .	528	68·0	1,277	—	—	—	—	—	—	—
2 . .	779	62·6	1,975	—	—	—	—	—	—	—
3 . .	660	56·5	1,628	—	—	—	—	—	—	—
4 . .	530	65·5	1,147	—	—	—	—	—	—	—
5 . .	743	45·4	1,746	—	—	—	—	—	—	—
6 . .	573	53·7	1,487	—	—	—	—	—	—	—
7 . .	751	58·7	2,141	—	—	—	—	—	—	—
8 . .	627	44·2	2,280	—	—	—	—	—	—	—
9 . .	633	30·4	1,779	—	—	—	—	—	—	—
1850 . .	575	37·1	1,121	4·3	3,363	799	—	—	—	—
1 . .	486	49·9	1,661	3·8	4,318	569	—	—	—	—
2 . .	537	49·9	1,281	3·2	5,312	616	—	—	—	—
3 . .	421	43·1	998	3·9	4,612	477	—	—	—	—
4 . .	559	54·7	1,666	7·7	5,509	678	—	—	—	—
5 . .	515	50·6	1,757	8·3	8,598	594	—	—	—	—
6 . .	458	33·2	1,304	18·3	6,465	421	—	—	—	—
7 . .	550	60·4	1,545	21·4	20,012	443	—	—	—	—
8 . .	627	53·1	1,612	14·3	7,875	376	—	—	—	—
9 . .	542	45·1	1,553	13·1	3,683	752	—	—	—	—
1860 . .	600	55·1	1,705	14·7	6,850	842	—	—	—	—
1 . .	655	60·0	1,897	19·4	6,648	617	—	—	—	—
2 . .	615	48·8	1,830	33·3	4,916	933	—	—	—	—
3 . .	560	73·3	1,554	27·8	6,228	678	—	—	—	—
4 . .	522	37·0	1,281	25·4	7,686	699	—	—	—	—
5 . .	484	55·6	1,410	22·4	3,862	1,020	—	—	—	—
6 . .	601	76·0	1,770	34·6	4,866	1,550	—	—	—	—
7 . .	516	55·9	1,732	44·1	7,596	1,728	—	—	—	—
8 . .	637	70·1	2,928	44·3	4,373	2,037	—	—	—	—
9 . .	492	49·1	1,464	114·8	6,575	1,262	—	—	—	—
1870* . .	523	86·4	1,420	84·7	5,243	680	—	—	—	—

TABLE XLII—(*continued*)

Year	Sugar '000 cwt.	Coffee '000 cwt.	Rum '000 glns.	Logwood '000 tons	Pimento '000 lb.	Ginger '000 lb.	Bananas '000 stems	Oranges No. million	Coconuts '000	Cocoa '000 cwt.
1871 . .	629	50·1	1,628	57·7	6,858	632	—	—	—	—
2 . .	604	84·8	1,690	77·9	5,341	600	—	—	—	—
3 . .	483	64·3	1,309	50·4	6,025	816	—	—	—	—
4 . .	483	92·4	1,655	62·8	5,761	1,182	n.a.	—	—	—
5 . .	473	63·7	1,794	80·9	6,440	1,491	n.a.	4·7	—	—
6 . .	494	77·8	3,084	75·0	4,475	1,604	133	10·0	—	—
7 . .	520	85·1	1,735	46·8	6,761	1,098	163	8·2	—	—
8 . .	443	85	1,522	35·2	6,195	909	313	10·2	—	—
9 . .	496	97	1,580	55·4	5,881	770	n.a.	9·4	—	—
1880 . .	546	91	1,561	46·3	10,215	890	n.a.	14·6	—	—
1 . .	358	88	1,172	43·5	6,058	780	n.a.	23·6	—	—
2 . .	653	66	1,909	30·3	8,515	664	888	35·5	2,764	—
3 . .	616	84	2,009	29·8	9,552	837	938	34·2	3,760	—
4 . .	589	48	2,036	44·9	12,373	1,359	1,843	41·6	5,440	—
5 . .	500	81	2,199	56·6	9·794	1,379	1,417	22·6	5,116	—
6 . .	329	55	1,476	63·5	6,919	1,293	1,662	38·9	3,712	—
7 . .	461	59	2,413	58·9	7,336	1,112	1,460	42·4	2,400	—
8 . .	490	99	1,869	100·9	7,455	1,145	3,093	47·4	5,913	—
9 . .	323	85	1,375	115·5	5,172	1,003	2,881	35·4	4,832	—
1890† .	378	76	1,594	109·3	10,121	1,219	4,848	40·7	8,555	—
1 . .	426	87	1,705	86·7	7,138	1,823	3,503	19·4	7,858	5·5
2 . .	372	97	1,698	92·6	7,806	1,527	4,180	23·2	6,979	8·5
3 . .	411	88	1,461	89·7	9,834	1,672	5,163	12·4	9,171	10·3
4 . .	399	95	1,956	76·3	9,403	1,736	4,678	30·0	10,144	9·3
5 . .	391	84	1,881	84·5	9,408	1,961	4,221	97·0	9,443	10·3
6 . .	321	67	1,643	43·1	10,897	1,234	4,839	103·7	11,802	9·2
7 . .	284	85	1,379	42·6	11,155	1,408	6,982	88·0	11,534	16·0
8 . .	361	110	1,564	43·4	4,345	1,702	7,497	107·2	11,968	21·0
9 . .	390	84	1,569	28·9	8,725	2,263	8,046	107·4	18,012	20·0
[illegible]	[illegible]	[illegible]	[illegible]	[illegible]	[illegible]	[illegible]	[illegible]	[illegible]	[illegible]	[illegible]

1901 . .	322	103	1,422	41·1	11,236	2,391	11,004	79·1	17,663	40·0
2 . .	406	108	1,927	37·9	8,075	3,263	14,184	98·6	25,624	31·5
3 . .	270	80	1,294	42·3	12,880	3,171	7,803	82·6	14,951	22·0
4 . .	198	52	1,234	30·0	7,963	2,465	8,904	73·1	4,246	23·5
5 . .	239	81	1,131	29·5	17,281	2,218	14,981	74·5	7,092	31·1
6 . .	279	55	1,463	30·0	10,270	2,017	16,010	55·2	11,064	47·6
7 . .	212	94	1,312	30·3	9,553	1,780	13,943	64·8	13,744	47·5
8 . .	123	70	1,245	21·6	8,277	2,319	14,613	35·9	11,131	49·1
9‡ . .	198	74	1,653	25·4	24,573	2,352	16,712	33·1	13,401	59·5
1910 . .	399	87	1,347	30·1	12,376	2,651	14,095	47·3	18,094	35·0
1 . .	401	60	1,145	40·8	12,936	3,361	16,497	42·0	20,453	53·6
2 . .	198	90	895	37·3	12,040	2,824	13,382	30·7	22,949	65·7
3 . .	98	58	954	50·1	15,187	2,378	11,598	45·9	23,770	46·4
4 . .	308	80	1,113	52·1	9,665	2,158	16,202	14·7	29,124	72·3
5 . .	303	64	1,309	47·8	11,648	1,291	8,157	24·0	27,330	68·5
6 . .	567	66	1,798	75·1	7,145	1,908	3,450	13·9	27,181	64·4
7 . .	640	51	418	36·0	9,040	2,370	2,395	5·3	23,363	56·8
8 . .	533	91	191	15·5	6,409	3,017	3,201	5·3	14,211	59·3
9 . .	753	74	3,059	20·3	13,125	2,050	9,674	10·5	24,283	70·2
1920 . .	733	41	744	32·6	7,563	1,635	9,037	18·1	28,246	50·4
1 . .	537	65	959	4·5	9,015	1,384	9,959	n.a.	24,224	65·0
2 . .	1,013	63	809	25·4	11,499	1,474	12,714	12·5	30,401	76·8
3 . .	515	77	538	19·4	10,508	3,814	12,454	15·1	23,706	43·1
4 . .	458	52	730	22·9	9,075	1,725	11,971	12·2	21,567	59·2
5 . .	754	104	1,121	22·4	13,764	2,386	15,017	16·0	26,381	52·3
6 . .	963	66	693	30·2	8,658	3,069	18,301	18·7	23,041	60·2
7 . .	996	82	741	25·6	9,864	2,789	21,152	12·9	33,179	57·3
8 . .	974	79	807	27·9	8,653	2,370	17,081	9·8	31,105	45·0
9 . .	748	59	810	21·0	9,039	2,129	22,048	1·6	39,918	60·0
1930 . .	1,007	61	678	16·2	9,523	2,486	24,597	4·0	31,190	60·6
1 . .	886	82	409	18·8	12,215	1,997	22,336	5·3	35,716	52·9

* Year ended 30th September. † Year ended 31st March. ‡ Year ended 31st December.

Sources: *a.* Sugar, coffee and rum: 1830, Sel. Com. on East India Produce, BPP, 1840 (527), pp. 598–600. 1831–49, Sugar, etc., BPP, 1854 (237). 1850–1931, Statistical Abstracts for the Colonies.

b. Logwood, pimento, bananas, oranges, coconuts and ginger: 1850–1931, or as available in the Statistical Abstracts.

c. Cocoa: 1891–1912, STC. 1913–1931, Statistical Abstracts for the Colonies.

TABLE XLIII

Prices of the Major Exports in the Years 1830 to 1931

Year	Sugar *s.* per cwt.	Coffee *s.* per cwt.	Rum *s.* per gallon	Logwood *s.* per ton.	Pimento *d.* per lb.	Bananas *s.* per stem	Cocoa *s.* per cwt.
1830	24	60	2·89	n.a.	n.a.		
1	24	72	2·82	—	—		
2	28	91	2·88	—	—		
3	29	96	2·93	—	--		
4	32	94	3.03	—	—		
5	32	104	3·16	—	—		
6	41	105	3·81	—	—		
7	35	113	4·04	—	—		
8	35	110	4·22	—	—		
9	36	122	5·40	—	—		
1840	48	116	5·12	—	—		
1	41	102	4·52	—	—		
2	37	93	4·78	—	—		
3	33	86	n.a.	—	—		
4	35	84	2·68	—	—		
5	33	78	3·54	100	3·2		
6	33	52	3·65	92	3·8		
7	27	49	4·57	89	5·0		
8	20	40	3·75	81	3·9		
9	22	47	3·09	90	4·1		
1850	23	56	3·04	81	6·0		
1	23	50	3·00	70	5·0		
2	20	51	2·79	66	5·0		
3	22	56	3·68	99	6·1		
4	20	55	5·01	139	5·7		
5	24	56	4·34	109	5·2		
6	28	58	3·96	125	4·8		
7	34	67	4·76	102	4·6		
8	24	63	4·31	105	3·3		
9	23	67	4·20	90	3·2		
1860	24	68	4·08	91	3·6		
1	22	69	3·66	102	3·7		
2	20	81	3·18	116	3·0		
3	21	81	2·78	97	2·9		
4	26	77	3·05	86	2·5		
5	22	78	3·31	77	2·6		
6	21	79	3·18	92	2·6		
7	22	76	3·15	77	2·1		
8	22	71	3·13	89	2·2		
9	24	71	3·19	115	2·3		
1870	23	64	3·65	101	2·1		
1	25·5	67	3·67	100	2.3		
2	25·5	79	3·74	103	3·2		
3	25·5	100	4·09	104	2·8		

Year	Sugar *s.* per cwt.	Coffee *s.* per cwt.	Rum *s.* per gallon	Logwood *s.* per ton	Pimento *d.* per lb.	Bananas *s.* per stem	Cocoa *s.* per cwt.
1874	21·5	112	4·35	112·0	3·2		
5	20·0	105	4·08	131·2	3·1		
6	21·5	105	3·58	124·4	3·6		
7	24·5	102	3·17	113·4	4·1		
8	20·0	101	2·76	108·4	4·5		
9	19·0	90	2·76	114·6	5·0		
1880	20·5	87	2·87	120·8	4·6	1·75	
1	21·25	80	3·39	102·5	4·9	2·08	
2	20·0	65	3·24	103·4	3·9	2·00	40
3	19·0	76	2·78	106·2	3·3	2·00	38
4	13·25	62	2·63	105·2	2·6	2·00	40
5	13·5	60	2·80	99·4	2·3	n.a.	37·5
6	11·75	68	2·71	96·6	2·5	2·00	45
7	11·75	90	2·67	109·2	2·3	2·00	43
8	13·0	80	2.30	126·4	2·5	1·75	40
9	16·0	95	2·42	122·1	3·0	1·75	36
1890	13·0	101	2·73	121·5	2·4	1.83	45
1	13·5	101	3·52	116·3	2·5	1·50	45
2	13·5	104	2·79	122·4	2·8	1·63	50
3	14·25	103	2·48	141·6	2·9	1·83	52·5
4	11·25	102	2·27	144·8	2·7	1·83	44
5	10·0	98	2·13	124·4	2·6	1·50	34
6	10·75	95	2·43	122·0	2·4	1·25	33·3
7	9·25	95	2·01	103·8	2·8	1·25	46·8
8	9·5	92	1·96	106·4	4·6	1·25	50·8
9	10·5	90	2·22	101·8	3·9	1·50	60
1900	11·25	75	2·65	96·6	3·3	1·50	35
1	9·25	70	2·56	100·2	2·7	1·50	42
2	7·25	70	2·17	93·0	2·9	1·58	41·5
3	8·5	70	2·10	86·2	2·8	1·50	37·8
4	10·25	75	2.15	85·8	3·3	1·16	34·8
5	11·0	75	2·27	89·0	2·5	1·13	34·0
6	8·5	75	2·40	90·4	2·7	1·10	46·3
7	9·0	75	2·83	98·4	2·8	1·49	64·0
8	9·75	66	3·66	95·4	2·3	1·43	37
9	10·25	70	3.83	95·0	2·2	1·68	37
1910	11·0	69	3·11	97·0	2·3	1·62	36
1	11·5	83	3·19	101·6	2·3	1·77	37·8
2	11·0	87	3·40	106·6	2·6	1.86	42·6
3	9·5	81	4·19	103·4	2·3	1·70	49·5
4	11·75	79	4·13	110·0	2·0	1·94	42·3
5	14·5	79	5·05	130·8	2·1	1·47	59·7
6	24·25	78	6·83	295·0	3·3	1·29	52
7	31·5	95	10·80	235·0	4·0	1·90	41·5
8	33·0	128	n.a.	400·0	5·7	1·86	52
9	38·5	146	n.a.	318·4	5·1	2·36	81·7
1920	58·0	148	—	390·0	4·9	3·40	69·3
1	19·5	121	—	318·4	2·8	3·05	29·5

TABLE XLIII—*continued*

Year	Sugar *s.* per cwt.	Coffee *s.* per cwt.	Rum *s.* per gallon	Logwood *s.* per ton	Pimento *d.* per lb.	Bananas *s.* per stem	Cocoa *s.* per cwt.
1922	15·0	121	—	218·4	2·2	3·33	36·2
3	25·5	118	—	183·4	2·3	4·34	27·0
4	23·5	153	—	170·0	3·2	3·01	27·9
5	16·25	154	—	160·4	4·7	2·92	36·8
6	17·5	155	—	153·4	7·0	3·24	41·5
7	16·5	144	—	n.a.	8·2	3·46	55·2
8	13·5	144	—	—	9·1	3·36	44·3
9	11·25	141	—	—	n.a.	3.51	34·3
1930	8·75	107	—	—	—	2·66	24·2
1	7·75	101	—	—	—	2·65	17·2

Sugar, coffee, rum, logwood and pimento prices are c.i.f. London. Banana and cocoa prices are f.o.b. Jamaica.

Sources: *a.* Sugar and coffee: 1830–44, Prince's Price Current quoted by Tooke, T. and Newmarch, W., *History of Prices*, London, 1838–57, vols. 2, 3 and 4. 1845–1931, Sauerbeck, A. 'Wholesale Prices of Commodities', *Journal of the Royal Statistical Society*.

b. Rum, logwood and pimento: Calculated in the same manner as by Sauerbeck: i.e. an arithmetic average of monthly price quotations published in the *Economist*. Quotations cease for rum in 1917, for logwood in 1926 and for pimento in 1928.

c. Bananas and cocoa: Up to 1913, STC. 1913–31, BBJ.

(i) *Sugar and Rum*

Exports of sugar declined from about 1·4 million cwt. in 1830 to about half that quantity ten years later (Table XLII). This decline, however, was not a new development. Looking at exports before 1830 we see that the decline was already evident in the early 1820's when output began to fall from the 1·7 million cwt. level which in turn represented a considerable reduction from the previous peak of 2·4 million cwt. achieved in 1805.[1]

Indeed, to judge by the experience of other sugar colonies such a diminution in output was to be expected. The history of the sugar colonies in the Caribbean since their settlement from east of the Atlantic is one of fluctuating fortunes. As each island was settled and opened up for sugar planting it quickly reached peak production, declined and gave way to a younger colony. The oldest—Barbados—

[1] RWIC, BPP, 1897 (C 8655), p. 139. The actual quantity is given as 150,352 Hhds. The weight of a hogshead varied greatly during the century. Here we have taken the ratio of 1 Hhd. = 16 cwt.

had been the first to experience diminishing returns. Then came the turn of the smaller islands, St. Kitts, Nevis and Antigua. Much later, towards the end of the eighteenth century, Jamaica reached her Golden Age of sugar planting. The decline after a brief span of prosperity was generally found to be due to widespread absenteeism resulting in poor management, antiquated techniques and capital withdrawal.

But in Jamaica this sequence was especially disastrous because the peak came so shortly before the abolition of the slave trade and thus prevented the introduction and maintenance of an adequate force. As we have already seen the slave population began to decline after 1808 and in the years 1817–34 alone fell by 10 per cent. Half of the decline in sugar exports in this period can therefore be attributed to the smaller labour force. In addition, the high prices ruling during the Napoleonic Wars had stimulated production beyond the normal geographical boundaries of sugar planting. The record crop in 1805 was not again approached for another 140 years and then only as a result of considerable technical progress. The earlier record clearly could only have been achieved by planting the less suitable areas and these were the first to be abandoned with the return of peace.

A certain diminution was thus inevitable with the return to normal trading patterns and a declining population. Nor is there any reason why Jamaica should not have followed the cycle of prosperity and decline already so familiar elsewhere in the Caribbean. But because of emancipation the decline became much more rapid than it would have been otherwise. The accelerated downward trend of the 1830's is all the more remarkable in that most of it actually occurred before 1838—the year when emancipation became fully effective. Thus it was not the actual outcome of emancipation that caused the decline but its possible effect on the supply of labour together with the recognition that much of the cane land in cultivation was uneconomic.

As expected the immediate effect of full emancipation on output was dramatic. The freed slaves refused to work for their former masters on the old terms and conditions of employment. Exports dropped from an average amount of 1 million cwt. in the years 1836 to 1838 to about 0·6 million cwt. in the years 1839 to 1841. This result of emancipation was the same throughout the British West Indies but in one way or another the other colonies found some means of solving the labour problem. In Barbados this was relatively easy: there was no cultivated land to which labour could withdraw. In Trinidad and British Guiana, on the other hand, the situation was more comparable with that of Jamaica. Available land caused a similar exodus of emancipated slaves from the estates but, unlike in Jamaica, planters there responded by bringing in indentured labour from the Far East. It is at this point that the history of the Jamaican sugar industry begins to diverge from that of the other colonies. Unlike the rapid recovery of the sugar industries of British Guiana, Trinidad and Barbados, exports in Jamaica rose only slightly to a little below 0·8 million cwt. in 1842 and then began to fall again until in 1853 they amounted to only 0·4 million cwt. The ostensible reason for this is that Jamaican planters failed either to turn the emancipated slaves into regular wage labourers or to supply the deficiency by indentured labour. Yet this was only the result and not the cause of the continued decline: immigration facilities were the same for Jamaica as for Trinidad and British Guiana. The real reason was that many estates were still uneconomic and that their land was poor having regard to the higher costs of labour and the rate of investment needed after emancipation. For estates these two events in the late forties—the Sugar Duties Act and the commercial crisis of 1847—were the last straw. (See Ch. 1, D.)

The Sugar Duties Act of 1846, which provided for the gradual abolition of preferential duties in the United Kingdom by 1854, caused an uproar in the West Indies and representations on behalf of the sugar planters in the United Kingdom led to the appointment of the Sugar and Coffee Planting Committee in 1846. The subsequent report of the committee put forward the view that, as surplus sugar was available in slave owning countries, such as Cuba and Brazil, free trade would force the price of sugar down to 15*s*. per cwt., well below production costs.[1] Subsequent events, however, proved this estimate wrong. Increasing population and rising living standards in the United Kingdom actually caused prices to rise once the worst phase of the 1847 slump had passed. The London c.i.f. price of sugar rose from its depth of 20*s*. per cwt. in 1848 to 34*s*. in 1857 (Table LXI).

Internal conditions were, at this time, no less favourable. The abandonment of estates during the previous decades had eliminated the least suited areas for cane cultivation. There were now also fewer opportunities for independent land settlement and with rapid population growth planters no longer had any just cause to complain of labour shortage. For two decades from 1854 sugar exports remained stable at about half a million cwt.

[1] BPP, 1847–8 (245), p. 153.

But in 1875 sugar exports began to decline once more. Commodity prices had begun to fall already in 1873. The decline in sugar prices during the seventies and early eighties was not as great as that in other commodities: in 1882 sugar prices were only 10 per cent below those of 1861, compared with reductions of over 20 per cent for tea, timber, wool and rice.[1] Nevertheless, the fall was disastrous for the West Indian cane sugar industry because it was not matched by increased productivity. Elsewhere prices had fallen as a result of increased investment. This was particularly true of the European beet sugar industry which had been revolutionized during the sixties by improved production techniques. As a result of the unequal progress made in the two industries, beet production expanded rapidly while cane production increased only slowly and, in the British West Indies, actually declined. It was claimed that beet production was stimulated by unfair competition. In fact, fiscal policy in France, Germany and Austria at first did no more than stimulate an already expanding industry. In these three countries, the government levied duties on an estimated yield of the beet but paid back duties on actual exports. Thus if yields increased above the amount estimated for fiscal purposes, exporters actually received a bonus. The system of drawbacks on exports thus provided a powerful incentive to improve yields and extraction processes.

Beet sugar competition did not become openly unfair to cane producers until world production began to outstrip demand. In 1888, Austria replaced the drawback of duties with a direct bonus. Her example was followed by Germany in 1892. As this left the French indirect bonus still above the direct bonus paid by Austria and Germany, these two countries were driven to double their bonuses in 1896, in turn leading the French government, in the following year, to pay a direct bonus in addition to its existing indirect bonus. In 1903 the total value of the bounties was estimated at £5 per ton.[2]

As a result sugar prices fell rapidly and, as seen from Table XLIII, at 10*s*. per cwt. (London c.i.f.) in 1895 were only half of those in the early eighties. Prices continued to fall until in 1902 they touched bottom with 7*s*. 3*d*. per cwt. (London c.i.f.). West Indian producers were temporarily protected from the worst effects of this catastrophic deterioration of the United Kingdom market by selling their

[1] Progress of the Sugar Trade, BPP (325).

[2] Martineau, G. *Sugar*, London, 1918, p. 135.

sugar to the United States where countervailing duties on bounty-fed sugar and higher freight charges for beet sugar from Europe kept prices above those ruling in the United Kingdom. In 1890 the differential in freight and insurance charges alone amounted to 30*s*. per ton.[1] This advantage, however, proved only short-lived. Beginning in 1901 the United States granted special terms to Porto Rico, the Philippines and Cuba and sugar from these islands increasingly replaced that from the British West Indies. By 1900 total sugar exports from Jamaica had dropped to less than 300,000 cwt. In the other British West Indies the position was no less distressing. In the fifteen years up to 1900 exports from Trinidad had declined by about one-third and from British Guiana and Barbados by about one-fifth.

Beet sugar bounties, however, were injurious not only to the cane producers. In the long run they were bound also to be damaging to the countries exporting the bounty-fed sugar. Bounties cause distortions in the economy because they stimulate the production of one commodity artificially at the expense of others and they also involve large transfer payments from the community as a whole to one section. If other countries, in self-defence, adopt similar policies of promoting exports then, as we have seen, the advantages are nullified unless bounties are increased. This in turn leads to further grants of bounties elsewhere and so the process continues until governments are burdened with intolerable costs.

From time to time efforts were made to secure international agreement to abolish all bounty-systems. The first conference was held in Brussels as early as 1875 at which Great Britain, France, Belgium and Holland were represented. A convention was drafted two years later but the United Kingdom refused to ratify the clause under which consenting countries were to be protected from competition from bounty-fed imports coming from countries outside the agreement. Meanwhile the situation continued to deteriorate and a second convention was signed in 1889 but again the United Kingdom refused to ratify the agreement. A third abortive effort was made in 1898. The British government was finally induced to co-operate only when the Colonial Office and Foreign Office began to argue in its favour and the Congress of Chambers of Commerce of the Empire pressed for action in 1900.[2] Accordingly in 1901 a new conference was con-

[1] Correspondence re Treaty regulating Trade, BPP, 1892 (C 6680).

[2] Martineau, 'The Brussels Sugar Convention', *Economic Journal*, 1904, vol. XIV.

vened in Brussels at which eleven countries, consisting of Belgium, Austria, Hungary, Germany, France, Spain, Great Britain, Italy, Holland, Roumania and Sweden, were represented.

The conference agreed to abolish all direct and indirect bonuses, to require that all sugar be refined in bond—to avoid the possibility of making profits out of drawbacks—and to give all contracting parties security against outside competition by imposing countervailing duties on bounty-fed imports. The agreement was subsequently ratified and came into force in 1903.

World production, however, was still excessive and prices recovered only slightly: in 1913 the London c.i.f. price was still only 9·5*s*. per cwt. In the same year the Brussels Treaty came up for renewal for the second time but the British government decided to withdraw. Any effect this decision might have had on the sugar market, however, was obscured by the outbreak of war.

The most important effect of the Brussels Convention was that it restored confidence in the cane sugar industry. After the abolition of the bounties, world production of cane sugar increased more rapidly than beet sugar and the outbreak of war, reducing beet sugar exports from Europe, gave an additional stimulus to expansion. Prices rose rapidly. In 1916 the price per cwt. (London, c.i.f.) had already risen to 24·25*s*. By the beginning of 1920 it was 63·5*s*. and by the early summer months had reached the record figure of 95·75*s*. Like cane producers elsewhere those of Jamaica took advantage of the higher prices. Exports from Jamaica rose from their depth of 98,000 cwt. in 1913 to nearly 733,000 cwt. in 1920.

But once again prosperity was only short-lived. With the return of peace, European beet producers quickly regained their pre-war level of output and late in 1920 the sugar boom broke. What made the situation different from and more disastrous than that of the 1890's was the small size of the open market. Special treaties were in force linking Porto Rico, Hawaii and the Philippines to the United States by complete remission of duties and Cuban sugar was admitted on preferential terms. The British West Indies enjoyed preferential treatment in the United Kingdom and Canada. The major danger to the security of these protected trading patterns, however, arose from the surplus available for the open market in Cuba and Java. Both islands, enjoying the lowest production costs in the world, increased their output by over 50 per cent during the 1920's.[1] The Cuban

[1] WISC, BPP, 1930 (Cmd. 3517), p. 30.

producers, moreover, were able, by virtue of their preferential treatment in the United States market, to dump surplus production elsewhere. Because of this dumping the price of sugar continued to fall and this fall led to demands for increased protection which, when granted, in turn encouraged further expansion. Between 1923–9 an unmarketed surplus of 3½ million tons had been accumulated in the world and a further 1·2 million tons had been added a year later.[1] There appeared to be no prospect of relief. Attempts to restrict production had been made in Cuba in 1926 but had to be abandoned because it was not possible to bring Java, the other major producer, into the scheme. The WISC appointed to enquire into the causes of the depression and advise on the steps to be taken to place the industry in the 'best possible position for the future' concluded, as had the 1897 RWIC, that the difficulties of the West Indian Sugar Industry was not to 'any material degree due to comparative ill-adaption . . . or to imperfect techniques or defects of the industry'. The main cause was the competition of protective tariffs, bounties and subsidies and under such conditions the Commission could see no prospect for 'an early restoration . . . of the market prices of sugar to figures which will enable the present rate of production to be maintained without loss to unprotected or unsubsidized producers'.[2] Before the Commission had published its findings, the Jamaican government granted a temporary relief of £2 per ton for the 1930 export crop and a total subsidy of £60,000 in the following year.[3] The WISC report resulted in additional preferential assistance in the form of Colonial Sugar Certificates. Altogether the preference of colonial producers thus amounted to £4 15*s*. per ton.[4] Even so, this was still below the advantages given by the United States and France to their producers.[5] As a result of competing tariffs and increasing production the world price continued to fall and this fall led finally to the International Sugar Agreement in 1937 which introduced quotas for exporters.

Exports of rum like those of sugar declined by over half from 3·2 million gallons in 1830 to 1·3 million gallons ten years later. But unlike sugar, rum exports were subsequently stabilized until the 1890's. Here the relatively higher prices induced planters to take advantage of the fairly wide range possible in the output ratio of

[1] WISC, BPP, 1930 (Cmd. 3517), p. 30. [2] *Ibid.*, p. 11.
[3] Report of the SIC, J. Govt. Printer, 1945, p. 8.
[4] RWIC, BPP, 1945 (Cmd. 6607), p. 25. [5] *Ibid.*, p. 26.

sugar and rum (Ch. 14, B). In the 1890's exports began to decline slowly and by the outbreak of war had dropped to less than 1 million gallons but, unlike sugar, exports of rum did not recover subsequently. World demand for the Jamaica-type rum did not grow and after the war rum exports remained stable at around 0·7 million gallons.

(ii) *Coffee*

Next to sugar, coffee was the most valuable export crop before emancipation. The Jamaican coffee industry owed its rapid expansion after 1790 to the decline in exports from San Domingo. In 1789 St. Domingo exported over 678,600 cwt.[1] and production was still expanding when the rebellion in 1792 interrupted coffee cultivation. 'Upwards of 1,000 coffee plantations were destroyed.'[2] Jamaica was in a good position to take their place. Coffee exports there had increased from 7,600 cwt. in 1783 to 20,100 cwt. eight years later.[3] In 1792 there were already 607 estates employing 21,011 slaves.[4] Many French Royalists sought refuge in Jamaica bringing with them their knowledge to the expanding industry. By 1799 the number of estates had risen to 686[5] and production multiplied five times and continued to grow thereafter.[6] But such expansion could be achieved only by planting inferior land. This, together with poor cultivation techniques and absenteeism—though not as serious as in sugar cultivation—caused contraction long before the abolition of slavery. As shown in Table XLII coffee exports after reaching a peak with 304,000 cwt. in 1814 began to decline. There was another peak of 247,100 cwt. ten years later but thereafter exports fell rapidly until in the three years between 1836 and 1838 they averaged only 106,000 cwt. Complete emancipation in 1838 caused a further fall to 76,300 cwt. in the years 1839 to 1841. But, unlike the sugar industry, the coffee industry did not recover subsequently and exports continued to decline until in the years 1848 to 1850 they averaged only 37,200 cwt.

Scarcity of labour combined with overseas competition to make

[1] Edwards, B. *History of the British West Indies*, London, 1819, vol. II, p. 354.
[2] *Ibid.*, p. 355.
[3] Sel. Com. East India Produce, BPP, 1840 (527), p. 590.
[4] Ragatz, L. J. *Statistics for the Study of British Caribbean Economic History*, New York, 1928.
[5] Gardner, *op. cit.*, London, 1873, p. 321.
[6] Sel. Com East India Produce, *op. cit.*, p. 590.

coffee planting unprofitable. In 1835 the West Indian coffee monopoly in the United Kingdom was partially destroyed with the admission of Ceylon coffee on equal terms. Seven years later East Indian coffee was accorded the same treatment. Here rising prices, equal ranking with colonial coffee together with the reduced supplies from the British West Indies proved a springboard for European investment. £3 million were invested in coffee planting in Ceylon during these years.[1] In 1847 over 240,000 cwt.[2]—about half of the imports into the United Kingdom—arrived from Ceylon.[3] Three years earlier the differential on foreign coffee had also been reduced but because of loose wording in the Act foreign coffee could enter as colonial by the simple device of re-shipment at an Empire port. A 'great quantity' of Brazilian coffee was landed at the Cape of Good Hope for reloading in British vessels.[4] As a result of increased supplies from elsewhere the London c.i.f. price of coffee fell sharply from 122*s*. in 1839 to 40*s*. per cwt. in 1848. Subsequently prices recovered only partially but estates continued to be abandoned in Jamaica.

The Jamaican coffee industry produced three distinct types of coffee: the high quality mountain grade, the middling grade grown on the less elevated hill slopes and the low quality grade of the lowlands. Most of the overseas competition affected the poorer grades. Hence abandonment of production was mainly among the estates producing these types while those in the Blue Mountains remained relatively immune to overseas competition.

The partial recovery of coffee exports that began in the early fifties was the result of an increase in the poorer quality grades grown by the peasantry. From this time onwards, coffee exports followed the trend in prices. Exports continued to increase until in 1879 they reached a peak with 97,000 cwt. The fall in prices which began in 1874 caused a decline until the middle 1880's but thereafter exports rose again to 110,000 cwt. in 1898. From then onwards, however, Brazilian competition caused a fall in the production of the poorer qualities again and exports subsequently were stabilized at around 70,000 cwt.

(iii) *Minor Exports*

There remain a number of other commodities which appeared in the export returns. With the exception of logwood, however, none

[1] SCP, BPP, 1847-8 (230), Qs. 14,310–11.
[2] *Ibid.*, Q. 14,312. [3] *Ibid.*, Q. 14,543. [4] *Ibid.*, Q. 14,298.

of them was ever very important in value; they accounted for at most 6 per cent of total exports. Only logwood differed from the other 'minor' products in its growing importance during the seventies and eighties and in the years 1888, 1889 and 1895 its export value actually surpassed that of any other commodity.

The logwood tree was introduced into Jamaica from Honduras in 1715.[1] Its original use was medicinal but this became less important with the discovery of its dye content. Logwood was usually self-sown and, as abandoned properties quickly testified, thrived in practically any part of the island. Hence the value of exports depended only on prices and the costs of collection and transport. After emancipation the trade was carried on chiefly by the peasantry. In 1850 only 4,300 tons were exported but ten years later had already risen to nearly 15,000 tons and in 1869 reached a peak with 114,800 tons. By this time, the large landowners had discovered that their 'ruinate' land had value after all and logwood exports became a recognized business in which labour was employed in cutting down trees and conveying it on board ship. Quantities exported declined steeply during the seventies and the early eighties, in spite of stable prices, probably because of excessive cutting in earlier years: it was said that even the roots of trees cut twenty or thirty years earlier were being dug up for export.[2] But by the late eighties exports had recovered again and in 1889 a new export peak of 115,500 tons was reached. The trade remained very profitable until 1895 but then received a setback first from competition of higher quality woods from Haiti and Campeachy[3] and later all natural dye exporters were affected by the development of the synthetic dye industries. Formerly used for all black and brown shades logwood was superseded by azo dyes, which were much cheaper to produce and apply, retaining a smaller market only for luxury cloths. Quantities exported fell rapidly and by 1908 amounted to only 21,600 tons. The trade recovered temporarily during the war but during the 1920's fell back again to about 25,000 tons per annum.

The dyewood extracting industry, developed in the first place in response to foreign dyewoods competition by saving transport costs, began exporting extracts in 1894. Decreasing demand for natural dyes offered little incentive to expansion and the export value of extracts provided only partial compensation for the loss of trade in

[1] *Jamaica in 1912*, p. 138.
[2] *Ibid.*, p. 139.
[3] Col. Rep., BPP, 1898 (C 8650), p. 23.

the raw product. In *1910* the value of exports was only £147,600 and in *1930* had fallen to £82,200 (Table XL).

Like logwood, exports of ginger and pimento began to increase after emancipation. Jamaica ginger enjoyed a good reputation abroad and invariably commanded higher prices than that produced elsewhere. Exports rose from about 0·4 million lb. in the late fifties to 2½ million lb. in the late 1920's. Pimento exports doubled between 1850–60 and after remaining fairly stable at about 6 million lb. for two decades began to increase again averaging about 10 million lb. after the turn of the century. The annual yield of both, however, was subject to considerable fluctuations and as seen from Table XL was apt to fall by as much as two-thirds from one year to the next. This appears to have been due chiefly to climatic factors. We do not have any prices for ginger but those for pimento show far less fluctuation than do the quantities exported (Table XLIII).

(iv) *Bananas*

The history of the banana as an export crop begins in 1869 when Captain Baker, an American sea captain, took the first shipload of the fruit to the United States and thus demonstrated that the fruit could be marketed in temperate climates in good condition. From that time onwards, combining later with others to form the powerful United Fruit Company, he organized a regular freight service to carry bananas to the United States. Annual returns of exports begin in 1882; these, as seen from Table XLII, grew rapidly thereafter. In 1884 exports exceeded 1 million stems and by 1901 had increased elevenfold, in spite of a slow downward trend in prices from 2*s*. per stem in the early 1880's to 1·5*s*. at the turn of the century. Prices, however, began to fall more rapidly during the first decade of the twentieth century and as a result exports ceased to expand after 1906 and remained stable at around 16 million stems until the outbreak of war. Lack of shipping and three devastating hurricanes reduced exports during the war to about 2 million stems but with the return of peace production recovered again and quickly surpassed pre-war records. In 1927 21 million stems were exported and three years later the quantity had increased further to 24½ million stems.

With the development of the banana trade, attempts were also made to promote exports of other fruit. Oranges were indigenous to the island but their cultivation was neglected until a subsidized steamer service made exports to the United States possible. Even then development was slow compared with the banana trade. The largest quantity exported in the eighties was only 35·5 million. The industry received a temporary stimulus from the failure of the Florida crop in the years 1898–9 when exports rose to 107 million but the subsequent recovery of Floridan supplies again checked Jamaican exports which declined until in the twenties they averaged only 1·2 million per annum. Lack of markets also prevented grapefruit and other fruits from developing on any important scale, with the single exception of coconuts which expanded fairly steadily from about 4 millon nuts in the eighties to about 28 million in the 1920's.

B. The Terms of Trade

We have seen how, beginning in the 1850's, the composition of exports began to change in response to price movements. The question to be answered here is how these changes affected the external purchasing power of Jamaicans. To what extent were changes in composition in exports accompanied by improvements in the terms of trade? Did imports, in fact, become more or less expensive in terms of exports?

TABLE XLIV

The Terms of Trade

1910 = 100

Year	Export Prices	Import Prices	Terms of Trade
1832	116	98	118
1850	115	84	137
1870	119	121	98
1890	126	92	137
1910	100	100	100
1930	111	132	84

Source: Appendix I.

We have computed the terms of trade for the six national income years from *1832* to *1930*. Details of the calculations are given in Appendix I. Here it need be noted only that the calculation of the price index for exports raised a special problem because of the drastic change in the composition of exports which occurred in the years between *1870* and *1890*. The method used to compute the export price index is not entirely satisfactory. Nevertheless, the results of the computations are sufficiently significant to enable us to indicate broad movements. The terms of trade here are calculated by dividing export prices by import prices. A rise in the index thus indicates an improvement and a fall a deterioration.

The Jamaican terms of trade deteriorated throughout the period except for the years from *1832* to *1850* and from *1870* to *1890* (Table XLIV). This is of interest because elsewhere the terms were improving between *1850* and *1870* and deteriorating sharply between *1870* and *1890*. The Jamaican terms of trade, in fact, fell sharply from 137 to 98 in *1870* and rose equally sharply during the following twenty years. Thereafter, the deterioration was continuous until in *1930* the terms stood at only 84. Most of these violent changes were the result of fluctuations in import prices. As seen from Table XLIV, the index of export prices shows much smaller variations than that of import prices.

The export price index, in fact, remained fairly stable for most of the nineteenth century. Such changes as occurred in export prices,

TABLE XLV

Price Indices of the Major Exports

(f.o.b. prices *1910* = 100)

Year	Sugar	Rum	Coffee	Ginger	Pimento	Logwood	Bananas
1832	151	80	172	192	274	202	—
1850	143	135	105	204	188	113	—
1870	148	149	142	93	78	94	65
1890	102	135	182	135	122	156	99
1910	100	100	100	100	100	100	100
1930	88	112	146	120	337	135	117

Source: Ch. 1, E.

shown in Table XLV, were offset by adjustments in exports. Thus up to *1850* the decline in sugar and coffee prices and the rise in rum prices were offset by reductions in sugar and coffee exports and increases in rum exports. Again the fall in sugar prices and increases in logwood and banana prices up to *1890* resulted in a shift in exports from sugar to bananas and logwood. Subsequently, the prices of all commodities except bananas fell steeply until the outbreak of World War I, but because banana exports continued to expand relatively the export price index fell by only 26 points between *1890* and *1910*, After the war, the index rose by 11 points owing chiefly to the increase in banana prices by 17 per cent. The prices of coffee, rum, ginger and logwood also increased, but this did not result in increased exports (Table XLV). By contrast, sugar exports actually increased, although f.o.b. prices in *1930* were appreciably below the pre-war level.

Movements in the import price index, on the other hand, were dependent entirely on what was happening to prices in the rest of the world. As the bulk of imports consisted of essential foodstuffs, clothing and raw materials, there was no possibility of offsetting price changes by changes in the composition of imports. Moreover, as most of the imports came from North America and the United Kingdom, the price index reflects fully changes in the price levels in these countries. Thus up to *1850*, prices of food and raw materials fell as the result of the opening of the North American continent and prices of manufactures fell as a result of advanced techniques applied in the United Kingdom. Civil War in North America brought about considerable increases in food, raw material and textile prices during the 1860's. After *1870*, increased output in the United States and further advances in the United Kingdom brought about a renewed fall in import prices. Import prices began to rise again, however, after *1890* (Table XLVI).

TABLE XLVI

Price Indices of Imports

(c.i.f. prices)

1910 = 100

1. Food:

Year	Flour	Meal	Codfish	Herrings	Beef and Pork	Bacon and Ham	Butter
1832	131	125	84	132	82	61	53
1850	113	68	44	101	67	68	48
1870	153	124	91	105	128	98	89
1890	94	96	78	98	79	91	64
1910	100	100	100	100	100	100	100
1930	102	149	153	181	134	172	145

TABLE XLVI—*continued*

2. Drink and Tobacco:

Year	Ale and Beer	Spirits	Tea	Tobacco	Wines
1832	44	48	359	311	70
1850	53	50	210	44	92
1870	91	94	242	148	142
1890	108	101	200	133	140
1910	100	100	100	100	100
1930	196	223	—	411	164

3. Clothing:

Year	Cotton	Leather	Linen	Woollen
1832	230	90	63	65
1850	115	75	44	41
1870	133	135	64	66
1890	83	117	72	108
1910	100	100	100	100
1930	176	238	163	115

4. Other Consumer Goods:

Year	Candles	Soap	Paper	Hardware	Oil
1832	197	178	(350·0)	274	762
1850	182	124	(300·0)	(230)	907
1870	240	125	277	186	450
1890	133	91	156	127	117
1910	100	100	100	100	100
1930	n.a.	120	122	206	290

5. Non-Consumption Goods:

Year	Coal	Wood	Metals	Live-stock	Mach-inery	Cement	Bags and Sacks	Cordage
1832	17	111	274	12	—	—	—	(90)
1850	58	56	(230)	16	(230)	—	—	92
1870	63	139	186	15	186	—	135	—
1890	87	70	127	31	127	137	117	100
1910	180	100	100	100	100	100	100	100
1930	808	121	45	552	206	152	128	152

Note: Prices in parenthesis are estimates.

Source: Ch. 1, E.

C. Imports

As we saw in Ch. 10, the pattern of production remained broadly unchanged. Agriculture continued to dominate output throughout the period, while manufacturing accounted for only a small proportion of total gross domestic product. Thus Jamaicans were almost entirely dependent on imports for their manufactures. Moreover, even agriculture did not satisfy the domestic demand for food. Of the total agricultural output exports accounted for between 35 and 47 per cent in the years between *1850* and *1930* and even more in *1832*. Of the remaining 53 to 65 per cent, an overwhelming amount was accounted for by ground provisions (Table XXV). There remained thus a remarkably small share of resources devoted to meat and dairy products and the quantity of fish caught locally was negligible. In short, production for the home market provided for only a low and monotonous mode of existence. Given such a pattern of production the need for imports becomes obvious.

TABLE XLVII

Per Capita Values of Imports

Year	Per Capita Value of Imports at *1910* Prices*	Per Capita Value of Imports at Current Prices
	£	£
1832	3·2	3·2
1850	3·2	2·7
1870	2·0	2·4
1890	3·2	3·0
1910	3·2	3·2
1930	4·3	5·7

* For method of computing imports at *1910* prices see Appendix I.
Sources: Chs. 2–7.

In Table XLVII we show the per capita value of imports at current and at *1910* prices. It will be seen that per capita imports, at *1910* prices, remained remarkably stable at £3·2 for most of the period. It was considerably below this level, at £2, in *1870* and above it, at £4·3, in *1930*. This remarkable stability in per capita imports in the face of considerable variation in output was due to changes in the terms of trade and in the balance of payments.

Per capita imports remained stable between *1832* and *1850*, in spite of the sharp fall in output, partly as a result of an improvement in the terms of trade from 118 to 137 but mainly owing to the decline in payments abroad. With the reduction in plantation activity after emancipation the transfer of profits abroad almost disappeared. As the size of these payments was of about the same order as the reduction in output, incomes available in the island for domestic production remained almost unchanged and hence also imports. After *1850*, however, changes in the balance of payments became much less important. Henceforward, the level of imports was determined chiefly by changes in output and in the terms of trade. The sharp fall in per capita imports to £2, for example, was caused by the considerable fall in the terms of trade to 98 in *1870*. The renewed fall in the terms of trade, beginning in the nineties, also explains why per capita imports did not rise as early and as quickly as output after *1890*. The fall in the terms by 37 points up to *1910* offset the rise in output completely, and the further fall by 16 points up to *1930* prevented imports from rising proportionately to output.

In short, the trend in imports diverged from that in output during the early years because of the disappearance of exported profits and after *1850* as a result of changes in the terms of trade. This divergence also resulted in a changing ratio of imports to national income. This rose from about 23 per cent in *1832* to 28 per cent in *1850* but fell thereafter and did not begin to rise again until after *1890* (Table XLVIII).

TABLE XLVIII

Imports and National Income

Year	Total Value of Retained Imports at Current Prices	Total Value of Retained Imports at *1910* Prices*	Imports as Percentage of Gross Domestic Product at Current Prices
	£'000	£'000	%
1832	1,175·6	1,195·4	23·3
1850	1,065·9	1,276·4	28·1
1870	1,223·9	1,015·4	21·6
1890	1,897·9	2,054·2	21·7
1910	2,645·4	2,645·4	23·4
1930	5,765·1	4,370·8	28·9

* For method of computing imports at *1910* prices, see Appendix I.
Sources: Chs. 2–7.

The increase in the ratio of imports up to *1850* was also accompanied by relative increases in imports of food and clothing and a decline in production materials. This is to be expected because of the greater equality of incomes after emancipation (see Ch. 15, A, (ii)) and the decline in production for export. Imports of production materials, in fact, began to recover again substantially only towards the end of the century with the growth in exports and increasing domestic investment. Production materials had, by *1930*, become the largest single group accounting for nearly 36 per cent of total imports (Table XLIX).

There were also some interesting changes within the different groups. The increase in food imports in the early years, for example, was accompanied by an increase in the share of cereal imports from 19 to 30 per cent and a decline in protein foods, such as meat and dairy products, from 45 to 28 per cent of total food imports. This again was due partly to changed income distribution but partly also to increased home production of animal products. Cereals continued to gain relative to animal products subsequently but after *1850* it was mainly the result of increased peasant production for the export market which resulted in the substitution of imported cereals for locally grown ground provisions. Again the clothing group underwent considerable changes. In *1832* the most important single item was linen which accounted for 37 per cent of the total, followed by woollen piece goods with 19 per cent. Both textiles were increasingly replaced by cotton piece goods which after *1870* accounted for over half of the total clothing imports.

The level of non-consumption goods, on the other hand, depended on the export trade and the development of secondary industries. The initial decline in exports decreased the demand for production materials while its recovery in later years was accompanied by changes in the import-content of exports. This can be seen in the sharp decline of timber imports. In the early period wood was imported to provide containers for the export crops as well as for domestic construction. With the decline in the chief exports, however, less timber was needed. In later years the higher degree of refining reached in sugar manufacture eliminated the need to drain sugar on the voyage, thus making possible the substitution of bags for wooden containers. Reduction in sugar manufacture also affected metal imports. Copper and brass sheeting was used extensively in the old type of factories. With the abandonment of so many estates fewer metals

TABLE XLIX

The Composition of Retained Imports

(Total Value of Retained Imports at *1910* Prices)

Part 1

	1832		*1850*		*1870*		*1890*		*1910*		*1930*	
	£'000	%	£'000	%	£'000	%	£'000	%	£'000	%	£'000	%
1. Food	388·7	32·5	461·3	36·1	376·8	37·1	703·9	34·3	917.0	34·7	1,239·1	28·3
2. Drink and Tobacco	79·0	6·6	91·4	7·2	61·4	6·0	86·9	4·2	78·1	2·9	113·9	2·6
3. Clothing	350·9	29·4	434·9	34·1	369·4	36·4	634·7	30·9	693·5	26·2	657·8	15·1
4. Other Consumer Goods	93·4	7·8	89·4	7·0	101·4	10·0	266·4	13·0	330·8	12·5	795·2	18·2
5. Production Materials	283·4	23·7	199·2	15·6	106·5	10·5	362·3	17·6	626·0	23·7	1,564·8	35·8
	1,195·4	100·0	1,276·2	100·0	1,015·5	100·0	2,054·2	100·0	2,645·4	100·0	4,370·8	100·0

Part 2. Food

	1832		*1850*		*1870*		*1890*		*1910*		*1930*	
	£'000	%	£'000	%	£'000	%	£'000	%	£'000	%	£'000	%
1. Cereals	73·5	18·9	137·8	29·9	124·0	33·0	279·6	39·7	404·3	44·1	432·9	34·9
2. Fish	124·8	32·1	168·5	36·5	135·7	36·1	221·2	31·4	212·2	23·2	235·1	19·0
3. Dairy Products	97·6	25·1	55·4	12·0	30·3	8·1	53·8	7·7	91·9	10·0	148·3	12·0
4. Meat	75·3	19·4	75·6	16·4	27·9	7·4	22·0	3·1	58·9	6·4	71·4	5·8
5. Other Foods	17·5	4·5	24·0	5·2	57·9	15·4	127·3	18·1	149·7	16·3	351·4	28·3
	388·7	100·0	461·3	100·0	375·8	100·0	703·9	100·0	917·0	100·0	1,239·1	100·0

T

Part 3. Drink and Tobacco

	1832		1850		1870		1890		1910		1930	
	£'000	%	£'000	%	£'000	%	£'000	%	£'000	%	£'000	%
1. Wines	53·0	67·1	22·7	24·8	11·1	18·1	15·9	18·3	15·8	20·2	13·3	11·7
2. Beer and Ale	2·9	3·7	21·9	24·0	32·1	52·3	42·6	49·0	31·1	39·9	39·8	35·0
3. Spirits	21·1	26·7	21·2	23·2	7·7	12·5	12·5	14·4	15·8	20·2	22·4	19·6
4. Tobacco	1·4	1·8	24·7	27·0	9·9	16·1	9·5	10·9	11·9	15·3	28·7	25·2
5. Other	0·6	0·7	0·9	1·0	0·6	1·0	6·4	7·4	3·4	4·4	9·7	8·5
	79·0	100·0	91·4	100·0	61·4	100·0	86·9	100·0	78·0	100·0	113·9	100·0

Part 4. Clothing

	1832		1850		1870		1890		1910		1930	
	£'000	%	£'000	%	£'000	%	£'000	%	£'000	%	£'000	%
1. Cottons	53·9	15·4	177·0	40·7	145·1	39·3	372·8	58·7	437·0	63·0	344·8	52·5
2. Linens	130.2	37·1	86·5	19·9	33·2	9·0	9·0	1·4	6·1	0·9	3·6	0·5
3. Haberdashery	37·4	10·6	50·4	11·6	123·0	33·3	146·6	23·1	97·0	14·0	47·2	7·2
4. Woollens	67·0	19·1	45·3	10·4	21·6	5·8	33·0	5·2	43·4	6·3	46·8	7·1
5. Leather	56·6	16·1	71·5	16·4	45·7	12·4	69·6	11·0	90·9	13·1	165·9	25·2
6. Other	5·8	1·7	4·2	1·0	0·8	0·2	3·7	0·6	19·1	2·7	49·5	7·5
	350·9	100·0	434·9	100·0	369·4	100·0	634·7	100·0	693·5	100·0	657·8	100·0

PART 5. OTHER CONSUMER GOODS

	1832		1850		1870		1890		1910		1930	
	£'000	%	£'000	%	£'000	%	£'000	%	£'000	%	£'000	%
1. Soap	19·1	20·5	25·5	28·5	20·6	20·3	33·3	12·5	35·5	10·7	85·8	10·8
2. Candles	11·3	12·1	11·1	12·4	17·5	17·2	1·9	0·7	1·8	0·5	—	—
3. Hardware	9·8	10·5	7.5	8·4	30·4	30·0	68·9	25·9	58·1	17·6	15·7	2·0
4. Earthenware	0·7	0·7	1·4	1·6	1·1	1·1	2·3	0·9	10·4	3·1	6·7	0·8
5. Stationery	3·3	3·5	3·2	3·6	2·9	2·9	8·9	3·3	14·8	4·5	73·6	9·2
6. Books	1·9	2·0	2·9	3·2	2·0	2·0	8·9	3·3	15·6	4·7	19·6	2·5
7. Oil	1·3	1·4	1·5	1·7	5·1	5·0	13·5	5·1	43·5	13·2	123·3	15·5
8. Carriages	—	—	2·7	3·0	—	—	—	—	29·5	8·9	290·8	36·6
9. Other	46·0	49·3	33·6	37·6	21·8	21·5	128·7	48·3	121·6	36.8	179·7	22·6
	93·4	100·0	89·4	100·0	101·4	100·0	266·4	100·0	330·8	100·0	795·2	100·0

PART 6. PRODUCTION MATERIALS

	1832		1850		1870		1890		1910		1930	
	£'000	%	£'000	%	£'000	%	£'000	%	£'000	%	£'000	%
1. Wood	90·8	32·0	88·4	44·3	34·7	32·6	125·8	34·7	191·7	30·6	240·1	15·3
2. Metals	12·3	4·3	15·9	8·0	2·5	2·3	18·5	5·1	86·0	13·7	407·7	26·1
3. Coal	9·7	3·4	21·9	11·0	40·5	38·0	40·7	11·2	48·1	7·7	81·4	5·2
4. Oil	—	—	—	—	—	—	1·1	0·3	2·7	0·4	239·9	15·3
5. Cement	—	—	—	—	—	—	4·1	1·1	24·2	3·9	43·6	2·8
6. Manure	—	—	1·2	0·6	3·4	3·2	1·5	0·4	7·2	1·1	7·3	0·5
7. Cordage	3·8	1·3	4·8	2·4	—	—	4·9	1·4	8·5	1·4	12·2	0·8
8. Bags and Sacks	—	—	—	—	0·6	0·6	4·5	1·3	16·8	2·7	37·2	2·4
9. Livestock	150·4	53·2	36·1	18·1	4·0	3·7	53·8	14·9	3·6	0·6	0·6	0·0
10. Machinery	—	—	4·1	2·1	14·7	13·8	25·9	7·2	72·1	11·5	65·5	4·2
11. Agricultural Implements	0·5	0·2	1·8	1·0	0·4	0·4	0·8	0·2	22·6	3·6	40·4	2·6
12. Vehicles	—	—	—	—	1·7	1·6	22·6	6·2	22·4	3·6	63·4	4·0
13. Other	15·9	5·6	25·0	12·5	4·0	3·8	58·1	16·0	120·1	19·2	325·5	20·8

were needed and when the sugar industry was rehabilitated later factories were equipped on completely different lines. The increased value of metal imports towards the end of the period was mainly the result of constructional work and manufacturing industries. The recovery of sugar and the development of other factories is seen in the increasing amounts of machinery imported especially during the years *1890* to *1910*. The relatively large increase in coal imports between *1850* and *1870* was due to the construction of public utilities and the railway.

D. The Geographical Pattern of Trade

Until the 1840's the external trade of Jamaica—in common with that of all the other British West Indian colonies—was governed by the provisions of the Navigation Laws. In so far as these related to the geographical pattern of trade, they compelled the colonies to obtain all their imports from the United Kingdom in return for the monopoly of their produce in the home market. These laws were amended and modified from time to time—such as permitting a limited entrepôt trade with South America—but no fundamental changes occurred as far as the British West Indies were concerned until restrictions on the North-American trade were partially relaxed in 1830. Thus by *1832* already 8·2 per cent of Jamaican imports came from the United States. But by far the greatest trade was still conducted with the United Kingdom. As shown in Tables L and LI 78 per cent of imports in *1832* came from the United Kingdom which also took the same proportion of Jamaican exports. Most of the remaining imports came from Canada while in the case of exports the balance was made up of trade with Latin America.

But from the 1830's onwards, the importance of the British West Indies as producers of tropical food and raw materials for the United Kingdom declined. Growing population and national income in the United Kingdom demanded larger supplies than could be furnished by the West Indies and this need for alternative sources was accentuated by the decline in production during the 1830's. At the same time, expanding production in the United Kingdom required larger markets than those provided in the West Indies. These two forces led the United Kingdom to adopt gradual trade liberalization culminating in the complete removal of all protective duties in 1854. As we have already seen the West Indian coffee monopoly began to be reduced in 1835 with the admission of Ceylon coffees on equal terms, to be followed in 1842 by the admission of East Indian (A, (ii) above). The sugar monopoly had been attacked already in 1825 with the inclusion of Mauritius in the preferential class and in 1841 the same privilege was extended to all cane produce from East India. Five years later the Sugar Duties Act provided for the gradual reduction in colonial preference and by 1854 all sugars were admitted to the United Kingdom on equal terms. The corollary to abolition of market preference, that of removing restrictions on all imports, was effected during the 1840's.

The share of imports from the United Kingdom had fallen to 65 per cent already in *1850* and continued to fall subsequently until in *1930* it accounted for only 28 per cent of total imports for home consumption (Table L). Until *1910* most of the decline was made up by American imports while Canada's share remained relatively low, except in *1870*, until the 1920's.

By contrast, the reduction and final abolition of protective duties was slow in affecting the destination of exports. Although Jamaicans were immediately able to take advantage of the freeing of the import market, their exports to countries other than the United Kingdom had to await liberalization of foreign trade. Hence until the 1870's most of Jamaican exports continued to be sent to the United Kingdom, which continued to take 78 per cent of Jamaican exports until *1870* (Table LI). Subsequently, however, the export trade changed dramatically: the share of the United Kingdom continued to decline until in 1910 it accounted for only 18·7 per cent of the total. Most of the loss was made up by the United States and to a lesser extent by Canada in *1910*. But after World War I the pattern of the export trade changed once more; the share of the United States declined to 33 per cent while those of the United Kingdom and Canada increased to 26 and 25 per cent respectively.

It will be seen that these three countries together accounted for the bulk of the external trade. Until *1910* they supplied about 95 per cent of Jamaican imports and took 84 per cent or more of her exports. The remaining exports in the early years consisted mainly of re-exports of British merchandise to the South American continent. This trade virtually disappeared after *1850* and was partly replaced by the trade in domestic product to France, Germany and a few other European countries. In the case of imports other countries did not become important until *1930* when the British West Indies supplied nearly 6 per cent of imports and 'Others'—including

TABLE L

Origin of Imports

(Total Imports)

	1832		1850		1870		1890		1910		1930	
	£'000	%	£'000	%	£'000	%	£'000	%	£'000	%	£'000	%
United Kingdom	1,209·4	77·7	769·2	64·6	770·6	60·0	1,053·7	53·9	1,177·0	43·9	1,638·8	28·4
United States of America	127·5	8·2	243·7	20·4	281·9	21·9	667·9	34·2	1,182·1	44·1	1,818·0	31·6
Canada	122·9	7·9	121·4	10·2	195·0	15·2	174·0	8·9	209·0	7·8	1,153·5	20·0
France	—	—	—	—	3·5	0·3	5·7	0·3	2·9	0·1	46·5	0·8
Germany	0·6	0·1	11·4	1·0	10·5	0·8	5·8	0·3	55·5	2·1	121·9	2·1
Portugal and Spain	21·8	1·4	—	—	—	—	—	—	0·9	—	13·8	0·2
India and Ceylon	0·1	0·0	4·4	0·4	7·7	0·6	16·5	0·8	6·9	0·3	153·0	2·7
British West Indies*	—	—	—	—	4·4	0·3	11·1	0·6	22·1	0·8	326·7	5·7
Foreign West Indies†	39·3	2·5	10·3	0·9	7·4	0·6	3·6	0·2	3·8	0·1	198·3	3·4
South America‡	34·1	2·2	26·6	2·2	3·9	0·3	8·1	0·4	—	—	25·8	0·4
Other	—	—	3·9	0·3	—	—	8·4	0·4	20·5	0·8	271·5	4·7
	1,555·7	100·0	1,190·9	100·0	1,284·9	100·0	1,954·8	100·0	2,680·7	100·0	5,767·8	100·0

* Includes British Guiana, British Honduras and Bermuda.
† Includes Cuba and Haiti.
‡ Includes Central American States.

Sources: 1832, Customs 6/1 and 2.
1850, Customs 6/18, 19 and 20.
1870, Customs 6/83, 84 and 85.
1890, 1910, 1930, BBJ.

TABLE LI

Destination of Total Exports

(including re-exports)

	1832		1850		1870		1890		1910		1930	
	£'000	%	£'000	%	£'000	%	£'000	%	£'000	%	£'000	%
United Kingdom	2,072·8	78·1	926·8	77·9	925·6	77·7	597·2	32·7	507·0	18·7	1,036·9	25·7
United States of America	78·9	3·0	72·0	6·0	102·5	8·6	968·0	53·1	1,611·1	59·3	1,328·6	32·9
Canada	94·9	3·6	4·6	0·4	20·9	1·8	45·5	2·5	198·3	7·3	1,005·8	24·9
France	—	—	—	—	22·2	1·9	63·7	3·5	124·3	4·6	155·0	3·8
Germany	2·8	0·1	22·6	1·9	6·8	0·6	52·4	2·9	68·0	2·5	271·5	6·7
British West Indies*	—	—	—	—	12·1	1·0	23·9	1·3	60·5	2·2	33·3	0·8
Foreign West Indies†	126·0	4·8	25·5	2·1	73·0	6·1	4·8	0·3	5·3	0·2	6·9	0·2
South America‡	271·7	10·2	139·2	11·7	23·1	1·9	—	—	—	—	29·2	0·7
Other	5·0	0·2	0·2	—	4·7	0·4	67·5	3·7	140·4	5·2	174·3	4·3
	2,652·1	100·0	1,190·9	100·0	1,190·9	100·0	1,823·0	100·0	2,714·9	100·0	4,041·5	100·0

* Includes British Guiana, British Honduras and Bermuda.
† Includes Cuba and Haiti.
‡ Includes Central American States.

Sources: 1832, Customs 12/1 and 2.
1850, Customs 12/18, 19 and 20.
1870, Customs 12/83, 84 and 85.
1890, 1910 and 1930, BBJ.

chiefly Japan, Belgium, Holland, Switzerland and the Scandinavian countries—4·7 per cent. We turn next to consider the reasons for these shifts in trade after *1832*.

(i) *Trade with the United States*

The 1830 Reciprocity Act opened the trade between the United States and the West Indies. Under this Act each country admitted the other's ships without imposing discriminatory duties. In *1832* already most of the lumber, flour, meal and Indian corn[1] were obtained in the West Indies in spite of the American duties payable by Jamaican consumers. These discriminatory duties were abolished with the repeal of the Navigation Laws and the trade received a new stimulus. By *1850* food supplies from Europe had virtually disappeared from the Jamaican CR except for bacon and butter. In 1832 wheat flour valued at £19,000 was imported from the United Kingdom but by 1850 this had been reduced to £760. In the case of beef and pork the change was even more striking: the share of imports from the United Kingdom fell from 78 per cent to 5 per cent in these years. The opening of the American market also affected imports from Canada. The share of Canadian exports of meat was reduced from about 20 per cent in 1832 to 0·4 per cent in 1850 and part of the timber trade likewise passed to the United States. The trade in manufactures, on the other hand, did not begin to shift from the United Kingdom until the turn of the century.

In contrast with the early growth of American imports, exports were slow to expand. In 1832 the most important exports were pimento and rum valued at £46,082 and £21,795 respectively. In the same year, however, coffee was freed from customs duties, provided it entered the United States in American vessels. This proviso was dropped in 1846 when a free trade doctrine was adopted. In *1850*[2] 28 per cent of Jamaican coffee was sent to the United States and nearly half of the pimento exports. The financial crisis of 1857 and the Civil War, however, led to a reversal of tariff policy. In 1861 duties were imposed on articles hitherto free and increased on others. This affected sugar, coffee and spices but was partly compensated by growing exports of logwood which, as raw materials, entered

[1] All statistics relating to the origin and destination of individual commodities used in Sections i to iv have been taken from CR until 1853 and from the STC thereafter.

[2] Relates to 1850 and 1851 only.

free of duty. But from 1870 onwards, non-protective duties were gradually removed culminating in the freeing of sugar in 1890.

At the same time as freeing sugar, however, the McKinley Tariff of 1890 introduced a new policy of reciprocity. Something similar had already been attempted in 1884. In that year the United States signed a number of most-favoured-nation treaties with the Sandwich Islands, Mexico, Central America, the Spanish West Indies and San Domingo. The purpose was to secure 'more intimate commercial relations with the countries of the American continent which can best be obtained through arrangements giving specific and exceptional advantages and therefore not falling within the most-favoured-nation clauses of existing treaties'.[1] Such treaties were viewed unfavourably by the United Kingdom because they would give American goods preference over those from the United Kingdom. Sugar planters were very worried. The mere news of the proposal was enough to induce them to curtail production and merchants to stop advances.[2] Mr. Lubbock, of the West India Committee, was sent to Washington to assist in the negotiations. Offers were made, on behalf of the West Indies, to abolish duties on goods coming principally from the United States. These included bread and biscuits, flour, lard, lumber, kerosene oil, oil cake and meal. Jamaica offered remissions for all these except lumber, oil cake and meal. But these concessions were not acceptable to the Americans who tendered an alternative proposal under which the West Indies would free ninety commodities including manufactured metal goods and textiles in return for the free entry of sugar, fruit, vegetables etc. The counter-proposal was turned down because it was considered too high a price to pay for a doubtful advantage. The free entry of sugar was an advantage only as long as duties continued to be levied on the produce from other countries but since the United States was negotiating treaties with all suppliers this favourable treatment was not likely to last long.[3]

In 1890, however, American policy was reversed. Under the McKinley Tariff Act raw sugar was added to the free list and bounty-fed sugar made subject to a countervailing duty, but, at the same time, power was given to the President to impose duties on imports from those countries which did not reciprocate the advantage on

[1] Trade between B.W. India Colonies and the United States, BPP, 1885 (C 4340), p. 3.

[2] *Ibid.*, No. 9.

[3] *Ibid.*, No. 18.

American goods. The implied threat could not be ignored. Since the 1884 negotiations the West Indian producers had come to rely on the American market because prices there were higher than in the United Kingdom. In *1890* as much as 83 per cent of Jamaican sugar was sold in the United States. The West India Committee forwarded a memorandum from planters, merchants, bankers and others drawing attention to the 'most urgent need and importance that sugar, the produce of the British West Indian colonies, should not be made subject to duties while sugar, the produce of other countries, continued to be admitted free'.[1] They also pointed out that West Indian duties were imposed for revenue purposes only and were therefore 'equal and reasonable in character, and such as may fairly be accepted by the government of the United States'.[2] But this did not satisfy the American demand for 'more satisfactory trading relations'.[3] Moreover, they were in a strong position to insist on their terms for the British West Indian contribution was too small to affect sugar prices. Refusal to negotiate would force the West Indies to accept lower prices—that is the prices obtained by foreign competitors less the amount of duty.

Jamaica's position, however, differed from that of the other British West Indies because she exported relatively little sugar. The big increase in the share of exports sent to the United States between *1870* and *1890* followed the expansion of the fruit trade. This was in the hands of the Americans and hence not subject to any restrictions. Refusal on the part of Jamaicans to assent to the McKinley proposals was therefore unlikely to lead to punitive action against her fruit trade. For the benefit of her sugar producers Jamaica signed a separate treaty in 1891 under which many commodities previously subject to a 12½ per cent *ad valorem* duty were freed—including manufactured foods, books, bottles, brooms, brushes, paper and watches—and duties on bacon, ham, beef, bread and biscuits, butter, cheese, corn, lard, lumber, meal, oats, petrol, pork and wheat considerably reduced.[4] The total cost of these concessions was estimated at about £35,000 per annum.[5]

The treaty, in the end, remained in force for only two years. In 1894 duties on raw sugar were reimposed. At first the import duty was 40 per cent *ad valorem* on raw sugar but three years later this

[1] Treaty Regulating Trade, BPP, 1892 (C 6680), No. 6.
[2] *Ibid.* [3] *Ibid.* [4] *Ibid.*
[5] Rept. on Finances of Jamaica, BPP, 1899 (C 9412), p. 3.

was replaced by a specific duty of about double that amount and although the policy of imposing countervailing duties on bounty-fed sugar was continued, the United States market became less attractive. In 1901 sugar from Porto Rico was admitted free of duty and in 1902 and 1903 the Philippines and Cuba were granted special terms. With the agreement of the Brussels Convention to abolish all bounty systems in 1903, the United States thus provided no further advantage to outside growers. As a result the share of Jamaica sugar sent to the United States declined from about 50 per cent in *1890* to 1·9 per cent twenty years later. Brazilian competition had also reduced the share of coffee bought by the United States from nearly half to about one-quarter in the same period. Spices and logwood exports, on the other hand, continued to expand but again it was the expansion of the banana trade that accounted for the increase in the total share of the American trade. By *1930* bananas, coconuts and spices made up practically the whole of the export trade to the United States.

Meanwhile changes had also taken place in the composition of imports from the United States. Towards the end of the century, these were no longer confined to food and raw materials. In addition to all those commodities enumerated in the McKinley treaty for preferential treatment, the share of other manufactures coming from the United States also began to increase. In *1910* more than half the electrical equipment, railway materials, machinery, carriages and carts and drugs and medicines imported into Jamaica came from the United States. In spite of unfavourable import tariffs after the war the American imports of some manufactured articles such as manufactured cottons, and hardware, continued to increase while, broadly, only in the case of food and raw materials did she lose part of her trade to other countries, particularly to Canada.

(ii) *Trade with Canada*

Until shipping communications to Lake Superior began to be improved in 1867 Canada was dependent on the transit traffic through the United States. This trade was encouraged by the Americans by drawback legislation and possibly part of the American exports originated in Canada. In order to promote direct trade with the West Indies, Canadians mooted proposals for the mutual abolition of customs duties in 1855.[1] Because this conflicted with the new

[1] Customs Duties (Canada—West Indies), BPP, 1856 (431), p. 3.

free trade doctrine, however, it was frowned upon by the Imperial government and no further discussions took place and the Canadian trade, apart from fish, continued to languish.

In 1890 Canada's interest was reawakened by the growing volume of the West Indian–American trade. Proposals for commercial reciprocity, however, met with little favour because of the pending negotiations under the McKinley Tariff Act and the fear that reciprocal preference with Canada would be penalized by the Americans through sugar. The West India Committee supplied another reason for refusal by pointing out that the Dominion could consume only one-third of the West Indian sugar crops.[1] But in 1899 Canada included the British West Indies in their preferential tariff without demanding reciprocal concessions. This entitled West Indian raw sugar to admission at a duty 25 per cent below the current rate, applying also to refined sugar if manufactured from colonial produce. This policy did not result in appreciable diversions of sugar from the United States to Canada. A year later the preferential reduction was raised to 33⅓ per cent. What results did come about, however, were not so much due to this as to other causes: among them the Brussels treaty—which by ending the countervailing duties on bounty-fed sugar in the United States made the American market less attractive—the surtax on German imports and increasing consumption in Canada. The preferential tariff, amounting to between 8*s*. and 10*s*. per ton,[2] appears to have had little to do with increasing exports to Canada. Indeed Mr. Cork, the Colonial Secretary, stated that the Jamaican sugar producer had not received any benefit from the preference at all—'so far as he knew, it had been a subsidy to the merchants of Canada'.

Partly for this reason Jamaicans were still hostile to reciprocal trade agreements when the subject was reopened in 1908.[3] But the main reason appears to have been the declining importance of the sugar industry. By *1910*, the share of sugar had dropped to 8 per cent of total exports. Because of this, it was thought that 'the value of the tariff preference given by Canada is not so great as to justify the colony offering tariff advantages with a view to its retention at the present time'.[4] This view received support from Jamaican merchants who had built up trading connections and shipping communications with the United States and who, accordingly, felt their interests

[1] Royal Commission on Trade Relations between Canada and the West Indies, BPP, 1910 (Cd. 5369), p. 3. [2] *Ibid*., p. 26. [3] *Ibid.* [4] *Ibid.*

threatened by any agreement that might result in a shift of trade to Canada.[1]

The position was different with most of the other British West Indian colonies because, there, sugar was the principal export. These colonies signed agreements with Canada in 1912 providing for mutual preference.[2] Thus in *1910*, apart from sugar, of which nearly 72 per cent was sent to Canada, and the growing export of oranges, trade with Canada was small. Canadian exports to Jamaica, too, continued to suffer from American competition. In *1910* 33 per cent of butter, 12 per cent of flour, 98 per cent of mackerels, 90 per cent of herrings, 67 per cent of dried fish and 1·5 per cent of timber imports came from Canada. Only in the first three commodities had the share increased while dried fish and, particularly, timber had declined.

World War I, however, was followed by closer trading connections between Empire countries. Preferential tariffs with the United Kingdom came into force in 1919, and a year later Jamaica signed a reciprocal trade agreement with Canada.[3] Under this Canada undertook to admit colonial produce at half the duty imposed on foreign produce and Jamaica to grant a preferential reduction of at least 25 per cent. By *1930* most of the sugar and coffee was sent to Canada, while imports of fish and flour from Canada were increasingly substituted for those from the United States, and those of condensed milk replaced previous imports from Germany.

(iii) *Trade with the United Kingdom*

Imports from the United Kingdom, as we saw above, declined quickly with the opening up of the United States market for food and raw materials. Free trade also destroyed a considerable part of the United Kingdom re-export trade in European produce. The one exception to this was the trade with Spain and Portugal. In *1832* Jamaica bought more than half of her wines directly from these countries, but subsequently the trade passed increasingly to British vintners. The reasons for this are to be found in the superior merchanting and transport facilities linking the Mother Country with her overseas territories. This also explains why Eastern products such as rice, when they entered international trade, were obtained through Britain.

[1] Royal Commission on Trade Relations between Canada and the West Indies, BPP, 1910 (Cd. 5369), p. 26.

[2] Agreement between Canada and West Indian Colonies, BPP, 1912 (Cd. 6092).

[3] Canada-West Indies Trade Agreement, BPP, 1920 (Cmd. 864).

On the other hand, the share of exports going to the United Kingdom did not begin to decline until after *1870*. Although the United Kingdom had begun to import tropical produce from outside the West Indian possessions before free trade was fully implemented—the share of Jamaican sugar in United Kingdom consumption had already declined from 40 per cent[1] in the 1820's to 13 per cent[2] in 1847, i.e. by more than the total output of sugar—Jamaica did not find alternative outlets for her traditional staples until tariffs and consumption standards elsewhere became more favourable. In 1840

TABLE LII

Imports of Raw Sugar into the United Kingdom

	1852		*1880*		*1890*	
	'000 cwt.	%	'000 cwt.	%	'000 cwt.	%
Cane Sugar, British	5,837·7	84·7	4,829·9	28·4	2,334·5	14·8
Cane Sugar, Foreign . . .	927·2	13·4	6,973·2	41·0	3,315·1	21·1
Beet Sugar . . .	131·8	1·9	5,198·5	30·6	10,067·9	64·1
	6,896·7	100·0	17,001·6	100·0	15,717·5	100·0

Sources: 1852. Progress of the Sugar Trade, BPP, 1884 (325), p. 33.
1880 and 1890. Correspondence re Brussels Conference, BPP, 1898 (C 8938).

the rest of the importing countries were still too poor or too protectionist to admit sugar from the British West Indies. France and Spain protected imports from their own colonies, the rest of Europe had its domestic supplies, and the United States obtained what sugar she needed from the large surplus available in Cuba.[3] Thus the British West Indian sugar producer still had to rely on the United Kingdom market. But already in the 1850's substantial amounts of sugar began to be imported into the United Kingdom from foreign cane-growing countries, and after 1870 the home market began to deteriorate

[1] SCP (361), App., p. 63, and Table XL above. [2] *Ibid.*
[3] Sel. Com. on East India Produce, App. No. 42.

rapidly with the growing volume of beet imports. In Table LII we see that the share of beet imports into the United Kingdom had risen from barely 2 per cent in 1852 to 30·6 per cent in 1880, and by 1890 exceeded all other raw sugar imports. If we include refined sugar as well the total share of beet imports in 1890 is increased to 74 per cent of total sugar imports.

The share of other Jamaican products going to the United Kingdom also declined rapidly. The share of coffee fell from 59 per cent in *1870* to 35 per cent in *1890* and further to 14 per cent in *1910*; that of logwood fell from 69 per cent in *1870* to less than half twenty years later. Again ginger fell from 96 per cent to 61 per cent, and pimento from 61 to 48 per cent in the same period. An attempt to supply the United Kingdom market with fruit in the early years of the twentieth century failed for lack of shipping communications (see subsection v).

A change in these trends came only after the war when the United Kingdom abandoned her free trade policy in favour of preferential treatment for Empire countries. Imperial preference, as we saw in subsection ii, had come into existence already at the turn of the century, but the United Kingdom did not support the ideal of closer co-operation among Empire countries until 1919 when she began to admit Empire produce at a preferential tariff amounting on the average to one-sixth of the full duties. In some cases, such as sugar, the remission was one-third. In return Jamaica agreed to grant preferential treatment amounting to between one-quarter and one-third of the general tariff. As a result, exports to the United Kingdom increased, and by *1930* accounted for the bulk of rum exports, nearly one-third of banana exports and about two-thirds of logwood extracts. British imports into Jamaica, however, continued to decline relatively partly as a result of continuing competition from the United States and partly owing to the substitution of direct trade with Empire countries: in *1930*, for example, 99 per cent of rice imports into Jamaica came directly from the growing countries.

(iv) *The Entrepôt Trade*

The entrepôt trade is as old as colonization in the Western hemisphere. It did not, however, receive legal recognition until the Free Ports Act was passed in 1766. This Act opened ports in the British West Indies to national ships coming from the South American continent and the French West Indies. Subsequent legislation altered the specifications of boats and their cargoes but, throughout, the trade, because the Spaniards did not enact complementary legislation, depended on smuggling. The trade consisted mainly in the re-export of manufactured cottons, linens and woollens from the United Kingdom to Guatemala, Colombia and the Spanish West Indies. The return trade, much less important, was made up of livestock, hides, indigo and hardwoods.

The trade reached its zenith during the Napoleonic wars principally because the European blockade made British manufacturers go

TABLE LIII

The Entrepôt Trade

Year	Total Value of Entrepôt Trade	Specie	Value of Re-export Trade in Commodities	Total Exports	Ratio of Re-exports to total Exports
	£'000	£'000	£'000	£'000	%
1832 . . .	450·9	—	450·9	2,644·3	17·1
1850 . . .	158·5	—	158·5	1,082·1	14·6
1870 . . .	95·7	—	95·7	1,229·1	7·8
1890 . . .	95·7	72·9	22·8	1,766·4	1·3
1910 . . .	147·3	110·2	37·1	2,715·3	1·4
1930 . . .	83·7	26·1	57·6	4,041·5	1·4

Note: The total value given here for the entrepôt trade does not always account for the difference between Domestic and Total exports shown in Tables L and LI.

(i) For the years 1832 and 1833 values and quantities are available only in manuscript and do not give the total for the detailed commodity analysis to check against that for the geographical analysis. The difference of £7,800 is probably a computing error.

(ii) For the years 1849, 1850 and 1851 the large difference of £108,800 may be due to the different sources used: BBJ and CR.

(iii) For the years 1869 and 1870 the Blue Books give different totals for the commodity and the geographical classifications. In 1870 the difference is actually £121,934. It has not been possible to check this as the commodity classification gives details of destination only for quantities and not for values.

(iv) For reasons for the difference in *1890* see Ch. 5.

further afield in search for markets. The Napoleonic wars, however, had a secondary effect which was ultimately to destroy the entrepôt trade itself. The defeat of Spain caused the South American colonies to revolt and as independent republics they were free to regulate their own commerce without having recourse to the more costly indirect trade. Henceforth trade was increasingly conducted with 'foreign houses established in their own territories'.[1] In the 1820's the importance of the entrepôt trade in Jamaican exports was already declining, yet in *1832* it still amounted to the considerable sum of £450,900. The value of the trade in *1850* was only one-third of that of *1832*, and it continued to decline subsequently. Table LII shows that the importance of the trade—taken as a percentage of total exports—declined from over 17 per cent in *1832* to a mere 1·3 per cent in *1890*. The loss of trade with Latin America after 1850 was temporarily made good by trade with Cuba in 1869–70, and was followed by a much smaller trade with the other British West Indies.

(v) *Shipping Communications*

One important aspect of changing geographical patterns of trade is that of adequate shipping services. While in general it may be true that shipping will be available if the demand for it exists there may be cases where trade fails to develop or expand for lack of enterprise in starting shipping services or because such enterprise is strangled by competing interests.

While sugar was the chief export no difficulties over shipping services arose. Planters usually consigned their output to British merchants, who provided suitable ships when they were wanted as part of their services as agents for the planters. Since these ships usually carried plantation stores, food and other consumer goods on the return trip, shipping communications with the United Kingdom were quite adequate at that time.

Apart from several British lines on the United Kingdom–Jamaica run a number of foreign shipping lines began to include Jamaica on their schedules towards the middle of the century. A French company began to call at Jamaica in 1865, thus providing communications with Cuba and the French Antilles—aiding the entrepôt trade with Cuba at that time—but by the early nineties this service ceased. The Central American line provided communications with Honduras and the Cunard Line maintained an intermittent service with Canada.[2]

More problematical, however, was the North American trade. Until the 1880's trade with the United States was not sufficient to maintain regular shipping services, and this lack was thought to hamper trade. Accordingly the Jamaican government was persuaded to arrange for regular communications with an American company.

[1] Hill, R. *Lights and Shadows of Jamaican History*, Jamaica, 1859, p. 65.
[2] HBJ, e.g. for 1895, pp. 422–3.

Under the agreement signed in 1872 the Pacific Mail Steam Ship Company agreed to call at Kingston twice per month on payment of a yearly subsidy of £5,000.[1] But with the development of the banana trade it was found that there was no lack of shipping since the banana companies provided their own boats. Moreover, their control over supplies of fruit in the island and of the American market meant that the subsidized steamers got only a small share of the trade. In the years from 1878 to 1882 they carried only one-fifteenth of banana exports.[2] The Jamaican government, on the recommendation of the Royal Commission on Public Revenues of 1884, therefore decided to discontinue the subsidy and although the Pacific Mail Steam Ship Company continued to call at Jamaica their connection with the fruit trade subsequently became even less important.

Competition among the banana companies was gradually eliminated, and by the 1890's the United Fruit Company (formerly the Boston Fruit Company) was left in virtual control of the Jamaica–United States run. This not only had the obvious disadvantage of leaving the Jamaican grower at the mercy of a monopolistic buyer for bananas, but it also prevented him from developing the citrus fruit trade since the banana companies were not interested in this. It is true that there was a protective duty on citrus in the American market for most of the time, but it is an open question whether the Jamaican producer might not have competed successfully in the New York market with the inland supplies from Florida.

Once the monopoly was established banana prices began to fall. Complaints of low prices and arbitrary rejection of fruit aroused, not unnaturally, widespread discontent and led to the demand, not only by the small settlers but also by the large planters, for alternative outlets. Since the United Fruit Company dominated the United States market as well as the shipping trade, the only alternative open to Jamaican producers was the development of the United Kingdom market. In 1896 this had already been demonstrated as a practical proposition.[3] The scheme for marketing fruit in the United Kingdom received further encouragement from the RWIC of 1897 and led finally to the establishment of the 'Direct Line'.

In 1901 the Imperial and island governments agreed to subsidize the 'Direct Line' with £20,000 each per annum for a provisional

[1] Rept. with BBJ, BPP, 1873 (C 709).
[2] BPP, 1884 (C 3890), p. 220.
[3] Lord Olivier, *Jamaica: The Blessed Island*, p. 382.

period of ten years. A contract was signed with the fruit and shipping company of Elder Dempster and Co., to provide a regular service of suitable ships between Jamaica and England.[1] The ships were to be loaded with the fruit supplied by contracting growers. The project, however, immediately ran into difficulties in Jamaica when it became clear that the United Fruit Company would make every effort to divert fruit from their competitors by tempting the contracting growers with higher prices. Consequently the 'Direct Line' was unable to fill their ships and had to come to terms with the United Fruit Company. The outcome of this was that the United Fruit Company gradually acquired a controlling interest in Elder Dempster and Co., and diverted the ships of the 'Direct Line' to Costa Rica and by 1904 had once more regained the monopoly of the Jamaican market.[2]

After the war the need for shipping communications received official attention again. The government no longer undertook the payment of subsidies but limited its assistance instead to guarantees. The two most important developments were the provisions for the Canadian trade and for the fruit trade with the United Kingdom. Under the Canada–West Indies trade agreement of 1920 the former undertook to provide fortnightly passenger, freight and mail steamship services to Jamaica,[3] and in 1929 a new Direct Line between the United Kingdom and Jamaica, the Jamaica Direct Fruit Line, Ltd., came into existence again to serve the fruit trade (Ch. 12, C, (iv)).

E. The Balance of Payments

Diagram I shows that both imports and exports declined during the fifteen years from 1832. The latter fell more steeply than imports, so that by the late forties the two were about equal. From 1850 onwards the two rose slowly until World War I but, on the whole, imports tended to grow slightly more quickly than exports. After the war there was a great increase, but this time the excess of imports was substantial and of long duration. Thus, whereas up to 1849 export surpluses were the rule, deficits became more frequent subsequently. Apart from the minor import surpluses of 1849–52, 1863–5, 1904–5, 1908 and 1912–13 which were due to special causes such as the sus-

[1] Contract between the Crown Agents for the Colonies and Messrs. Elder Dempster and Co., BPP, 1900 (Cd. 175).

[2] Olivier, *op. cit.*, pp. 377–98. [3] Canada–West Indies Trade Agreement.

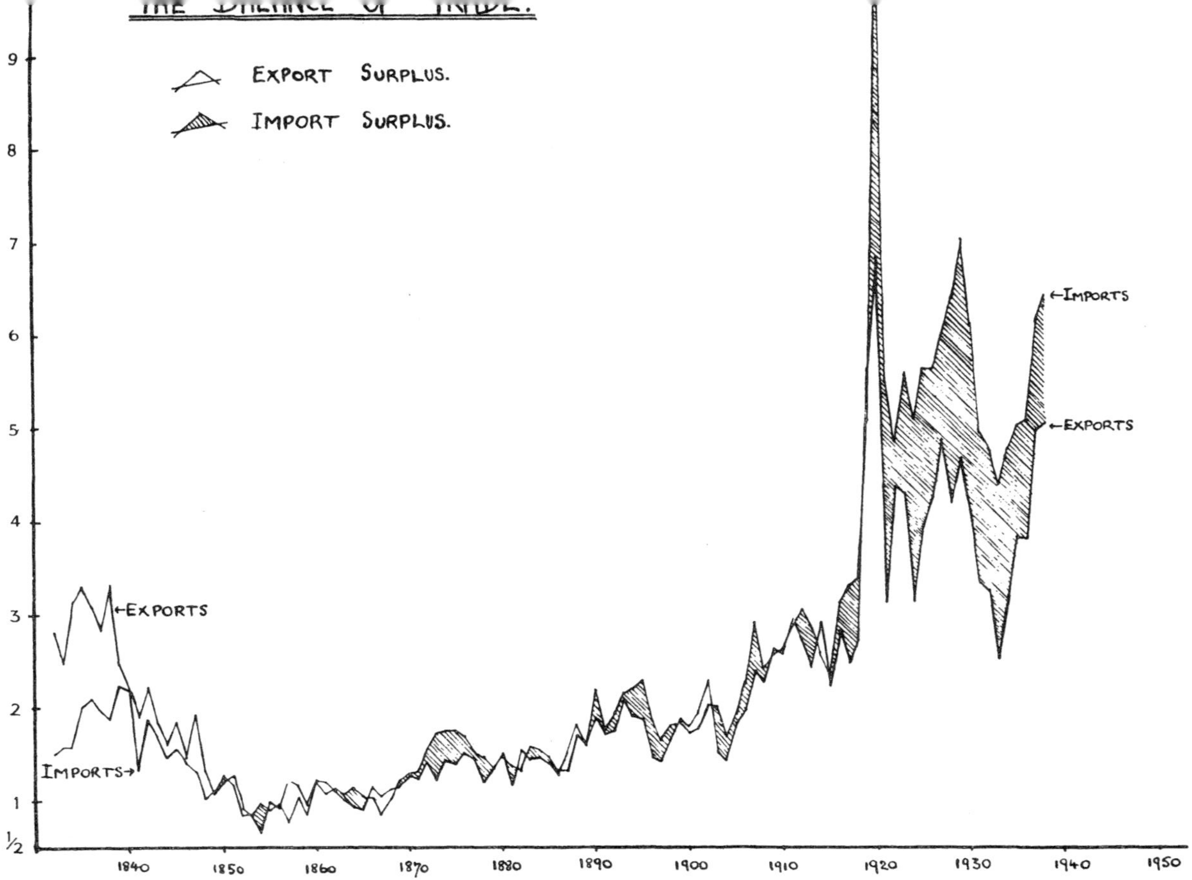

EXPORT SURPLUS.
IMPORT SURPLUS.
←EXPORTS
IMPORTS→
←IMPORTS
←EXPORTS
9
8
7
6
5
4
3
2
1
½
1840
1850
1860
1870
1880
1890
1900
1910
1920
1930
1940
1950

pension of import duties, during the first years of adverse balance, and droughts, storm damage and the Kingston earthquakes in later years, and which were generally followed by export surpluses, there were four chief periods of negative trade balance. These occurred in the years 1869–78, 1883–6, 1890–9 and from 1917 onwards.

Unfortunately our information about invisible earnings and payments abroad is very poor. Since for the most part we have been able to make only very crude estimates of these items we have decided to refer, as explained in Ch. 1, I, to the resultant balance simply as Foreign Balance. Not much accuracy can be claimed for the results. As indicated in the notes accompanying the estimates in Part I, however, the probable errors are not likely to change the sign of the net balance in any of the years. Before interpreting the results of these estimates it may be useful to comment briefly on the conclusions we reached in compiling them. As far as invisible earnings are concerned these do not appear to have been of much consequence during the nineteenth century. They consisted mainly of earnings from the entrepôt trade and receipts from religious societies. It was only after the turn of the century that emigrants' remittances and receipts from the tourist trade became substantial. For most of these items we have been able to make estimates. Payments abroad, however, were rather more difficult to estimate. We have not been able to make any estimates at all for profits sent abroad or other payments except those made by public authorities. The resultant foreign balance, together with the balance of trade, is shown in Table LIV.

TABLE LIV

The Balance of Payments

Year	Balance of Trade	Foreign Balance	Foreign Balance as % of GDP
	£'000	£'000	%
1832	1,017·8	1,090·4	21·9
1850	– 142·3	– 93·1	– 2·5
1870	– 79·7	– 109·8	– 1·9
1890	– 227·2	– 264·0	– 3·0
1910	– 77·3	– 75·9	– 0·7
1930	– 1,807·3	– 1,540·6	– 7·7

What emerges from Table LIV is, first, the persistently negative foreign balance from *1850* onwards, and secondly, the relatively much smaller share of this balance in the national income for most of the period. In *1832* the positive balance accounted for as much as 22 per cent of Gross Domestic Product, but by *1850* it had dropped to 2·5 per cent and continued at around this level until *1930*, when it had risen again to nearly 8 per cent.

As a general rule, we should expect the inflow of capital to be heavy when exports are profitable or when the government is borrowing abroad. Neither condition applied before 1865. Exports were not flourishing not so much because prices were adverse—they actually began to improve again in the fifties—but because the other pre-requisites to an expanding industry, as we saw in Ch. 11, were not present. At the same time the government was neither strong enough nor interested in construction schemes in the island and hence no borrowing took place. As a result there was a net outflow of capital in the early years. The negative balance of *1850* was only temporary and was due to the legislative deadlock which, because of the expiry of the Import Duties Act, resulted in an unusually heavy volume of imports. It was only after the establishment of the new government that conditions for foreign investment changed. The new government began to raise funds abroad to finance its public works programmes, but towards the end of the century private foreign investment also became important.

With government borrowing profitability is not the immediate criterion in public investment provided the government is securely established and there is confidence that interest payments will be met. The negative balance in the years between 1869 and 1878, in spite of unfavourable price movements, was due to the public works programme undertaken by the island government with loans floated in London with the backing of the Imperial government. These were the years following the change in constitution, during which much needed to be done to make up for past decades of neglect and mismanagement. Obviously the guiding principle was the firm establishment of the new government if confidence in the economic future of the island was to be restored. Accordingly the government began by improving public buildings, roads, bridges, railway services and other communications.

We have summarized the value of all loans raised under the authority of the government, including those raised for special purposes such as irrigation schemes (Table LV). It will be seen that during the first fifteen years of the life of the new government, between 1865 and 1879, a total of £731,300 was raised—that is a sum considerably in excess of that raised in the preceding years. Government policy for improving public services received a new impetus with the development of the fruit trade. Better communications were needed and there was also scope for government assistance in bringing new land under production. Hence the years between 1880 and 1894 saw an even greater expansion in government borrowing for railway extension, irrigation works and road improvements.

TABLE LV

Gross Government Borrowing for All Purposes during the Years 1860 to 1934

Years	£'000	Years	£'000
1860–64	107·7	1900–04	165·9
1865–74	731·3	1905–09	30·0
1875–79	155·0	1910–14	143·0
1880–84	1,044·2	1915–19	217·0
1885–89	2,800·1	1920–24	1,515·5
1890–94	820·9	1925–29	429·6
1895–99	40·0	1930–34	86·5

Source: HBJ, for 1932.

Beginning in the middle nineties, however, government borrowing had to be curtailed drastically as a result of the combined effects of depression in the sugar industry and the failure of the Jamaica railway. Thereafter a series of unfortunate events—hurricanes and the earthquake of 1907—prevented further expansion of public works and it was not, in fact, until the early twenties that government borrowing regained its former importance. In the two years 1922 and 1923 alone the government borrowed over £1½ million to finance railway improvements and schools, water and sewage developments. During the second quinquennium of the twenties total borrowing by the government had again declined to less than £½ million—most of which was destined for railway improvement.

Beginning in the eighties foreign private investment was also becoming important. Unfortunately we have no statistical information about this. Our estimate of the balance of payments for *1890* gives only a very imperfect indication of the level of capital imports because we have been unable to include profits sent abroad and, moreover, a substantial part of the capital imports at that time were, as we have seen, the result of government borrowing. It appears that the American banana companies, finding local supplies of fruit inadequate, began to invest in banana plantations directly. By 1893 the United Fruit Company owned 15 estates and seven years later their number had risen to 32.[1] Investment by banana companies directly in planting was reduced subsequently, no doubt because of local difficulties arising from their monopolistic position in the island and possibly also because at this time the United Fruit Company was investing heavily in plantations in Costa Rica. Due to this and also to reduced government borrowing abroad the estimated amount of capital imports in *1910* had declined to £75,900—that is less than one per cent of Gross Domestic Product and may have been even lower since our estimates of emigrants' remittances are rather doubtful.

It is, however, during the twenties and thirties that the most interesting balance of payments situation developed. After the boom at the end of the war prices of most exports began to fall catastrophically. London c.i.f. prices fell between 1920 and 1921 from £58 to £19·5 per ton of sugar; from 148*s*. to 121*s*. per cwt. of coffee; from 69·25*s*. to 29·5*s*. per cwt. of cocoa; from 390*s*. to 318·4*s*. per ton of logwood, and, apart from a partial recovery in the middle twenties, continued to fall subsequently. Only banana prices showed a much slower downward trend: the price per stem fell by only 0·35*s*. from 3·40*s*. in 1920 to 3·05*s*. in the following year. Yet during the twenties the trade balance was persistently negative, averaging about two-fifths of total exports, and the estimated amount of capital imports in *1930* is about one-quarter of total exports.

There is no mystery about the level of capital imports immediately after the war. During the early post-war years and the middle twenties sugar estates re-equipped their factories, but, as, according to our information, most of the sugar estates were Jamaican-owned, investment must have been financed either out of previous earnings or with loans raised abroad. Investment in sugar factories practically ceased during the latter part of the twenties and government borrowing, as we saw above, also accounted for only a negligible part of the foreign balance. In the absence of information any attempt to account for the persistently negative balance during these and subsequent years can be little more than guesswork. However, several explanations offer themselves.

[1] HBJ for 1895 and 1902.

Perhaps the most obvious is the possibility that our estimates of invisible earnings are understated. Yet no reasonable margin in the estimates of the tourist trade and profits from abroad can possibly account for the large gap.

A second explanation for the continuing capital imports may be the borrowing from abroad by sugar and banana estates. The willingness to lend may have been encouraged by the policy of Imperial Preference and the knowledge that the United Kingdom would protect colonial producers from the worst consequences of world competition: a belief not, in fact, without foundation. As we saw in Section A, (i), preferential duties and direct subsidies kept the price to Jamaican growers considerably above the world price. The effect of this policy was that up to 1930 no sugar estate had been abandoned as a consequence of the depression of the sugar market.[1] We have also seen that the price of bananas fell much less than that of the other commodities during the twenties. All the same, it is hard to see how borrowing by either sugar or banana estates owned by Jamaicans could account for more than a fraction of the total capital imports. In our examination of the estate economy we found no evidence to suggest that partnerships with overseas capitalists were being formed and, since only relatively few estates were owned by corporate enterprises, access to overseas finance must have been difficult for the majority of the estates. It appears more likely that most of the investment during the late twenties was made by foreigners directly. The number of banana estates increased from 329 to 505 in the ten years beginning in 1920.[2] Of interest in this context, however, is the fact that of this considerable expansion, the United Fruit Company alone was responsible for twenty.

The third, and most likely, explanation is to be found in the expansion of new enterprises. There was, as we saw in Ch. 10, C, some growth in manufacturing industry. There was also considerable expansion in retail trading. Larger stores began to be built in Kingston and a few of the other more populous centres. But perhaps the most important development took place in the tourist trade. With improved communications with North America and publicity of the island's attractions, Jamaica was quickly becoming a fashionable tourist centre for Americans. Again, the information about the size and origin of investment in the tourist trade is scant. According to the HBJ the number of hotels and boarding-houses had been more

[1] WISC, p. 13.

[2] HBJ for 1921 and 1932.

than doubled from 54 in 1910 to 114 in 1930. Overseas investment appears to have been an important factor in this development. Some of the largest and most famous hotels—among them the Myrtle Bank in Kingston and the Titchfield in Port Antonio—were either built or bought by American companies.[1]

[1] HBJ, for 1928.

CHAPTER 14

PRODUCTIVITY

THE basic ingredients for increases in productivity are techniques, capital and a favourable attitude to economic progress. In this chapter our first task is to measure changes in productivity and our second, to account for them.

A. PRODUCTIVITY

As a first measure of productivity we take our estimates of gross domestic product, prepared in Part I for selected years from 1832 to 1930, and divide them by total population. Eliminating price changes, as shown in Table LVI, we see that the per capita product fell sharply

TABLE LVI

Per Capita Output at 1910 Prices

Year	Gross Domestic Product £'000	Per Capita Product £
1832	5,772·5	15·6
1850	4,886·5	12·2
1870	6,006·0	11·9
1890	7,925·3	12·4
1910	11,361·9	13·7
1930	15,969·5	15·7

Source: Ch. 8, Table B.

after emancipation, and continued to fall until the arrival of the banana. Not until the 1890's did a significant rise begin. Between *1832* and *1850* per capita output fell by more than one-fifth from £15·6 to £12·2. During the forty years beginning in *1850* the rise in the total product kept approximately in step with population growth; the rise was slightly slower up to *1870* so that the per capita product fell to £11·9 but somewhat higher thereafter, thus bringing about a rise to £12·4 in *1890*. After *1890*, however, per capita output rose rapidly: between *1890* and *1910* it increased by about one-twelfth and during the last twenty years at an even higher rate until in *1930* it amounted to nearly £16.

In Table LVII, Part I, we make an attempt to estimate productivity in agriculture and in the non-agricultural sectors, using the revised estimates of the working population. It is important to note, however, that for the purposes of this table we have adjusted our estimates of agricultural output to conform to the census definition

TABLE LVII

Output per Earner in Agriculture and in the Non-Agricultural Sectors

PART 1. OUTPUT AT *1910* PRICES

Year	Agricultural Output £'000	Labour Force '000	Per Capita Agricultural Output £	Non-Agricultural Output* £'000	Labour Force '000	Per Capita Non-Agricultural Output £
1832 . . .	3,396·5	116·0	29·3	1,874·7	51·0	36·8
1850 . . .	2,518·0	121·5	20·7	1,850·2	50·2	36·9
1890 . . .	3,957·1	172·5	22·9	3,085·9	102·2	30·2
1930 . . .	7,703·3	223·0	34·5	6,626·1	188·9	35·1

PART 2. OUTPUT AT CURRENT PRICES

Year	Agricultural Output £'000	Labour Force '000	Per Capita Agricultural Output £	Non-Agricultural Output* £'000	Labour Force '000	Per Capita Non-Agricultural Output £
1832 . . .	2,932·7	116·0	25·3	1,556·3	51·0	30·5
1850 . . .	1,904·7	121·5	15·7	1,403·5	50·2	28·0
1890 . . .	4,421·2	172·5	25·6	3,306·7	102·2	32·4
1930 . . .	9,014·1	223·0	40·4	8,391·0	188·9	44·4

* Excludes rent.

Sources: For output figures see Part I.
For population data in *1832* and *1890* see Ch. 9, Table XIX; estimates for *1850* are based on the assumption of even growth between 1844 and 1861; for *1930* we have assumed even growth for the total labour force between 1921 and 1943 but in the case of the agricultural labour force have added 31,000 to the 1921 number to allow for increasing employment in ground provision and banana cultivation—the non-agricultural labour force thus represents the difference between the two calculations.

of agricultural employment. Thus agricultural output here includes all manufactured sugar and rum and also the value of distribution services performed by workers in agriculture; but it excludes the estimated value of distribution services performed by the specialized transport and distributive workers. What we are, in fact, measuring here is the productivity of all workers engaged in the agricultural industry and not that of primary production. In order to bring our estimates in Part I, which show output at final value at factor cost, into line with the census definition we have taken out the estimated value of distribution services performed by non-agricultural workers. This was possible only for those years for which we have been able to estimate income distribution, and hence no values are shown in Table LVII for the years *1870* and *1910*.

According to Table LVII the series for agricultural per capita output broadly followed that of total per capita output. There was a similarly sharp fall in output between *1832* and *1850*, and again a sharp increase after *1890*. Only in the years between *1850* and *1890* was there a tendency to diverge: in these years per capita agricultural output actually rose by about £2 from £21 in *1850* to £23 in *1890*, compared with the relative stability in the total per capita product. Per capita output in the non-agricultural sectors, on the other hand, began to fall only after *1850* and also recovered more slowly after *1890*.

Per capita output in agriculture declined during the early years because production for the export market declined. Since export crops have a much higher per capita value than production for the domestic market, and no relative expansion of domestic agriculture took place to compensate for the reduction in exports, there was a net decline in per capita output of nearly £9. During the following forty years there were only slight increases in exports (coffee and the minor products) and in domestic agriculture (exports retained for home consumption) relatively to growth in the agricultural labour force. But from *1890* onwards exports and retained exports increased relatively rapidly bringing about the large increase in per capita output from about £23 to £35.

Variations in the per capita output of the non-agricultural sectors were also due to changes in composition. Broadly, there was a decline in the occupations with a high income and an increase in those with a low per capita income. We have already seen in Ch. 2, A, how the number of professional people began to decline in the 1830's and continued to fall until the 1870's and that, at the same time, there was an increase in the ranks of the lower-paid professional people and, even more important, in industrial, domestic and commercial workers. As a result, per capita output fell from £37 in *1850* to £30 in *1890*, and began to recover only subsequently with the relative growth in the number of civil servants, professional workers and merchants.

This shift from the higher- to the lower-income occupations also brought about a narrowing in the margins between agricultural and non-agricultural per capita output after *1850*. The difference between the two series declined from about £16 in *1850* to less than £1 in *1930*. The result is almost the same if we take output at current prices. According to Table LVII, Part 2, non-agricultural per capita output also declined and, in spite of a substantial recovery after *1890*, exceeded agricultural per capita output by only £4 in *1930*. But in considering these differences it is important to bear in mind that the estimates of agricultural output include much manufacturing and a great deal of distribution. Agricultural output according to the standard definition (i.e. excluding all manufacturing and distribution) would be lower and hence the margin between the agricultural and non-agricultural series greater.

But, whichever definition of agricultural output is adopted, there can be no doubt that the margin between agricultural and non-agricultural per capita output had narrowed over the years. This was the result of the relative decline in agricultural employment and the growth in the number engaged in the service trades. As we have already seen, the labour force increased more quickly than employment in agriculture. People unable to find work on the land or ancillary occupations moved to badly paid jobs in the towns. Practically all the jobs which accounted for the large increase in the non-agritural labour force—the independent workers after the middle of the century and, particularly, domestic servants and petty traders after the eighties—were characterized by a low per capita output. Since our estimates of non-agricultural output exclude all output of factories, except the small amount produced by the secondary industries established after *1890*, and also a great deal of distribution, Table LVII thus brings out the effect of the movement of the surplus working population out of agriculture into the service trades on the relative per capita output.

We conclude, then, that the variations in per capita output were due to changes in both agricultural and non-agricultural productivities. The variations in our estimates of non-agricultural per capita output are accounted for by changes in the composition of the labour force. They have been calculated on a per capita basis, and thus do not take account of any changes in the quality of services. Undoubtedly, some services became more efficient and others less so: medical practitioners were better trained in the 1930's than in 1830 and the improved hospital facilities enabled them to make fuller use of their skill; public administrators similarly were relieved of the more repetitive burdens by the increasing employment of clerks and shorthand typists. Such factors are difficult to measure, as is also the decrease in efficiency of domestics and petty traders resulting from the splitting up of available employment. We have therefore been compelled to ignore such changes in quality and hence, except for changes in composition, we must expect per capita output in the non-agricultural sectors to remain constant.

In the agricultural sector, on the other hand, variations in per capita output were the result not only of changes in composition but also of changes in techniques. Ideally, we should proceed next to trace changes in per capita output for the different agricultural products. Unfortunately, this task has proved impossible partly owing to the structure of the industry and partly to the peculiarities of wage employment. In the first place, much of the agricultural output was contributed by small settlers whose cultivation, as we have seen, was mixed: estimates of productivity for different crops are therefore out of the question. Secondly, where agriculture was specialized, as in the case of sugar, coffee and later bananas, the available returns of the labour force are not suitable because there was no standard working week. The number of hours per day and days per week worked varied greatly and, although later censuses give details of employment according to crop, the accompanying data of duration of employment are not available.

Alternatively, productivity may be estimated by taking acreage, instead of labour, as a unit of measurement. But here again the problem of mixed cultivation arises. Nor did the specialized estates often furnish the necessary information. Only in the case of the sugar industry has it, in fact, been possible to calculate acreage yields for a number of years. These, shown in Table LVIII, have been collected from a variety of sources, and not all can be taken as representative of the sugar industry for that particular year: those for 1837 and 1846 are average yields based on three successive years for a single estate; those for 1859 and 1870 refer to estates in Hanover where acreage yields were below the island average, while those for 1896 and 1929 are taken from returns submitted to public commissions, which are not necessarily random samples. Only the years 1880 and 1890 refer to data for the whole industry: 1890 being based on a three-year average and 1880 on one year only (and that a very favourable one compared with 1879 and 1881). Because of the possibility of bias in the data due to their selection, we have to be wary about attaching significance to small differences. Thus all that can reasonably be claimed for the years up to 1890 is that there was some suggestion of rising yields and that it was only after 1890 that a definite upward

TABLE LVIII

Sugar Yields

Year	Average Yield per Acre (tons)
1837[1]	0·63
1846[1]	0·74
1859[2]	0·64
1870[3]	0·78
1880[4]	0·80
1890[5]	0·80
1896[6]	0·92
1929[7]	1·91

Sources: 1. Sugar and Coffee Planting, BPP, 1847–8 (167), Q. 4434.
2. PPSC, BPP, 1861 (2841), p. 7.
3. JA, 1870.
4. HBJ, 1883.
5. HBJ, 1890, 1891 and 1892.
6. BPP, 1897 (C 8669), Pt. XIII (751).
7. This yield is calculated from the average yield of canes per acre—21·2 tons—and the ratio of cane to refining sugar—11·0965 tons. WISC, BPP, 1930 (Cmd. 3517), p. 43, and SSIJ, J. Govt. Printer, 1929, pp. 88–9.

trend began. As seen from Table LVIII yields per acre rose by less than one per cent per annum in the first seventy years after emancipation and by more than three per cent per annum between 1896 and 1929. That acreage yields actually show an upward trend when abandonment of cultivation was so widespread may cause surprise. But we must remember that the least efficient producers were the first to suffer and that average output would, for this reason alone, increase without any improvement in techniques.

What happened in the sugar industry after the 1830's, however, had little effect on agricultural productivity because the share of sugar in output declined throughout the years. It is for this reason that productivity in the agricultural industry fell in spite of the rise in the sugar industry during the nineteenth century and also rose much more slowly than that of sugar thereafter.

Throughout this section we have stated that the per capita return in domestic agriculture was lower than that in exports. As pointed out above we have no direct information about productivity. In fact all we can say is that productivity in the production of the staple foods remained approximately stable. This rests on the assumption we made in Ch. 1, D, that per capita consumption of the stable starch foods remained constant throughout the years. The number of those employed in cultivating ground provisions also appears to have remained a stable proportion of the total population. According to Table XXVII, Ch. 10, the number of men engaged in provision growing varied between 14 per cent in 1891 and 13 per cent in 1921. Before 1891, the relative fall in the total agricultural labour force is accounted for by the decline in sugar and coffee planting. Thus it would seem that productivity must also have remained constant.

The large differences in the productivities in export and home production were mainly due to the techniques employed. By tradition, both private and public concerns centred on the export industry while, for the greater part of the period, little interest or capital was expended on production for the home market. Indeed the important contribution of ground provisions to the domestic food supply was not recognized until national income estimates began to be prepared during World War II,[1] and other activities, such as stock-rearing, hardly fared any better. Our main concern in the remainder of this chapter, therefore, will be with exports. We shall try to show how changes in productivity in exports were brought about and, in the process, attempt to explain why progress in other spheres was so slow.

B. Technological Changes

(i) *Sugar Industry*

Before emancipation, production methods employed in the sugar industry relied heavily on manual labour and only infrequently were attempts made to substitute animals or machinery for the simpler tasks. Where machinery was employed it was crude and, compared with other countries, antiquated. Briefly, cane juice was extracted by primitive mills operated by water or wind, sometimes by animal but more often by human labour. Sugar boiling was done in a series of

[1] Benham, *op. cit.*, Bulletin No. 5.

open pans fired by bagasse—the stalks of the cane left after the sugar had been extracted—and coal and the separation of molasses from raw sugar was accomplished by leaving the casks to drain. Yields per acre were low; the extraction rate was also extremely low and losses due to drainage during the long voyage to the United Kingdom and spoiling were high.

Of the total capital needed to start a sugar plantation in 1819 in Jamaica only one-sixth was actually invested in factory buildings and equipment while the cost of slaves and stock accounted for as much as one-half—the remaining one-third representing the cost of land.[1] The estate described by Bryan Edwards manufactured about 200 hogsheads per annum, but most of the factories appear to have been smaller. It is interesting to note that in 1846 the factory of the Cuban estate Ingenio Saratoga had a capacity of 800 tons. Although still using slaves their dependence on manual labour was considerably less than it had been in pre-emancipation Jamaica. The share of slaves was only one-third, while that of buildings and equipment was almost as high. Steam engines, mills and railed transport were already in use.[2]

Many technical improvements were, in fact, available long before this date. During the twenties, thirties and forties a number of guides to sugar planting, describing improved methods of cultivation and manufacture, were published.[3]

The most obvious improvement was the plough to replace the arduous manual labour involved in cane hole digging. In some instances the plough was tried but, for many estates, it was said to be unsuitable because of the type of soil and the number and cost of traction cattle required.[4] Cane hole digging with spade and hoe thus remained the standard practice until the twentieth century. The substitution of cattle for human labour for cartage and in the sugar mill was carried out more universally. Apart from providing motive power the cattle also supplied manure: but this was not always used in the best possible way.[5] Instead of preparing the manure in the

[1] Edwards, B. *The History of the British West Indies*. London, 1819, vol. II, pp. 292–7.

[2] Deerr, N. *The History of Sugar*, London, 1950, vol. II, p. 337.

[3] Porter, G. R. *The Nature and Properties of the Sugar Cane*, London, 1843.
Roughley, T. *The Jamaican Planter's Guide*, London, 1823.
Wray, L. *The Practical Sugar Planter*, London, 1848. In addition see list given by Burns, W. L., *Emancipation and Apprenticeship in the B.W.I.*, London, 1937 p. 44n.

[4] SCP, BPP, 1847–8 (167), Qs. 4,520–1 and 6563. [5] *Ibid.*, Qs. 6747–50.

yard and applying it to the tilled land, cattle were penned in the field. But on exhausted soils animal manure was not sufficient. Bryan Edwards, writing in 1819, had already pointed to the 'great room for improvement, by way of judicious rotation of crops, and artificial assistance' and enumerated a number of locally available materials.[1] Small amounts of guano began to be imported in the middle of the century. In *1850* the value of imported manure was only £1,924, but twenty years later it had risen to £10,076.[2]

The type of cane planted in Jamaica was the Bourbon or Otaheite. This yielded well and ratooned over a long period, but being a shallow rooter it was susceptible to drought and fungus diseases.[3] The effect of dry seasons is shown clearly in the large annual fluctuation in output, but evidence of diseases is rather harder to discover. This may, of course, have been due to the lack of diagnosis. In any case, the need for different cane varieties was sufficiently obvious to encourage the Botanical Gardens to sponsor their introduction after 1870. Of the varieties tried out the most successful was the White Transparent.

To improve the manufacturing process there was the steam mill to replace the water and cattle mills, and the vacuum pan to improve the method of separating the sugar from the molasses. But both required skilled mechanics for their maintenance. Engineers and sugar boilers had to be brought from Europe, and that was worth while only if the price for the improved quality of sugar was increased sufficiently to make up for the higher costs, or yields increased sufficiently to reduce total costs. In the case of vacuum pan sugar apparently the higher prices obtained for the improved quality were not enough to offset the increased costs. The reason for this in 1846 was said to be that the vacuum pan sugar 'did neither for one thing nor the other; it was neither a fit article for the grocer nor a fit article for the refiner; that it was something in between the two; that under no circumstances was it of much greater value than 3*s*., which would not pay the increased expense of manufacture'.[4] Only five or six vacuum pans were in operation in Jamaica at this time.[5] As for the steam mill, the experience of Mr. Price had discouraged other planters. Mr. Price had imported 'a very fine and large mill; being so large and fine a mill, in all probability there was nobody in the island competent to

[1] *Op. cit.*, p. 257.
[2] See Appendix I, Sections 2, B and C.
[3] Deerr, N. *Cane Sugar*, London, 1921, p. 51.
[4] SCP (184), Q. 9136.
[5] *Ibid.*, Q. 9141.

mend it when it was out of repair'.[1] In a society lacking industrial skills the introduction of mechanical equipment was, undoubtedly, a hazardous undertaking; where a planter relied entirely on the new machinery he risked the loss of his whole crop if any breakdown could not be repaired locally. Mr. Price's estate, for example, was said to have got into financial difficulties as a result of his experiments.[2]

Instead of adopting improved techniques planters generally chose the negative policy of restricting output. Average output per factory decreased from 104 tons in 1832 to 56 tons in 1852 (Table LXI). In view of the deterioration in the conditions of production it is surprising that it was possible for Jamaican estates to survive at all, especially with an even lower average output.

If profitability of sugar estates had solely depended on size—capacity of factory or area under cultivation—we should have expected output per factory to increase in spite of the reduction in the number of estates and total output. But this was not the case: the loss in this period was clearly not confined to the smaller estates. Unfortunately we have no information about estates' acreages for these years. An indication of the trend can, however, be obtained from the geographical distribution of estates. From Table LIX we see that the decline in the number of estates between 1836 and 1852 was greatest in St. Andrew, Portland, St. Elizabeth, St. Thomas, and St. Catherine and least in Westmoreland, Trelawny and Clarendon. Comparing these relative losses with the extent of cultivation in 1910, when sugar production was at its lowest and hence confined to the most productive areas, we see that the three parishes losing the least number of estates during the first twenty years cultivated about 70 per cent of total estates' sugar acreage in 1910.[3] This suggests that the declining cultivation in the early years was primarily due to unfavourable location—soil or situation—for sugar planting, and that size of estate became an important factor only later.

Another way of reducing losses that was open to sugar planters lay in varying the proportion of sugar and rum manufacture. Though theoretically it was possible to concentrate on the production of either sugar or rum the extreme cases were rarely found. Generally cane juice was boiled and the molasses reboiled once or twice to extract crystallizable sugar and the remainder left to ferment for rum. By changing the number of reboilings the proportion of rum and

[1] SCP (163), Q. 4551. [2] *Ibid.*, Q. 4544. [3] HBJ, 1911.

sugar could be varied with their relative prices. After 1830 planters took advantage of relatively higher rum prices. Table LX shows that the rum ratio increased sharply between *1832* and *1850*, and again between *1870* and *1890*. Though lower in *1870*, when the price of sugar had increased slightly, it was still above that of *1832*.

TABLE LIX

Geographical Distribution of Sugar Planting in 1836 and 1852

Parish	Number of Estates		1852 as Percentage of 1836
	1836[1]	1852[2]	
Westmoreland . . .	48	40	83
Trelawny	84	62	74
Clarendon	70	49	70
Hanover	59	41	70
St. Ann	32	22	69
St. Mary	60	41	68
St. James	89	56	63
St. Catharine . . .	56	32	57
St. Thomas. . . .	82	47	57
St. Elizabeth . . .	27	13	48
St. Andrew. . . .	17	7	41
Portland	46	17	37
Total	670	427	64

Sources: 1. Papers re Abolition of Slavery, BPP, 1836 (166), Pt. III–I, p. 24.
2. PAIJ, BPP, 1854 (1848), p. 55.

Possibly also ratooning was more widely adopted after emancipation. Ratoons are the growth of cane roots left in the ground after the first year's crop. These roots can be left to ratoon for several years, but each season the length and circumference of the shoots are smaller and yield less juice. But this method also has certain advantages. Holing and planting were physically the most exacting part of sugar planting, and with ratooning only weeding, loosening of the soil and manuring are required. In a well cared for ratoon field the yield was estimated by Bryan Edwards to be as much as 0·55 tons per acre,[1] which did not compare too unfavourably with the average yield of

[1] Edwards, *op. cit.*, pp. 244–5.

plant cane at that time. So long as the reduction in output was not greater than the saving in labour costs it was clearly more profitable to ratoon canes. In Bryan Edwards' day it was already standard practice to plant only one-third of the land each year. With the more expensive and uncertain labour supply in the post-emancipation period the incentive to extend ratooning was even greater. Unfortunately, the evidence about ratooning is rather indeterminate. In

TABLE LX

Ratio of Sugar and Rum Output

Year	Exports		Ratio Gallons per cwt.	Prices f.o.b.		Price Index	
	Sugar '000 cwt.	Rum '000 glns.		Sugar cwt.	Rum glns.	Sugar	Rum
1832 .	1,362	3,166	2·32	19*s.*	1*s.* 7*d.*	100	100
1850 .	565	1,760	3·11	17*s.* 10½*d.*	2*s.* 8*d.*	95	169
1870 .	545	1,504	2·76	18*s.* 7*d.*	2*s.* 11½*d.*	98	186
1890 .	376	1,558	4·15	12*s.* 10½*d.*	2*s.* 8*d.*	68	169

Sources: For Quantities see Table XLII, Ch. 13, and for prices Ch. 1, E.

1870 the Governor of Jamaica spoke of a 'system of permanent ratooning—where on some estates a complete field of yearling plants is hardly ever seen, the plants that fail being replaced yearly plant by plant'.[1] At the end of the century ratooning was still an important method of reducing costs for the 'general practice is to establish from 10–30 per cent of plant canes each year according to the special circumstances of the estates to replace an equivalent acreage of ratoon suffered to drop out'.[2] However, it is also possible that ratooning increased only where estates were on the verge of abandonment.

Abandonment of unsuitable land, a higher rum ratio and possibly also ratooning, enabled some estates to continue production without the introduction of technical improvements. Mortality of sugar estates throughout this period, however, remained high and with the fall in prices, beginning in the seventies, it became clear that a more

[1] Report with the BBJ, BPP, 1872 (C 523).
[2] RWIC, BPP, 1897 (C 8669), Pt. XIII, No. 739.

venturesome attitude to production was needed if sugar planting was to survive. The beet-sugar industry in Europe had been revolutionized by the invention in 1860 of the diffusion process which made possible a rate of extraction far higher than that obtained from the existing mills in the cane-sugar industry. As a result of this, and of the improvements in acreage yields to which it gave rise, beet-sugar production in Europe doubled between 1864 and 1871 and in 1881 world production of beet began to exceed that of cane.[1] It was this final blow that stimulated the search for improved methods, which eventually were also introduced into Jamaica.

Briefly, there are four ways of raising productivity per man. These are increased cane yields, reduced labour requirements per acre, higher extraction rates and improved methods of manufacture. We have already seen that by the 1890's the White Transparent cane was replacing the Bourbon and Otaheite varieties. Much was claimed for its disease-resistant qualities, but after World War I an outbreak of Mosaic disease led to renewed search for suitable varieties. Altogether fifty-three varieties were tried out, and between 1920 and 1929 nearly 3½ million cuttings were distributed by the Department of Agriculture.[2] The Uba cane, introduced from Natal during the war, came to the rescue of many estates hit by the disease.[3] Its sucrose content, however, was not high and it was difficult to cut and handle in the factories.[4] When superior canes became available it found its proper place in the poorer soils.[5] More promising varieties were obtained from the Department of Agriculture in Barbados. Experimental work in seedling canes had produced the B.H.10(12) and the Ba 6032. In the late twenties the increased cane yields were mainly due to the former; in many instances its yields were more than double those of other varieties.[6] In the years 1929–30, 7,633 acres were planted in B.H.10(12). The White Transparent was the next in importance with 7,339 acres, and thirdly the Uba with 6,644 acres.[7] Together with the increasing use of fertilizers the new cane varieties made possible far more intensive cultivation.

Apart from increasing cane yields improvements in cultivation were confined to the adoption of the plough. No method of mechanizing reaping was found and canes continued to be cut and cleaned manually. The scale of operation in cultivation was thus not as

[1] Deerr, N. *The History of the Sugar Cane*, *op. cit.*, pp. 490–1.
[2] SSIJ. J. Govt. Printer, 1929, p. 60. [3] *Ibid.*, p. 58. [4] *Ibid.*, p. 76.
[5] *Ibid.*, p. 58. [6] *Ibid.* [7] *Ibid.*, pp. 62–3.

important as in manufacture. The main advantage to factories growing their own cane lay in the certainty and proximity of supplies, and after the turn of the century manufacturing estates found it worth while to buy canes from outside growers (Ch. 11, I).

In the manufacturing processes, too, striking advances were made. Once centralization was started modernization proceeded rapidly.

TABLE LXI

Average Output of Sugar Factories

Year	Number of Factories	Total Output tons*	Average Output tons
1832	653[1]	68,100[5]	104
1846	513[1]	34,450[5]	67
1852	427[2]	24,067[5]	56
1869	266[3]	27,553[5]	104
1880	202[4]	29,221[4]	148
1890	162[4]	24,164[4]	149
1900	111[4]	20,762[4]	187
1910	74[4]	21,312[4]	288
1920	66[4]	37,015[4]	561
1930	39[4]	61,293[4]	1,572

* Represents average of three successive years for all years except 1880.

Sources: 1. SCP, BPP, 1847–8 (245), App., p. 153.
2. PAIJ, BPP, 1854 (1848), p. 55.
3. BBJ, 1869.
4. HBJ relating to these years.
5. Table XLII, Ch. 13. Figures here are three-year averages.

The progress made is indicated by the capacity of factories. Table LXI shows the average output of sugar factories between 1832 and 1930. It should be noted that up to 1880 output includes exports only; for 1880 and subsequent years it represents total production—i.e. sugar sold in the home market as well as exports. The large rise in average output between 1869 and 1880 may be largely accounted for by this difference in content, but it is not likely that earlier years would be affected significantly by the inclusion of domestic consumption. However, our interest here is confined to the last fifty years. Between 1880 and 1930 output per factory rose more than ten-fold; the most spectacular increases taking place in the twentieth century. In the last ten years alone capacity was nearly trebled.

Inside the factory considerable changes had taken place. Extracting techniques were the first to be improved. This was due to the profitability of the rum market. So long as the maximum cane juice was extracted the efficiency of manufacturing could be neglected since the sugar remaining in the molasses could always be recovered in the distillery. Of the 162 factories operating in 1890 as many as one hundred were using steam mills, while a further 19 used both steam and water. Twenty years later 75 per cent of estates were using steam mills, and by 1930 only mills driven by steam or electricity were in operation.[1] The rate of extraction in 1897 was 65 per cent, though one planter obtained as much as 70–75 per cent.[2] In 1930 two factories recorded extractions of 82–85 per cent while the remainder obtained 72 per cent or less.[3] Compared with the recovery of about 88 per cent obtained in other British West Indian territories there was thus still room for improvement.[4]

Even more remarkable, during this period, were the improvements in the manufacturing processes. Of the 162 factories in 1890 only five used vacuum pans; another 73 had installed centrifugals but 64 were still manufacturing with the old methods only—'common', 'old' and 'open battery of boilers'. In 1910 only 14 retained the old equipment and the number of vacuum pans had risen to 21. By 1930 all sugar was manufactured by vacuum pans and centrifugals.[5] In 1929 the average recovery was one ton of refining sugar for 11·1 tons of cane.[6]

(ii) *Other Agricultural Industries*

Apart from sugar the most important crop in 1830 was coffee. As far as technological changes in this industry are concerned, however, there is little to record. Coffee cultivation by estates declined throughout our period without any serious attempts being made to arrest the decline. Part of the reason for this was the widespread conviction that 'many coffee plantations are worn out. Coffee is planted in what is called virgin soil, and can only be once planted'.[7] The life of coffee trees was said to be only 15 years[8] and many had

[1] HBJ relating to these years. [2] RWIC (C 8669), Pt. XIII, Q. 328.
[3] WISC, BPP, 1930 (Cmd. 3517), p. 115. [4] *Ibid.*, p. 95.
[5] HBJ relating to these years. [6] SSIJ, p. 89. Average of returns listed.
[7] SCP (184), Q. 8,984. [8] *Ibid.* (230), Q. 14,320.

already exceeded this period by the 1840's. Yields per acre at this time were only 271 lb.[1] compared with about 560 lb.[2] in Bryan Edwards' day. Because of the reduced yields it was only the high quality mountain coffee that could compete with Ceylon for these continued to secure a 'fancy price' [3] and hence estate cultivation came to be increasingly concentrated in the Blue Mountains. Here the 'common cry' of soil exhaustion was not heard. Sir Henry Barkly quotes the owner of one of the most thriving plantations in St. Andrew as saying that 'since the plan of manuring the roots of the old trees with guano or bone dust has been introduced, no more complaints of the want of virgin land were made in his neighbourhood; and that he himself considered it just as rational to talk of a coffee piece in Jamaica being worn out as it would be to say that the cornfields of England were unfit for further cultivation'.[4] The peasants, as we have seen, were also exposing the long-held fallacy of soil exhaustion.[5] But settlers' coffee, on the whole, was of inferior quality. This was due not only to the fact that they obtained land abandoned as unsuitable because of exhaustion or elevation, but also to their poor curing techniques. Where they sold their produce to central coffee factories for curing its value was said to be doubled.[6] By the end of the century Liberian coffee was increasingly replacing Arabian. Although the weight of the dried bean per fruit was less in Liberian coffee it was much hardier and more resistant to disease.

Ginger, too, was subject to diminishing yields and again methods of manuring had to demonstrate the fallacy of 'ruinate' land.[7] Ideally planted at elevations of about 2,000 ft. this cultivation had serious consequences later when it became evident that continuous cultivation, without interplanting of deeper rooting trees or crops, led to soil erosion.

Pimento was a spontaneous crop which, it was believed, could be sown only by birds until it was realized that the surrounding pulp had to be removed—as done by the birds—before it was sown.

The great technical problem of the banana industry in the twentieth century was disease. The banaua grown for the export market was the Gros Michel. From the point of view of cultivation and

[1] SCP (245), App., p. 165.
[2] *Op. cit.*, calculated from details given on p. 343.
[3] PAIJ, BPP, 1854 (1848), p. 7. [4] *Ibid.* [5] See Ch. 12, C, (ii).
[6] RWIC (C 8669), Pt. XIII, Q. 1,235.
[7] Col. Rep. BPP, 1898 (C 8650), p. 24.

transport this strain was excellent but the inevitable effects of continual planting over several decades without rotation or chemical aids began to appear early in the twentieth century. Panama Disease and Leafspot were diagnosed in 1911.[1] The former attacked the roots and destroyed the plant completely while the latter reduced yields. Panama Disease spread over large areas and by 1931 already 15,660 acres had been lost of which Portland alone accounted for 9,000 acres.[2] No remedy was found until the disease-resistant Lacatan strain was introduced after World War II.

Finally we turn to production serving purely domestic needs. As already seen in Ch. 12, C, (ii), methods of cultivating food crops employed by the peasantry remained virtually unchanged throughout the century. As far as meat production was concerned the livestock industry—admirably suited to parts of the island—failed to develop a good tropical strain of cattle. The Department of Agriculture began to specialize in dairy cattle breeding in the early years of the twentieth century but attempts to combine the characteristics of quality of the British with the hardihood of the Indian cattle were not successful until the Jamaica Hope was reared after World War II.

C. Investment

Increases in productivity depend, of course, on investment as well as on improvements in technology. Whatever the methods employed to raise output—clearing new land, improving soil fertility, building roads or mechanizing manually performed operations—resources have to be diverted from immediate consumption to capital formation. The rate of investment needed to secure a given increment of output is likely to vary among different types of economies but the experience of a number of countries suggests that there is a fairly general relationship between the rate of investment and of economic progress. Where progress is rapid the annual rate of net investment usually amounts to 10 per cent or more of national income and where the economy is stationary—that is per capita output remains unchanged—the rate is usually 5 per cent or less.[3]

In Jamaica, the rate of gross investment was below 7 per cent for most of the nineteenth century. Only towards the end of the century

[1] Col. Rep., BPP, 1912 (Cd. 6007–39). [2] Report of JBC, 1935, p. 83.

[3] Measures for the Economic Development of Under-developed Countries, United Nations, 1951, p. 35.

did the rate become significantly greater. Gross investment is estimated to have taken only about 5 per cent of the national income in *1832* and *1870* (Table LXII). The ratio was slightly higher in *1850* but it did not begin to show any sustained upward trend until after *1870* when it increased from 5·6 per cent to over 7 per cent in *1890* and continued to rise subsequently until in 1930 it exceeded 10 per cent.

From *1832* to the end of the century net investment thus cannot have been more than about 4 or 5 per cent of national income and as about half of this investment was in houses it is not surprising that no industry in Jamaica during these years showed any significant increase in productivity. During the nineties the rate of net investment began to increase mainly because of larger public capital formation and investment in bananas and in some factories. The same years also saw a rise in per capita output, at *1910* prices, on an average of about 0·6 per cent per annum.

TABLE LXII

Gross Capital Formation and Gross Domestic Product

Year	Gross Capital Formation	Gross Domestic Product	G.C.F. as Percentage of G.D.P.
	£'000	£'000	%
1832	263·8	5,041·9	5·2
1850	257·4	3,724·4	6·9
1870	320·1	5,676·9	5·6
1890	638·7	8,746·6	7·3
1910	908·3	11,361·9	8·0
1930	2,049·4	19,951·6	10·3

Sources: Ch. 8, Tables A and E.

We can trace this growth in the per capita product in the changing composition of total investment. Building and construction accounted for about 80 per cent or more of total investment until World War I (Table LXIII). Moreover, of this total between one-half and two-thirds was taken up by residential housebuilding. Public works accounted for most of the remainder from *1870* onwards but in the early years commercial construction was relatively more important. It should be noted that commercial construction includes estimates for business premises and sugar factories only. A decline in its share is therefore to be expected as sugar estates were abandoned. Subsequent recovery in sugar planting was not accompanied by a proportionate increase in construction because centralization of sugar manufacture reduced the number of factories. By contrast agricultural investment, that is the cost of opening up new land, accounted for only 1–2 per cent of the total in the years between *1850* and *1910* while in *1832* and *1930* no investment appears to have taken place at all.

Finally, the share of durable producer goods fell sharply from about 20 per cent in *1832* and *1850* to 12·5 per cent in *1870*. It began to recover again thereafter but it was during the last twenty years that the most rapid increase took place. In discussing the share of producer goods, however, it must be borne in mind that the estimates include only the c.i.f. value of imported capital goods. As explained in Ch. 1, F, we have not added any margin for installing imported equipment nor have we included any estimate of locally produced goods or of changes in inventories. It may be for this reason that the share in 1930, at about 27 per cent, is still relatively low compared with that of between 35 and 40 per cent usually found in other countries. If we allow, say, 25 per cent for these omissions, then the share of producer goods would be increased to 31 per cent and the share of investment in Gross Domestic Product to 10·9 per cent. All the same it can hardly be expected that the share of durables would be as high in Jamaica as, for example, in the United States or Western Europe for even in *1930* mechanization of production and distribution had not proceeded very far.

In relating changes in the composition of investment to growth in national income we are concerned only with those forms of investment which are directly reproductive—that is those which bring about immediate increases in output. From this point of view investment in residential housing is less important because although the average standards of housing were poor and, in spite of the high share in total investment still far below the quality needed to ensure healthy and efficient workers, this type of improvement affects output only very slowly and is difficult to separate from other types of welfare services. Thus ignoring investment in houses we see that the total share of reproductive investment began to increase after *1870*—that is at around the same time as the per capita output.

The share of agricultural investment remained, as seen from Table LXIII, fairly stable between *1850* and *1910*. The actual amount spent on this type of investment was small because most of the new land brought into cultivation had already been cultivated at one time or another in the past, and preparing it for production again thus involved only the removal of secondary growth in place of the much more formidable task of clearing virgin land (see Ch. 1, F). Opening up new land, however, raises productivity only if it is accompanied by other investment, such as labour-saving equipment. By itself it is of importance only if population is growing and needs more food. That is why in the years between *1850* and *1890* productivity did not rise in spite of agricultural investment. It was only later when investment in public works and durable producer goods increased that agricultural investment contributed to increases in per capita output.

TABLE LXIII

The Composition of Investment

	Residential Building		Public Works		Commercial Construction		Agricultural Investment		Durable Producer Goods		Total Investment	
	£'000	%	£'000	%	£'000	%	£'000	%	£'000	%	£'000	%
1832	129·6	49·1	43·7	16·6	38·0	14·4	Nil	—	52·5	19·9	263·8	100·0
1850	122·5	47·6	28·7	11·1	50·3	19·6	2·4	0·9	53·5	20·8	257·4	100·0
1870	185·7	58·0	64·1	20·0	29·4	9·2	2·3	0·7	38·6	12·1	320·1	100·0
1890	281·0	44·0	220·6	34·5	32·3	5·1	5·5	0·9	99·3	15·5	638·7	100·0
1910	428·7	47·2	249·4	27·4	55·5	6·1	15·1	1·7	159·6	17·6	908·3	100·0
1930	912·4	44·5	512·2	25·0	82·9	4·0	Nil	—	541·9	26·5	2 049·4	1 0 0

The share of public works began to increase after 1865 when the new government began to assume greater responsibility for extending and maintaining communications in the island. A considerable part of the increase in output was due to improvements in access to remote areas, thus facilitating the exchange of production that was surplus to requirements. Most of this took the form of roads and bridges but in some areas the extension of the railway system was also important. It should be noted that the cost of laying and maintaining the railway track is included under public works while that of rolling stock is shown under durable producer goods. The distinction between the two types of investment is thus somewhat misleading.

The government also sought to encourage economic development more directly with the construction of irrigation systems in hitherto arid regions. In 1876, the Rio Cobre irrigation scheme came into operation, and in 1903, the Vere works were completed.

Durable producer goods, in fact, did not become an important factor in raising productivity until *1890.* Up to that time they consisted mainly of materials and plant for the sugar industry which were not sufficient to keep the industry alive, much less efficient. It will be noted that the shares of durable producer goods in *1832* and *1850* were considerably higher than in *1870.* In *1832* the high proportion is merely the result of a low investment ratio and in *1850* it was probably due to the overdue replacement of worn-out equipment in sugar factories: there is no evidence to suggest that it represented additions to capital. Presumably it was the neglect of even replacements that accounts for the extraordinarily low share of durable producer goods in *1870.* The increase in the share subsequently, however, was due at first mainly to investment in transport, public utilities and some non-sugar manufacturing industries. The railway system was being extended rapidly during the 1890's. Between 1890 and 1896 the track was lengthened from 38 to 184 miles (see Ch. 10, D). In some cases, private enterprise was also providing its own means of transport. The United Fruit Company built a narrow-gauge line to their shipping point at Bowden in St. Thomas[1] and in the Catadupa area installed rope haulage to connect with the public line.[2] Yet another track was laid down by the Vere Estate Company in St. Catherine.[3] But after the turn of the century heavy investment began also to be made in the sugar industry. The share of producer goods reflects this to some extent but it should be noted that the most important period of capital formation occurred in the early 1920's. From £19,110 in 1919 imports of sugar machinery shot up to £477,671 in the following year and £353,364 in 1921. After declining it reached another peak in 1925 with £117,881.[4]

D. Enterprise

In the two preceding sections we saw that both techniques and the rate of investment began to change significantly only towards the

[1] Col. Rep., BPP, 1907 (Cd. 3729–13).
[2] Hammond, F. D. *Transport Problems in Jamaica,* Crown Agents, 1923, p. 22.
[3] Col. Rep., BPP, 1907 (Cd. 3729–13). [4] SSIJ, p. 64.

end of the century. This raises the question whether this was solely due to lack of opportunities or partly also to lack of enterprise. Did Jamaicans, in fact, grasp all the opportunities open to them or did they allow some of them to slip by?

These questions are best answered by finding out who was best placed to respond to opportunities. For this we look at the social structure of Jamaica. The first point to note is that, at the time of emancipation, social and economic divisions closely corresponded to racial groupings. At the top of the scale were the whites who enjoyed all the privileges of the ruling class: in 1830 they owned nearly all the patented land, provided most of the professional people and controlled internal affairs by electing members of the House of Assembly and staffing public offices from their own ranks. They also conducted most of the business. Next came the free coloured community. Since 1813 they had been free to inherit property and to pursue most occupations except those on estates owned by white persons. They were also still subject to certain other civic disabilities such as the holding of public offices and debarred from the voters' roll. These limitations were not removed until 1831. Since the Privileged Act of 1813, however, they had managed to penetrate a wide variety of occupations ranging from landed proprietorship to manual work. Indeed in the 1820's it was claimed that they owned some coffee estates and all the pimento plantations.[1] Some were also found in the offices of counting-houses and solicitors.[2] Thirdly, the slave population was wholly engaged in manual occupations—usually unskilled though some were employed on semi-skilled jobs in sugar factories. They were generally illiterate and the available evidence—such as the number of paid-for manumissions—does not suggest that they were either able to, or in fact often did, accumulate appreciable savings.

(i) *The White Community*

When we look for the most likely source of enterprise we naturally turn first to the white population. In the past some of them had shown considerable initiative in developing the plantation system and facing the risks inherent in sugar planting while others had conducted an often equally risky entrepôt trade with Latin America. The latter found it more profitable after 1820 to trade directly with

[1] Dr. Lushington, Hansard, New Series, 1827, vol. XVII, p. 1,244.

[2] Wesley, C. H. 'The Emancipation of the Free Coloured Population in the British Empire,' *Journal of Negro History*, 1934, vol. 19.

the United Kingdom and left the island for the South American continent. But in the case of large-scale enterprise, planters failed after emancipation to develop new methods of running estates. Ch. 13, A, showed that similar changes did not have the same results elsewhere in the Caribbean. Barbados, Trinidad and British Guiana experienced only temporary setbacks and, in the last two, subsequent progress was rapid. Investment in the sugar industries in these colonies was already substantial in the 1850's and Trinidad led the way with centralization nearly thirty years before the first central factory was established in Jamaica.

The Jamaican failure was usually attributed to the way of life of the island's plantocracy. It was pointed out that under slavery planters had been accustomed to live luxuriously in spacious residences, to employ innumerable servants and to entertain lavishly. This way of life was said to be inimical to enterprise because it destroyed initiative and discouraged saving. The view was also taken that in the changed social conditions the planters, no longer enjoying the statutory privileges which had formerly made them superior to the black population in every respect, felt compelled to assert their dominance in ways that were still open to them. For example, J. Bigelow, visiting the island in 1850, wrote that 'every house and shop is filled with black servants . . . the most modest and economical establishment in the country will have four to five domestic servants . . . and the amplest provision is always made to prevent the possibility of the ruling race being compelled to do anything themselves which can be done by servants'.[1]

This, however, still leaves us to explain why the attitude to progress in Jamaica should have been so different from that in the other sugar colonies where it certainly did not check the inflow of capital or the adoption of improved techniques. Part of the reason, as we saw in Ch. 11, was that the sugar industry had been overstimulated before emancipation. Many estates had poor soils, were badly situated for rainfall and also too small and scattered for centralization. For these adoption of the improvements available after emancipation would not have brought production costs down to a competitive level. But, as shown in Section B above, even on the more favourably placed estates few improvements were made before the 1880's in cultivation techniques or in mechanical equipment. Only in the amalgamation of some small estates does there appear to

[1] *Op. cit.*, p. 125.

have been some progress before the nineties. If such improvements were worth while during the depth of the sugar depression, why could they not have been made earlier?

The reason seems to have been a general loss of confidence in the sugar industry of Jamaica. We have seen that output was already declining before emancipation and that this decline conformed to the usual experience of the sugar cycle in the older colonies. Thus even before emancipation planters were facing a much more difficult future: yields were bound to decline and costs to rise. Without any other changes planters would presumably have accustomed themselves to the new situation either by improving techniques or by going out of business. But before they had time to adjust themselves to the more difficult conditions emancipation struck a new blow and its coincidence with declining yields appears to have been the last straw. In general no attempt was made to face the problem. Proprietors simply abandoned their estates. This willingness to withdraw was naturally greater among the absentees and among those who still had connections at home and had already made a fortune in the island.

As a result of the withdrawal of so many absentees the white population in the island after 1834 came to differ radically from that of the pre-emancipation days. They increasingly came to regard themselves as Jamaican[1] and this attitude was reinforced by their inability to continue sending their children to schools abroad. Local facilities for secondary and higher education, however, were limited and those for technical training completely lacking (Ch. 15, B). The change in education together with the decline in absenteeism reduced contact with the outside world and new ideas and hence also affected the attitude to progress. Witnessing the destruction of the system that had in the past brought them rich returns and consequently left them relatively much poorer they not unnaturally felt themselves unjustly treated. For the time being, in the absence of other opportunities, they directed all their energies to protesting against their misfortunes. As legislators their record of obstructionism during these decades is truly remarkable. They had always enjoyed a reputation for independence in their legislative capacity by holding up the passage of bills introduced into the House of Assembly by the governors but after emancipation they resorted to even stronger measures to publicize their desperation (Ch. 16). Except for the two decades

[1] See Ch. 9, D.

beginning in the 1850's conditions in the sugar industry continued to deteriorate forcing many of the resident whites to withdraw from planting and their children to seek other occupations mostly in the more secure openings of government service and the independent professions.

Thus when, towards the end of the century, the banana provided a new investment opportunity not many of the old plantocracy or their descendants were still connected with planting. But even among those that remained there was a marked slowness in changing over to banana planting. Part of the reason for this was the mistaken belief that old cane land was not suitable[1] but there was also the tendency to dismiss fruit growing as a 'backwoods nigger business'.[2] Those who made the change had no reason to regret their decision because, as we saw in Ch. 11, it yielded handsome dividends which planters were able to invest in sugar when the market for that commodity improved. However, where sugar planters were unwilling to make the change and unable to make their properties pay, there was no lack of willing purchasers. In addition, many banana plantations were also opened up in new areas or in areas where sugar had long been abandoned. As a result of this development most of the new banana planters were members of quite different sections of the community. They were often merchants or professional men. Both were distinct from the old plantocracy. Professional people like Dr. John Pringle were more recent arrivals in the island[3] and among the new merchant-planters were many Jews, who, though old-established in the island, had no previous connection with planting. Like the free coloured people before emancipation they were subject to civil disabilities and achieved full civil status only a little earlier than the former. Until the banana offered a better investment opportunity they tended to keep to the professions and trade. In 1860 G. W. Sewell referred to unsubstantiated reports that Jews were buying up sugar estates in the Montego Bay district.[4] Certainly in the 1890's the list of banana proprietors included several Portuguese Jewish names and in the second decade of the twentieth century many more well-known merchant names are found.[5]

Once the banana was adopted by local interests, enterprise did not rest there. Plants were set up to process bananas into various products

[1] RWIC (C 8669), Pt. XIII, Q. 2,637.
[2] Olivier, *op. cit.*, p. 379.
[3] *Ibid.*, p. 379.
[4] *Op. cit.*, p. 212.
[5] HBJ for 1895 onwards include returns of banana properties.

such as banana meal and figs and, where coconut trees were also grown, fibres and copra were produced. Local enterprise was also responsible for the various other factories that began to be established in the nineties such as tobacco, matches, beer, soft drinks, soap, etc.

(ii) *The Middle Classes*

We have already seen that the free coloured population had for some time before emancipation been free to enter a wide variety of occupations and to acquire property. Among them some had been educated in the United Kingdom and others in the island. In their pursuit of equality with the whites they had also shown themselves capable of concerted and sustained effort and among them some, like Edward Jordan, the editor of the *Watchman*, prepared to risk personal safety in the struggle for their rights. In 1838 there appeared to be no reason why they should not continue to progress further into an enterprising middle class.

But in fact there appears to have been little progress among the coloured community in agriculture until the end of the century. In planting they seem to have been affected by the same pessimistic outlook as the whites and like them it was not until the banana was introduced that they were successful in agriculture. In trade they appear to have made rather more progress in the earlier years. G. W. Gordon, for example, starting off 'with nothing but his own energy and business habits as his stock in trade' in Kingston in 1836, had already built up a business worth £10,000 in 1843.[1] It is difficult to discover to what extent his case may have been typical for only rarely does literature record the more humble success stories and even more rarely does it distinguish between the races. What evidence we have, however, suggests that the coloured community was not widely successful in trade for, towards the end of the century, the mercantile establishments appear to have been mainly in the hands of Jews and subsequently Syrians and Chinese (see subsection iii).

The greatest advance was made in the professions and public life. One of the first to achieve fame in public life was Edward Jordan. In 1835 he was elected to the House of Assembly and proved himself to be one of the few people capable of pursuing a positive policy and by the late 1850's emerged as the leader of the Town Party.[2]

[1] Roberts, W. A. *Six Great Jamaicans*, Kingston, 1952. Ch. 3.
[2] *Ibid.*, Ch. 2.

By this time, altogether seventeen out of the forty-seven members of the House were coloured.[1] Another coloured man to reach prominence during this era was Richard Hill, the author of *Lights and Shadows*, and a number of pamphlets, memoranda and contributions to learned journals on local topics. He played an important role in the formation and administration of the Society of Arts and other institutions designed to further economic and social progress in the island.

Their conspicuous success in the professions and in public life, in contrast to their failure in agriculture and in trade, was also partly the result of their intermediate racial position. Ever since they had been freed their position in society had been delicate. At first there were positive restrictions on their opportunities. To remove these it was necessary to demonstrate equality through the attainment of education and living standards. Removal of civil disabilities, however, still did not bring acceptance by the whites and the need to prove equality remained. This need was met by acquiring advanced educational qualifications and entering the professions and especially by the prestige and power conferred by public service. However, it also meant the emulation of the living standards of the whites—the employment of innumerable servants and lavish hospitality—and this made it difficult to save for investment in agriculture and in trade.

(iii) *The New Immigrants*

The fact that the banana became an export crop at all was due to the initiative of an American—Captain L. D. Baker. Perceiving its possibility on the American continent he induced the peasantry of Portland to grow bananas for export.[2] He organized the collection, shipping and marketing of the fruit and his interests grew quickly into the powerful United Fruit Company (Ch. 13, D, ii). Other American companies also became interested in the banana industry subsequently.

Yet another group of outsiders showed considerable initiative in completely new directions. Syrians and Chinese began to arrive in the 1890's. Traditionally they are said to have come to Jamaica during the Exhibition held in 1891 and being so impressed with the potentialities of the island had decided to stay. Generally they began as itinerant traders and, living thriftily, they quickly amassed sufficient capital to build up large and efficient retail stores—a field

[1] Sewell, *op. cit.*, p. 254. [2] RWIC (C 8655), p. 140.

hitherto completely neglected. The Chinese tended to specialize in grocery stores while the Syrians more often dealt in dry goods. In 1935 the number of Chinese and Syrian traders engaged in dry goods and grocery distribution numbered 1,731 and the number holding spirit licences 933. At that date they also owned 44 manufacturing establishments.[1] Prominent among the Syrians was the Issa family who later were to extend their activities to the tourist trade and textiles.

The success of the Chinese and Syrians raises the question why such activities should be left to outsiders. The answer is to be found partly in the well-known fact that opportunities are always more easily recognized by new arrivals than by the inhabitants. Another reason why none of the many Jamaican itinerant petty traders shared their success also appears to be that most of them were women with family obligations and hence less able to save than the new immigrants. There may also be substance in the widely-held belief that the immigrants, less concerned about following the customary methods of conducting business and about personal appearances, found it easier to amass capital than the Jamaicans.

(iv) *Conclusion*

What emerges from the foregoing is that there was a general failure of enterprise immediately after emancipation. This failure resulted in a sharp fall in the share of profits. Once plantation profits had disappeared income distribution became more egalitarian and this also made it more difficult to save. There was, at the same time, also little foreign investment in Jamaica, unlike in Trinidad and British Guiana, because local enterprise showed itself so incapable of making the most of local opportunities. As a result the investment ratio remained low and productivity continued to decline until the banana reawakened local enterprise.

What Jamaicans needed for agricultural development in the second half of the nineteenth century was roads, water supplies, agricultural research and extension services; and for development in manufacturing, trained artisans and engineers. Both required much more education at all levels. One reason why factories did not pay in Jamaica was that so much expatriate personnel from skilled workers up had to be employed because of lack of trained Jamaicans.

All these problems require government action. But the Jamaican

[1] Syrian and Chinese Traders, J. Council Mins., 1935, vol. 76, App. LVIII.

government failed to initiate effective schemes for education above primary level. The attempt to introduce industrial training was unsuccessful, and agricultural research and education suffered from lack of funds and poorly trained personnel. It is worth noting that at the same time the government of Japan was taking vigorous action in all these spheres.

Behind the government's failure to assume responsibility for economic development lay the failure on the part of Jamaicans to recognize the importance of public expenditure on education, on health and on public works. Up to the middle of the 1860's, the Assembly was preoccupied with restoring the sugar industry instead of thinking of the economy as a whole. What little action was taken by them was designed to aid the plantations and to restrict the growth of small-scale agriculture. But, on the whole, the dominant creed was laissez-faire. The government's proper function was the maintenance of law and order, while economic development was best left to private enterprise. This philosophy was still current after the change in the constitution in 1865. Jamaicans subsequently were no longer responsible for their government's actions but they were able to influence it. That is why, when Jamaica did get governors who recognized the needs of the island they failed to get the support of the community. Sir J. P. Grant initiated many schemes which, if subsequently improved and expanded, would have easily repaid their cost. He established industrial schools and, for the first time in the history of the island, a proper public works programme. He also initiated the Rio Cobre irrigation scheme which, although benefiting chiefly the sugar estates, was hotly opposed. Sir A. Musgrave, too, was responsible for vast improvements in road and rail communications. However, neither was able to convince the vocal sections of the Jamaican community that such schemes would benefit them as well as the peasants. On the contrary, the coloured middle classes joined the whites in their cry against mounting public expenditure and finally also in their demand for more local control over government policy.

CHAPTER 15

SOCIAL CONDITIONS

SOCIAL conditions at once result from, and are determined by, economic progress. They depend on economic activity: the population can only consume what it produces. But at the same time the ability to produce depends on the level and pattern of consumption and on the level of savings. This chapter therefore concerns itself as much with the effects of the level and distribution of income and of education and health on economic development, as with measuring the results of development on the standard of living.

We begin with personal consumption, showing first the level of consumption, secondly, the distribution of income and thirdly the pattern of consumption. The second and third sections deal with education and health and the chapter is concluded with an account of employment opportunities.

A. PERSONAL CONSUMPTION

By personal consumption here we mean expenditure on consumer goods and services by people resident in Jamaica. This concept differs from that of gross domestic product, used in previous chapters, in that it excludes the amount spent by the government on goods and services, the value of payments made abroad less income received from abroad and the amount saved by Jamaicans. When the two sets of estimates are revalued at constant prices another difference is introduced, because, in eliminating price changes in the consumption series, we use import price indices for imported consumer goods while in the productivity series exports are revalued with export price indices. In short, per capita consumption is determined not only by productivity but also by the share of the government in national income, by invisible items in the balance of payments, by domestic savings and by the terms of trade. Furthermore, the level of savings and, to some extent, the foreign balance also depend on the distribution of income changes which, in turn, determine the pattern of consumption. In this section, therefore, we shall deal first with the level of consumption, accounting for differences between this and productivity, secondly with the distribution of income and finally with the pattern of consumption.

(i) *The Level of Consumption*

As is to be expected from the productivity series given in the previous chapter there were no phenomenal changes in per capita consumption—though there were some important differences between the two series which will be dealt with below. From Table LXIV which shows per capita expenditure at *1910* prices, we see that the average level of consumption rose by £0·3 between *1832* and *1850*, fell during the following twenty years by £0·8 but from *1870* onwards increased again.

TABLE LXIV

Per Capita Personal Consumption

(at *1910* prices)

	£
1830	11·2
1850	11·5
1870	10·7
1890	11·9
1910	12·0
1930	13·5

Source: Ch. 8, Table F.

The rise was relatively rapid in the years *1870* to *1890* and again between *1910* and *1930* so that by *1930* per capita consumption amounted to £13·5 thus exceeding the *1832* level by more than one-fifth.

In the years between *1832* and *1850* consumption diverged sharply from productivity. The former actually increased by about five per cent while productivity declined by more than one-fifth. Most of this was due to changes in income distribution (see subsection ii). In these years profits of planters fell sharply while those of the peasantry rose. This meant that the considerable positive foreign balance,[1] accounting for 21·9 per cent of gross domestic product in *1832*, was turned into a negative balance of 2·5 per cent in *1850* and since this was not offset by increased domestic savings a far higher share of the gross domestic product was available for consumption. The

[1] For definition of Foreign Balance see Ch. 1, I.

terms of trade also became more favourable during these years—rising from 118 to 137—but this was a less important source of increased consumption than the changes in income distribution because imports accounted for only about one-quarter of national income.

During the years *1850* to *1870*, however, per capita consumption declined by £0·8. Part of this fall was due to the lower per capita output which declined by £0·4 mainly because exports did not keep pace with population growth. As we saw in Ch. 5, the most important export, sugar, remained stable while food production and services for local consumption generally expanded only with population growth. Thus the share of exports in gross domestic product fell from 24·3 per cent in *1850* to 20·2 per cent in *1870* and, as a result, the per capita output. The remainder of the fall was the result of the sharp deterioration in the terms of trade from 137 in *1850* to 98 in *1870*. This does not appear to have been due to a reversal in the previous trend towards greater income equalization for, although we have no estimates of income distribution for *1870*, savings remained low and the foreign balance actually declined.

During the following twenty years there was a sharp recovery in personal consumption amounting to £1·2 per capita. This was partly the result of higher output, which increased by £0·5 mainly as a result of expanded home production and possibly due to further income equalization. Most of the increased consumption, however, appears to have been due to the considerable improvement in the terms of trade which, according to our calculations, rose from 98 to 137.

By *1910* the two series had again diverged sharply; productivity rose relatively quickly from £12·5 in *1890* to £13·7 in *1910* while the rise in consumption was negligible, amounting to only £0·1 per capita. The rise in output was brought about by expansion in production for the home market and for export. The latter rose relatively faster so that by *1910* its share had risen to 22·6 per cent. However, since prices of Jamaican exports—except bananas—fell catastrophically while those of food and manufactured goods bought from abroad rose, most of the increased exports were needed to pay for the same amount of imports. This deterioration in the terms of trade was further aggravated by the reduction in the negative foreign balance. Hence, in spite of the considerable increase in production, average consumption showed practically no change.

During the last twenty years of our period both productivity and consumption increased again but that of productivity once more rose much faster than that of consumption. This divergence, as in the years *1890* and *1910*, was due mainly to the worsening in the terms of trade which fell from 100 to 84. That personal consumption did not fall proportionately to this deterioration in the external bargaining position was the result of the rise in net income from abroad from 0·1 per cent to 1·3 per cent and the substantial growth in the negative foreign balance from 0·7 per cent to 7·7 per cent.

One of the conclusions that emerges from these comparisons is that most of the rise in personal consumption up to *1850* and a small part of the rise up to *1890* were the consequences of changes in income distribution.

(ii) *The Distribution of Income*

For reasons given in Ch. 1, we have been unable to prepare distribution estimates for the years *1870* and *1910*. Thus Table LXV, showing the distribution of income among the main classes of income receivers, refers to only four of our national income years. The classification adopted here is self-explanatory except for groups 1 and 2 in *1832*. As we saw in Ch. 4, there were no peasants in *1832* that corresponded to the independent settlers of the post-emancipation era. The value shown under peasants' income in *1832* refers to the value of food raised by predial slaves in their employers' time on their employers' land, while the amount of agricultural wages shows only the income in kind received by predial slaves. The distribution between the two groups is therefore somewhat artificial, because it refers to the same group of income earners, but we decided to adopt it for two reasons. First, the relative shares of incomes received in kind and produced by slaves themselves furnish an interesting aspect of the plantation economy, and secondly, after emancipation the two groups tended to become increasingly distinct—the one becoming whole-time wage earners and the other independent peasants—and their separation in *1832* thus makes possible an estimate of this movement during the crucial post-emancipation years. However, when we come to compare the share of agricultural wage labour between *1832* and *1850* we must add groups 1 and 2 together in the earlier year.

The outstanding feature of Table LXV is the increase in the combined share of agricultural labourers' wages and small-settlers' profits between *1832* and *1850* and the big fall in plantation profits.

Compared with these changes in income distribution subsequent shifts were inconsiderable as were also those in other groups throughout the period.

Between *1832* and *1850* the combined share of groups 1 and 2 rose sharply from 29·6 per cent to 44·3 per cent but remained at around this level thereafter. The big increase in the initial years was due entirely to the growth in settlers' incomes. The share of agricultural

TABLE LXV

The Distribution of Income

	1832	*1850*	*1890*	*1930*
	%	%	%	%
1. Agricultural Labourers' Wages	12·8	17·5	6·2	7·2
2. Small-Settlers' Gross Profits .	16·8	26·8	36·5	34·8
3. Planters' Gross Profits . . .	26·8	5·5	7·8	6·7
4. Other Wages and Salaries . .	21·4	24·0	22·0	26·1
5. Merchants' Gross Profits . .	11·1	13·1	14·4	14·8
6. Professional Profits	4·1	4·6	1·9	1·7
7. Independent Workers' Profits .	7·0	8·5	11·2	8·7
	100·0	100·0	100·0	100·0

Source: Ch. 8, Table D.

wages fell by more than one-third from 29·6 per cent (combining groups 1 and 2) to 17·5 per cent while that of the peasantry amounted to 26·8 per cent in *1850*. After *1850* the peasantry continued to expand in numbers relatively to wage labour so that by *1890* their share had increased further to 36·5 per cent and that of agricultural wages had fallen to 6·2 per cent. Only after *1890* is there a suggestion of a reversal of this trend with the peasants' share falling to 34·8 per cent and wages rising to 7·2 per cent.

Plantation profits fell by more than four-fifths from 26·8 per cent to 5·5 per cent in *1850*. This decline was the result of lower average profits which caused many estates to be abandoned; this in turn brought about a lower share of profits in total incomes. The relatively greater fall in profits than in agricultural wages is to be expected because, as we saw in Ch. 11, B, it was precisely the inability of planters to reduce labour costs that caused the abandonment of so many estates. The recovery of plantation profits to 7·8 per cent in

1890 was due to the expansion of banana production. This increase was not, however, accompanied by a rise in the share of agricultural wages partly because the banana is less labour-intensive and partly because real wages had been reduced.

Movements in the shares of 'Other Wages and Salaries' were relatively small (Table LXV). During the first eighteen years incomes arising out of public administration fell from their exceptionally high share of 5·1 per cent in *1832*, caused by the slave rebellion, to 3·9 per cent in *1850*. This decline, however, was more than offset by the increased shares of domestics', construction and distribution workers' wages. Subsequently, incomes of those engaged in public administration, education, distribution and construction increased continuously but in *1890* the total share of this group fell as a result of the relative reduction in domestic servants' income.

Merchants' profits began to increase after *1850* partly because of the rising volume of imports and partly because of their growing participation in the export trade. Earnings in the professions, on the other hand, fell relatively to total incomes because of the changing composition of this group which resulted in a decline in those with a high per capita income—doctors and lawyers—and an increase in the number of those with a low per capita income—the clergy. Finally the share of independent workers rose until *1890* but thereafter productivity fell and they retained less of the total product.

In sum, there was a considerable shift in the distribution of incomes between *1832* and *1850* but thereafter changes were relatively unimportant. The redistribution of the early years was characterized by a general reduction in the higher incomes and the increase in the lower income groups—i.e. from planters, doctors, lawyers, etc., to small-settlers—resulting in a less uneven income distribution. Unfortunately, we cannot verify this more directly as we have no data on size distribution (Appendix III)—but there are two pieces of evidence which bear out this contention. In the first place the shift in income distribution between *1832* and *1850* was roughly one from incomes from property to incomes from work. Taking planters' and merchants' profits together as an indication of income from property we see that after emancipation income from property accounted for only about 20 per cent of the national income, which is considerably below the share of about 30 per cent found, say, in the United Kingdom. The comparison is not strictly valid because the profits of planters and merchants includes some income from work, especially that of petty traders, and the profits of peasants some income from property. All the same the comparison does suggest that after emancipation income distribution was much less unequal than formerly and probably also more egalitarian than in most other countries at this time. It also helps to explain why savings were so low after emancipation. Secondly, the contention that income distribution became less unequal is also borne out by the pattern of consumption to which we now turn.

(iii) *The Pattern of Consumption*

The shares of different consumption goods may change either because total consumption rises or because income distribution changes. As average incomes rise expenditure on essential goods does not rise proportionately and thus relatively more is available for luxuries or semi-luxuries. Hence, when living standards rise we should expect the shares of food and clothing to decline and those of other consumption goods and services to increase. If, on the other hand, the same total output is merely reallocated from the richer to the poorer, we should expect the opposite—that is an increase in the shares of the essential goods and a decrease in services—since the poorer generally are too poor to have reached the point where extra income can be spent on luxuries.

From Table LXVI, showing the pattern of consumer expenditure, we see that between *1832* and *1850* the share of food increased from 44·4 per cent to 49·5 per cent, clothing remained stable while other consumer goods declined from 8·9 per cent to 8·4 per cent and rent proportionately even more from 16·5 per cent to 12·4 per cent. Since total personal expenditure actually increased during these years, the rising share of food confirms our previous conclusion that the lower share of plantation profits in national income and the increased share of peasants' incomes implied a less unequal distribution of incomes.

Between *1850* and *1870* the share of food rose even further to nearly 54 per cent while all other groups, except other consumer goods, declined. These changes were due in part to lower per capita expenditure, which we should expect to result in an increase in the share of essential goods and, possibly, also to further income equalization. The evidence for the latter lies in the accompanying decline in the shares of professional and domestic service. We know from the population censuses that the white population continued to decline

TABLE LXVI

The Pattern of Consumer Expenditure

(current values)

	1832		1850		1870		1890		1910		1930	
	£'000	%	£'000	%	£'000	%	£'000	%	£'000	%	£'000	%
Food	1,486·2	44·4	1,655·4	49·5	2,771·5	53·9	4,271·6	53·8	5,382·2	53·7	9,044·0	49·4
Clothing	648·9	19·4	603·1	18·0	792·1	15·4	1,228·4	15·5	1,605·3	16·0	2,225·1	12·1
Other Consumer Goods	299·0	8·9	280·2	8·4	517·2	10·0	689·9	8·7	787·4	7·9	2,355·0	12·9
Personal Services	363·2	10·8	393·4	11·7	444·8	8·6	646·8	8·1	859·3	8·6	1,765·4	9·6
Passenger Transport	—		—		23·7	0·5	89·7	1·1	165·3	1·7	386·5	2·1
Rent	552·9	16·5	416·2	12·4	595·7	11·6	1,018·7	12·8	1,215·7	12·1	2,546·5	13·9
	3,350·2	100·0	3,348·3	100·0	5,145·0	100·0	7,945·1	100·0	10,015·2	100·0	18,322·5	100·0

Source: Ch. 8, Table E.

relatively to the total population. This reduction occurred mainly among planters and professional people—that is those with the highest average income—leading in turn also to lower employment of domestic servants.

During the following forty years, between *1870* and *1910*, the shares of the main consumption groups remained fairly stable. Income distribution probably did not change very greatly during these years. On the other hand, the fact that per capita consumption actually rose during this period suggests that general consumption standards were still so low that the mass of the population had not yet reached a sufficiently high level of food consumption to enable them to spend more on non-essentials.

It was only after *1910* that these trends were reversed. The proportion spent on food declined from 53·7 per cent to 49·4 per cent and that of clothing from 16·0 per cent to 12·1 per cent while the shares of other consumer goods, personal services and rent increased (Table LXVI). Since, at the same time, per capita expenditure increased appreciably and there are no grounds for believing that income distribution became less unequal—as would be shown, for example, by increased savings—we conclude that these changes in the pattern of consumption represented a real rise in average living standards.

B. Education

(i) *The State of Education before 1834*

The BBJ for 1833 lists thirty-six schools, in thirty-one of which 2,759 pupils were taught. These returns may be incomplete, for, between 1820 and 1834 alone, forty-seven schools are reported to have been opened.[1] No doubt some of these did not survive until 1834. But even if some of them had been omitted from the BBJ returns the total number of schools would still be negligible for a population of about 371,070. Taking the most optimistic view—that is assuming that half of the new schools had been omitted and that they were also of the same size as those reported—the total number of schools cannot have provided education for more than about one in every fifteen children aged between five and fifteen years.

[1] Educational Systems of the Chief Colonies of the British Empire, BPP, 1901 (Cd. 416), p. 577.

The reason for this state of affairs is not far to seek. It was customary for planters and the more prosperous merchants and professional people to send their children to the United Kingdom; as for the slaves, literacy was considered to be beyond their intellectual capacity by one school of thought, while another argued that it would make them unfit for their work as manual drudges. As a result, such schools as were established catered mainly for the children of the poorer whites and the free coloureds. With growing missionary activity after the abolition of the slave trade, however, education of the slaves also began to receive attention. Of the forty-seven schools opened between 1820 and 1834 forty were designed for the children of slaves.[1]

Such education as existed in the island at this time was indeed mainly due to the efforts of missionaries and private benefactors. The government took no direct responsibility for education but some of the parochial authorities made small contributions towards the upkeep of schools run by the Church of England. From time to time individuals endowed schools for the children of the free population which became known by the names of their benefactors. Woolmer's, Manning's, Rusea's, and Munro and Dickenson were the best known. The majority of the schools opened for the slaves, on the other hand, were conducted by the churches. Of the forty schools opened between 1820 and 1834 nine were run by the Church of England, twelve by the Moravian, six by the Presbyterian and four by the Baptist missions.[2] The remainder were established by proprietors of estates. Schools run by the Church of England probably had no financial difficulties as the Church was relatively wealthy and also received assistance from public funds. The Nonconformist churches, however, depended for their income on voluntary gifts from congregations, but frequently these were insufficient and they had to draw on the funds of their parent societies. The Baptists, alone, had no such overseas sources for education but far from discouraging them this seems to have acted as a stimulus. Certainly their record of school building during the Apprenticeship was much better than that of the other missionary societies.[3]

Standards in most of these schools do not appear to have been very high. The endowed schools were generally badly administered and according to one writer 'it would not be too much to say that

[1] *Ibid.* [2] *Ibid.*
[3] Negro Education, Jamaica, BPP, 1837–8 (113), pp. 8–9.

the bulk of the money left for educational purposes was squandered or stolen'.[1] As for the mission schools, little could be expected from the poor resources at their disposal coupled with the constant threat of closure under which most of them laboured owing to their unpopularity with the slave owners.

(ii) *Education in the Post-Emancipation Years*

With emancipation, however, education received a great deal of attention. The Apprenticeship had been designed to prepare the slave for freedom and one way of carrying this into effect was to send him to school. By 1836 already the number of schools had shot up to 307 with a student body of 16,592. In addition, there were 139 Sunday schools and 95 evening schools with 20,870 and 5,304 pupils respectively.[2] Taking account only of those attending day school the ratio of pupils to child population (5–15 years of age) was about 1 in 5, representing a threefold improvement on that before emancipation.

This great increase had taken place mainly among the mission schools. The Imperial government aided expansion by making funds available for school buildings. Between 1837–42 Jamaica received £30,000 annually and further grants on a decreasing scale until 1846.[3] It had been intended that the island legislature would follow the example of the Mother Country but in the end it contributed only about £5,000 up to 1836 and subsequently even less.[4] For running costs, most schools were thus still dependent on other sources of income. Since voluntary gifts and mission funds were often inadequate for the increased activity of Nonconformist churches it became customary to charge about threepence per week, though teachers were always ready to waive this if parents were unable to find the money.[5] There was also much enthusiasm on behalf of the freed slaves in the United Kingdom and this resulted in the donation of considerable funds to the religious societies for education.

However, enthusiasm and money are not enough. It is the lack of educational organization rather than the meagre financial assistance that stains the island government's record. It may, of course, be objected that at this time it was not fashionable for governments to

[1] Educational Systems, *op. cit.*, p. 577.
[2] Negro Education, *op. cit.*, pp. 72–3. [3] Educational Systems, p. 578.
[4] Schools and Education (Jamaica), BPP, 1837 (353).
[5] Negro Education, p. 13.

interest themselves in popular education, but then it was equally unfashionable to free slaves and to make financial provisions from public funds for their education.

The precedent having been set it was only common sense that some authority should be responsible for seeing that these efforts were not wasted. However, the island government made no provisions for controlling expenditure or for inspecting schools. It is not very surprising, therefore, that much of the money was wasted. The Imperial government's grants were allocated to the various religious bodies on the basis of hastily prepared plans and realization of such schemes varied widely.[1] No records appear to have been kept of this expenditure and very little of any other aspect of education. Most of the missionary bodies were also ignorant not only of each others' activities but even of the existence and conduct of their own schools so that Mr. C. J. Latrobe, sent to Jamaica in 1837 to investigate the state of education in the island, was compelled to compile his own statistics by personal visits to schools.[2]

Schools were thus established haphazardly (or where missionary activity was greatest) without adequate provision for their future. Apart from uncertain income, the problem encountered by most schools was to find teachers. In 1836 there were only 381 teachers[3]—that is little more than one for each school. But even among these not many were qualified for their work. Those recruited in England were said to be efficient but the white and coloured people appointed locally, often only the product of the schools in which they were to teach, were usually inferior.[4] No facilities for training teachers existed in the island at this time. The first training college to be opened was Lady Mico's Charity which began to concentrate on teachers' training shortly after its establishment in 1836. Seven years later the Baptists opened Calabar College. These colleges turned out sound teachers but could not keep pace with the demand.[5]

As is to be expected standards were low. Because of the few and poorly qualified teachers, teaching was almost entirely by rote.[6] Large claims were actually made about the scholastic attainments of pupils during these years: magistrates were reporting that 'there is scarcely one above seven years who cannot read the Bible or Testament'.[7] But others soon discovered that a child's prodigious memory

[1] Negro Education, pp. 4–5. [2] *Ibid.*, p. 4. [3] *Ibid.*, p. 73. [4] *Ibid.*, p. 13.
[5] PPSC, BPP, 1854–5 (1919). [6] Educational Systems, *op. cit.*, p. 579.
[7] PWI, Pt. II, Jamaica, BPP, 1841 (344), p. 160.

rather than knowledge of the three R's brought about such remarkable feats. 'So far as I have seen, the children repeat like parrots and scarcely know their letters.' [1]

(iii) *The Years of Neglect, 1846–65*

During the forties expansion appears to have been halted. Statistics of enrolment begin only during the following decade but as these returns were made voluntarily they have to be treated with some reserve. The first return, relating to 1852, shows the number of scholars as 12,792.[2] In the following year the number jumped to 19,662[3] but thereafter fell back again to 16,389 in 1856.[4] Subsequently the numbers fluctuated but generally showed an upward trend until in 1864 30,514 pupils[5] were reported to be enrolled in 475 schools. If we deduct pupils attending Sunday schools conducted by the Baptist mission—possibly the other Nonconformist churches also include Sunday school pupils—the number attending day school was 22,988. Most of the variations during the fifties were probably due to omissions and part of the upward trend merely the result of better coverage. At all events, the figures suggest that no expansion had taken place during the forties and that during the following decade the increase was hardly enough to keep pace with population growth. In 1864 the ratio of pupils to children of school age (5–15 years of age) was only 1 in 5·4.

What is surprising about these figures is not the failure of school facilities to expand relatively to population but the fact that they grew at all; once the post-emancipation enthusiasm had spent itself there was little to encourage the establishment of new schools. The Imperial grants ended in 1846 and the island government spent even less on education than before. The House of Assembly had, in fact, set up a Board of Education in 1845 but failed to vote enough funds to make it effective. The Board was launched with the meagre sum of £751[6] and subsequent grants averaged less than £2,000 p.a.[7] After the last stoppage of supplies in the years 1849–53[8] the House refused to make any provisions at all on the 'plea that a new system of public instruction was contemplated'.[9] However, no plan materialized and the grants, when they were resumed, were even smaller

[1] PWI, Pt. II, Jamaica, BPP, 1841 (344), p. 153. [2] PPSC.
[3] *Ibid.* [4] *Ibid.*, 1859 (2567). [5] *Ibid.*, 1866 (3719).
[6] PAIJ, 1849 (1065), p. 111. [7] *Ibid.*, p. 105.
[8] See Ch. 16. [9] PPSC, 1854–5 (1919), p. 41.

than previously. In the financial year 1854–5 only £573 was paid out of central government funds and, though the amount was increased subsequently, by 1863–4 had reached only £4,165.[1] The importance of this, however, must not be exaggerated as mission schools had never received more than a fraction of their income for current expenditure from public funds. Even during the most favourable years they had depended mainly on contributions from private sources and fees. Unfortunately, interest abroad in the freed slaves began to flag and less money was forthcoming and often the missionary societies themselves lost interest. Some missionaries even were recalled for work in other parts of the world. Beginning in the middle forties, too, difficulty was experienced in collecting fees. Those who had been most anxious for education—the peasants—were, as we have seen, suffering a setback and it was also said that parents became less keen on an education that did not fit their children for the most ordinary duties much less for the social advancement they had hoped for.[2]

In view of the difficulties under which the schools laboured little could be expected in the way of improved standards. Teachers continued to be scarce and poorly qualified. In 1847 a Committee set up by the President of the Board of Education proposed a scheme for encouraging pupil teachers at existing schools[3] but, needless to say, nothing came of this and the task of training teachers continued to be left to private efforts. In 1861 the Presbyterians opened a training college in Montego Bay, thus bringing the number of training colleges up to three. It was not until the early sixties that public conscience was aroused sufficiently to enquire into the state of elementary education. In 1864 an Englishman, Mr. Savage, was appointed Inspector of Schools and asked to carry out this task. After examining 289 of the existing schools he reported that only 25 could be classed as efficient.[4]

If the denominational schools left much room for improvement the conduct of the endowed schools was also not above reproach. More often than not their funds were mismanaged or misappropriated. Two examples will suffice as illustration. One of the schools, the Titchfield School, was supported by a trust which yielded an income of about £400 p.a. Up to 1852 the school was reported to be a flourishing and useful institution. 'But in that year the trustees, or

[1] REJ, BPP, 1881 (285).
[2] Educational Systems, p. 579.
[3] PAIJ, p. 111.
[4] Educational Systems, pp. 579–80.

such of them as acted, quarrelled with their schoolmaster, and consequently refused to pay him the arrears of his salary lawfully due. The schoolmaster was obliged to prosecute for his dues, and obtained a judgement for £161 9*s*. 7*d*. debt, with £100 15*s*. 5*d*. costs. But instead of paying the debt from ample trust funds at their disposal, the trustees drove the trust into chancery. The usual course was then proceeded with. Instead of selling a few houses, by which the debt might have been paid off in a month or two, the estate was placed under receivership. The income as it accrued was absorbed, and the property meanwhile allowed to go waste. The school was necessarily abandoned very early in the operation. The schoolmaster and his representatives have never received a farthing of their dues.'[1] The free school of St. Jago de la Vega and Smith's Charity had also become 'all but useless for any educational purpose'.[2] The clergymen in charge had evolved a novel method of discharging their duties by appointing masters at low salaries to teach badly a small number of subjects, 'the main part of the income being retained for superintendence, which if not quite nominal was quite futile'.[3]

(iv) *The Beginning of an Educational System, 1865–90*

Progress in education, as so much else in Jamaica, dates from the year 1865. The new government interested itself in education and soon after its establishment took steps to lay the foundations of a sound educational system. Its first act, in 1867 was to implement some of the recommendations proposed by Mr. Savage three years earlier. Under these the government did not undertake direct responsibility for education but left control with existing bodies. Henceforth the denominational schools were to provide elementary and the endowed schools secondary education.

The denominational schools received public grants but were, at the same time, placed under the supervision of an official inspectorate. They were examined regularly and graded according to their efficiency. The amount of aid depended on this grading and could be received only if fees were collected. The amount of fees ranged between 1½*d*.–6*d*. per week and proved a considerable addition to school incomes.[4] In 1871–2 they amounted to £5,873 compared with the government grant of £9,897.[5] In the following years, the number of school places increased rapidly and by 1890–1 there were 836

[1] Report with the BBJ, 1870 (C 85), p. 4. [2] *Ibid*., 1871 (C 334), p. 6.
[3] *Ibid*. [4] Report with the BBJ, 1873 (C 709). [5] *Ibid*., 1875 (C 1183).

elementary schools with an enrolment of 80,199 pupils,[1] representing a spectacular rise in the ratio of enrolment to children of school age to one in two. Progress in raising teaching standards, on the other hand, was much slower. In 1871 there were only six schools in the first grade while 239 were placed in the third[2] and twenty years later the proportion qualifying for first class grants had risen to only 14 per cent.[3]

TABLE LXVII

Literacy

Year	Population 5 Years of Age and Over	Able to Read and Write		Able to Read Only		Total Literate	
	'000	'000	%	'000	%	'000	%
1861	380·1	50·7	13·3	68·3	18·0	119·1	31·3
1871	435·2	71·1	16·3	81·4	18·7	152·5	35·0
1881	505·2	115·4	22·8	115·8	22·9	231·2	45·7
1891	556·4	177·8	31·9	114·5	20·6	292·3	52·5
1911	716·6	338·3	47·2	108·5	15·1	446·8	62·3
1921	746·5	389·4	52·1	65·7	8·8	455·0	60·9

Sources: CP.

Endowed schools received no public assistance. Such funds as remained after the years of neglect were secured on the public debt but in some cases mismanagement had gone too far and it became necessary to close some schools and to amalgamate others such as the Free School of St. Jago de la Vega with Smith's Charity.[4] We have no information about their efficiency for it was only in 1879 that the endowed schools came under the supervision of the Jamaica Schools Commission.

Shortage of teaching staff was still proving a considerable obstacle to raising standards. In 1870 the government added to the existing training facilities with the opening of the Government College. The number of teachers increased gradually. But even in 1890 the staff-student ratio was still only 1 : 97. Added to this was the fact that 42 per cent of the teachers were still untrained.[5]

[1] BBJ, 1890–1.
[2] Report with the BBJ, 1873 (C 709).
[3] BBJ, 1890–1.
[4] Law 30 of 1869.
[5] BBJ, 1890–1.

Nevertheless these years saw a remarkable growth in literacy. From Table LXVII, comparing census returns of literacy with the number of people aged five years and over, it will be seen that total literacy had increased from 31·3 per cent in 1861 to 52·5 per cent in 1891. Even more telling than this total increase is the rising proportion of those able to write as well as read from 13·3 per cent to 31·9 per cent compared with the rise of only 2·6 per cent of those able to read only.

(ii) *Further Progress, 1890–1930*

Once the framework for an educational system was established the government was faced with the problems of increasing the number of school places, improving attendance and raising teaching standards.

Average attendances had always been far below enrolment. Even after emancipation when popular enthusiasm was at its highest, attendances averaged only 78 per cent[1] and in subsequent years fell to less than 60 per cent. This was largely due to climate and poverty. Attendances always fell during the rainy season because of the physical difficulties of getting to school. The fall in attendances was particularly evident during hurricanes not only because of road blockages but also because the storms often left parents destitute who, unable to afford the fees or even food and clothing for their children, were unwilling to send them to school. The hurricane of 1880, for example, resulted in a fall in attendances from 32,871 to 26,649 in the following year[2] and it was not until 1883 that the former level was regained.

One solution to this problem was compulsion but this in turn raised the question of school accommodation and fees. The first step was taken in 1892 with the abolition of school fees. A Central Board was set up charged—among other things—with the responsibility of recommending the enactment of compulsory education in certain areas.[3] School attendances increased temporarily but no further steps were taken to make attendances compulsory. Indeed this was impossible with the existing state of schools. Not only was total accommodation below requirements but also existing facilities were badly distributed. The government had begun to build public elementary schools in 1885 but most of the expansion during these years had taken place among the denominational schools. The disadvantage of this policy was that there was considerable rivalry

[1] Negro Education.
[2] Col. Rep., 1884 (C 4193).
[3] Law 31 of 1892.

among the churches and this led to duplication of school facilities in some areas while others were less well provided for. It also meant that schools had, on the average, only 130 pupils.[1] Since such small schools could pay only low salaries they tended to attract inferior teachers. Moreover, they were relatively expensive to maintain and supervise. The Education Commission of 1897 accordingly recommended that no new denominational schools should be opened and that existing ones should be amalgamated.

TABLE LXVIII

Child Population, School Enrolment and Attendance

Year	Number of Children of School Age (5–14 years)	Number of Children Enrolled	Percentage of Children Enrolled	Average Attendance in Elementary Schools
	'000	'000	%	%
1861	110·5	40·8	36·9	n.a.
1871	123·8	30·0*	24·2*	59·1
1881	146·9	67·4	45·9	54·8
1891	164·5	99·8	60·7	54·8
1911	216·4	125·5	58·0	62·6
1921	226·0	129·6	57·3	61·4

* Elementary schools only.
Sources: CP and BBJ.

But since even this would not provide enough places for the whole child population they sought to overcome the difficulty by proposing a reduction in the school age from 5–14 to 6–12.[2] The policy of amalgamation was adopted immediately and between 1899 and 1909 the number of schools had fallen from 776 to 693.[3] Implementation of the Commission's proposals for compulsory education, on the other hand, would have resulted in considerable increases in school grants, necessitating in turn additional taxation which, at that time, was not possible.[4] It was not until 1923 that attendance was made compulsory for children aged 8–14 in certain urban areas.[5]

The policy of not allowing new denominational schools to be

[1] Col. Rep., 1902 (Cd. 788–43).
[2] Summarized in Educational Systems, *op. cit.*, pp. 624 et seq.
[3] Col. Rep., 1902 (788–43), and BBJ, 1909. [4] Col. Rep., *ibid.*
[5] Order in Council dated 21 August, 1923.

established meant that school facilities could no longer keep pace with the growth in the child population: government schools were not built in sufficient numbers to take their place. In 1929 the government had direct responsibility for only 134 schools out of a total of 664.[1] The percentage of those of school age enrolled in schools declined from 60·7 per cent in 1891 to 57·3 per cent in 1921 (Table LXVIII). At the same time, however, there was a remarkable increase in literacy. The percentage literate rose from 52·5 per cent in 1891 to 62·3 per cent twenty years later. By 1921 the percentage had dropped again slightly to 60·9 per cent but it will be noted that the proportion of those able to read and write had increased very rapidly to 52·1 per cent while, at the same time, those able to read only declined relatively as well as absolutely. These figures suggest that after 1891 the government concentrated on better tuition rather than on increasing the number of school places.

The government's policy for raising standards is also reflected in its interest in higher education. After reorganization of the endowed schools only ten were left which, together, in 1890 had a student body of only 878,[2] which meant that only about one school child in every hundred received secondary education. This dearth of schools led the government to pass a law in 1892 empowering the Governor to establish new secondary schools and to award scholarships to promising pupils from elementary schools.[3] In 1896 the first school under this law was opened in Montego Bay. Beginning in 1920 the government also made grants available to the endowed schools provided they attained the specified level of efficiency. The number of secondary schools increased gradually until in 1929 there were 25 with a student body of 2,677,[4] thus providing secondary education for about one school child in every fifty.

The numbers receiving higher education was even smaller. Provisions for taking external examinations were made in the 1880's. The Cambridge Local Examinations, at the Matriculation level, were established in 1881. To this were added facilities for studying for the external degrees of London University under the supervision of the Jamaica Schools Commission. The obstacles to pursuing courses at such great distance were, of course, formidable and not many were able to persevere with such studies. The HBJ for 1928 lists only seventeen people as having successfully taken degrees up to that date. Most of the people with higher educational qualifications in

[1] BBJ, 1929. [2] BBJ, 1890–1. [3] Law 32 of 1892. [4] BBJ, 1929.

Jamaica had studied abroad. Some of them were helped by the Jamaica Scholarship, which was awarded to boys and girls, and Rhodes Scholarships.

C. Public Health

(i) *The State of Public Health before Emancipation*

Health, like every other facet of the social condition of the population at this time, was considered to be the responsibility of the individual. The only official requirements relating to public health, in fact, were the clauses contained in the Slave Acts compelling owners to provide a certain amount of food and medical attention for their slaves.[1] The slave owners had, of course, every reason to keep their labour force physically fit, with the result that the legal requirements generally appear to have been complied with. Most estates employed doctors to visit estates regularly to attend to the slaves and in addition often provided hospital facilities for the more serious cases. Doctors usually received a fixed sum—about 6*s*. p.a.[2]—for each slave on the plantation. In the case of the white people the fees were considerably higher.[3] Medical practitioners were thus assured of a steady income and many of them were said to be extremely prosperous. As a result there was no difficulty in attracting doctors to the island and for 1830 their number is returned as 200:[4] that is one for every 1,855 people.

In Ch. 9, A, we estimated the death-rate among the slave population at about 32·7 per 1,000, of which about 3 or 4 per 1,000 were due to the high average age of the population, and concluded that general health standards and hence medical attention among the slaves were as good as might be expected at this time. Among the white population, on the other hand, mortality and sickness was, as we have seen, considerably higher. We do not have any information about the civilian population but certainly among the military the ratio of sickness was high. Between 1817 and 1836 admissions to hospitals averaged 1,812 per 1,000[5] p.a. Even if we deduct all the admissions for fevers—a risk to which the military were especially exposed owing to the location of some of their stations—admissions still amounted to over 900 per 1,000.

[1] Laws of 1827 and 1831.
[2] Ragatz, *The Decline of the Planter Class in the British Caribbean, 1763–1833*, New York, 1928. [3] *Ibid.* [4] *Jamaica in 1912*, p. 62.
[5] Statistics of Health of the Troops since 1803, BPP, 1837–8 (138), pp. 44–6.

(ii) *The Decline in Health Standards after Emancipation*

After emancipation general health deteriorated. Dr. Milroy, sent out from England to investigate the causes and course of the cholera epidemic, reported that the incidence of certain diseases, notably tuberculosis, stomach disorders, yaws and leprosy, had been increasing since emancipation[1] and that this made the population more susceptible to the more virulent diseases. Data about epidemics are hard to come by but Dr. Milroy, at any rate, was of the opinion that epidemics had also become more frequent and more severe. Yellow fever was said to occur in most years, smallpox also visited the population from time to time and in 1850 the most catastrophic of all—cholera—broke out, exceeding in its duration and destruction of lives any previous outbreak (Ch. 9, B).

As far as preventive measures were concerned, no effective legislation existed to safeguard the public from the outbreak and spread of diseases. Quarantine was a farce. Enforcement varied greatly from port to port since no regulations existed to guide health officers in the duration of quarantine or the type of disease against which it was to be enforced. In the towns the state of sanitation did nothing to hinder the outbreak of diseases. Refuse was left to decay in the streets and no regulations existed to enforce the safe disposal of sewage or for the supervision of markets, water supplies and cemeteries. Graveyards were numerous in Kingston and located near residential areas. During the cholera epidemic the death-rate was so high that fresh graves had to be reopened with consequent nuisances to nearby residents. In other cases people were left dying unattended and several days elapsed before the dead were buried. The handling of food for human consumption also left much to be desired. The office of Clerk to the Markets existed but, instead of being used to supervise the sale of food, was regarded as a mere sinecure.[2] Open swamps in or near towns were also a constant source of malaria and while a number of private water companies had existed for some time providing an indifferent service[3] the bulk of the population depended on wells and ponds of questionable purity.

Poor housing often also contributed to ill-health. While the houses of the peasantry were often a distinct improvement on those during slavery those occupied by estate labour and squatters appear to have

[1] Cholera (Jamaica), BPP, 1854 (235), p. 91. [2] *Ibid.*, p. 105.
[3] HBJ, e.g. for 1905.

fallen below them. A number of contemporary observers, between 1843 and 1862, testified to the improvement among the peasantry.[1] Although they undoubtedly described the exception the gap between their description and our knowledge of the slave huts is too wide for their claims of improvement to be discounted. Estate labourers, on the other hand, generally continued to live in huts provided on the property. After the initial attempts to charge rent or evict labour, planters usually undertook the provisions of housing as a matter of course and labourers took this to be their due. But since no legal compulsion existed neither owners nor labourers had any interest in improvements. For the most part, huts were mere shacks roughly constructed with 'some thatch rudely thrown over them'.[2] The bare earth served as flooring. The thatch itself was said to be a 'receptacle for filth and vermin'.[3] Bad as the accommodation was it was made worse by overcrowding. Into 'a room 8 or 9 feet square as many as 6, 8 or 10 persons are often crowded at night . . . on the ground'.[4] A measure of the general state of overcrowding is unfortunately not available before 1861. The 1844 census enumerated only 34,624 houses but this number probably omits all peasants' and labourers' huts. According to the 1861 census there was one house for every 5·1 persons. Since the majority of houses had only one or two rooms each this ratio suggests a fairly high degree of overcrowding.

Another cause of the deterioration in health standards was the inadequacy of medical attention. By 1846 the number of doctors had already fallen to 139 and continued to decline until in 1860 only 50[5] remained, thus reducing the ratio of doctors to population to 1 in 8,822. With emancipation the estate owners' obligation to provide medical attention for their labour ceased and henceforward workers were responsible for their own health. It was said that the freed slaves did not accept this new obligation and computations were actually made to show that doctors' fees were well within a labourer's wages packet provided he worked a full week.[6] We need not examine this line of argument any further: the ending of the old system of fixed annual payments, the impoverishment of the white population and the more widely dispersed population are quite sufficient to explain the declining attraction of Jamaica to the medical profession.

[1] E.g. Phillippo, J. B., *op. cit.*, p. 220. PAIJ, 1854 (1848), pp. 44–5. Sewell, *op. cit.*, pp. 195–7, and Underhill, *op. cit.*

[2] Cholera (Jamaica), *op. cit.*, p. 111. [3] *Ibid.*, p. 103. [4] *Ibid.*, p. 111.

[5] *Jamaica in 1912*, p. 62. [6] Cholera (Jamaica), p. 94.

An attempt to arrest the decline in the number of doctors was made in 1846 with the passing of the Dispensary Act. Under this public dispensaries were set up. Doctors were to be paid £40 each from general revenue but their chief income was to be derived from regular subscriptions by members of the public in exchange for free medical attention and medicines during sickness. The scheme failed because in the absence of compulsion, not enough people supported it.[1]

On the whole, residents in Kingston were rather better provided for than those in the country parishes since most of the remaining doctors preferred to practise in the city. The population was dense and relatively richer. Fees ranging from £1 12*s.* 6*d.* and £5 6*s.* 8*d.* per visit are said to have been charged.[2] For some of those unable to pay these exorbitant fees the Kingston Metcalfe Dispensary, maintained voluntarily, was opened in 1842. This was designed for the 'relief of the industrious poor' but its services were restricted to people earning less than 5*s.* per week.[3] In the country parishes medical aid was often unobtainable. All parishes had medical appointments but the holders of these offices did not always reside in the parish town. The parish of St. John, for example, had been without a resident medical practitioner for several years before 1851.[4] Consequently an accident such as a broken leg, in rural areas, was likely to prove fatal.[5]

(iii) *The Elimination of Epidemic Diseases*

Complaints about the number of deaths due to preventable causes were voiced from time to time but no steps were taken to deal with this problem, as with so many others, until after the change in constitution in 1865. During Sir J. P. Grant's administration the various aspects of public health were tackled: a Public Medical Service was established, attempts were made to control epidemics by regulating quarantine, vaccination and sanitation and, thirdly, existing public utilities were taken over and expanded. The success of these measures is evident in the effective prevention of serious epidemics. The 'normal' death-rate did not, apparently, fall below about 23–4 per 1,000 but, at the same time, it did not rise very much above this level as it had done during the outbreaks of cholera, yellow fever and smallpox.

[1] Cholera (Jamaica,) p. 93. [2] PWI, Pt. II, Jamaica, p. 177. [3] JA, 1846.
[4] Cholera (Jamaica), p. 16. [5] Report with BBJ, 1870 (C 85).

The Public Medical Service, established in 1869, was designed to obtain a more equitable distribution, as well as to encourage an influx, of medical practitioners. The island was divided into forty medical districts, on the basis of population and area, to each of which a Government Medical Officer was appointed. A fixed salary varying between £200 and £300 p.a. was guaranteed to each officer. This payment was intended partly as an inducement to doctors to settle in districts that would otherwise be unattractive and partly as a payment for services rendered in looking after paupers and prisoners and public vaccination. Medical officers were also expected to start private practices in their own districts. However, the choice among local practitioners was so limited that at the end of the year five appointments were still vacant.[1] Subsequent legislation widened the scope of the service: the ticket system was devised in 1880 for those unable to pay; the number of medical districts was increased to forty-five and the public hospitals and the Lunatic Asylum were included in the service. In time all vacancies were filled. Outside the service, however, the number of doctors was slow to increase and in 1921 there were still as many as 6,129 persons for each doctor.[2]

At the same time as making provisions for vaccination, quarantine regulations were enforced and Visiting Officers appointed at all ports to carry them into effect. The number of other preventive measures adopted during the following years also makes an impressive list. Under Law 21 of 1874 the May Pen estate, purchased in 1851, was turned into a cemetery for Kingston and burial grounds in the city were gradually closed thereafter. During the 1870's the government also took over and began building on its own initiative a number of public utilities. In 1871 the Kingston and Liguanea water works were bought.[3] Completely new works had to be built to ensure an adequate supply of water for the town at sufficient pressure to extinguish fires—a calamity with which Kingston was frequently afflicted. Unlike the old supply, the new works provided filtered water. In 1899 Kingston suburbs were supplied from the Constant Spring Reservoir and of the thirteen chief towns or parishes nine had acquired water works.[4] The Kingston slaughterhouse, which assured the city of a safe and clean meat supply, was opened in 1876, by which date all private slaughtering yards were to have ceased operation.[5] In the following year the Kingston gasworks were completed. Markets were

[1] *Ibid.* [2] CP, 1921. [3] Law 15 of 1871.
[4] Col. Rep., 1894 (C 7319). [5] Law 37 of 1872.

also being built in most urban areas and after 1899 the sale of fresh meat, poultry and game outside these was prohibited.[1] In 1890 commissioners were appointed charged with the duty of collection and discharge of sewage in Kingston.[2] Five years later the town had been equipped with street sewers and work was begun on linking them with private premises. By 1905 1,896 houses had been connected.[3]

(iv) *The Development of Curative Medicine*

By the end of the century, the government, having succeeded in bringing epidemics under control, began to turn its attention to the slower-developing debilitating diseases. More information about their incidence was collected. The most widespread disease apparently was hookworm. An examination of prisoners in the General Penitentiary in 1910 disclosed an incidence of about 70 per cent.[4] This was confirmed for the general population when a survey, carried out during the Hookworm Campaign, showed that 16,712 people out of a total of 24,008 were afflicted.[5] Yaws was also widespread and about 8,000 cases were treated annually after the Yaws Notification Law came into operation.[6] But this number by no means gives a complete indication of the numbers affected since many sufferers remained reluctant to seek medical aid, believing the disease to be incurable. Malaria was found in most areas near swamps and this meant that many of the sugar workers were liable to get the disease. The areas surrounding Spanish Town, parts of St. Thomas, St. James and Westmoreland had a high incidence of malaria. Extension of banana cultivation to some of these areas also made malaria a typical disease of banana workers. Statistics relate only to those admitted to hospital and thus certainly understate the incidence. In 1916 5,495 people were admitted into hospitals.[7] Vomiting sickness did not occur very frequently but caused much distress when it did appear. It was said to be due to poisoning from the ackee fruit[8] which was eaten widely but the Jamaican government did not follow the example of Trinidad in cutting down all ackee trees. Venereal disease was also said to be prevalent, but since not all cases presented themselves for treatment no estimate of its incidence is possible. Tuberculosis was also believed to be increasing but again no statistics are available.

[1] Law 38 of 1889. [2] Law 31 of 1890. [3] HBJ, 1905.
[4] Col. Rep., 1912 (Cd. 6007–3), p. 31.
[5] Col. Rep., 1933 (Col. No. 1603), p. 8.
[6] Col. Rep., 1919 (Cmd. 1–3), p. 17.
[7] Col. Rep., 1917 (Cd. 8434–30), p. 17. [8] *Ibid.*, p. 18.

One of the earliest measures adopted was the Yaws Notification Law of 1910.[1] Under this, rural constables were used to find and persuade affected people to undergo treatment in out-patients' clinics. Elimination of malaria was more difficult because it involved considerable capital expenditure. While steps were taken to fill in or drain some of the swamps near towns, short-run relief began to be afforded in 1912 with the sale of quinine at cheap rates.[2] Malaria continued to receive attention and in 1928 a survey was carried out[3] which led to malaria control in several endemic areas.[4] In the same year a survey was also made of tuberculosis resulting in the establishment of a Tuberculosis Dispensary and Health Unit. Treatment of venereal disease was free and in 1918 made compulsory.[5]

More long-term measures designed to raise the general standard of health were adopted after the end of World War I. In 1919 a school for sanitary inspectors was opened to provide efficient officers in rural areas. The Bureau of Health Education was established in 1926 and its monthly journal *Jamaica Public Health* reached a circulation of 20,000.[6] The importance of the health of the school child was also beginning to be recognized and in the late twenties medical examinations and dental treatment were carried out in Kingston and St. Andrew schools.

Lack of public resources continued to limit the government's activities and hence there remained many opportunities for private enterprise. The United Fruit Company set an excellent example to private employers in 1919 with the inauguration of a scheme for medical attention for their employees.[7] In the same year work was begun on the Hookworm Campaign under the auspices of the Rockefeller Foundation. Financial responsibility for this was increasingly taken over by the Jamaican government until, in the late twenties, this provided the larger share.[8] An account of the campaign is of special interest here because it illustrates the methods needed to achieve results in the eradication of diseases and the cost in time and resources involved. In this instance the problem of covering the whole island was solved by selecting Demonstration Areas in each parish. The actual work was carried on in two parts. In the first place, a sanitary unit was set up in the Area with the object of providing a sanitary

[1] Law 32 of 1910.
[2] Col. Rep., 1914 (Cd. 7050–24).
[3] Col. Rep., 1929 (Col. No. 1458), p. 7.
[4] Col. Rep., 1930 (Col. No. 1509), p. 26.
[5] Law 6 of 1918.
[6] Col. Rep., 1931 (Col. No. 1550), p. 28.
[7] Col. Rep. (Cmd. 1103–10), p. 7.
[8] HBJ, 1928.

latrine for each house. When this was completed the second unit moved in to examine each resident for hookworm and to treat all cases until cured.[1] Progress in this work was necessarily slow and in 1931—after eleven years' work—the campaign was expected to require a further two or three years.[2]

Statistics of incidence and causes of death are, unfortunately, too poor to enable us to judge the efficacy of these measures directly. Of their success, however, there can be no doubt because the death-rate began to fall during the early twenties when some of the government's curative measures had already been in existence for some years and others were being introduced.

We conclude therefore that the years from about the turn of the

TABLE LXIX

Number of Persons per House and per Room

Year	Number per House	Number per Room
1861	5·1	n·a.
1871	4·9	n·a.
1881	4·7	n·a.
1891	4·8	n·a.
1911	4·5	2·4
1921	4·5	2·3
1943	3·8	2·0

Sources: CP. The ratio of persons per room is calculated by taking the mid-point of each class interval as weights—i.e. 1, 2, 3·5, 6 and 8 rooms per dwelling.

century were remarkable for the improvement in education, health and per capita consumption. The same upward trend is also evident in housing statistics. The housing ratio fell slowly from 5·1 persons per dwelling in 1861 to 4·5 in 1921 and more rapidly during the next inter-censal years to 3·8 in 1943 (Table LXIX, col. 2). The reduction in the number of persons per dwelling was also accompanied by a reduction in the number of persons per room from 2·4 in 1911 to 2·0 in 1943. This decrease in overcrowding was also accompanied by rising standards of construction. According to the census returns the proportion of unfloored houses declined from 49 per cent in 1881 to 17 per cent in 1921. In this period shingle, concrete and metal

[1] Col. Rep., 1933 (Cd. No. 1603), p. 13.   [2] *Ibid.*

roofs were also replacing thatch so that the percentage of houses using these improved building materials rose from 17 to 57 per cent.

But at the same time as general health standards improved new problems of public health were created by the movement of people into Kingston in search of work. Many of them lived under appalling conditions and were chronically short of food. The subject of malnutrition did not receive attention until the thirties and forties when the situation was probably much worse as a result of depression, increasing unemployment and war-time shortages. According to the Nutrition Committee of 1937, malnutrition affected 'a very high percentage of the population'.[1] Compared with the daily intake of 2,700 calories recommended by the Hot Springs Conference the 1945 Committee on Nutrition found that the average Jamaican consumed only 1,800,[2] of which 70 per cen twere obtained from the bulky starches.[3] However, the 1945 Committee based its calculations of food consumption on Dr. Benham's estimate for 1943 which, as pointed out in Part I, Ch. 1, D, may have been too low. It is unlikely that the average diet during the twenties was insufficient in bulk; but that it was ill-balanced there can be no doubt. (For composition of home-produced food see Ch. 10, Table XXV, and for that of imports Ch. 13, Table XLIX.) Furthermore, these conclusions relate to the average Jamaican: among the unemployed and the intermittently employed in the towns, consumption was undoubtedly much lower.

The problem of insufficient diet does not appear to have arisen in the country districts because there were usually wild or semi-wild foods such as mangoes, citrus and coconuts which, though they do not ensure a well-balanced diet, at any rate prevent outright starvation. Nevertheless, malnutrition among agricultural workers has frequently been used to explain the customary short working week. Labourers, so it is argued, are so exhausted after three or four days' work that they have to use the remainder of the week to rest. This explanation is not satisfactory because it does not consider whether a full week's earnings could purchase a more adequate diet. If the argument proves anything at all it is that wages were too low to keep a man in good health and, since they failed to do this, workers preferred leisure to hard work for inadequate returns.

[1] J. Govt. Printer, 1937. [2] J. Govt. Printer, 1945, p. 9.
[3] *Ibid.*, p. 13.

D. Employment Opportunities

(i) *Labour Scarcity*

The supply of labour, as we saw in Ch. 9, began to fall short of demand immediately after the abolition of the slave trade. Output of the major exports declined between abolition and emancipation and, although part of this decline was attributable to unfavourable prices after the end of the Napoleonic wars, there is no doubt that it would have fallen less steeply but for the decrease in the working population. Labourers were, of course, prevented from taking advantage of their scarcity because as slaves they were tied to the plantation of their owners.

After emancipation all restrictions on movements were lifted, and henceforth labour was free to seek work where it was offered. As before estates continued to offer employment. There was also plenty of land available for those willing to bear the risks of crop failure and the other disadvantages to which independent small-scale cultivation was liable. In the towns, too, opportunities in the service industries were growing with the breaking down of the isolation of estates. There were thus plenty of opportunities even for those without the capital to acquire a freehold.

The level of employment offered by estates, however, was the same as before emancipation only if workers were willing to accept the same real wages as before (or possibly even less owing to the increased working capital required to finance payments in cash). However, at this wage, independent cultivation or employment in the towns was more attractive to the freed slaves not only because of the higher returns in the new occupations, but also because these offered other advantages such as independence or regular wage payments. Not many estates were in a position to offer wages high or regular enough to compete with the new opportunities and as a result workers left the estates (Ch. 11, B).

The drain of labour from estates, in turn, resulted in their abandonment, and hence reduced opportunities for wage employment in agriculture. But, at the same time, abandonment of estates increased the land available for independent settlement. Moreover, so long as the peasantry continued to expand and so long as they produced more than their own subsistence there were also opportunities in non-agricultural employment. In Ch. 12 we saw that, beginning in the late forties, the peasants began to sell surplus food to estate labour and to the towns and subsequently expanded production of export crops as well. With their earnings they were able to buy imported goods, but also goods and services produced in the island. As a result 'Industrial' employment, in the census sense, increased from 18,500 in 1844 to 32,000 in 1861. We do not know in which occupations this expansion took place, but according to subsequent trends it must have been mainly in those catering for consumers directly, e.g. dress and shoemakers.

(ii) *The Crisis of 1865*

Early in 1865 E. B. Underhill wrote to the Secretary of State for the Colonies pointing to the general distress prevailing in the island: 'the simple fact is that there is not enough work available for the people; neither work nor capital to employ them'.[1] In the same year, a group of settlers in St. Ann petitioned the Queen for the grant of cultivable land,[2] and in other parishes there were also signs of lack of employment opportunities. This situation had arisen because crop failure and higher prices of imports forced peasants to seek wage employment on estates. But since fewer estates were still in production there was little opportunity for temporary wage employment.

The causes that had led to this situation were, however, only temporary. More favourable rainfall and the decline in import prices subsequently restored the peasants' prosperity, and the continuing abandonment of estates made more land available for small-scale agriculture. The fact that much of it had to be occupied illegally made no practical difference until 1865 to the peasants' ability or willingness to produce, because the inefficiency of the administration under the old constitution made the chance of eviction practically non-existent. After the beginning of Crown Colony government proceedings began to be taken against squatters, but these did not become effective until the end of the seventies and since much of the acreage recovered was released to the occupants on favourable terms it did not result in a reduction of opportunities.

The decline in estate employment therefore affected the peasant adversely only in so far as it deprived him of a means of tiding over temporary periods of adversity. It meant, in fact that henceforth he had to rely on his own cultivation entirely and, as we saw in Chapter 4, this had a salutary effect on his capacity to produce. Thus, although abandonment of estates and increasing population

[1] Papers re the Affairs of Jamaica, BPP, 1866 (3595), p. 1. [2] *Ibid.*, p. 136.

had raised the numbers seeking work, employment opportunities expanded sufficiently to absorb them. By 1866 the number of small-settlers is estimated to have increased further to 60,000 and 'Industrial' employment and retail trade also continued to increase, as one would expect, from the growing production for exchange.

(iii) *The Turning Point of the Eighties*

During the eighties, the first signs of scarcity of employment opportunities appeared. We have already seen in Ch. 10, that during this decade there was a sharp fall in the percentage of the working population employed in agriculture and also a big jump in the numbers entering domestic service and that these trends continued subsequently. Population had been growing at approximately 1·4 per cent per annum since the middle of the century and cultivated acreage was being extended at an even greater rate. But in spite of this employment opportunities in agriculture failed to grow proportionately to the increase in the working population because the banana was supplanting sugar and this involved a reduction in the labour requirements per acre cultivated.

Between 1871 and 1911 labour requirements per acre in agriculture appear to have been nearly halved. The cultivated acreage per person employed in agriculture rose from 0·771 in 1871 to 1·393 in 1911 (Table LXX). During the same period the total area under cultivation rose nearly two and a half times. But this increase was not sufficient to offset the effects of lower labour requirements and increasing population, and hence the percentage of the working population engaged in agriculture fell continuously from 68 per cent in 1871 to 58·5 per cent in 1911.

What happened to those seeking work who failed to be absorbed in agriculture? As we saw in Ch. 14, A, the relative decline in agricultural employment was accompanied by a sharp rise in per capita output at *1910* prices, from £22·9 in *1891* to £34·5 in *1930*. A rise in productivity in agriculture should bring with it an expansion in non-agricultural employment, because, as the agricultural community becomes richer its demand for non-agricultural goods and services increases, and this in turn stimulates investment in manufacturing industries. But as we saw in Ch. 10 the development of secondary industries during these years was negligible. There are several reasons for this. First of all, most of the rise in productivity was offset by a deterioration in the terms of trade, and hence real incomes hardly rose at all. Secondly, the redistribution of incomes that had taken place in earlier years had favoured those with a high propensity to consume.

It is true that the share of incomes of those most likely to invest in secondary industry—the merchants—is estimated to have risen slightly up to 1891. They, in fact, initiated most of the development that took place during these years. Finally, and this is the chief

TABLE LXX

Cultivated Acreage and Labour Requirements per Acre*

Year	Total Acreage Under Care and Cultivation	Cultivated Acreage Only	Cultivated Acreage as % of Total Acreage	Number of Cultivated Acres per Person Employed in Agriculture
	'000 acres	'000 acres	%	acres
1871	516·9	113·4	21·9	0·771
1881	547·1	121·7	22·2	0·721
1891	626·8	139·2	22·2	0·807
1911	926·8	273·0	29·5	1·393
1921	1,074·7	307·7	28·6	1·603
1943	1,062·8	382·9	36·0	1·729

* There were several changes in classification during this period. The distinction between cultivated acreage and acreage under care may not have been consistently adhered to.

Sources: Acreage statistics are taken from BBJ and HBJ and the numbers employed in agriculture from Table XIX, Ch. 9.

reason, there were few opportunities for establishing industries able to compete with imports. There were, as we saw, no cheap supplies of power and no local raw materials, apart from some agricultural by-products, to stimulate manufacturing. Nevertheless, there were some products not dependent on either local raw materials or cheap power. Locally manufactured textiles, for example, could compete successfully with imports if labour costs were sufficiently low. But Jamaica lacked skilled workers of all grades. There were no local facilities for training artisans and engineers. Hence Jamaican industry was dependent on overseas for its technical staff and this inevitably raised costs.

The only developments of importance during the nineties were the expansion of the transport system and public works. The former, however, employed relatively little labour and the latter was only temporary. Thus, in the absence of expansion in the productive sectors to compensate for the decline in agriculture, the working population increasingly had to seek employment in the service trades. According to the censuses an increasing proportion went into domestic service and petty trading. Employment in domestic service increased steeply in the 1880's and by 1891 accounted for 13·5 per cent

TABLE LXXI

Occupational Distribution of Women

(revised estimates)

	1891		1911		1921	
	Nos. '000	%	Nos. '000	%	Nos. '000	%
1. Agriculture . .	34·3	37·6	36·1	31·5	30·0	24·4
2. Personal Service .	31·8	34·8	44·2	38·5	55·0	44·7
3. Milliners and Dressmakers . .	19·0	20·8	21·5	18·7	24·9	20·3
4. Petty Traders . .	1·5	1·6	3·2	2·8	3·7	3·0
5. Other	4·7	5·2	9·8	8·5	9·4	7·6
Total	91·3	100·0	114·8	100·0	123·0	100·0

Source: Ch. 9, E.

of the working population. It continued to increase further subsequently until in 1921 it accounted for nearly 18 per cent. The proportion engaged in the 'Commercial' group also increased from 3·0 per cent in 1881 to 5·9 per cent in 1911. Apart from growing employment in transport much of this increase was due to petty traders. 'Industrial' employment, on the other hand, continued to increase only with population growth, as, indeed, we should expect, from the lack of any important growth in secondary industries and a constant level of consumption.

This movement of labour into the service trades occurred mainly among women. Table LXXI shows the main categories of female employment according to our revised estimates of the working population. The miscellaneous group comprises chiefly teachers, shorthand-typists and other service occupations. A rise in these is to be expected with the growth in the educational system, commercial services and catering. What is important in this table, however, is the changing shares in the other groups. The number of women employed in agriculture fell from 37·6 per cent in 1891 to 24·4 per cent in 1921. This fall was compensated by a rise in domestic service and petty trading.

These trends are symptomatic of a lack of employment opportunities because the expanding occupations, marked by a low per capita output and under-employment, are in the nature of job creation rather than in response to a real demand for their services. The large increase in female domestic servants was not evidence of a high standard of living enjoyed by a small section of the community. On the contrary, it was the response of a much wider community to the needs of surplus rural population. By the end of the century the custom had grown up to provide shelter, food and training to 'schoolgirls' in return for service. This cheap labour supply enabled far lower income groups to enjoy personal services than is usually found in more fully developed societies. Though adding something to national income the value of such employment, in the absence of social insurance, lay chiefly in its provision for the unemployed. Similarly, the more than proportionate growth of female petty traders indicates under-employment. The function of petty traders is to buy and sell small quantities of, usually, local produce. We should expect their number to grow with the expansion in production for exchange—as it did during the post-emancipation years. But there is no reason to believe that the proportion of produce entering exchange increased during these years and hence we conclude that the growth in the number of petty traders was mainly the result of the splitting up of existing work. The result of these trends was that per capita output in the non-agricultural sectors had fallen considerably by *1890* and also recovered much more slowly than agriculture. (Ch. 14, A.)

For the men no comparable opportunities for job-creation presented themselves with the result that they responded to emigration opportunities with alacrity. The volume of emigration, as we saw in Ch. 9, C, (iv), was considerable during the eighties and again after the turn of the century. Emigration may, of course, be due as much to the attraction of the work offered abroad as to the need to seek it because of failure of domestic employment or ignorance of local opportunities or unwillingness to enter certain types of domestic employment. No doubt the first exodus during the years 1853–4 was due to the attraction of the higher and regular wages offered abroad but after 1880 this explanation is no longer convincing. In the first place, wages were undoubtedly higher, but, according to the available evidence, this was largely offset by higher living costs and less attractive living conditions. Moreover, each boom abroad usually lasted only a short time and was, each time, succeeded by unemployment and much hardship. Similarly the explanations of unwillingness or ignorance are not convincing because during the nineties there was a considerable west to eastward movement from sugar estates to banana estates.

It is true that complaints about the labour supply continued to be heard as late as 1910.[1] But such scarcity applied only to certain districts. The availability of Jamaican labour now depended largely on whether or not the labourer had a plot of land. Where labour was wholly dependent on estate work for its livelihood it was said to be 'abundant, inexpensive and obtainable'.[2] Shortages occurred only where estates were dependent on small-settlers for their labour. In 1891 an attempt was made to encourage workers seeking employment to enter into contract with sugar and other proprietors through the Immigration Department in the hope of dispensing with immigration altogether. 'No result accrued from this law, the native labourer being unwilling to bind himself to work regularly for hire.'[3] A further attempt to even out local surpluses and scarcities of labour was made in 1902. This time the Immigration Department was to be used merely as a Labour Intelligence Office without requiring both parties to enter into a contractual relationship. This experiment was also considered a failure because workers migrating to other parishes demanded higher wages than those paid to local labour—a demand which employers were not prepared to meet.[4] We do not, unfortunately, have further information about these attempts at setting up labour exchanges. That they were considered a failure is rather surprising because other evidence, such as the growth in the number of banana workers and internal migration during these years, does not support the conclusion that labour was unwilling to migrate or to enter agricultural wage employment.

[1] Letter from P. C. Cork to Secretary of Jamaica Baptist Union, J. Council Min., 1910, vol. 51.
[2] RWIC, 1897 (C 8669), Pt. XIII, No. 754.
[3] *Ibid.*, No. 757.
[4] Letter from P. C. Cork, *op. cit.*

On the contrary, fears were beginning to be expressed that the introduction of immigrants might reduce employment for native labour and force them to seek work abroad.[1] In the case of the United Fruit Company this policy appears to have been pursued deliberately. The United Fruit Company planted in predominantly peasant areas, and since they were interested as much in buying as in planting bananas they had nothing to gain from persuading the peasants to work for their own estates. The labour needed for their own properties, therefore, had to be recruited from other parishes but was found to be unsatisfactory. The steady attention needed in fruit growing was said to be obtainable only from the East Indians.[2] Captain Baker, the promoter of the scheme, claimed that the Jamaican made a much better wage labourer abroad. This is hardly surprising because, apart from the fact that a strange country offers no inducement to idleness, the Costa Rican planters were also supported by a stringent vagrancy law under which anyone unable to show means of subsistence or work was arrested and sent to employers needing labour. Refusal to work could mean expatriation. Reference to Tables X and XI in Ch. 9 shows that immigration can only have been the cause of a small part of emigration. The objections raised against immigration are nevertheless interesting because they show that a lack of employment opportunities was already evident at this time.

We conclude, therefore, that growth in domestic employment opportunities first fell short of that of the working population during the eighties, but that this was masked temporarily by emigration of men and the growing entry of women into domestic service and petty trade. During the nineties there was a partial improvement in local opportunities due to expansion in banana planting by estates, public works and railway construction, but after the turn of the century opportunities began to fall short of the labour supply once more but this was again masked by emigration and a further increase in job-creation.

(iv) *The Growth of Unemployment*

By 1921 only 55·3 per cent of the working population were occupied in agriculture. This was again due to a further reduction in labour requirements per acre and to the failure of cultivated acreage to expand sufficiently to make up for the lower labour requirements and population growth. The cultivated acreage per agricultural

[1] *Ibid.*

[2] *Ibid.*

worker had risen to 1·603. The sugar industry began to expand again during the war, but this did not improve employment opportunities significantly partly because in 1921 it was still relatively unimportant and partly because it had become more efficient and hence less labour-intensive. The prospect of extending the area under cultivation was by now also much less hopeful. Cultivated acreage had begun to encroach on pasture land already during the first decade of the century, and total acreage 'under care or cultivation' increased only slightly between about 1910 and 1920 and thereafter not at all. This suggests that by about the second decade of the century the limit to agricultural expansion had been reached and that cultivation henceforth could be increased only by taking over inferior land.

The need to find work outside agriculture had thus become greater than before, but the chance of finding it even less. The considerable rise in the productivity of the agricultural sector was also accompanied by a rise, though less rapid, in the standard of living. There was some investment in manufacturing industries which used local agricultural raw materials or replaced bulky imports (see Ch. 10, C). As for other manufacturing, however, there was little prospect of overcoming inherent handicaps without the restriction of comparable imports or some other form of government stimulus. Hence in *1930* the manufacturing industry was still an insignificant sector in the economy.

Until 1921 the situation had been relieved by a further growth in the proportion of domestic servants to 17·9 per cent and by emigration to Cuba. The exodus to Cuba, however, virtually ceased in 1921 and, beginning in 1923, there was a net inflow of emigrants. Like the previous waves of emigration to Central America this movement also ended in unemployment and hardship and, again, does not appear to have resulted in considerable savings or remittances to relatives at home. Unfortunately we have no information about the value of remittances sent home or of savings. The only figure available is that of the Unemployment Bureau of Jamaica[1] which estimated the average value of remittances from overseas between 1883 and 1935 at £125,000 p.a. But this figure is of little help since the value of remittances must have fluctuated considerably from decade to decade. Neither is there any evidence that emigrants added significantly to domestic incomes in enterprise or in capital when they came back.

[1] Quoted in Labour Conditions in the West Indies, BPP, 1938–9 (Cmd. 6070), p. 78.

The original desire of emigrants to save while abroad and establish themselves in some independent enterprise on their return does not often appear to have been realized. And failure to achieve this meant joining the ranks of those seeking wage employment.

Owing to the absence of unemployment statistics, we have no direct evidence of the growth of unemployment after 1921. No attempt to collect statistics was made until 1936, and even these are incomplete.[1] However, we can deduce the growth of unemployment from the movement of people into Kingston. Between 1921 and 1943 the increase in the city's population (73 per cent) and in that of St. Andrew, which included much of suburban Kingston (135 per cent), was far in excess of the island increase (44 per cent). This disproportionate growth was also accompanied by a deterioration in health standards.

[1] Rep. Com. on Unemployment, J. Govt. Printer, 1936.

CHAPTER 16

PUBLIC FINANCE

In this chapter we consider the share of the government in national income. There are many ways in which a government can affect expansion. How much it can do in stimulating production depends, in the first place, on the wealth of the community. If the country is poor then scope for raising revenue is small, and hence there is little opportunity of spending on services which, in turn, encourage progress. But for a given taxable capacity the willingness and ability of a government to encourage progress also depends on how much power it has and whose interests it represents. We therefore begin this chapter with a brief outline of the constitutional history of Jamaica. In the following section we compare the level of government expenditure first with national income and secondly with the assumption of public responsibility for various services. The third section deals with the sources of public revenues, and the final section with local government finance.

A. Constitutional Changes

Until 1865 Jamaicans were governed under the Old Representative System—a form of constitution they had possessed since 1661. This provided for a nominated Legislative Council and an elected House of Assembly with the Governor at its head. They were empowered to legislate on matters relating to internal affairs, but Imperial confirmation had to be obtained before the Acts came into force. It was the Governor's duty to uphold Imperial interests and to execute Imperial policy. But in practice this was often difficult. The House of Assembly, elected on a narrow franchise and representing mainly the planting and commercial interests in the island, had developed a powerful weapon in passing revenue bills that were valid for a short time only. When Imperial policy clashed with local aspirations pressure, in the form of stoppage of supplies, was thus quickly brought to bear on the Queen's representative. Consequently, measures introduced by the Governor were enacted only with great difficulty and after considerable delay.

After emancipation the need for government services increased, and the Imperial government sought to introduce a number of social reforms. The result was that clashes between the Governor and the Assembly became all the more frequent. The first legislative deadlock occurred already in 1839 over the West India Prisons Bill. But the Sugar Duties Act of 1846 gave rise to the worst and most protracted crisis of all. Members of the House were convinced that free trade would finally ruin the sugar industry, and when it became clear that the home government would not change its policy the House decided that one way of preparing for the lean years was a reduction in public expenditure. The retrenchment crisis began in 1849 and lasted four years. Briefly, the crisis revolved round the conflict between the Assembly's determination to make substantial reductions in official salaries and terminate expenditure on some services, such as health, and the Imperial government's refusal to permit such violation of their obligations. Each time a revenue bill came up for renewal retrenchment clauses were inserted and the Bill was disallowed. Consequently no revenue bills were enacted, and in April 1853 the last to remain in force—the Import Duties Act—expired. By this time the Colonial Treasury was empty. Official salaries amounting to £101,664 were in arrears and, before any revenue could be raised by new legislation, liabilities were expected to increase by another £45,547.[1] Island cheques with a face value of £1 were being discounted at 12*s.*[2] The situation had become so desperate that it could only be relieved with external help. The Imperial government granted a loan to meet the deficit but, at the same time, used the opportunity to change the island constitution.

The new constitution, introduced in 1854, provided for an Executive Committee which was to be responsible for all financial bills to replace the previous custom by which it was open to any member to introduce money bills, and no one was ultimately responsible for financial matters. The reform, however, did not tackle the main problem: namely the ability of an opposing faction to retard business or to prevent it from being carried out. Consequently, only few bills reached the Statute Book and in 1865, after the outbreak of Morant Bay, the House of Assembly was at last persuaded of the failure of representative government under existing conditions and to surrender its constitution.

[1] Papers re Legislative Proceedings, BPP, 1854 (1806), p. 33.
[2] Gardner, *op. cit.*, London, 1873, p. 448.

In 1866 Crown Colony government was introduced and, apart from a concession to local opinion in 1884, retained until 1944. The new constitution provided, apart from the Governor and Privy Council, for a Legislative Council composed of ex-officio and nominated members. The privilege of introducing measures was restricted to the Governor and he, by virtue of the composition of the Legislative Council, was always able to carry through his legislation. This combination of autocratic rule and growing public expenditure, however, led to complaints, and in 1884 the Colonial Office was forced to make some concession to local opinion. The amended constitution provided for the election of half the members of the Legislative Council. At the same time, the Governor was instructed not to fill all the nominated seats, thus giving the elected members a majority. But in 1899 this gave rise to a legislative deadlock and resulted in a financial crisis. To avoid a repetition all nominated seats were filled subsequently.

B. The Level and Pattern of Government Expenditure

The significance of the constitutional change of 1865 for economic development is that the new government, unlike the old, was interested in maintaining an efficient and impartial administration and in providing basic social services and good communications. This change in emphasis can be seen both in the share of the government in national income and in the pattern of expenditure.

(i) *The Share of the Government in National Income*

Table LXXII shows the share of public administration (central and local government combined) in national income, excluding expenditure on trading services such as the Post Office and public utilities. Columns 2 and 3 give the value and share of goods and services, excluding transfers, and columns 4 and 5 the value and share of total expenditure. It should be noted that the year *1832* is not really comparable with later years, as it includes a large amount of defence expenditure for which the island was still liable at that time. We have, therefore, included an alternative set of figures which exclude defence expenditure.

Looking at column 3 first, we see that the share of the government's expenditure on goods and services, excluding defence, in national income rose rapidly from 4·1 per cent in *1832* to 6·2 per cent in *1850.*

This rise, however, was mainly the result of the big fall in gross domestic product during these years; the actual expenditure rose by only about ten per cent. For about two decades after *1850* the share declined, but after *1870* it began to rise again and by *1930* accounted for 8·5 per cent of gross domestic product.

If we include transfer payments—that is education grants, poor relief, subsidies and debt charges—we see from column 5 that the share of the public sector rose rapidly during the initial eighteen years from 4·8 to 7·3 per cent and also declined during the following twenty years and began to increase again subsequently. It will also be noticed that the increases between *1832* and *1850* and in the years *1870* to *1930* were more rapid than in the case of goods and services only, showing that transfer payments rose more than proportionately during both periods.

TABLE LXXII

The Share of the Public Sector in Gross Domestic Product

Year	Expenditure excluding Transfer Payments		Total Expenditure	
	Value £'000	% of G.D.P.	Value £'000	% of G.D.P.
1	2	3	4	5
1832 . . .	*381·2 (209·1)	7·6 (4·1)	415·6 (243·5)	8·2 (4·8)
1850 . . .	229·8	6·2	271·5	7·3
1870 . . .	324·4	5·7	393·9	6·9
1890 . . .	571·2	6·5	694·0	7·9
1910 . . .	695·4	6·1	970·7	8·5
1930 . . .	1,704·6	8·5	2,440·7	12·2

* Figures in parenthesis exclude defence expenditure.
Source: Pt. 1.

What emerges from these two series is that the share of government expenditure did not fall with economic activity up to *1850* but, on the other hand, also did not expand with increased output during the subsequent twenty years. In fact, total government expenditure actually fell during the fifties until in the financial year 1857–8 it amounted to only £198,200. Thereafter expenditure began to recover again slowly until in 1863–4 it reached £314,600. The rebellion in the following year caused a sharp increase to £377,100. Expenditure fell back again to £350,100 in the year 1865–6[1] but thereafter increased continuously.

What these statistics do not show, however, is the quality of the services provided. The change in government brought not only increased expenditure but also greater efficiency so that, in fact, as we shall see below, the value of government expenditure after 1865 increased more than its rising share in national income suggests.

(ii) *The Pattern of Central Government Expenditure*

In this and the following section we deal only with the activities of the central government. Except for the year *1870* the parochial authorities maintained separate services and raised taxes and loans to finance them. Information about their activities, however, is very poor and, rather than complicate our account with unreliable estimates, we have decided to deal with local government finance separately in section D. To make our data on central government expenditure, shown in Table LXXIII, comparable we have deducted expenditure on parochial services in *1870*. The corresponding adjustment in the revenue table, given in section C, was unfortunately not possible.

The change in government in 1866 is even more evident in the composition of central government expenditure than in the rising share of the public sector in national income. As seen from Table LXXIII, the main objects of expenditure in the early years were the administrative, defence, judicial and ecclesiastical establishments. Very little was spent on health—apart from the temporary rise in *1850*, which was caused by the cholera outbreak—on education or on public works. After 1866, on the other hand, communications and the basic social services received greater attention until by *1930* they accounted for 52·5 per cent of total government expenditure.

It is useful here to note how the composition of government expenditure in Jamaica in *1930* compares with that in other countries. W. A. Lewis and A. Martin, in 'Patterns of Public Revenue and Expenditure',[2] have calculated the various classes of government expenditure in sixteen countries as a percentage of gross national product. Our figures are not strictly comparable because they are based on gross domestic product and also because our latest year is *1930*, while Lewis and Martin's figures refer to 1953–4. Nevertheless

[1] REJ, 1882 (285).

[2] *Manchester School*, vol. XXIV, No. 3, 1956.

TABLE LXXIII

Expenditure of the Central Authority

(current values)

	1832		*1850*		*1870**		*1890*		*1910*		*1930*	
	£'000	%	£'000	%	£'000	%	£'000	%	£'000	%	£'000	%
Administration	47·2	17·3	94·7	46·5	166·5	47·7	182·4	31·8	210·1	26·1	595·5	29·3
Judiciary	7·1	2·6	20·6	10·1	27·4	7·9	38·6	6·7	35·8	4·5	58·5	2·9
Defence	172·1	63·0	0·9	0·4	2·9	0·8	8·3	1·5	7·9	1·0	15·6	0·8
Education†	—	—	1·8	0·9	9·1	2·6	40·9	7·1	71·6	8·9	200·1	9·8
Health	—	—	30·3	14·9	19·2	5·5	51·5	9·0	45·4	5·6	170·2	8·4
Ecclesiastic	14·6	5·3	26·4	13·0	22·1	6·3	6·0	1·1	1·2	0·1	—	—
Public Works	8·0	2·9	3·5	1·7	45·6	13·0	157·2	27·4	193·0	24·0	497·7	24·5
Debt Charges	15·2	5·6	17·9	8·8	56·7	16·2	77·9	13·6	224·5	27·9	295·2	14·5
Subsidies‡	9·2	3·3	7·5	3·7	—	—	10·2	1·8	15·4	1·9	198·8	9·8
	273·4	100·0	203·6	100·0	349·5	100·0	573·0	100·0	804·9	100·0	2,031·6	100·0

* Excludes estimated expenditure on parochial services.
† Includes grants to independent Education Authorities.
‡ Includes deficits of railway, post office and public utilities.
Source: Pt. I.

a rough comparison is possible and the results throw a useful light on the assumption of responsibility for the various services by the Jamaican government. For example, expenditure in Jamaica on administration at 3·3 per cent of gross domestic product was rather higher than that of the majority of the countries examined whose percentages lay between 2·77 and 3·22 of gross national product. Economic services, on the other hand, compared favourably at 3·5 per cent with a range between 3·35 and 4·16 per cent. In respect of both education and health, however, Jamaican expenditure at about 1 per cent of gross domestic product on each was less than half of that of most of the countries examined.

Before emancipation the central government assumed responsibility for the general duties of maintaining law and order only. It maintained a civil establishment consisting of the Governor and his secretary, the Island Agent and the Receiver-General and his local representatives. Administrative officials received salaries, but their offices often yielded supplementary incomes. It was not unusual for one person to hold several offices at the same time. William Bullock, for example, was at the time of his death in 1832 the holder of no less than five public offices, three of which alone provided him with an income of £4,000 p.a. apart from fees.[1] Preparation of financial accounts occurred infrequently. Like all other colonies Jamaica was expected to prepare returns for inclusion in the Blue Books. After many exhortations, a financial account was submitted in 1831 purporting to be 'an average of the preceding nine years'.[2] Submissions were more regular subsequently, but the form they took earned them the reputation of being the 'worst returns in the Colonial Office'.[3]

The Judiciary was composed of a Supreme Court and two courts of Assizes. Defence also absorbed a large part of expenditure as the island had to maintain a militia, recruited from the white and free coloured population, and contributed towards the upkeep of the West India Regiment stationed in the island. Expenditure was exceptionally heavy in *1832* owing to the outbreak of the last Slave Rebellion in December 1831 which raised normal defence expenditure by £161,596.[4] After 1832 Jamaica was relieved of the cost of Imperial troops, and subsequently defence expenditure was devoted mainly to

[1] *Lady Nugent's Journal*, London, 1939, p. 19n.
[2] Jamaica Establishments and Revenue, 1823–31, BPP, 1831–2 (58).
[3] Martin, R. M. *History of the British Colonies of the British Empire*, London, 1843, p. 17n. [4] *Ibid.*, p. 1.

the upkeep of fortifications. In addition, the government also provided the stipends and the pensions of the clergy of the Church of England.

After 1838 the need for administrative and judicial services increased. The more widespread incidence of taxation necessitated more staff and the increase in the number of people entitled to law and protection was beyond the capacity of the existing judiciary. A new judiciary was established in 1840 providing for the appointment of a Vice-Chancellor, a Chief Justice, two Puisne judges and nine chairmen of quarter sessions.

Between *1832* and *1850* expenditure on administrative services doubled and on judicial services nearly trebled (Table LXXIII). Expenditure, however, gives a misleading indication of the increase in the services provided because the administration was grossly inefficient. Among the collecting constables abuse was rife and no small part of the increased cost of collecting taxes was due to this factor. The collection of internal taxes was left to the discretion of parochial vestries, who had the power of exempting people from paying taxes on the grounds of poverty.[1] Apart from the injustices to which it gave rise, exercise of this power also made the amount of revenue likely to be available always uncertain. The person ultimately responsible for all revenue collected was the Receiver-General. He, as well as a number of other officials, had to give security before taking office. In 1848 the Receiver-General's sureties were under bond for £60,000, and when he died in January of the following year his sureties were called on to make good a deficiency of £12,000.[2]

Expenditure on the ecclesiastical establishment had also nearly doubled by *1850* owing to the increase in the number of clergy. The large expenditure on health in *1850*, on the other hand, was exceptional as a result of the outbreak of cholera. Compared with the cost of health services of £30,300 in *1850* expenditure during the rest of the decade was only about £9,000[3] and before *1850* even less.

By contrast, expenditure on defence in *1850* had declined to £900 and that on public works had also been reduced. Responsibility for maintaining roads and bridges during these years was left to parochial authorities, and the central government concerned itself only with the upkeep of public buildings. However, the parishes did little towards providing communications, and in 1858 responsibility for the

[1] Papers re Affairs of Jamaica, BPP, 1849 (1065), p. 86.
[2] *Ibid.*, p. 95. [3] REJ.

construction and maintenance of main roads was transferred to the central government to be dealt with under the Main Road Fund. Three qualified civil engineers were appointed to advise the Executive Committee on projects.[1] But the Fund never fulfilled its intended function because the House of Assembly took away its power of raising taxes with which the work was to be financed. By the time the Fund came to an end it owed £32,695 besides £100,350 of loan money raised in its name. 'It had achieved only some current repairs.'[2]

In short, under the old constitution most of the government expenditure was devoted to administration, justice and the ecclesiastical establishment but because the administration was so inefficient much of it was wasted. Before the new government could assume responsibility for new services, reform in the basic departments was therefore essential. Considerable economies were effected through the abolition of some offices which were mere sinecures, by the merging of others and by the reduction of salaries.[3] At the same time, collecting constables, hitherto paid on commission, were replaced by salaried officials. The increased tax yield in 1868 was attributed to more thorough collection and better supervision.[4] As a result of these reforms the share of the administrative and judicial departments fell subsequently not only relatively to total government expenditure but also relatively to national income; its declining share until *1930* was not merely the result of increased total government expenditure. In 1870 the government also disestablished the Church of England. Subsequently vacancies were left unfilled and ecclesiastical expenditure gradually decreased and after *1910* ceased altogether.

Greater efficiency in administration, reduction in ecclesiastical expenditure and a rising share in national income thus provided the means to expand existing services and embark on new ones. Expenditure on health, education and public works all increased rapidly (Table LXXIII). Between *1870* and *1930* expenditure on health services rose seven-fold, on public works eight-fold and on education twenty-four-fold.

At the same time the government also assumed responsibility for a number of trading services. As we saw in Chs. 10, B, and 15, C, these years saw an impressive development in public utilities and in railway expansion. To finance these projects as well as certain specific public works programmes loans were raised under government guar-

[1] PPSC, 1859 (2567), p. 37.
[2] Report with BBJ, 1872 (C 523).
[3] Report with BBJ, 1870 (C 85).
[4] *Ibid.*

antee. As a result debt charges mounted rapidly. By *1870* they already accounted for over 16 per cent of total expenditure. During the following twenty years there was only a small increase in expenditure, but by *1910* the share of debt charges had reached the record level of 27·9 per cent of total expenditure. This was mainly the result of the transfer of the railway to public ownership in 1901, but partly also due to the use of loan finance for some public works during the nineties.

Subsidies, consisting mainly of small payments to foreign companies for providing shipping and telegraphic communications and of deficits on trading services, remained relatively small until *1930*. The sharp increase in *1930* was mainly the result of the huge railway deficit which alone accounts for half the total subsidies.

C. Sources of Revenue and the Incidence of Taxation

Before 1834 most of the tax revenue of the central government was derived from the poll tax and rum and import duties. Slave owners had to pay a tax for every slave in their possession; customs duties were imposed, in conformity with the Navigation Laws, on goods from the United States and other foreign countries, while those from the United Kingdom were admitted duty free; and an excise duty was levied on every gallon of rum consumed in the island. A number of miscellaneous, low-yielding, taxes were also imposed on traders, horned stock and land, and the accounts were balanced by the issue of island certificates, i.e. debt creation.

The revenue derived in *1832* (Table LXXIV) does not give a representative picture of the relative importance of the various sources of income because payments of taxes in these years were affected by the slave rebellion. Many estate proprietors suffered considerable losses from the destruction of property and output and were unable to meet their obligations. Consequently payments of the rum duties and poll taxes fell short of the expected level. Had all the taxes been fully paid at the existing rate, the poll tax would have yielded about £90,000 and the rum duty £24,000,[1] making the former the largest single source of revenue. This, of course, came to an end with emancipation and the island had to find other methods of raising revenue. The condition of the colony precluded the imposition of alternate internal taxes, and no suitable sources of revenue were found until free trade

[1] Jamaica Establishments and Revenue, *op. cit.*

permitted a more comprehensive customs tariff. In 1838 tax revenue of the central government was only £162,283 compared with £239,877 four years earlier.[1] Finally an Import Duty Act was passed in 1843. This levied duties on all imported goods except coal, coke, manure and a number of unimportant miscellaneous articles. By 1846 65 per cent of total revenue was derived from import duties and 15 per cent from the excise duty on rum, while the remainder was raised by a number of low yielding taxes, fees and licences.

The change in the tax structure also affected the incidence of taxation. Whereas formerly taxation had been confined to a small, chiefly propertied, section of the community now everybody was liable to pay tax. Duties added on the average 15 per cent to the c.i.f. value of imports in *1850*, but for certain commodities the increase was even greater: for codfish and herrings it was 20 per cent, for flour 24 per cent, for rice 31 per cent and for beef as much as 42 per cent.[2]

However, it was not on grounds of equity but on the probable effects of higher import prices on the distribution of resources that criticism was first based. Lord Grey objected to the imposition of customs duties on food because this tended to raise the value of domestically produced food and hence encouraged the peasantry to grow provisions for sale to wage labour instead of working for estates directly. To make people work for wages, he suggested, taxation 'should be so designed as to stimulate the indolent. Imports should not be taxed, nor should tax fall heavily on the well-to-do and prosperous, but rather on those living above bare subsistence.'[3]

The argument did not meet with favour in the island. The chosen form of taxation had one great virtue from the administrative point of view—collection was easy. To have relied on any other form of revenue would have increased costs and strained even more the already creaking administrative machinery. The schedule of import duties was altered from time to time and new articles included and others taken out. Rates of duty were generally reduced during the forties and, after remaining fairly stable during the fifties, were increased again in 1859. By 1865 most import duties had risen considerably.

In his famous letter of 1865 E. B. Underhill[4] condemned the exist-

[1] SCP, 1847–8 (361–11), App., pp. 42–5.

[2] Rates of Duty are listed in the BBJ for 1850. For import prices see App. I, 1, B. ii.

[3] Colonial Policy of Lord John Russell's Administration.

[4] Papers re Affairs of Jamaica, BPP, 1866 (3595), pp. 1–2.

ing level of taxation as too heavy and called for a searching enquiry. In his earlier book he had already charged the Legislature with pursuing a discriminatory taxation policy.[1] He alleged that articles primarily consumed by the poorer sections of the community were subjected to heavy duties while others, such as production materials required by estates, escaped lightly. It is rather difficult to verify this charge since the basis on which duties were fixed varied during these years. As far as can be seen, however, there is little justification for Underhill's objections in the form in which they were stated. The level of duties appears to have been raised uniformly on all articles without favouring production materials which, in any case, would have been defensible in the interests of the export trade. What caused hardship during these years was the imposition of an *ad valorem* duty on articles—such as clothing—in common consumption. This obviously affected people adversely in the 1860's when prices were high. On the other hand, the benefits of lower prices were equally apparent in other years. The real charge against the existing structure of taxation lay in its unfairness. If the criterion of a just system of taxation is ability to pay then the Jamaican system could not be called just. The same rate of duty was payable irrespective of income and no attempt was made to single out for higher taxes the commodities consumed or property owned by the better-off.

Apart from objections on the ground of equity, customs duties were by no means an ideal source of revenue. Since the demand for imports was liable to fluctuate from year to year, the amount of revenue forthcoming could never be estimated correctly. But although other taxes were imposed from time to time, their yield never approached that of customs revenue which remained at about 60 per cent of total government income. The first task facing the new government, however, was the constant deficit. In 1868 import duties were raised by one-tenth but subsequently remained virtually unchanged, except for a temporary reduction of duties on American goods under the McKinley tariff,[2] until after the turn of the century. At the same time, production was aided by freeing agricultural implements, factory equipment, and railway materials of the four per cent *ad valorem* duty, but the rum duty was increased to five shillings per gallon.

Next to customs and excise duties, taxes on property were the most important source of revenue. These consisted of levies on horses and

[1] *The West Indies*, London, 1862, p. 217.

[2] See Ch. 13, 4, A.

horned stock—the latter was discontinued in 1892—quit rents, taxes on land, varying according to the use to which it was put, and the tax on houses. The last was raised for poor-relief and after 1885 was collected by the parochial authorities. In 1890 the Holdings Tax was instituted and two years later an additional tax on houses was imposed to make good the loss of income resulting from the abolition of school fees. Property in houses and land was now subject to five different taxes with the heaviest burden falling on the poorest class. In 1897 the total amount payable on the poorest houses varied from 6*s*. in Manchester to 10*s*. in St. James.[1] In the following years arrears and remissions became so frequent that the tax ceased to fulfil its purpose. There was also the difficulty and arbitrariness in assessing house values and, finally, the fact that land was taxed only lightly was thought to impose an unfair burden on the smaller properties. All these objections led to the adoption of an alternative method of raising revenue: one based on 'real value of property'. The valuation roll was prepared in 1901 and the tax, replacing all the previous levies, instituted two years later.

The decision to change the method of taxing property was one of the outcomes of the financial crisis of 1899. For some years past the government had been carrying out a programme of loan-financed public works. By 1890 it was recognized that the fruit trade was superseding sugar as the major export crop and further expansion made the provision of good roads and bridges imperative. But while fruit exports, particularly bananas, in the 1890's grew rapidly, world market conditions for most of Jamaica's other products deteriorated and this, in turn, was of course reflected in public revenues. The reduced value of exports was followed by declining imports. Consequently customs revenue fell and difficulty was experienced in collecting internal taxes. Such obstacles might well have been surmounted, with recovery in prices or further shifts in production, had not the railway company failed at the same time. In addition to the old railway debt the government now had to meet the charges of the new railway extensions. Together they amounted to £122,033, while the excess of receipts over running expenses amounted to only £40,253.[2] The government had also become liable for arrears of interest to the bondholders.

[1] Report on the Finances of Jamaica by Sir David Barbour, BPP, 1899 (C 9412), p. 12.

[2] Col. Rep., 1902 (Cd. 788–43), p. 17.

TABLE LXXIV

Sources of Revenue of the Central Authority

	1832		1850		1870*		1890		1910		1930	
	£'000	%	£'000	%	£'000	%	£'000	%	£'000	%	£'000	%
Direct Taxes:												
i. on income	—	—	—	—	—	—	—	—	—	—	98·2	5·5
ii. on property	59·8	31·3	12·1	6·2	58·5	14·1	17·3	3·0	35·9	4·5	77·9	4·4
Indirect Taxes:												
i. customs	69·7	36·5	136·5	69·6	221·3	53·4	344·2	59·9	469·3	58·7	1,102·2	61·6
ii. excise	17·3	9·1	17·3	8·8	75·9	18·3	127·3	22·1	122·9	15·4	268·4	15·0
iii. stamps	8·1	4·3	7·7	3·9	12·0	2·9	19·2	3·3	24·6	3·1	75·9	4·2
iv. Post Office surplus	—		—		0·4	0·1	—		6·2	0·8	8·5	0·5
v. Public Utilities surplus	—	—	—	—	—	—	—		0·3	0	0·8	0
vi. Railways surplus	—	—	—	—	—	—	10·9	1·9	62·8	7·8	—	—
Rent	—		—		1·6	0·4	—		4·5	0·6	5·7	0·3
Licences, fees, fines, etc.	35·9	18·8	22·5	11·5	44·8	10·8	35·7	6·2	55·8	7·0	125·7	7·0
Interest	—		—		—		20·6	3·6	16·9	2·1	26·9	1·5
	190·8	100·0	196·1	100·0	414·5	100·0	575·2	100·0	799·2	100·0	1,790·2	100·0

* Includes revenue raised for parochial purposes.
For sources and definitions see Part I.

Apart from the unfortunate consequences of the railway contract the crisis illustrated the real difficulty of estimating the future course of revenue where most of it depends on the fortunes of the export market. This is especially the case where the commodities exported fluctuate not only in value—owing to world conditions—but also in quantities produced for the export market—owing to the vagaries of the weather. Thus in Jamaica an adverse movement in the terms of trade reduced the cash incomes of the population. This led to smaller imports and customs revenues as well as difficulty in paying internal taxes. On the other hand, where hardship is caused by the inability to produce for the export market the effects on the exchequer tend, in the first place, to oppose those due to the terms of trade. An illustration of this is provided by the aftermath of the 1903 hurricane. The storm reduced the quantity of crops severely; in some areas foodstuffs grown for home consumption were destroyed and many houses were also ruined. Consequently imports of food, lumber, building materials and other necessities increased while other imported consumer goods declined, though not to the same extent. As a result revenue from customs duties at first actually increased, but fell during the following year. After the Kingston earthquake in January 1907 the results were even more remarkable—though external help accentuated the effects. Receipts from customs duties increased by over £100,000 between 1906–7 and 1907–8 while most of the other revenue items increased as well.[1] Such increases in customs receipts were, of course, needed to repair damages. Nevertheless, better market conditions during the decade restored finances, and by 1909 some reduction in the customs tariff was possible. Taxation subsequently remained virtually unchanged until after the war.

In 1918 expansion and increased cost of services led to higher taxation. Import and rum duties and the property tax were all increased. In addition three new taxes were introduced. In 1919 the package tax was levied as a temporary measure, but was retained subsequently until 1928. In 1920 income and entertainments taxes were introduced. The yield of the entertainments tax was only about £4,000 p.a., that of the package tax was about £45,000 and that of the income tax varied between £80,000 and £140,000 during the 1920's.[2] In 1930 the last provided only about 5 per cent of total revenue. It was imposed on incomes over £100 p.a. The rate of duty

[1] Report on the Finances of Jamaica by H. E. Dale, Crown Agents, 1924, p. 77.
[2] HBJ, relating to these years.

began at $2\frac{1}{2}d.$ in the £, increasing gradually to the maximum rate of 2*s*. in the £ on incomes over £10,000.

At this rate of duty the income tax cannot be said to have been either burdensome on the higher incomes or to have shifted the incidence of taxation materially from the lower income groups. This, in fact, was the conclusion reached by H. E. Dale in his analysis of sample budget data. Distinguishing between incomes from agriculture and other occupations he calculated the total tax liability of three different groups. In the case of agricultural incomes the burden of taxation increased from 8 per cent of incomes of £150 p.a. to 13·33 per cent of those of £1,000. For non-agricultural incomes the percentage paid in tax actually declined from 8·66 per cent in the lowest group to 7 per cent of incomes of £500 p.a. and rose to between 8 and 11·5 per cent on the highest incomes.[1]

D. A Note on Local Government Finances

Under representative government members of the parochial boards, like those of the House of Assembly, were elected by the freeholders of the parish. The boards enjoyed complete autonomy in all local affairs and do not appear to have been under any obligation to account for their actions to the central government. They had responsibility for the upkeep of local roads, poor-relief and police and they also maintained Courts of Common Pleas and contributed small sums to education. To meet the cost of these services they were empowered to raise taxes and loans on the security of 'parish papers'.

We know little about their income and expenditure because records are scant. The BBJ for 1833 includes financial returns for nineteen out of the twenty-one parishes in existence at that date, but most of them give only the total income and expenditure. According to these, total expenditure of the nineteen parishes amounted to £181,000 currency and revenue to £185,400 currency, or £129,300 and £132,400 sterling respectively. From the fragmentary returns available it appears that expenditure on poor relief was negligible, that on education rather more, and that the lion's share went to public works. Taxes were raised on the same basis as those of the central government, with the exception of customs and excise duties, but rates of duty differed among the parishes. The most important source of

[1] *Op. cit.*, p. 33.

revenue appears to have been the poll tax with the tax on other property coming a close second.

After emancipation parochial authorities, like the central government, had to face the problem of finding an alternative for the poll tax. In general they appear to have found the answer in reduction of expenditure. By 1851 local government expenditure amounted to only £48,808, and two years later this had fallen further to £8,642.[1]

Local administration appears to have been even less efficient than that of the central government. We have already seen that parishes had the power to exempt persons from paying taxes. They also had the privilege of nominating collecting constables. No records were kept of commissions paid out and of collection expenses. As before emancipation, most of the revenue was devoted to public works. Between 1843–7 expenditure on public works averaged £25,234[2] but, as we saw in Ch. 10, D, there was usually little to show for it.

The first step to curb parochial autonomy was taken in 1854 with the withdrawal of the power to levy taxes and raise loans. The parishes still retained control over expenditure, but although their affairs were henceforth controlled by the Executive Committee supervision does not appear to have been very effective. Parochial expenditure began to increase again after 1854, and by the financial years 1858–9 had reached £71,663.[3] But, as in the case of the central government, much of this increase in expenditure was not matched by an expansion of services. The cost of services differed greatly between parishes for no apparent reason. The expenditure for medical services in one parish, for example, was four times as great as that in another similarly placed.[4] Their record in road maintenance continued to be poor, and in 1858 responsibility for main roads was transferred to the central authority to be dealt with under the provisions of the Main Road Fund.

With the substitution of Crown Colony government for representative government the parochial authorities also lost all their powers. The parochial boards were replaced by nominated municipal boards and henceforth, until 1885, parochial services were administered by the central government. While assuming direct responsibility for local affairs the government also embarked on considerable administrative reforms. The first was to reduce the number and to change the boundaries of parishes to make them more equal in size

[1] REJ. [2] Papers re Affairs of Jamaica, *op. cit.*, p. 25. [3] REJ.
[4] Report with the BBJ, 1870 (C 85).

and population.[1] Parishes had been created haphazardly from time to time with a tendency to concentrate near the seat of the government. In 1842 Metcalfe was created, bringing the total number of parishes to twenty-two. Thus the eastern half of the island contained fifteen parishes, while the western half was divided into only seven, but in spite of this large variation in size and population each parish maintained the same establishment. Apart from the possible savings in administration costs, the object of reform was to make each parish into a self-contained unit for judicial, revenue, poor relief, medical and road services.[2] For this purpose the boundaries were so drawn as to make the thirteen country parishes more equal in size and population. The seven parishes in the western half of the island, Hanover, Westmoreland, St. James, St. Elizabeth, Trelawny, Manchester and St. Ann, were left unchanged, but in the east the existing fifteen were reduced to seven. Vere was merged with Clarendon, St. Dorothy, St. Thomas in the Vale and St. John with St. Catherine and Metcalfe with St. Mary. The town of Port Royal and a part of St. Andrew were incorporated with Kingston, and the remaining parish of Port Royal with St. Andrew. St. George and a part of St. Thomas in the East were merged with Portland and St. David with the remainder of St. Thomas in the East.[3]

With the introduction of semi-representative government in 1885, the municipal boards were replaced by elected boards and that of Kingston received the title of council with a mayor at its head. These boards were free to develop water, gas and sanitation services and to care for paupers. To meet the cost of these services they were empowered to levy specific taxes, but they also received part of general internal taxes. From this time onwards there grew up a complicated financial relationship between the local and central administration under which the Parochial Boards ceded part of their revenue from property taxes to the central government in return for part of the proceeds of the package and entertainment taxes. Parochial expenditure increased gradually from about £85,000[4] in 1880 to double that amount twenty years later. By 1910 expenditure exceeded £200,000 and by 1930 amounted to £432,000.[5]

[1] Law 20 of 1867. [2] Report with the BBJ, 1868–9 (4090).
[3] *Journal of the Institute of Jamaica*, 1894, vol. I, p. 238. [4] REJ.
[5] Report on the Finances of Jamaica by H. E. Dale.

APPENDIX I

TERMS OF TRADE

1. Method of Constructing the Price Index of Exports

The construction of a price index of exports raises a special difficulty because the composition of exports changed so radically in the years between *1870* and *1890*. As seen from Table XLI, Ch. 13, this remained fairly stable up to *1870* and again after *1890*. But linking *1870* to *1890* is a problem, since, if one uses *1870* weights, the result is *m*, while if one uses *1890* weights one gets the very different result ***n***. One could take an average of the two, but the result would not be meaningful.

In these circumstances it has seemed best to go behind the commodity to the factorial terms of trade. It is assumed fairly realistically that there were no relative changes in productivity. Thus one export commodity may be translated into another if a set of equilibrium prices at any given date is known.

Here we have taken the following f.o.b. prices as equilibrium prices:[1]

Sugar	18*s*.	7*d*.	per cwt.
Coffee	73*s*.	7½*d*.	per cwt.
Rum	2*s*.	11½*d*.	per gln.
Logwood	63*s*.	11½*d*.	per ton.
Pimento	17*s*.	2*d*.	per cwt.
Bananas	2*s*.	0*d*.	per stem.

Using these prices to convert the different exports into tons of sugar we get quantities in *1870* equivalent to 70,300 tons and in *1890* to 90,400 tons.[2] These quantities are divided by their corresponding export values.[3] The average price per ton in *1870* is accordingly £15·55 and in *1890* £16·56 and the price increase 6·5 per cent.

For the years from *1832* to *1870* we have used the current weighted index with *1870* as base year. This gives us:

1832 = 98·0
1850 = 96·0
1870 = 100·0

[1] For method of deriving f.o.b. prices, see Ch. 1, E.
[2] Ch. 13, Table XLII. [3] Ch. 13, Table XL.

Similarly, for the years from *1890* to *1930*, the current weighted index gives us:

1890 = 126·2
1910 = 100·0
1930 = 111·0

Linking these three indices we get the price index of exports:

Year	Price Index of Exports *1910* = 100
1832	116·1
1850	114·5
1870	118·5
1890	126·2
1910	100·0
1930	111·0

2. Method of Constructing the Price Index of Imports

The problem of changing composition does not arise in connection with imports, because there was relatively little change between the five main categories of imports. There were changes (Ch. 13, C) within most of the groups but these took the form of substitution of similar rather than the introduction of different commodities. We, therefore, use the ordinary current weighted index. The price index of imports is accordingly computed as:

Year	Price Index of Imports *1910* = 100
1832	98·3
1850	83·5
1870	120·5
1890	92·4
1910	100·0
1930	131·9

3. The Terms of Trade

Finally we compute the terms of trade by dividing the import price indices into the export price indices:

Year	Terms of Trade *1910* = 100
1832	118·1
1850	137·1
1870	98·3
1890	136·6
1910	100·0
1930	84·2

APPENDIX II

COST OF LIVING INDEX

THE method of constructing a cost-of-living index depends on the use to which it is to be put. The most frequent object is to obtain an indication of the purchasing power of wages. The appropriate index for this purpose measures the commodities most generally consumed by the wage earners. Such an index would also have been useful here to calculate the real wages of agricultural workers. Unfortunately, we lack the necessary information about the pattern of expenditure of wage earners. Instead we have used the pattern of total personal expenditure estimated in Part I above as weights. The resultant index therefore tells us the cost of living of the average Jamaican. It is misleading for the wage earning class in so far as it gives greater weight to the more expensive commodities than would a typical wage earner's budget. On the other hand, it is more reliable for the middle class incomes than would be an index based on wage earners' budgets.

METHOD OF CONSTRUCTING THE COST OF LIVING INDEX

For our base year weights we have used the *1910* pattern of personal expenditure at market prices. This is derived from the personal expenditure at factor cost (Ch. 6) by adding all indirect taxes and subtracting subsidies. The resultant weights are thus:

Weights for the Cost of Living Index

	Weights
1. Food, Drink and Tobacco: imported	141
home-produced	403
2. Clothing: imported	92
home-produced	70
3. Other Consumer Goods: imported	47
home-produced	35
4. Personal Services: professional	22
domestic	59
5. Passenger Transport	16
6. Rent	115
	1,000

The weights altogether cover 76 items: imported food, drink and tobacco 28, home-produced food, drink and tobacco 11, clothing 10, other consumer goods 16, personal services 5, passenger transport 2 and rent 4.

The problem of changing composition is not as serious as in the case of exports because, as we have seen, the average standard of living did not vary greatly over the years. It is only in the years *1832* and *1930* that differences were at all noteworthy: in *1832* relatively to the years *1850–1910* because the distribution of income was more unequal and hence gave rise to a different pattern of expenditure and in *1930* because the standard of living had risen. The choice of the year *1910* as a base is therefore as good as any other and the resultant index probably reflects changes in the cost of living fairly accurately except for *1832* and possibly *1930*.

The method of obtaining price relatives has already been explained in Ch. 1, E. Here it should be noted that market prices are calculated by adding specific and *ad valorem* customs and excise duties to all commodities subject to them.

Cost of Living Index

(*1910* = 100)

Year	Index
1832	93·3
1850	75·6
1870	100·8
1890	104·1
1910	100·0
1930	131·5

APPENDIX III

A NOTE ON WAGE STATISTICS

As explained in Ch. 1, we have not been able to estimate the income table separately because we lack sufficiently reliable information about the numbers employed in the various occupations and their incomes.

In Table I we have collected wage rates of predial workers, tradesmen and domestic servants over some years. It should be noted that the list is not exhaustive: beginning in the 1860's wage quotations covering these groups are available annually in the BBJ and for earlier years other wage quotations will also be found in contemporary literature, but because of their limited usefulness we reproduce only some of them. These statistics have, in fact, several drawbacks. In the first place it will be noted that most of the wage rates are quoted in ranges—some of them extremely wide—and as far as rates of predials and tradesmen are concerned, we do not know how far they reflect actual earnings. It has been said that rates and earnings were usually identical because workers tended to work only long enough to earn the rate.[1] Where rates differed among occupations or among districts it was also said that the actual earnings tended to be uniform because the differences usually reflected local conditions[2] —e.g. hard soil making it more difficult to earn the same wage as in working looser soil. But even if we were to assume that daily rates reflect daily earnings accurately we should still be unable to estimate workers' weekly or annual incomes because we lack the necessary data on duration of employment and accurate statistics of the numbers employed in different categories of work.

It will be seen that use of these data would have needed several assumptions, making the resultant estimates subject to considerable margins of error. Because of this we abandoned the attempt to calculate incomes independently and instead estimated them indirectly by allocating output to the several income earners on the basis of various data. In the case of plantation output, for example, we had

[1] SCP, 1847–8 (167), Q. 4,448.

[2] Labour Conditions in the West Indies, BPP, 1938–9 (Cmd. 6070), p. 74.

information about the pattern of production costs which enabled us to calculate the size of the wages bill in *1832* and in *1850*; for *1890* and part of *1930* information was available about labour costs per acre and per unit of output. It will be noted that in none of these cases did the calculation involve, or throw light on, wage or employment statistics. Similar methods were also used to calculate the incomes arising out of most of the other sectors. The only exceptions were professional workers (i.e. lawyers and doctors), independent craftsmen and domestics, where use of both wage and employment statistics was necessary in order to estimate output. The statistics used to estimate the incomes of these three groups are shown in parenthesis in Table I.

Wage Rates of Predial Workers, Tradesmen and Domestic Servants and Salaries of Professional Workers

Year	Predial per day	Tradesmen per day	Domestics per week	Professional per annum
1832		(£26 p.a.)		(£500) Lawyers (£609) Doctors
1836[1]	1*s.* 10*d.*–2*s.* 5*d.*	3*s.* 7*d.*	11*s.* 11*d.*	
1838[2]	7*d.*–1*s.* 2*d.*	2*s.* 4½*d.*		
1841[3]	1*s.* 2*d.*–1*s.* 9*d.*	2*s.* 6*d.*		
1843[4]	1*s.*–1*s.* 6*d.*			
1848[5]	1*s.* 6*d.*	7*s.* 6*d.* per week		
1850[6]	9*d.*–1*s.*	n.a.	n.a.	(£500) Lawyers
1854[7]	9*d.*–1*s.* 6*d.*	1*s.* 6*d.*–2*s.* 6*d.* (1*s.* 3*d.* and 2*s.* 6*d.*)	3*s.*–10*s.* 5*s.*	(£300) Doctors
1861[8]	1*s.*–1*s.* 6*d*	2*s.* 6*d.*–6*s.*	6*s.*–12*s.*	
1870[9]	1*s.* 2*s.*	1*s.* 3*d.*–2*s.* 6*d.* (2*s.* 10*d.*)	3*s.*–6*s.* (£15 12*s.* p.a.)	(£500) Lawyers (£300) Doctors
1890[10]	9*d.*–1*s.* 9*d.*	2*s.* 6*d.*–6*s.* (5*s.*)	5*s.*–10*s.* (5*s*)	(£600) Lawyers and Doctors
1910[11]	6*d.*–1*s.* 6*d.*	2*s.* 6*d.*–6*s.* (4*s.*)	3*s.*–12*s.* (5*s.*)	(£600) Lawyers and Doctors
1920[12]	3*s.* 6*d.*	7*s.* 3*d.*	5*s.* 9*d.*	
1930[13]	2*s.* 6*d.*–3*s.* 6*d.*	12*s.*–26*s.* per week (12*s.* and £1)	8*s.*–10*s.* (8*s.*)	(£800) Lawyers (£700) Doctors
1932[12]	1*s.* 9*d.*	5*s.* 5*d.*	6*s.*	

Note: *a.* Figures in parenthesis are wage rates and salaries used in National Income estimates.

(*Notes and references continued on next page.*)

b. Wages rates in 1836, 1838 and 1841 were actually quoted in currency. These have been converted into sterling at the ruling rate of exchange £140 = £100 (Martin, R. M. *History of the Colonies of the British Empire*, London, 1843, p. 19).

1. BBJ, 1836 (currency 2*s*. 6*d*.–3*s*. 4*d*, 5*s*. and 16*s*. 8*d*.).
2. Sel. Com. on East India Produce, BPP, 1840 (527), Predials, Q. 3691 (currency 10*d*.–1*s*. 8*d*.); Tradesman, Q. 3769 (currency 3*s*. 4*d*.).
3. Papers re to the West Indies. Pt. II. BPP, 1841 (344), Predials, p. 176 (currency 1*s*. 8*d*.–2*s*. 6*d*.); Tradesmen, p. 163.
4. Phillippo, J. M. *Jamaica: its Past and Present State*. London, 1843, p. 95.
5. SCP, 1847–8 (167), Predial, Q. 4455—Tradesmen, Q. 4462.
6. Bigelow, *op. cit.*
7. PAIJ, 1854 (1848), Predial, pp. 18 and 20; Tradesmen, pp. 18 and 25; and Domestic, p. 22.
8. BBJ, 1861.
9. *Ibid.*, 1870.
10. *Ibid.*, 1890.
11. *Ibid.*, 1910.
12. Labour Conditions in the West Indies. BPP 1938–9 (Cmd. 6070).
13. Predial: Col. Rep. 1931 (Col. No. 1603), Tradesmen and Domestic, BBJ, 1930.

BIBLIOGRAPHY

THE material listed here includes only those documents that have been useful directly or indirectly in this study.

1. OFFICIAL SOURCES

A. *Basic Statistical Sources.*

i. Blue Books of Jamaica. These are in manuscript until 1862 and printed thereafter. They are to be found in the Public Record Office under call number CO 142.

ii. Colonial Reports. These annual surveys by the Governors of Jamaica begin in 1845. They are variously called Governor's Report (from 1845 to 1850), Past and Present State of H.M. Colonies (from 1851 to 1866), Report with the Blue Book (from 1867 to 1879/80) and Colonial Reports (from 1880/1 to date). They were published as Parliamentary Papers up to the year 1919/20 and as Non-Parliamentary Papers thereafter.

iii. Customs Returns. These include detailed statistics of the external trade of Jamaica by commodity, origin and destination during the years 1832–53. They are in manuscript and are to be found in the Public Record Office under call numbers Customs 6/1–22 and Customs 12/1–22.

iv. Population Censuses. Population counts were made in Jamaica in 1844 and decennially between 1861 and 1921 with the exception of 1901. No complete copies of the first three enumerations have been found. An abstract of that for 1844 was published as a Parliamentary Paper under the title 'Population in the West Indies' in 1845 under the sessional number 426 and summaries of the censuses for 1861 and 1871 have been found in the West India Reference Library in Jamaica.

v. Statistical Abstracts. These are variously called Abstracts for the Several British Colonies, Possessions and Protectorates, for the British Self-Governing Dominions, Colonies, etc., and for the Several British Overseas Dominions and Protectorates. These are published annually beginning in 1865. Each publication covers 14–15 years. They reproduce only information contained in the Blue Books but they are useful as they are more generally available than the Blue Books.

vi. Statistical Tables for the Colonies. These were published triennially between 1856 and 1916, covering the years from 1850 to 1912, as Parliamentary Papers. Like the Abstracts they contain only information given in the Blue Books. Each volume covers only three years but, on the other hand, gives more detail than the Abstracts.

vii. Handbooks of Jamaica. These annual publications begin in 1880. They were preceded by the Jamaica Almanack—a much less ambitious publication. Copies of the Almanack are very scarce and only few have been found in the Colonial Office Library, the Royal Empire Society Library and the West India Reference Library.

viii. Jamaica in 1895, 1897, etc. This is a handbook of information for intending settlers and visitors with some account of the Colony's history. Published by the Institute of Jamaica.

B. *Other Parliamentary Publications*

A complete list of Parliamentary Publications up to 1870 is available in Volume II of the Cambridge History of the British Empire. Thereafter Parliamentary Papers may be found conveniently in the Decennial Indexes of Parliamentary Papers. Here we give a list only of those that have been found useful in this study.

1830, XXI (582). Return re Population of Colonies.
1830, XXI (674). Slave Population.
1830–1, VI (273). Estimates for Slave Registry.
1830–1, IX (120). West Indies—Statement re State of Colonies.
1830–1, XVI (302). Slave Manumission, 1817–26.
1830–1, XVI (305). Abstract of Slave Population.
1831, XIX (260). Date and Capture of Each Colony, Population, Trade.
1831–2, XX (721). Sel. Com. on the Extinction of Slavery.
1831–2, XX (381). Sel. Com. on Commercial State of West India Colonies.
1831–2, XXXI (275). Laws Passed for the Relief of Catholics, Removal of Disabilities of the Jews and Free Persons of Colour.
1831–2, XXXI (58). Jamaica Revenue and Expenditure.
1831–2, XLVI (No no.). Papers re Measures of Amelioration.
1831–2, XLVII (482). Jamaica—Papers re Slave Insurrection.
1831–2, XLVII (285). Correspondence re Slave Rebellion.
1831–2, XLVII (365). Jamaica: Manumissions Granted since 1825.
1831–2, XLVII (481). Reports from the Bishop of Jamaica.
1831–2, XLVII (561). Report on Injury Sustained during Slave Rebellion.
1833, XXVI (539). Slave Registrations: Jamaica.
1833, XXVI (540). Baptist Missionaries.
1833, XXVI (736). Amount Advanced for Assistance of West Indian Proprietors.
1833, XXVI (700). Slave Population.
1833, XXXIII (590). Report on Ure's Sugar Experiments.
1834, VI (570). Colonial Military Expenditure.
1836, XV (560). Sel. Com. on Negro Apprenticeship.
1836, XLVIII (166). Papers re West Indian Emancipation. Part III. Jamaica.
1833–8, XL (138). Statistics of Health of Troops since 1803.
1837–8, XLVIII (215). Slave Compensation Claims.
1837–8, XLVIII (113). Negro Education, Jamaica.
1837–8, XLIII (353). Schools and Education.
1838, XVIII (70). Jamaica: Return of Exports for 53 Years.
1838, XIV (24). Return re Church Establishment and Schools, 1831–6.
1839, XXXV (107). Jamaica—re State of Colony.
1839, XXXV (217). Account of Value of All Exports from Great Britain to Jamaica.

1839, XLI (541). Schools, Jamaica.
1840, VIII (527). Sel. Com. East India Produce.
1840, XXXIV (238). Jamaica—Annual Imports, 1835–9.
1840, XXXV (212). Papers re West Indies.
1841, III (344). Papers re West Indies, Part II. Jamaica.
1841, XVI (411). Jamaica—Abstracts of Net Revenue.
1842, XIII (479). Sel. Com. West India Colonies—Employers and Labourers.
1842, XXIX (374). Papers re to the West Indies.
1843, XXXIII (136). Immigrants into the British West Indian Colonies.
1845, XXXI (426). Population in the West Indies.
1847, LX (717). West Indies—Exports and Imports, Shipping etc.
1847–8, XXIII (123) (137) (167) (184) (206) (230) (245) (361–I) (361–II) (518) (361). Sel. Com. Sugar and Coffee Planting.
1847–8, XLIV (685). Despatches received from Sir Charles Grey.
1849, XXXVII (1065). Papers re to Affairs of Jamaica.
1849, L (351). Sugar, Molasses, etc.
1850, XXXIX (1139). Papers re Affairs of the Island of Jamaica.
1850, LII (280). Sugar Imported into Britain, 1793–1849.
1852, XXXI (231). Immigrants and Liberated Africans.
1852, XXXI (144). Exports and Imports (Colonies).
1852–3, LXII (836). Customs Duties.
1852–3, LXV (269). Immigrants and Liberated Africans.
1852–3, LXV (1655). Papers re Legislative Proceedings.
1852–3, LXVII (76). Sugar Growing Colonies.
1854, XLIII (1806). Papers re Legislative Proceedings in Jamaica.
1854, XLIII (1848). Papers re Affairs of the Island of Jamaica.
1854, XLIII (235). Cholera (Jamaica).
1854, LXV (237). Sugar, etc.
1856, XLIV (431). Customs Tariff with Canada.
1859, XX (31). Correspondence between Colonial Office and Governors of Colonies.
1862, XIII (390). Sel. Com. on Sugar Duties.
1863, LXVII (272). Imports into Britain from the West Indies.
1866, XXX (3682). Jamaica Royal Commission.
1866, XXXI (3683). Mins. of Evidence and Appendix.
1866, XXX (3683–I). Papers laid before the Royal Commission.
1866, LI (3695). Papers re Affairs of Jamaica.
1880, XII (332). Sel. Com. Sugar Industries.
1882, XLVI (285). Expenditure and Revenue (Jamaica).
1884, XLVI (C 3840). Royal Commission on Public Revenues, etc.
1884, LV (C 3982) Rep. on West India Incumbered Estates Court.
1884, LXXIV (325). Progress of the Sugar Trade.
1884–5, LIII (C 4234). Further Correspondence re West Indian Incumbered Estates Court.
1885, LXXI (C 4340). Correspondence re Negotiations of Treaty between West India Colonies and the United States.
1887, LXXVIII (312). Sugar Trade.

1888, XCIII (353). Sugar Trade.
1890, XLIX (49). Jamaica—Sugar Estates.
1890–1, LVII (C 6352). Correspondence re Sale of Jamaica Railway to an American Syndicate.
1892, LVI (C 6680). Customs Tariffs with the United States.
1892, LVI (C 6805). Rates of Import Duties in force prior and subsequent to Commercial Arrangement of 1891–2.
1897, L (C 8655) (C 8656) (C 8657) (C 8669). Royal West India Commission.
1897, LXI (C 8359). Correspondence re Sugar Industry in the West Indies.
1898, LXXXV (C 8706). Customs Tariffs of the United Kingdom from 1800 to 1897.
1898, XCII (C 8780). Correspondence re Sugar Bounties.
1898, XCII (C 8938). Correspondence re to the Conference at Brussels.
1899, LIX (C 9412). Rep. on Finances of Jamaica.
1899, LIX (C 9177). Correspondence re to the Public Finances.
1899, LIX (C 9413). Further Correspondence re to the Public Finances.
1900, XXI (Cd. 416). Educational System of the Chief Colonies.
1900, LV (Cd. 125). Further Correspondence re to the Public Finances.
1900, LV (Cd. 175). Jamaica: Contract between the Crown Agents for the Colonies and Messrs. Elder, Dempster and Co.
1904, CX (Cd. 1771). Convention between United Kingdom and France re Commercial Relations between France and Jamaica.
1906, LXXVI (Cd. 2901). Rep. on the Working of the Imperial Department of Agriculture for the West Indies.
1907, LXXXI (334). Sugar: World's Production, Consumptiòn etc.
1907, LXXXVII (Cd. 3565). Papers re Brussels Sugar Convention.
1908, CVII (Cd. 3960). Despatches re employment of British West Indian Labour in the Panama Canal Zone.
1909, LIX (Cd. 4589). Papers re Mechanical Transport in the Colonies.
1901, XI (Cd. 5369). Royal Commission on Canadian Trade Relations with the West Indies.
1911, LXXXVII (281). Sugar: World's Production, Consumption, etc.
1912, LX (Cd. 6092). Agreement between Canada and Certain West Indian Colonies.
1912–3, LX, XCIII (Cd. 6282) (Cd. 6325). Correspondence re Withdrawal of H.M. Government from the Brussels Convention.
1920, XXXIII (Cmd. 864). Canada—West Indies Trade Agreement.
1922, XVI (Cmd. 1679). Rep. by the Hon. E. F. L. Wood on his Visit to the West Indies and British Guiana.
1929, VIII (Cmd. 3517). Sugar: Rep. of the West Indian Sugar Commission.
1930, XXIII (Cmd. 3745). Further Correspondence re Position of the Sugar Industry.
1930, XXIII (Cmd. 3705). Correspondence re Position of the Sugar Industry.
1930, VIII (Cmd. 3523). Statement of Policy re West Indian and Mauritius Sugar Reports.

1938–9, XV (Cmd. 6070). Rep. on Labour Conditions in the West Indies.
1939–40, V (Cmd. 6174). West India Royal Commission—Recommendations.
1944–5, VI (Cmd. 6607). Rep. of the West India Royal Commission.
1944–5, VI (Cmd. 6608). Rep. on Agriculture, Fisheries, Forestry and Veterinary Matters.

C. *Non-Parliamentary Papers*

1930, HMSO (Col. No. 49). Rep. of West Indian Sugar Commission. Part IV.
1946, HMSO (Col. No. 195). Nutrition in the British West Indies.
1953, HMSO (Col. Res. Studies No. 10). Colonial Monetary Conditions.

D. *Crown Agents for the Colonies*

1923. Rep. on Transport Problems in Jamaica by F. D. Hammond.
1924. Rep. on Finances of Jamaica by H. E. Dale.

E. *Jamaica Government Printer*

1879. Rep. on the Juvenile Population of Jamaica.
1884. Jamaica at the World's Exposition.
1886. Rep. on System of Elementary Education.
1898. Rep. on System of Education in Jamaica.
1899. Rep. re Establishment of Agricultural Department.
1899. Rep. on Fruit Trade with England.
1900. Rules as to Sale of Lands by the Government of Jamaica to Small Settlers.
1905. Elementary Education in Jamaica.
1908. Proceedings of Conference on Trade Relations between the West Indies and the Dominion of Canada.
1914. Rep. on the Working and Administration of the Department of Agriculture.
1920. Rep. on Transportation and Power Problems in Jamaica.
1929. Statistics of the Sugar Industry of Jamaica.
1931. Syrian and Chinese Traders.
1931. Rep. on Immigration of Aliens into Jamaica.
1933. Sel. Com. on Cattle and Dairy Industry of the Colony.
1935. Rep. on the Beef Cattle Industry of Jamaica.
1935. Rep. on Dairy Industry in Jamaica.
1936. Rep. on Jamaica Banana Commission.
1936. Rep. of Committee on Unemployment.
1937. Rep. of Nutrition Committee.
1945. Rep. on Nutrition in Jamaica.
1945. Rep. of the Sugar Industry Commission of Jamaica 1944–5.
1945. Historical Supplement to Registrar-General's Annual Report.

See also annual Departmental Reports of—Tourist Development Board, Commissioner for Emigration in Cuba. Immigration Department, Collector-General's Department.

2. General Histories, Descriptions, etc. of Jamaica

A. *Pre-emancipation*

Barclay, A., *Practical View of the Present State of Slavery*, London, 1827.
Bridges, G. W., *Annals of Jamaica*, London, 1828, 2 vols.
Candler, John, *Extracts from the Journal of John Candler*, London, 1840.
Carmichael, Mrs., *Domestic Manners and Social Condition*, London, 1834, 2 vols. (This does not deal with Jamaica but is included here because it contains interesting descriptions of living standards of the various classes.)
Edwards, Bryan, *History of West Indies*, London, 1819, 5 vols.
Lewis, Matthew G., *Journal of a West India Proprietor*, London, 1834.
Marly or *Life of a Planter in Jamaica*, London, 1828, 2nd edition.
Nugent, Lady M., *Journal of a Voyage to, and Residence in, the Island of Jamaica from 1801 to 1805*. Ed. F. Cundall. London, 1939.
Roughley, T., *The Jamaican Planter's Guide*, London, 1823.
Stewart, J., *A View of the Past and Present State of Jamaica*, Edinburgh, 1823.
Whiteley, Henry, *Three Months in Jamaica in 1832*, London, 1833.
Williams, C. R., *A Tour through the Island of Jamaica*, London, 1826.

B. 1834–65

Bigelow, John, *Jamaica in 1850*, New York, 1851.
Biggs, John, *Observations on the Manufacture of Sugar and Rum in Jamaica*, London, 1843.
Bleby, H., *Death Struggles of Slavery*, London, 1853.
Buchner, J. H., *The Moravians in Jamaica*, London, 1854.
Free Trader, *A Letter on the West India Question*, London, 1848.
Grey, H. G., *The Colonial Policy of Lord John Russell's Administration*, London, 1853, 2 vols.
Gurney, Joseph John, *A Winter in the West Indies*, London, 1840.
Hill, Richard, *Lights and Shadows of Jamaican History*, Kingston, 1859.
Hincks, F., *The Results of Negro Emancipation*. Speech delivered in London, 1st August, 1859.
Hinton, J. W., *Memoir of William Knibb*, London, 1849.
Jelly, T., *A Brief Enquiry into the Conditions of Jamaica*, London, 1847.
King, D., *The State and Prospects of Jamaica*, London, 1850.
Martin, R. M., *History of the British Colonies*, London, 1834, 5 vols. New edition, 1843, 1 vol.
—— *Statistics of the Colonies of the British Empire*, London, 1839.
Maxwell, James, *Remarks on the Present State of Jamaica*, London, 1846.
Merivale, H., *Colonization and Colonies*, London, 1861.
Military Officer, *Jamaica As it Was, As it Is, and as it May Be*, London, 1835.
Phillippo, J. B., *Jamaica; its Past and Present State*, London, 1843.
Porter, G. R., *The Nature and Properties of the Sugar Cane*, London, 1843.

PORTER, G. R., *Tables of Revenue, Population, Commerce of the United Kingdom and its Dependencies*, London, 1835.

Royal Society of Arts, Jamaica, *Jamaica, its existing conditions with a few suggestions for its amelioration*, London, 1856.

SEWELL, WM. G., *The Ordeal of Free Labor in the British West Indies*, New York, 1861.

STURGE, J., and HARVEY, T., *The West Indies in 1837*, London, 1838.

Suggestions for a United West-India Government and Joint Stock Company, Jamaica, 1849.

UNDERHILL, E. B., *The West Indies*, London, 1862.

WHITEHOUSE, W. F., *Eight Treatises on the Sugar Cane*, Spanish Town, 1843.

WRAY, L., *The Practical Sugar Planter*, London, 1848.

C. 1865–1930

African Agriculture and the Native: Example of Jamaica. Supplement to the *African World*, 29th June 1929.

Alleged Distress in Jamaica, Kingston, 1883.

BLEBY, H., *The Reign of Terror*, London, 1868.

Canada and the West Indies, The West India Committee Circular. 19th November 1925.

Canadian Pacific Railway Co., *Trade with the West India Islands*, 1897.

BARBOUR, D., and BLAIN, W., *Suggestions for the Establishment and Regulation of Government Currency Note Issue in the West Indies*, 1900.

BRANFORD, V. V., *An Undeveloped Estate of the Empire*, London, 1899.

BROOKS, A. J., *The Cultivation of Citrus Fruit in the West Indies*, London, 1909.

COOK, E. M., *Jamaica. The Loadstone of the Caribbean*, London, 1924.

CRADWICK, WM., *Coffee Growing in Jamaica*, West India Committee Circular, 1927.

CUNDALL, F., *Political and Social Disturbances in the West Indies*, Kingston, 1906.

CUST, R. J., *A Treatise on the West Indian Incumbered Estates Act*, London, 1865, 2nd edition.

DE LISSER, H. G., *Twentieth Century Jamaica*, Kingston, 1913.

EDEN, C. E., *The West Indies*, London, 1880.

ESPEUT, W. BANCROFT, *The Advantages to Result from Railway Extension*, The Institute of Jamaica, Kingston, 1887.

FOSTER, G. F., *Canadian Trade with the West Indies*, Trinidad, 1890.

FROUDE, J. A., *The English in the West Indies*, London, 1888.

GARDNER, W. J., *History of Jamaica*, London, 1873, new edition, 1909.

HARVEY, T. and BREWIN, WM., *Jamaica in 1866*, London, 1867.

HUTTON, J. E., *A History of Moravian Missions*, London, 1922.

Jamaica Banana Producers' Association Ltd. Petition addressed to the Commission on the Banana Industry, Mimeograph, 1935. (Copy in the Library of the University College of the West Indies.)

Jamaica Producers' Association, West India Committee Circular, 19th November 1925.

JAMES, WINIFRED, *The Mulberry Tree*, London, 1913.
LINDO, A., *Dr. Underhill's Testimony of the Wrongs of the Negro in Jamaica Examined*, London, 1866.
LIVINGSTONE, W. P., *Black Jamaica*, London, 1899.
LUBBOCK, SIR NEVILLE, *The Present Position of Our West Indian Colonies*, London, 1900.
LUDLOW, J. M., 'The Cornwall Agricultural and Commercial Association of Jamaica', Extract from *Good Words*, 1866.
MACGLASHAN, J., *Jamaica—Review of Finances since 1866*, Jamaica, 1884.
MALCOLM, IAN, *The 'White Flag' in Jamaica, The Nineteenth Century*, 1907.
MARTINEAU, G., 'The Brussels Sugar Convention', *Economic Journal*, vol. XIV, March, 1904.
—— *Sugar*, London, 1910.
MUSGRAVE, A., Jamaica: 'Now and 15 Years Since', *Proceedings of the Royal Colonial Institute*, 1879–80, vol. XI.
NOEL, W., *The Case of George William Gordon, Esq., of Jamaica*, London, 1866.
PHILLIPPO, J. C., *Jamaica: its Government and its People*, Kingston, 1883.
PRICE, G. E., *Jamaica: Papers relating to Proposed Change in the Form of Government*, London, 1884.
PRINGLE, H., *The Fall of the Sugar Planters of Jamaica*, London, 1869.
PULLEN-BURRY, B., *Ethiopia in Exile*, London, 1905.
—— *Jamaica As it Is*, London, 1903.
'Railways and Roads in Jamaica', Extract from *Modern Transport*, 17th November, 1923.
RAWLINSON, SIR R., *Sanitary Improvement in Kingston, Jamaica*, London, 1888.
RHODES, T., *Jamaica and the Imperial Direct West India Mail Service*, London, 1901.
SALMON, C. W., *Depression in the West Indies*, London, 1884.
SCOTT, J. S. D., *To Jamaica and Back*, London, 1876.
SMITH, W. E., *The Fruit Industry of Jamaica*, Trinidad, 1904.
Times Trade and Engineering Supplement, *Problem of Making Jamaica Pay*, 25th September, 1926.
UNDERHILL, E. B., *The Tragedy of Morant Bay*, London, 1895.
WATTS, F., *Central Sugar Factories for Jamaica*, 1917.
WILCHER, F. H., *The Source of Discontent in the West Indies*, London, 1885.

D. *Modern*

ARMYTAGE, F., *The Free Port System in the British West Indies*, London, 1953.
BURN, W. L., *Emancipation and Apprenticeship in the West Indies*, London, 1937.
—— *The British West Indies*, London, 1951.
GIRVAN, D. T. M., *The Jamaica Agricultural Society, 1895–1951*. Typescript.
GRANT, J. T. C., *Early History of the Parish of Manchester*, Address, 1946.

HART, A., 'The Banana in Jamaica: Export Trade,' *Soc. and Econ. Studies*, vol. 3, no. 2, 1954.

HART, R., *The Origin and Development of the People of Jamaica*, Kingston, 1952.

HENRIQUES, F., *Family and Colour in Jamaica*, London, 1953.

Jamaica Agricultural Society, *Journ. of the J.A.S.*, vol. XLII, nos. 11 and 12, 1938.

KEPNER, C. D., and SOUTHILL, J. H., *The Banana Empire*, New York, 1935.

KERR, M., *Personality and Conflict in Jamaica*, Liverpool, 1952.

LEWIS, W. A., 'Industrial Development in the Caribbean', *Caribbean Econ. Review*, 1950.

—— and MARTIN, A. 'Patterns of Public Revenue and Expenditure', *The Manchester School*, vol. XXIV, no. 3, 1956.

—— 'Issues in Land Settlement Policy', *Caribbean Econ. Review*, vol. III, nos. 1 and 2, 1951.

MATHIESON, W. L., *British Slavery and its Abolition, 1823–38*, London, 1926.

—— *British Slave Emancipation, 1838–49*, London, 1932.

—— *The Sugar Colonies and Governor Eyre, 1849–66*, London, 1936.

MAUNDER, W. F., 'Development of Internal Transport in Jamaica', *Soc. and Econ. Studies*, vol. 3, no. 2, 1954.

OLIVIER, LORD, *Jamaica, the Blessed Island*, London, 1936.

—— *The Myth of Governor Eyre*, London, 1933.

PHILLIPS, ULRICH B., 'A Jamaica Slave Plantation', *The American Historical Review*, April 1914.

RAGATZ, L. J., *The Decline of the Planter Class in the British Caribbean, 1763–1833*, New York, 1928.

—— *Statistics for the Study of British Caribbean Economic History*, New York, 1928.

—— *Absentee Landlordism in the British Caribbean*, London, 1928.

Roberts, G. W., 'A Life Table for a West Indian Slave Population', *Population Studies*, vol. V, no. 3, 1952.

—— 'A Note on Mortality in Jamaica', *Population Studies*, vol. IV, no. 1, 1950.

—— 'Immigration of Africans into the British Caribbean', *Population Studies*, vol. VII, no. 3, 1954.

—— 'Mating and Fertility in the West Indies', *Population Studies*, vol. VIII, no. 3, 1955.

—— *The Population of Jamaica*, Cambridge, 1957.

ROBERTS, W. ADOLPHE, *Six Great Jamaicans*, Kingston, 1952.

ROTTENBURG, S., 'Entrepreneurship and Economic Progress in Jamaica', *Inter-American Economic Affairs*, vol. 7, no. 2, 1953.

SIMEY, T. S., *Welfare and Planning in the West Indies*, Oxford, 1946.

SIRES, R. V., 'The Jamaica Constitution of 1884', *Soc. and Econ. Studies*, vol. 3, no. 1, 1954.

—— *The Experience of Jamaica with Modified Crown Colony Government*, vol. 4, no. 2, 1955.

UKERS, WM. H., *All About Coffee*, New York, 1922, 2nd edition, 1935.

WESLEY, C. H., 'The Emancipation of the Free Coloured Population in the British Empire', *Journal of Negro History*, vol. 19 April 1934.

WRONG, H. H., *The Government of the West Indies*, Oxford, 1923.

3. NEWSPAPERS

Copies of nineteenth-century newspapers are very scarce. The Public Record Office possesses a few copies of the earlier papers and the British Museum Newspaper Library has copies of some of the later papers. Here we list only those copies that have been consulted for this study.

A. *Public Record Office*

Jamaica Watchman and Free Press, 1830–6.
Kingston Chronicle and City Advertiser, 1835–7.
Morning Journal, 1849–53.
Royal Gazette, 1832–8.
Jamaica Gazette, 1869–85.

B. *British Museum Newspaper Library*

The Semi-Weekly Gleaner, 1869, 1873 and 1874 (incomplete).
The Tri-weekly Gleaner, 1882–93 (incomplete).
The Daily Gleaner, 1866 to date (incomplete).
The Jamaica Creole and Daily Record, 1878–82 (incomplete).
Kingston Guardian, 1871.
Gall's Newsletter, 1882–88.
The Budget, 1877.

4. NATIONAL INCOME ESTIMATES OF JAMAICA

BENHAM, F., *The National Income of Jamaica, 1942*, Dev. and Welf. Bulletin No. 5, Barbados, 1942.

Central Bureau of Statistics, *The National Income of Jamaica, for 1943 and 1946*, Mimeograph, 1948.

DEANE, P., *The Measurement of Colonial National Incomes*, Cambridge, 1948.

THORNE, A. P., 'Size, Structure and Growth of the Economy of Jamaica', *Supplement to Soc. and Econ. Studies*, vol. 4, no. 4, 1955.

INDEX

www.ingramcontent.com/pod-product-compliance
Ingram Content Group UK Ltd.
Pitfield, Milton Keynes, MK11 3LW, UK
UKHW020204290926
15470UKWH00001B/4

9 780837 17157